Cheeky Angel ™

Vol. 17
Story and Art by
Hiroyuki Nishimori

Cheeky Angel
Vol. 17
VIZ Media Edition

Story and Art by
HIROYUKI NISHIMORI

Translation & English Adaptation/Joe Yamazaki
Touch-Up Art & Lettering/Susan Daigle-Leach
Cover and Interior Design/Izumi Evers
Editor/Gary Leach

Managing Editor/Annette Roman
Editorial Director/Elizabeth Kawasaki
Editor in Chief, Books/Alvin Lu
Editor in Chief, Magazines/Marc Weidenbaum
Sr. Director of Acquisitions/Rika Inouye
Senior VP of Marketing/Liza Coppola
Exec. VP of Sales & Marketing/John Easum
Publisher/Hyoe Narita

Printed in the U.S.A.

Published by VIZ Media, LLC
P.O. Box 77010
San Francisco, CA 94107

VIZ Media Edition
10 9 8 7 6 5 4 3 2 1
First printing, April 2007

www.viz.com
store.viz.com

RATED T+ FOR OLDER TEEN

PARENTAL ADVISORY
CHEEKY ANGEL is rated T+ for Older Teen and is recommended for ages 16 and up. This volume contains strong language, violence and sexual themes.

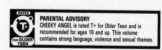

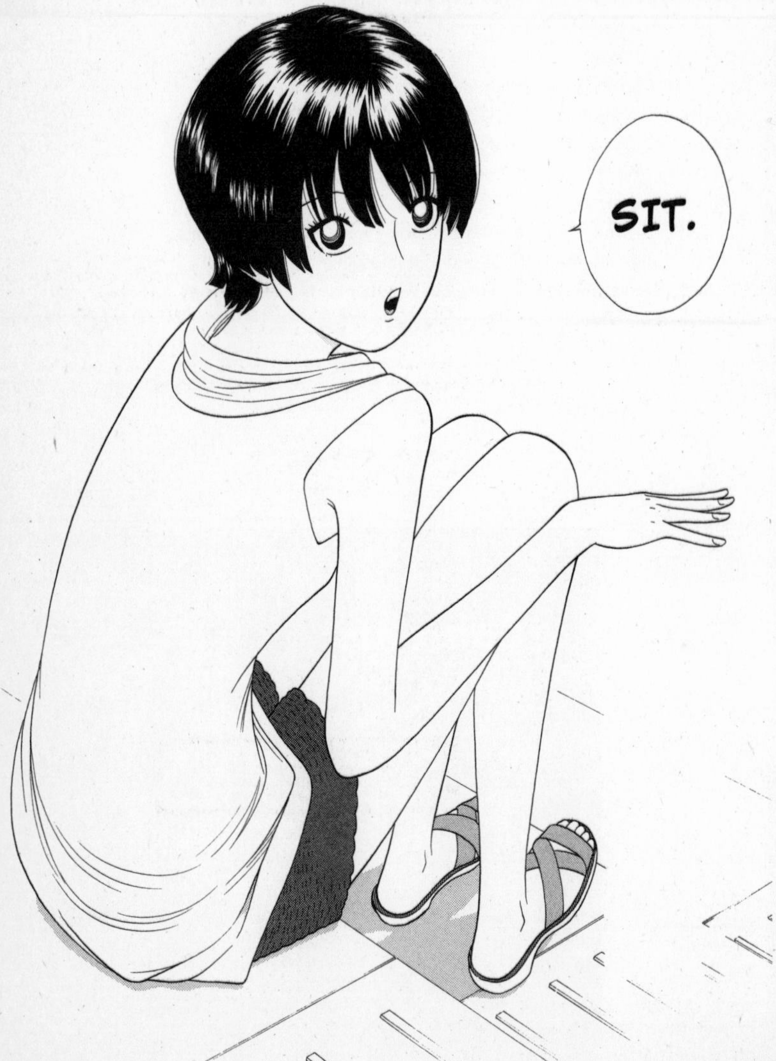
SIT.

STORY THUS FAR

Megumi's date with a prince doesn't go well, and she envisions her mother exiling her from Japan. However, her mother just considers it a learning experience. Meg's relief is short-lived when she learns that Miki is now determined to find a new magic book!

Genzo has gone all out to find Yanagisawa, the gang leader who attacked him and Megumi during the "Ideal Woman Cup." He's unaware that Yanagisawa has joined up with Takao Gakusan, Miki's former fiancé, who is again plotting revenge against Megumi and her friends.

Miki soon finds a new magic book—four, in fact! Meg and her pals summon the spirit of one that looks like the mythical kappa. This spirit seems benign, but why is it so focused on the group's Mr. Average, Ichiro?

Contents

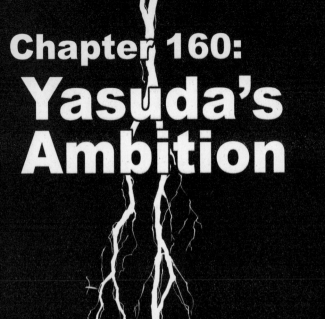

Chapter 160:
Yasuda's Ambition

OUTTA MY SIGHT.

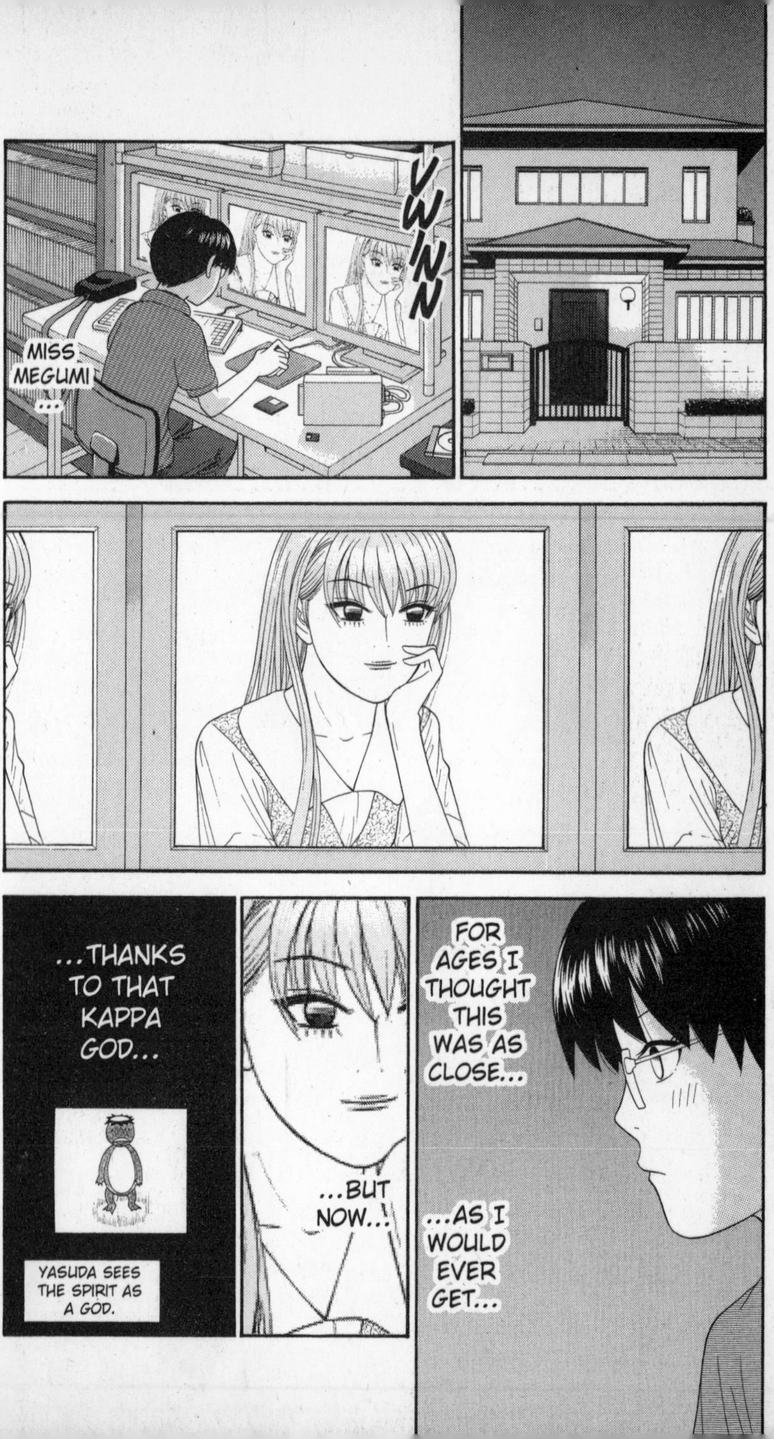
VWINN
MISS MEGUMI ...
FOR AGES I THOUGHT THIS WAS AS CLOSE...
...AS I WOULD EVER GET...
...BUT NOW...
...THANKS TO THAT KAPPA GOD...
YASUDA SEES THE SPIRIT AS A GOD.

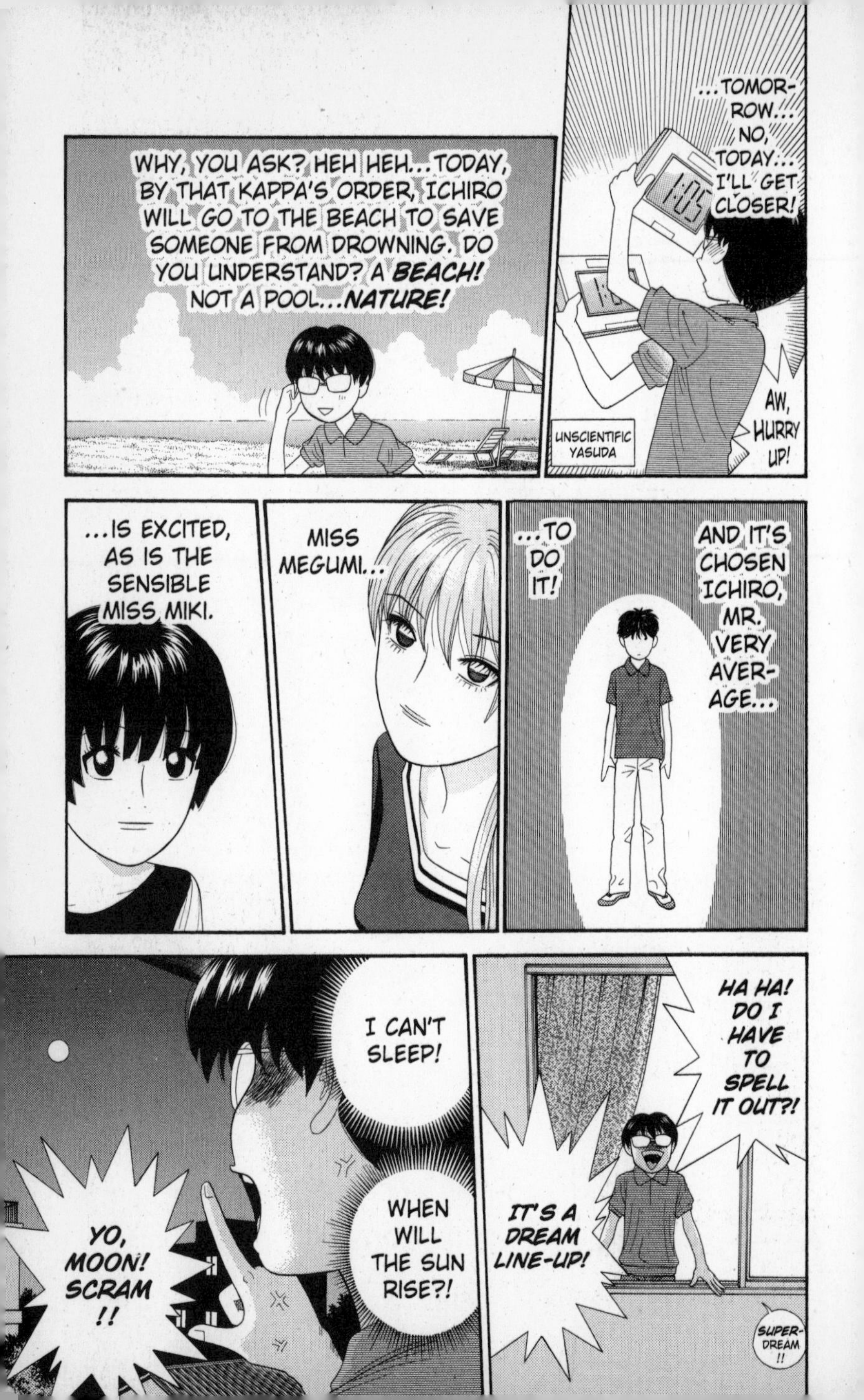
...TOMORROW... NO, TODAY... I'LL GET CLOSER!
AW, HURRY UP!
UNSCIENTIFIC YASUDA
WHY, YOU ASK? HEH HEH... TODAY, BY THAT KAPPA'S ORDER, ICHIRO WILL GO TO THE BEACH TO SAVE SOMEONE FROM DROWNING. DO YOU UNDERSTAND? A BEACH! NOT A POOL...NATURE!
AND IT'S CHOSEN ICHIRO, MR. VERY AVERAGE...
...TO DO IT!
MISS MEGUMI...
...IS EXCITED, AS IS THE SENSIBLE MISS MIKI.
HA HA! DO I HAVE TO SPELL IT OUT?!
IT'S A DREAM LINE-UP!
SUPER-DREAM !!
I CAN'T SLEEP!
WHEN WILL THE SUN RISE?!
YO, MOON! SCRAM !!

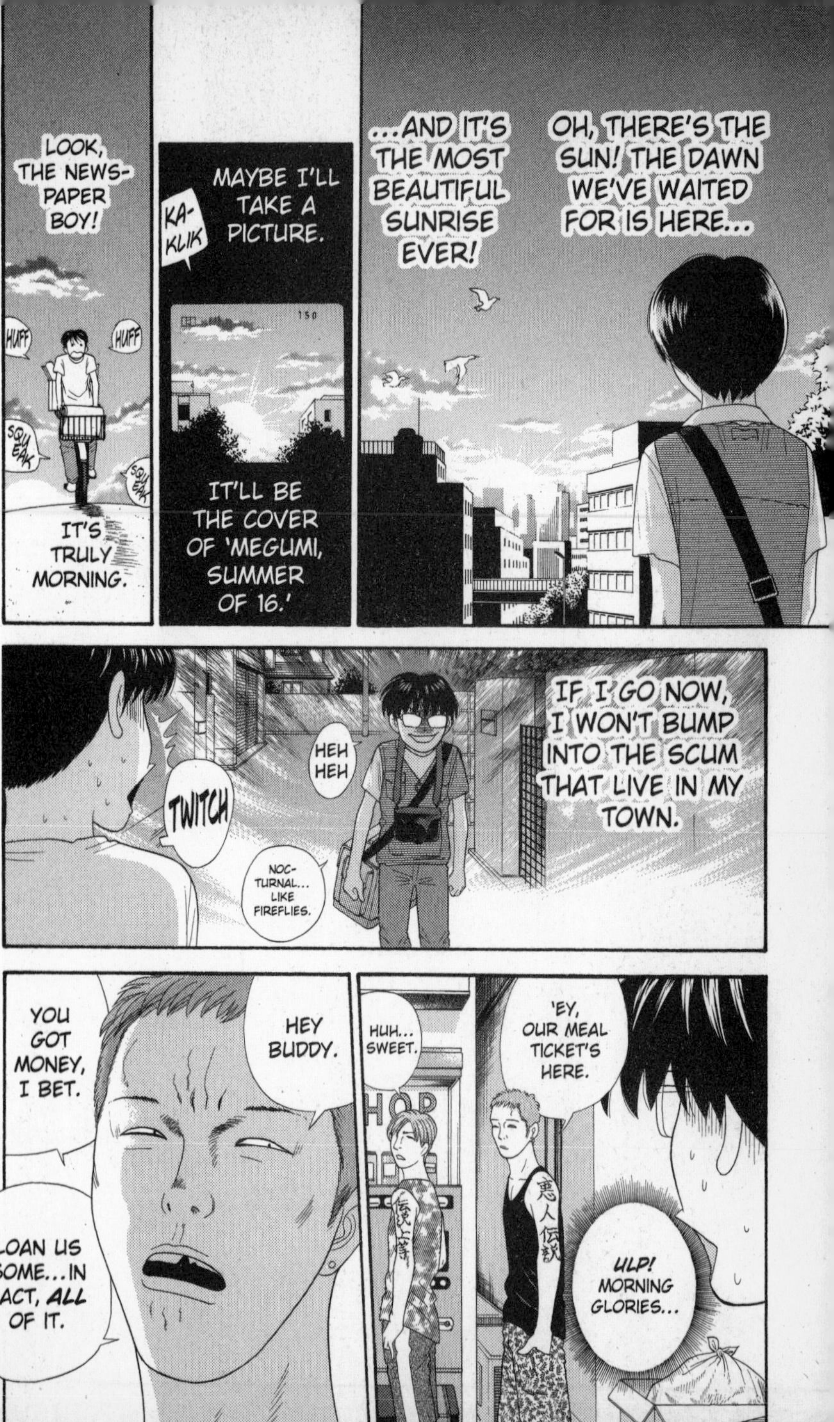
OH, THERE'S THE SUN! THE DAWN WE'VE WAITED FOR IS HERE...
...AND IT'S THE MOST BEAUTIFUL SUNRISE EVER!
MAYBE I'LL TAKE A PICTURE.
KA-KLIK
150
IT'LL BE THE COVER OF 'MEGUMI, SUMMER OF 16.'
LOOK, THE NEWS-PAPER BOY!
HUFF
HUFF
SQUEAK
SQUEAK
IT'S TRULY MORNING.
IF I GO NOW, I WON'T BUMP INTO THE SCUM THAT LIVE IN MY TOWN.
HEH HEH
NOC-TURNAL... LIKE FIREFLIES.
TWITCH
'EY, OUR MEAL TICKET'S HERE.
ULP! MORNING GLORIES...
HUH... SWEET.
HEY BUDDY.
YOU GOT MONEY, I BET.
LOAN US SOME...IN FACT, ALL OF IT.

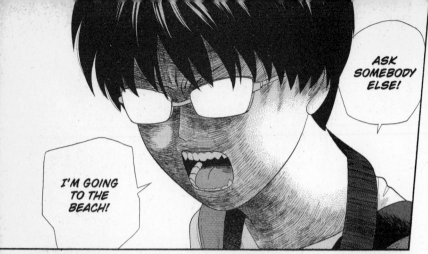

ASK SOMEBODY ELSE!

I'M GOING TO THE BEACH!

AN *ARMY* WOULDN'T STOP ME TODAY!

ZZZ

AK

ZZAK

EEE-YAK

ELECTRIC ARC!

HEY YOU...

GRIP

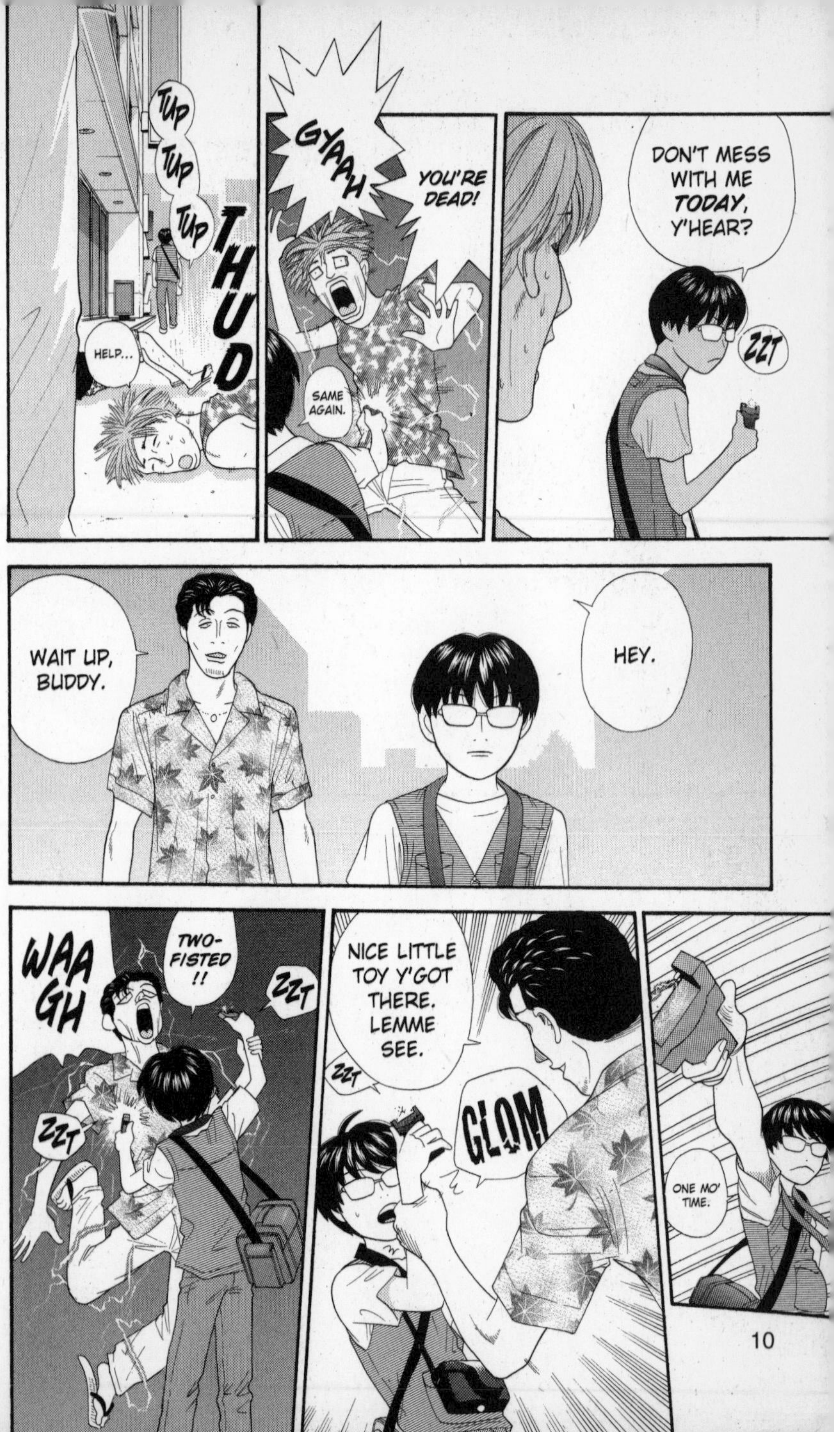
DON'T MESS WITH ME *TODAY*, Y'HEAR?
ZZT
GYAAAH
YOU'RE DEAD!
SAME AGAIN.
TUP
TUP
TUP
THUD
HELP...
HEY.
WAIT UP, BUDDY.
ONE MO' TIME.
NICE LITTLE TOY Y'GOT THERE. LEMME SEE.
ZZT
GLOM
TWO-FISTED !!
WAAGH
ZZT
ZZT

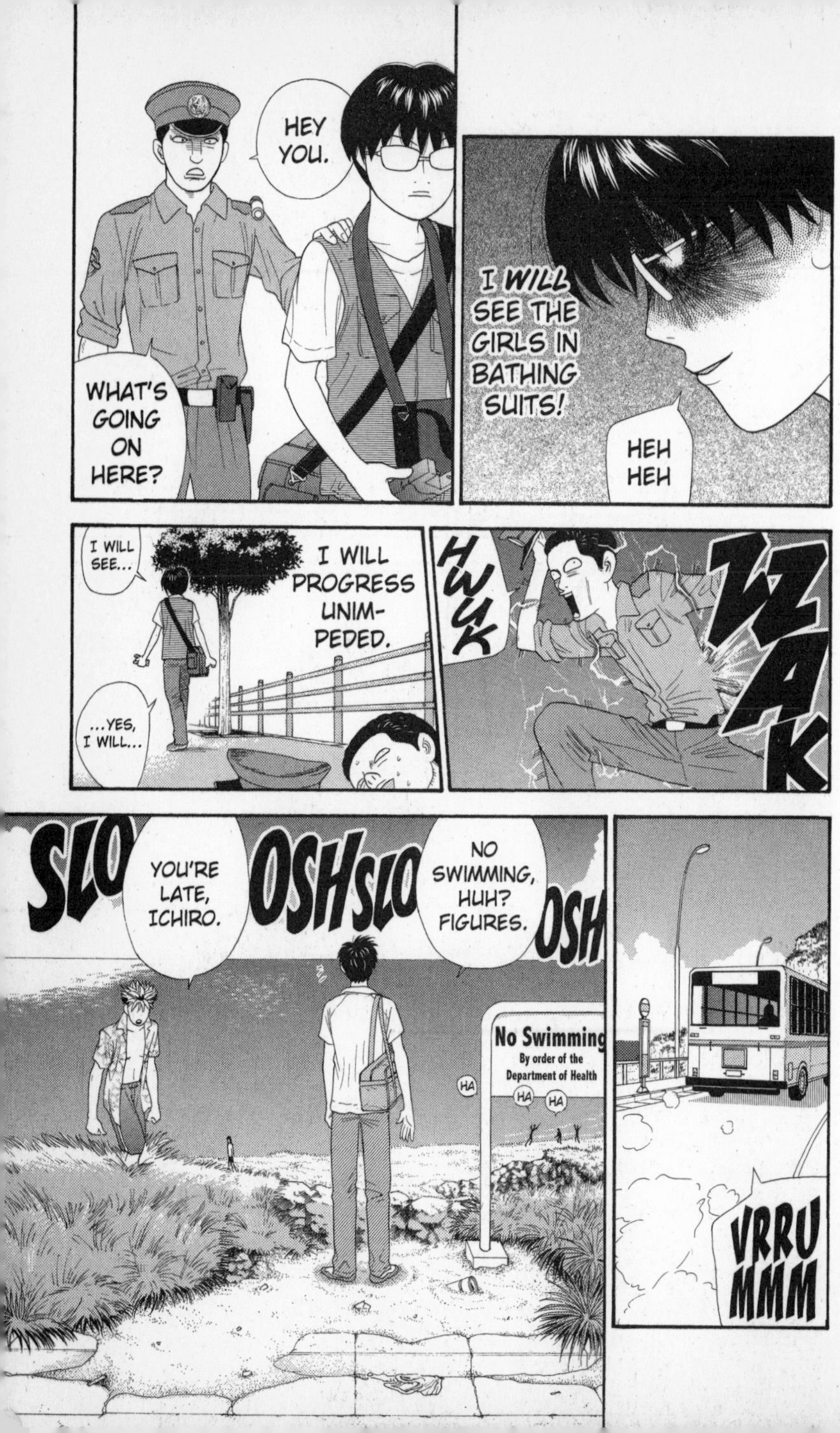
I WILL SEE THE GIRLS IN BATHING SUITS!
HEH HEH
HEY YOU.
WHAT'S GOING ON HERE?
HWUK
WAK
I WILL PROGRESS UNIM-PEDED.
I WILL SEE...
...YES, I WILL...
VRRUMMM
SLOOSH
NO SWIMMING, HUH? FIGURES.
SLOOSH
YOU'RE LATE, ICHIRO.
No Swimming
By order of the
Department of Health
HA
HA
HA

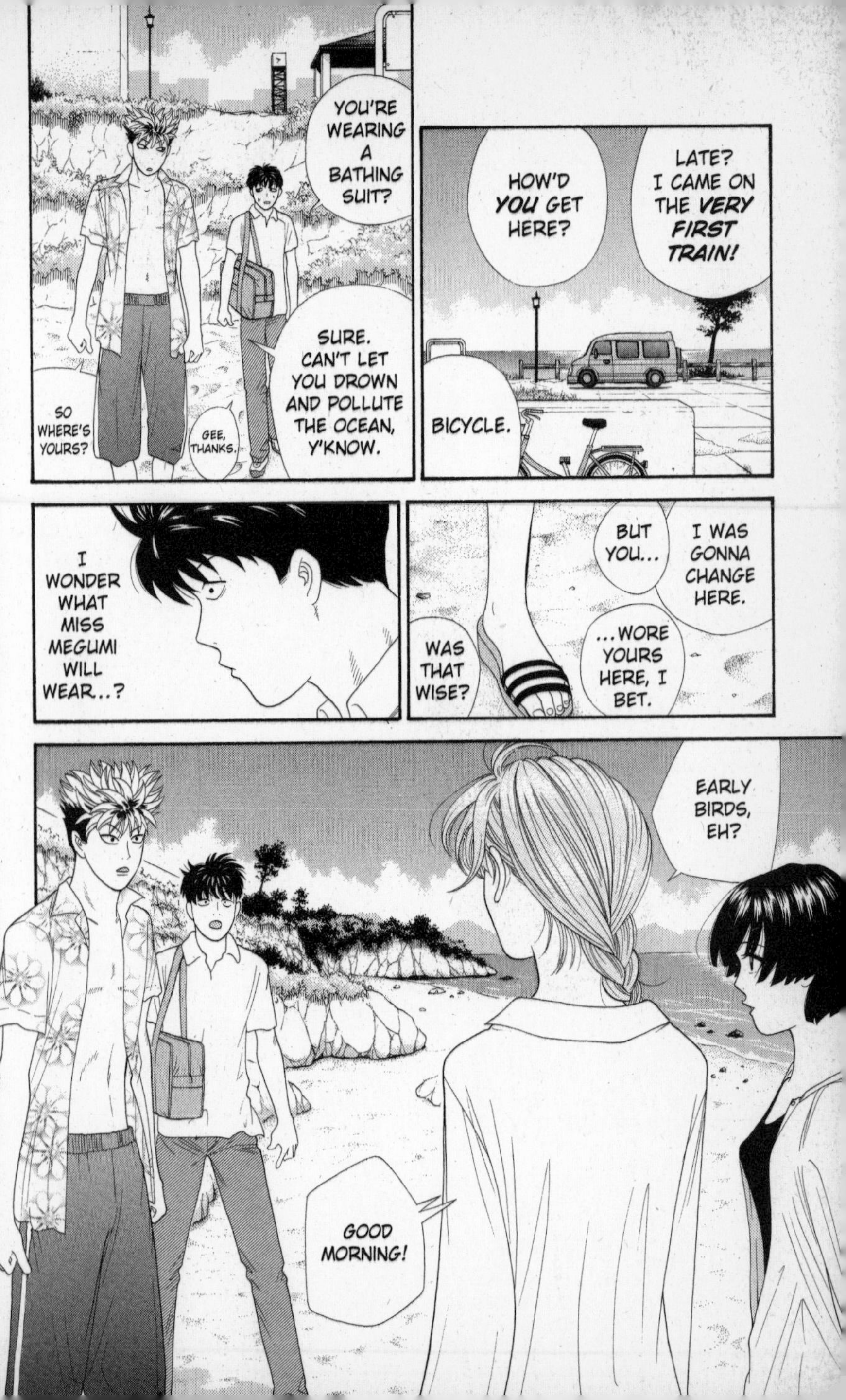
LATE? I CAME ON THE *VERY FIRST TRAIN!*
HOW'D *YOU* GET HERE?
BICYCLE.
YOU'RE WEARING A BATHING SUIT?
SURE. CAN'T LET YOU DROWN AND POLLUTE THE OCEAN, Y'KNOW.
GEE, THANKS.
SO WHERE'S YOURS?
I WAS GONNA CHANGE HERE.
BUT YOU...
...WORE YOURS HERE, I BET.
WAS THAT WISE?
I WONDER WHAT MISS MEGUMI WILL WEAR...?
EARLY BIRDS, EH?
GOOD MORNING!

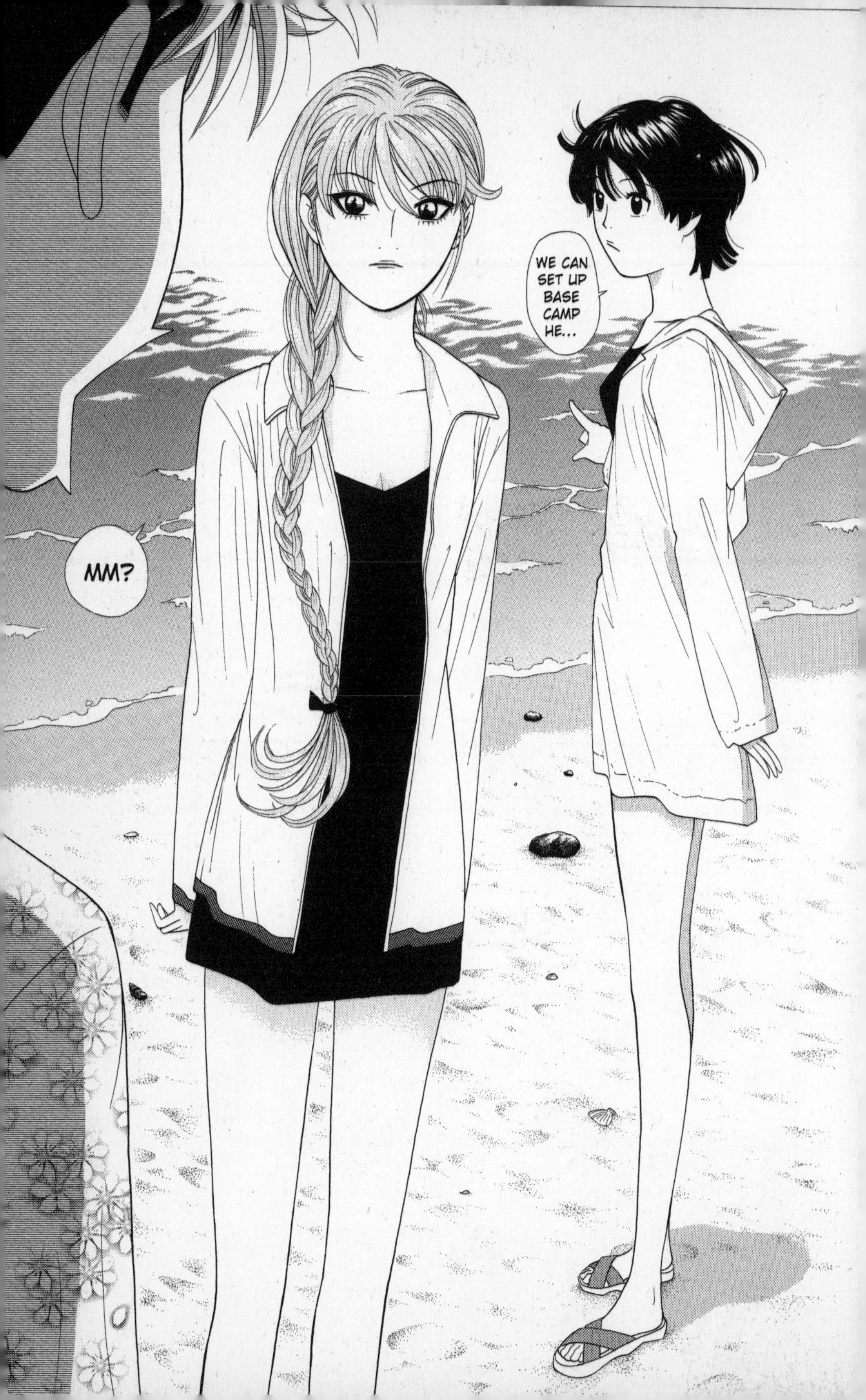
WE CAN SET UP BASE CAMP HE...
MM?

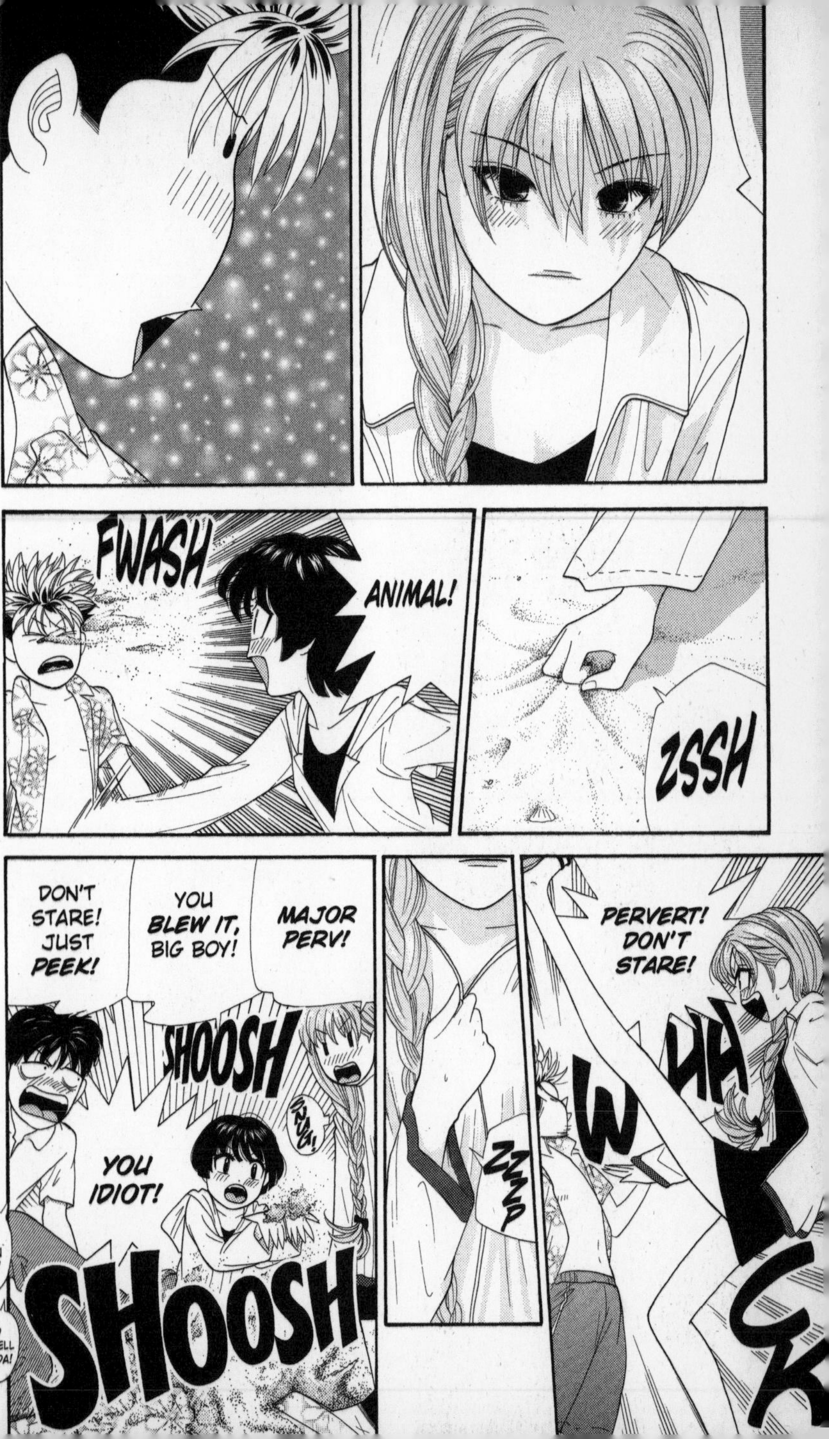
ZSSH
ANIMAL!
FWASH
PERVERT! DON'T STARE!
MAJOR PERV!
YOU BLEW IT, BIG BOY!
DON'T STARE! JUST PEEK!
SHOOSH
YOU IDIOT!
YOU BEEN BAD!
AND I'LL TELL YASUDA!
SHOOSH

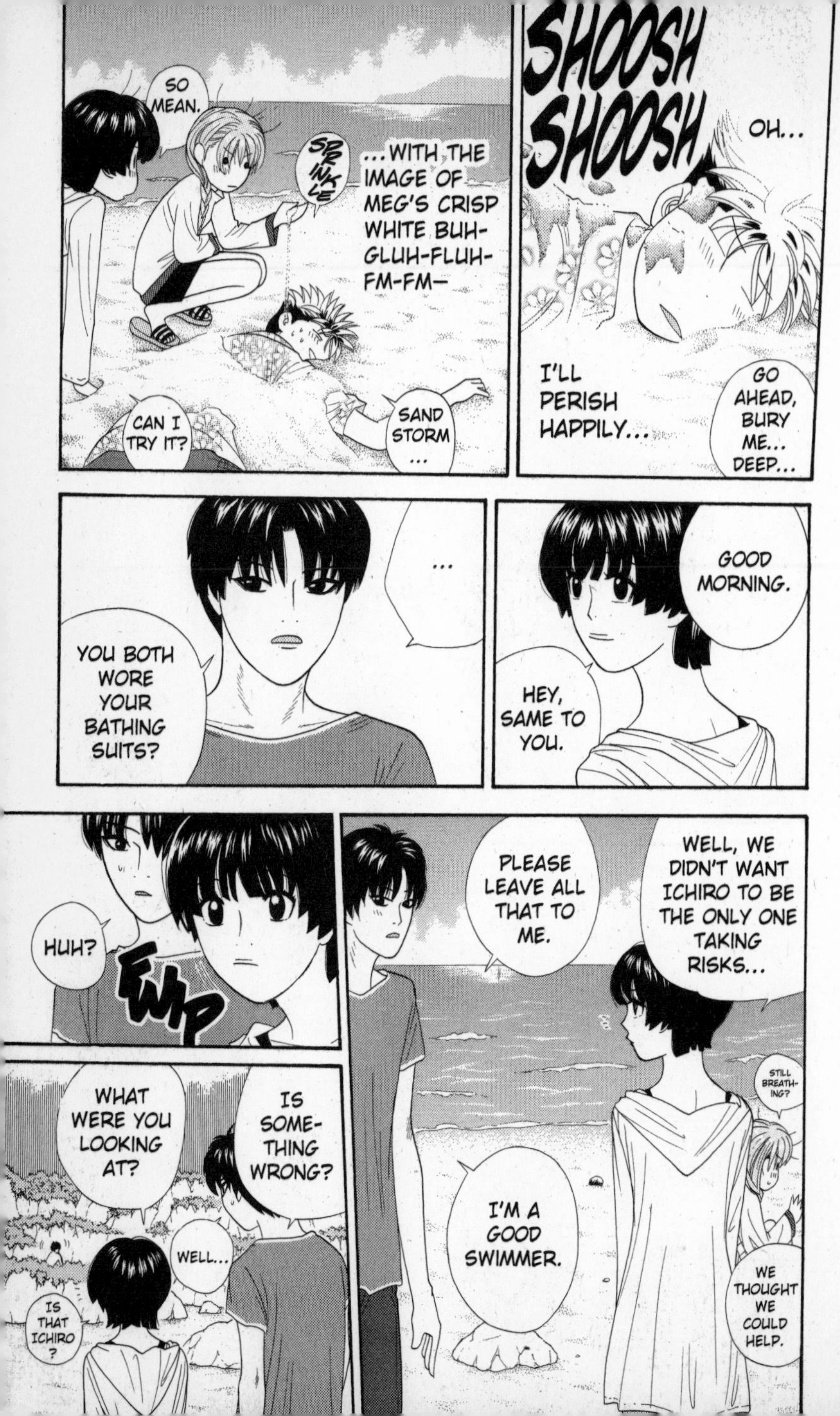
OH...
SHOOSH SHOOSH
GO AHEAD, BURY ME... DEEP...
I'LL PERISH HAPPILY...
...WITH THE IMAGE OF MEG'S CRISP WHITE BUH-GLUH-FLUH-FM-FM—
SPRINKLE
SO MEAN.
SAND STORM...
CAN I TRY IT?
GOOD MORNING.
HEY, SAME TO YOU.
...
YOU BOTH WORE YOUR BATHING SUITS?
WELL, WE DIDN'T WANT ICHIRO TO BE THE ONLY ONE TAKING RISKS...
PLEASE LEAVE ALL THAT TO ME.
STILL BREATH-ING?
WE THOUGHT WE COULD HELP.
I'M A GOOD SWIMMER.
HUH?
FWIP
IS SOME-THING WRONG?
WHAT WERE YOU LOOKING AT?
WELL...
IS THAT ICHIRO?

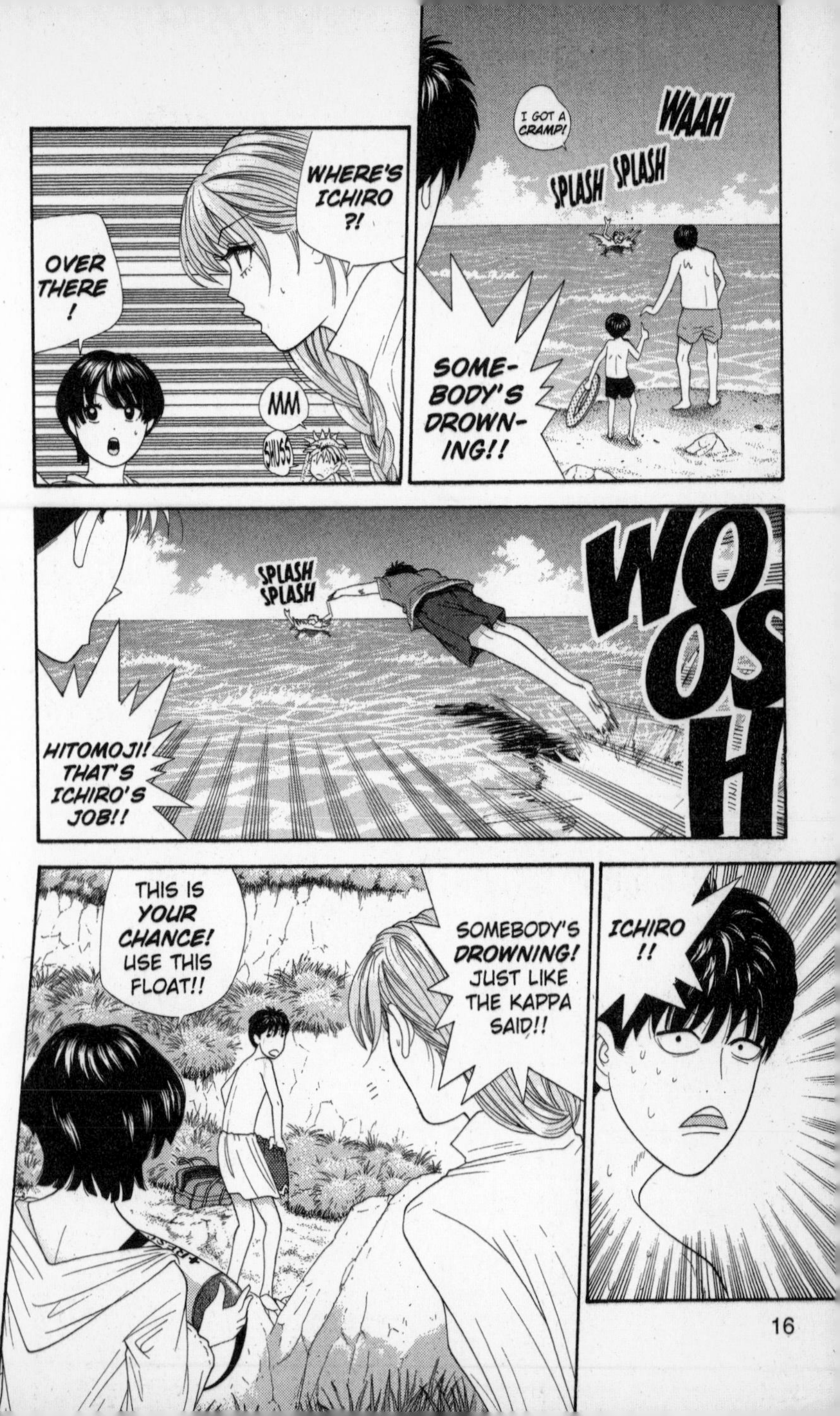

WAAH
I GOT A CRAMP!
SPLASH SPLASH
SOMEBODY'S DROWNING!!
WHERE'S ICHIRO?!
OVER THERE!
MM
SHUSS
WOOSH
SPLASH SPLASH
HITOMOJI! THAT'S ICHIRO'S JOB!!
ICHIRO!!
SOMEBODY'S DROWNING! JUST LIKE THE KAPPA SAID!!
THIS IS YOUR CHANCE! USE THIS FLOAT!!

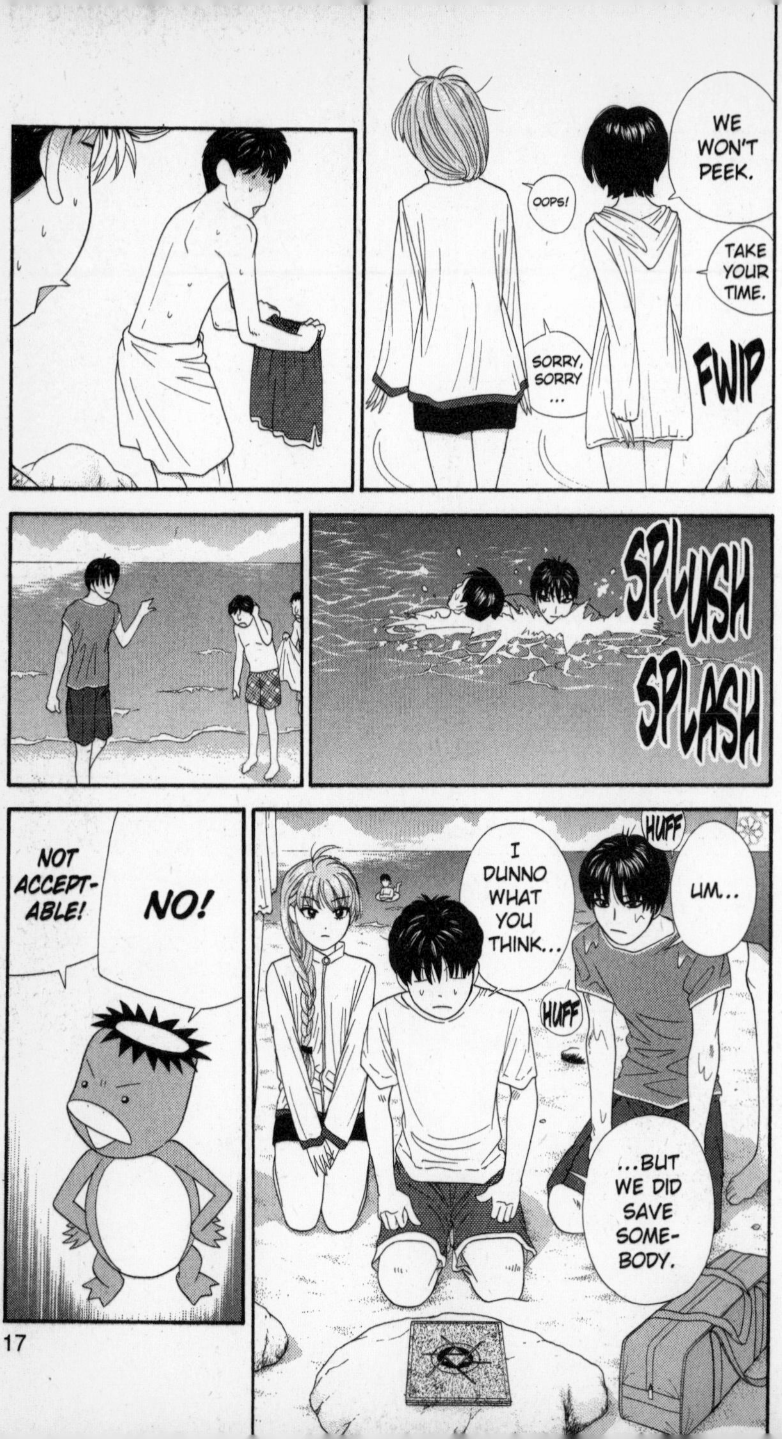
WE WON'T PEEK.
TAKE YOUR TIME.
OOPS!
SORRY, SORRY ...
FWIP
SPLUSH SPLASH
HUFF
UM...
I DUNNO WHAT YOU THINK...
HUFF
...BUT WE DID SAVE SOME-BODY.
NO!
NOT ACCEPT-ABLE!

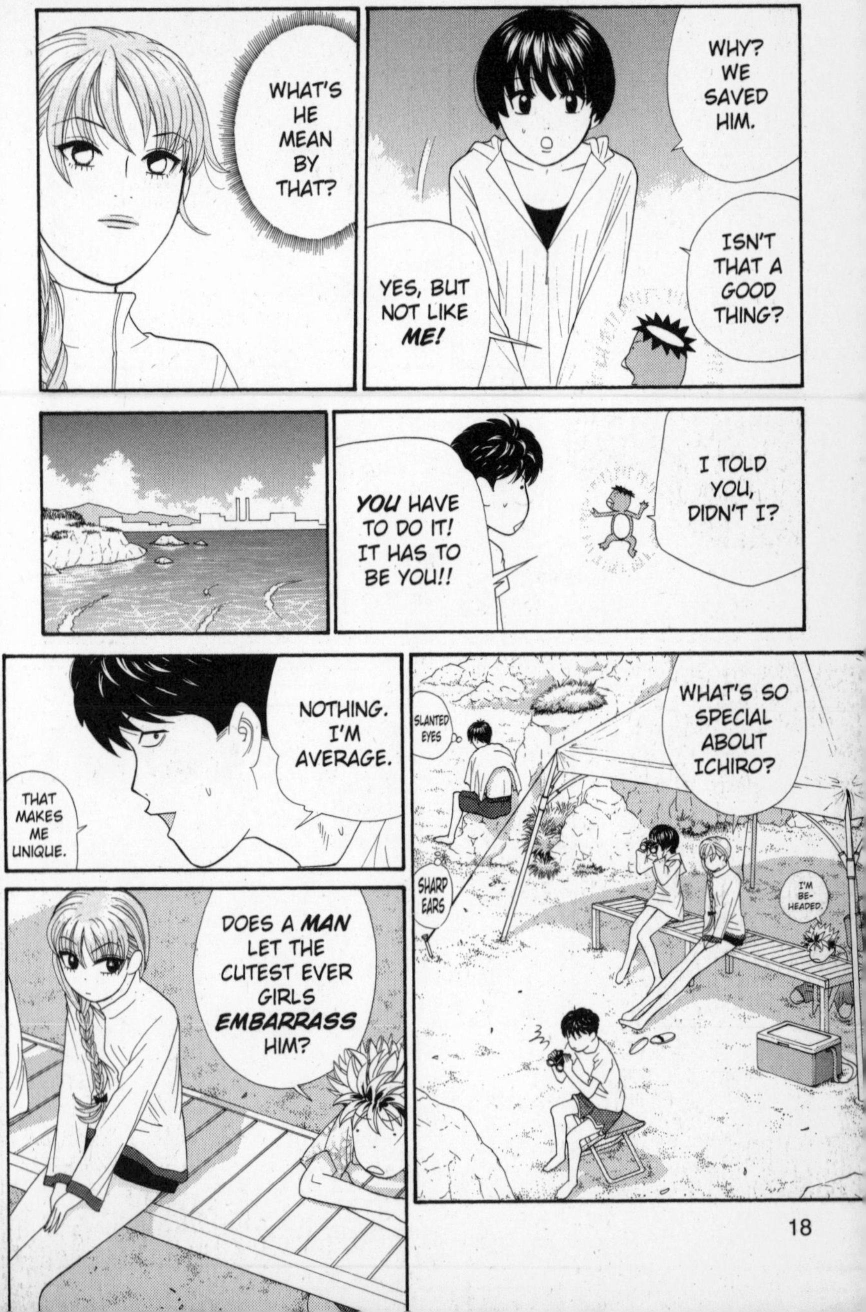
WHY? WE SAVED HIM.
ISN'T THAT A GOOD THING?
YES, BUT NOT LIKE ME!
WHAT'S HE MEAN BY THAT?
I TOLD YOU, DIDN'T I?
YOU HAVE TO DO IT! IT HAS TO BE YOU!!
WHAT'S SO SPECIAL ABOUT ICHIRO?
SLANTED EYES
SHARP EARS
I'M BE-HEADED.
NOTHING. I'M AVERAGE.
THAT MAKES ME UNIQUE.
DOES A MAN LET THE CUTEST EVER GIRLS EMBARRASS HIM?

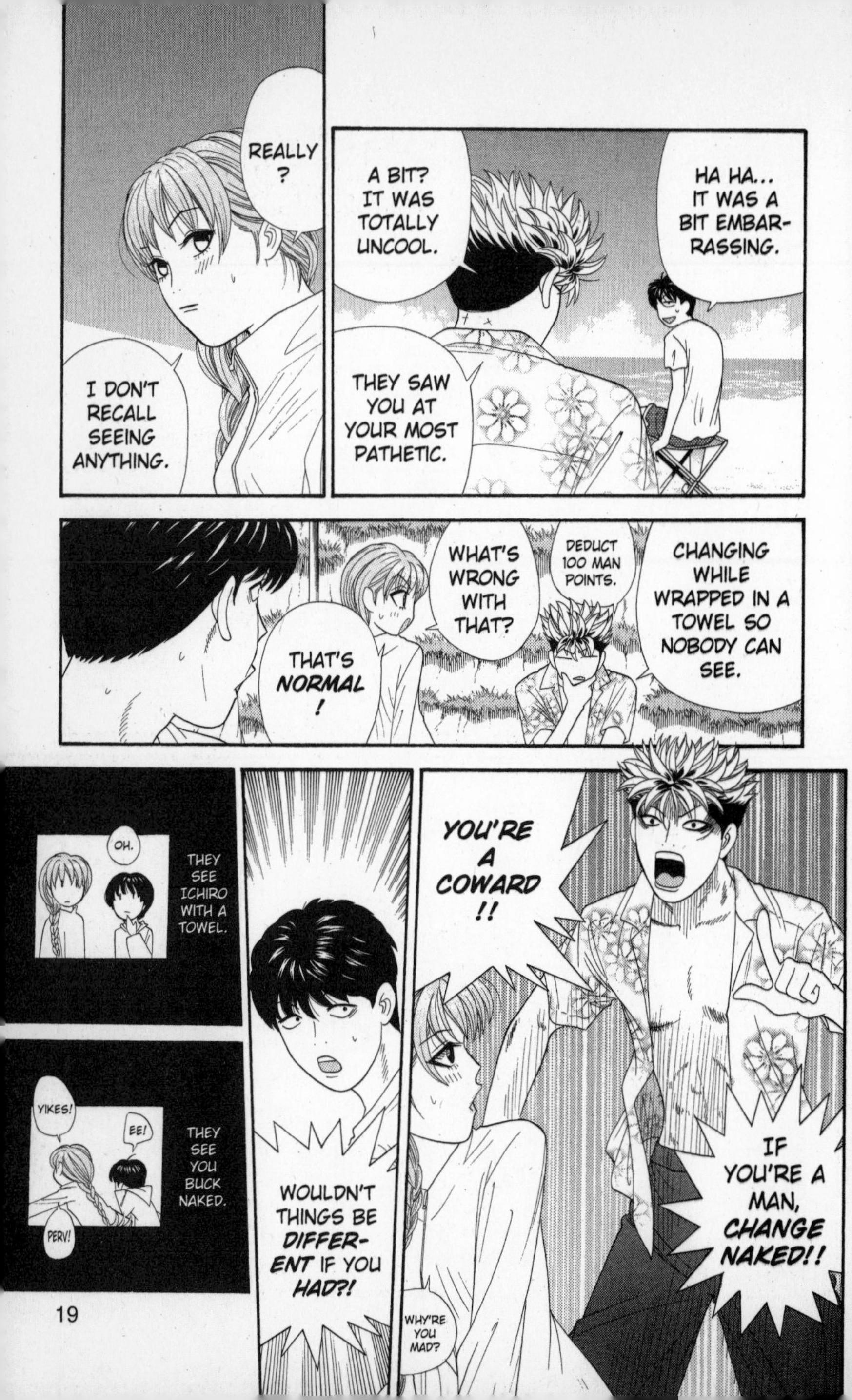
HA HA... IT WAS A BIT EMBARRASSING.
A BIT? IT WAS TOTALLY UNCOOL.
THEY SAW YOU AT YOUR MOST PATHETIC.
REALLY?
I DON'T RECALL SEEING ANYTHING.
CHANGING WHILE WRAPPED IN A TOWEL SO NOBODY CAN SEE.
DEDUCT 100 MAN POINTS.
WHAT'S WRONG WITH THAT?
THAT'S NORMAL!
YOU'RE A COWARD!!
IF YOU'RE A MAN, CHANGE NAKED!!
WOULDN'T THINGS BE DIFFERENT IF YOU HAD?!
WHY'RE YOU MAD?
OH.
THEY SEE ICHIRO WITH A TOWEL.
YIKES!
EE!
PERV!
THEY SEE YOU BUCK NAKED.

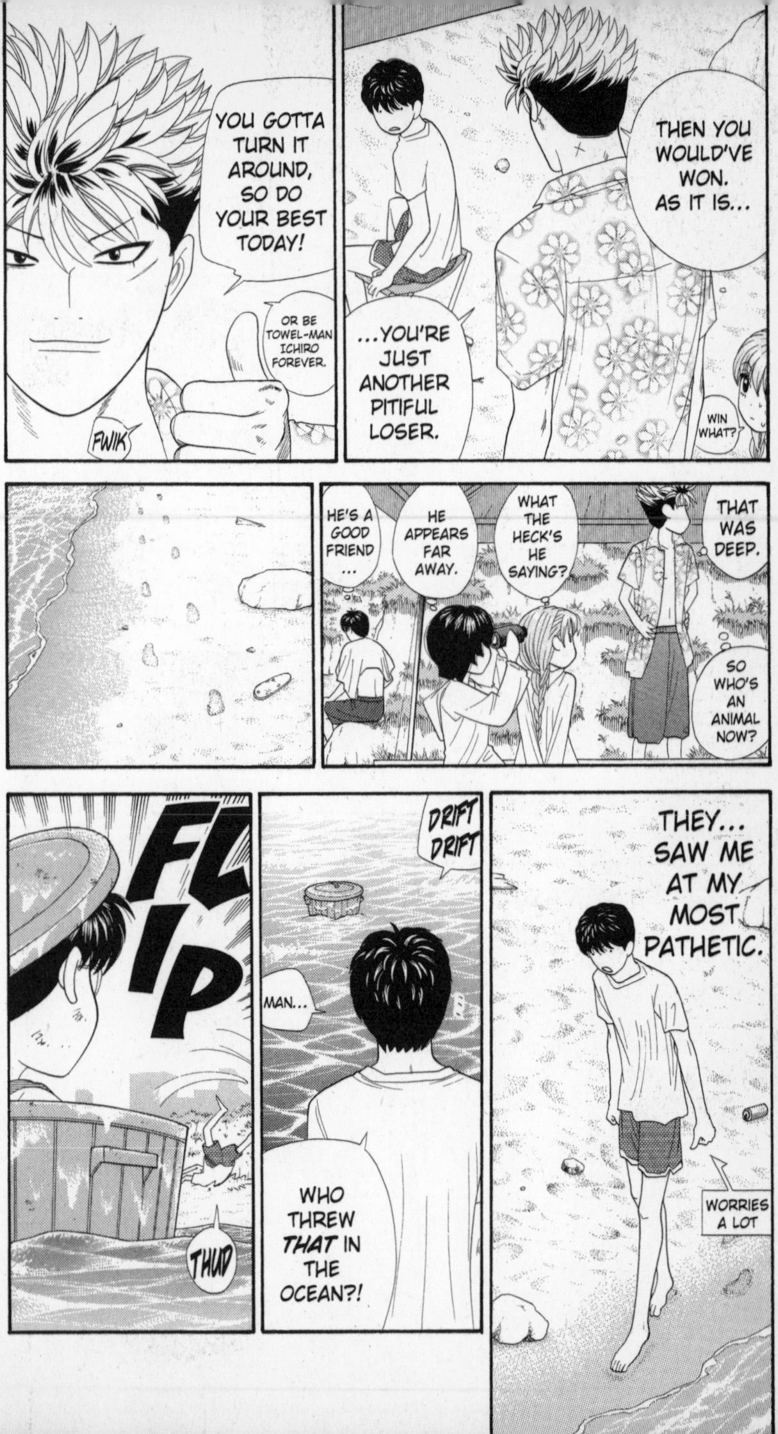

THEN YOU WOULD'VE WON. AS IT IS...
...YOU'RE JUST ANOTHER PITIFUL LOSER.
WIN WHAT?
YOU GOTTA TURN IT AROUND, SO DO YOUR BEST TODAY!
OR BE TOWEL-MAN ICHIRO FOREVER.
FWIK
THAT WAS DEEP.
SO WHO'S AN ANIMAL NOW?
WHAT THE HECK'S HE SAYING?
HE APPEARS FAR AWAY.
HE'S A GOOD FRIEND...
THEY... SAW ME AT MY MOST PATHETIC.
WORRIES A LOT
DRIFT DRIFT
MAN...
WHO THREW *THAT* IN THE OCEAN?!
FLIP
THUD

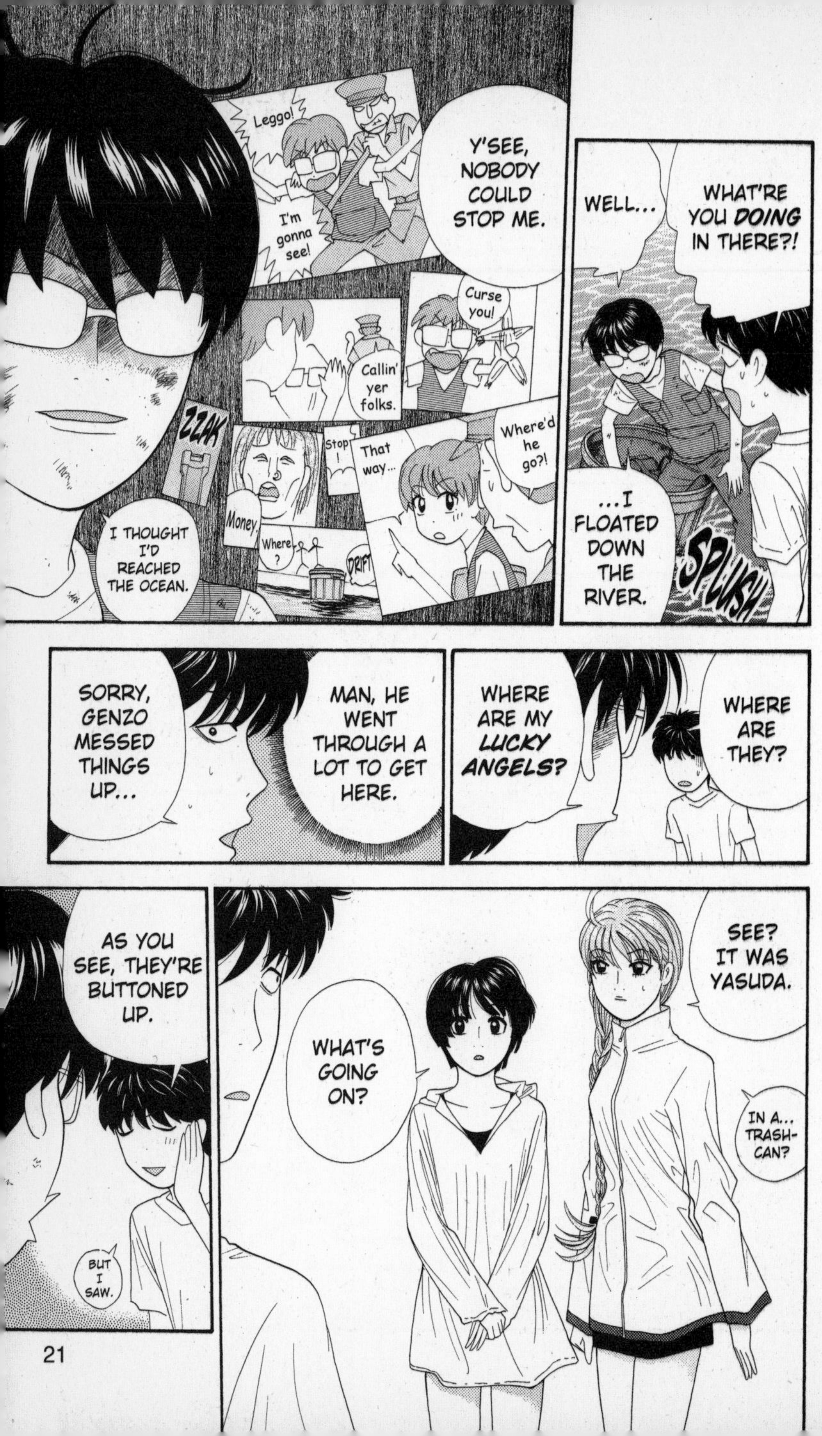
WHAT'RE YOU DOING IN THERE?!
WELL...
...I FLOATED DOWN THE RIVER.
SPLUSH
Y'SEE, NOBODY COULD STOP ME.
Leggo!
I'm gonna see!
Curse you!
Callin' yer folks.
Where'd he go?!
That way...
Stop!
ZZAK
Money.
Where?
DRIFT
I THOUGHT I'D REACHED THE OCEAN.
WHERE ARE THEY?
WHERE ARE MY LUCKY ANGELS?
MAN, HE WENT THROUGH A LOT TO GET HERE.
SORRY, GENZO MESSED THINGS UP...
SEE? IT WAS YASUDA.
IN A... TRASH-CAN?
WHAT'S GOING ON?
AS YOU SEE, THEY'RE BUTTONED UP.
BUT I SAW.

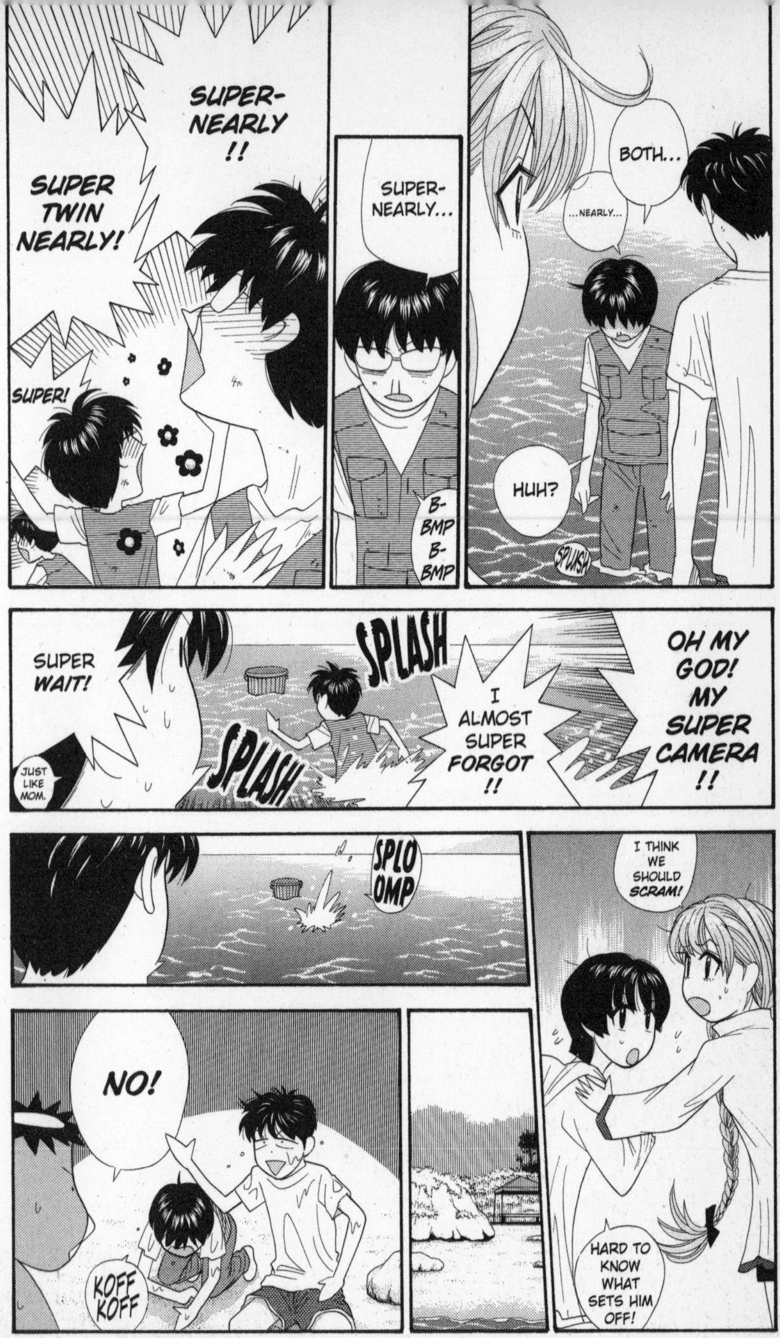
BOTH...
...NEARLY...
HUH?
SPLASH
SUPER-NEARLY...
B-BMP B-BMP
SUPER-NEARLY !!
SUPER TWIN NEARLY!
SUPER!
OH MY GOD! MY SUPER CAMERA !!
I ALMOST SUPER FORGOT !!
SPLASH
SUPER WAIT!
SPLASH
JUST LIKE MOM.
I THINK WE SHOULD SCRAM!
HARD TO KNOW WHAT SETS HIM OFF!
SPLOOMP
NO!
KOFF KOFF

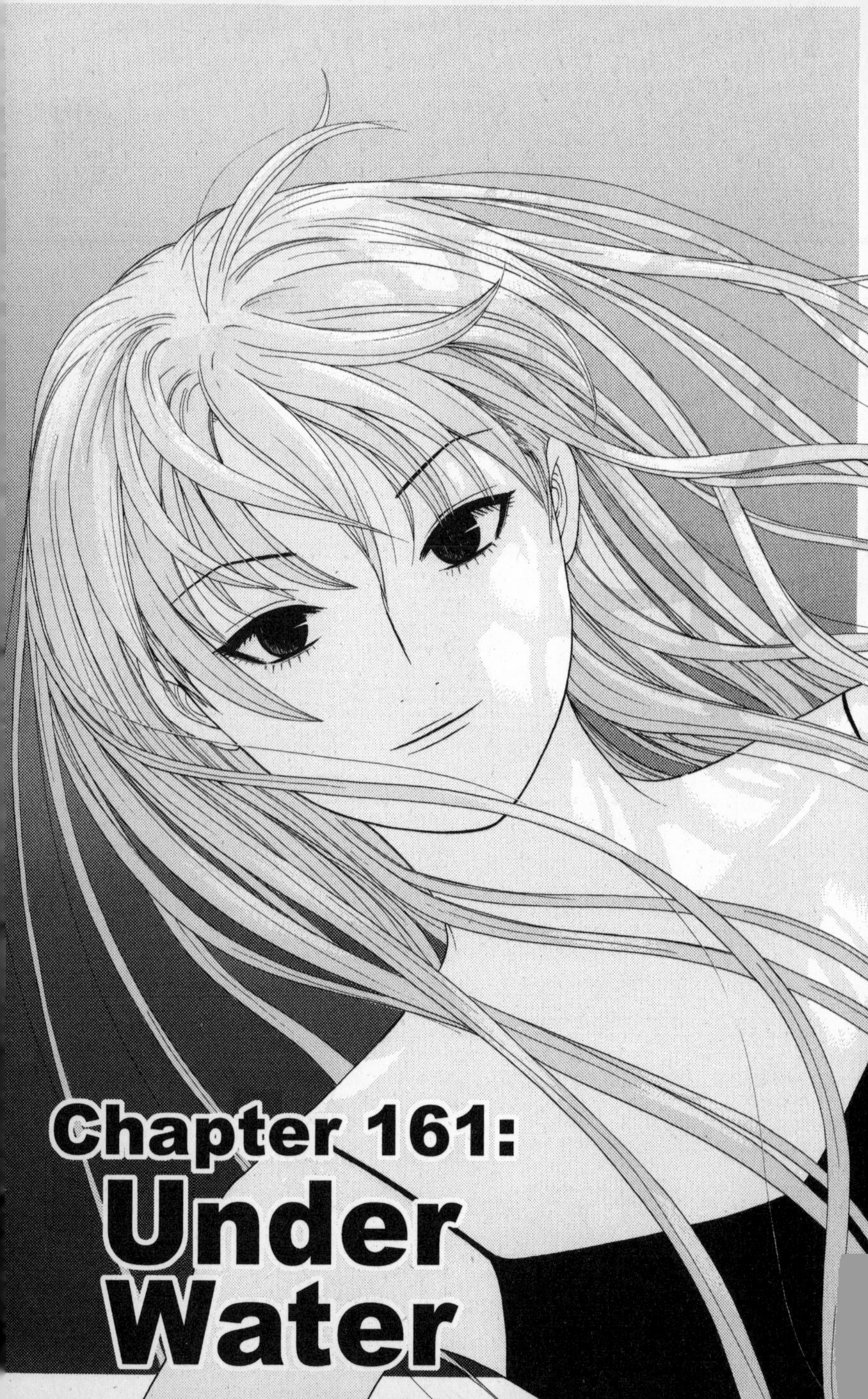
Chapter 161:
Under Water

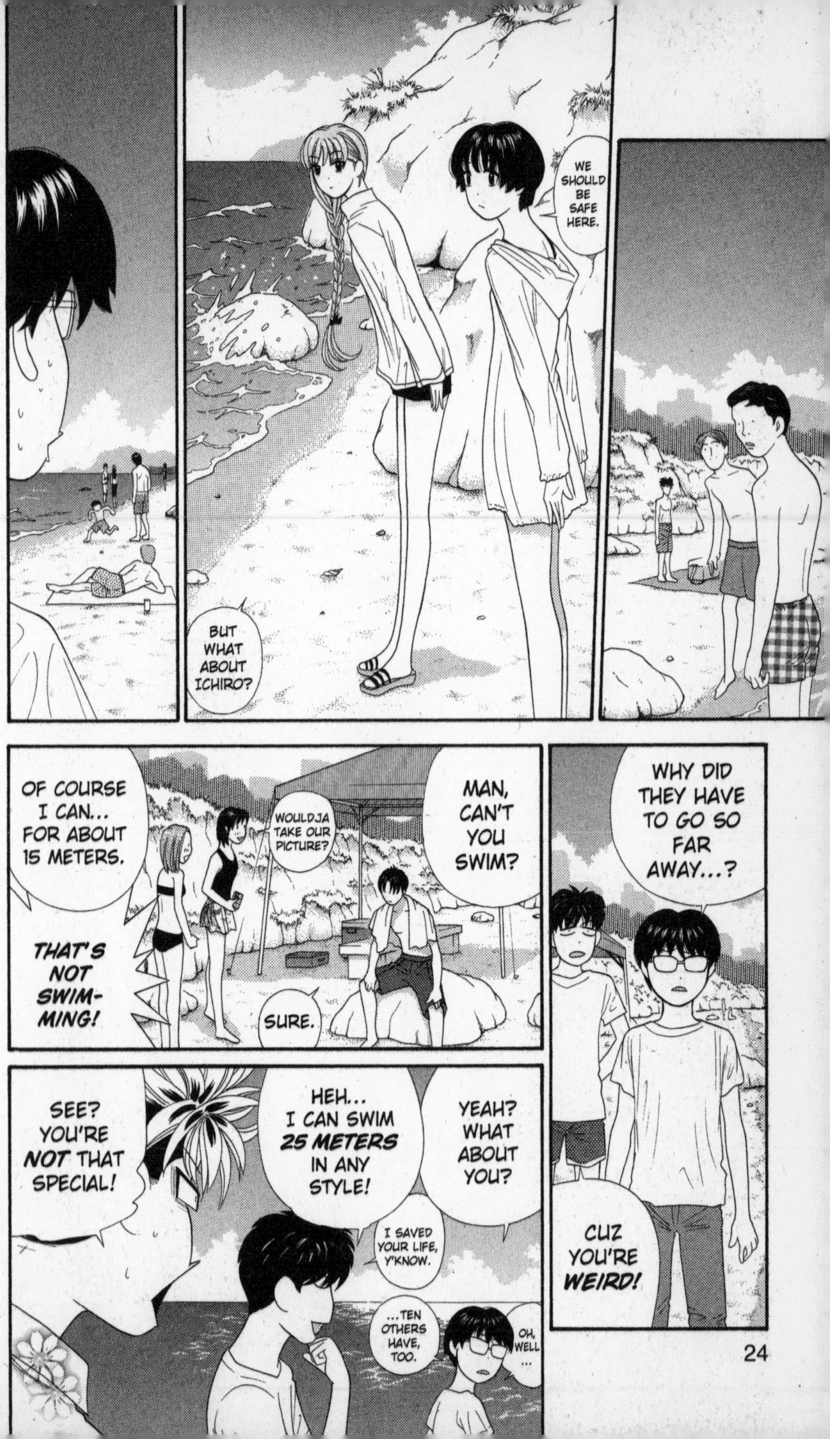
WE SHOULD BE SAFE HERE.
BUT WHAT ABOUT ICHIRO?
WHY DID THEY HAVE TO GO SO FAR AWAY...?
CUZ YOU'RE *WEIRD!*
MAN, CAN'T YOU SWIM?
WOULDJA TAKE OUR PICTURE?
OF COURSE I CAN... FOR ABOUT 15 METERS.
SURE.
THAT'S NOT SWIMMING!
YEAH? WHAT ABOUT YOU?
HEH... I CAN SWIM *25 METERS* IN ANY STYLE!
SEE? YOU'RE *NOT* THAT SPECIAL!
I SAVED YOUR LIFE, Y'KNOW.
...TEN OTHERS HAVE, TOO.
OH, WELL ...

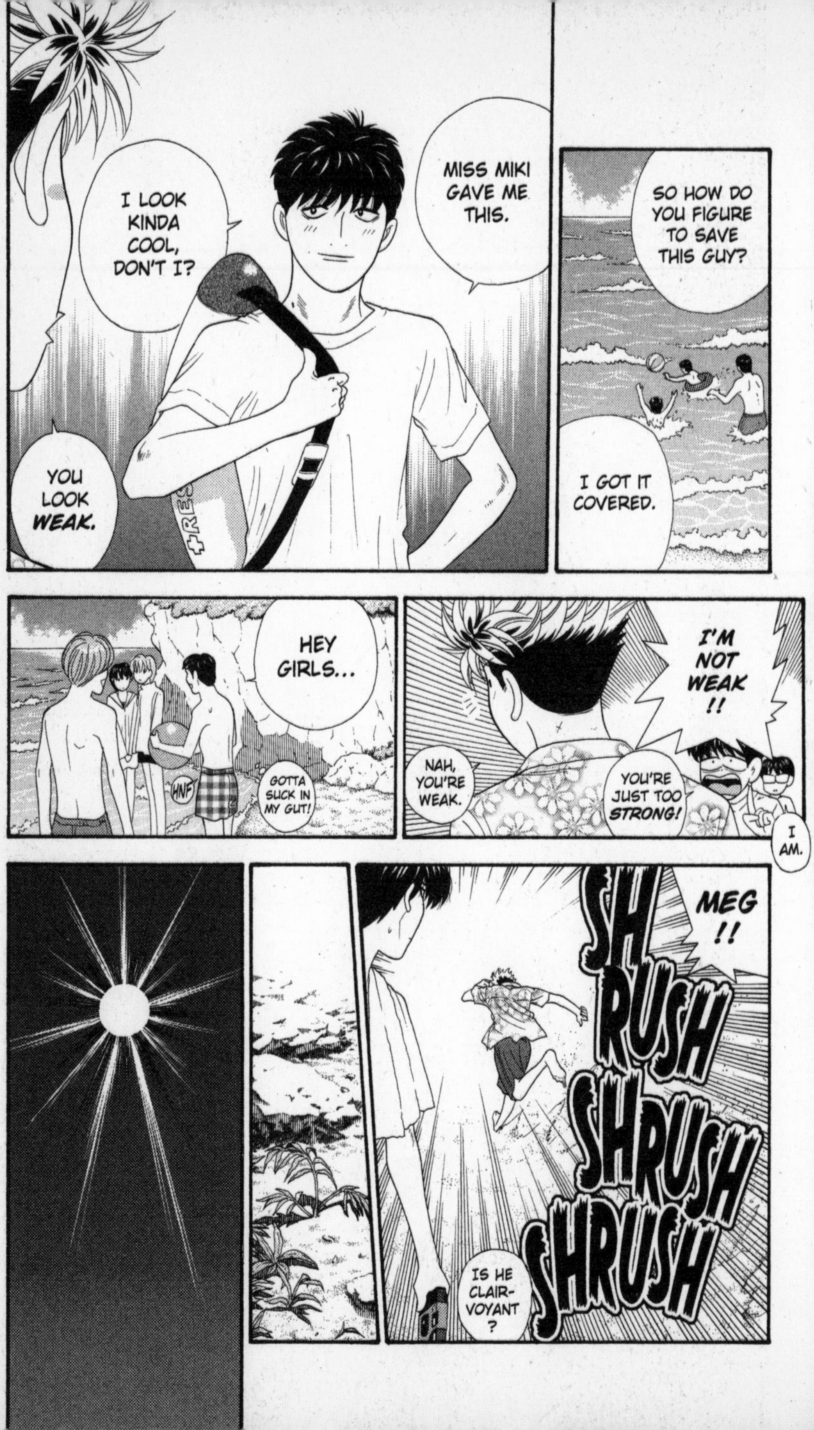
SO HOW DO YOU FIGURE TO SAVE THIS GUY?
I GOT IT COVERED.
MISS MIKI GAVE ME THIS.
I LOOK KINDA COOL, DON'T I?
YOU LOOK **WEAK.**
I'M NOT WEAK!!
YOU'RE JUST TOO **STRONG!**
NAH, YOU'RE WEAK.
I AM.
HEY GIRLS...
GOTTA SUCK IN MY GUT!
HNF
MEG!!
SHRUSH
SHRUSH
SHRUSH
IS HE CLAIR-VOYANT?

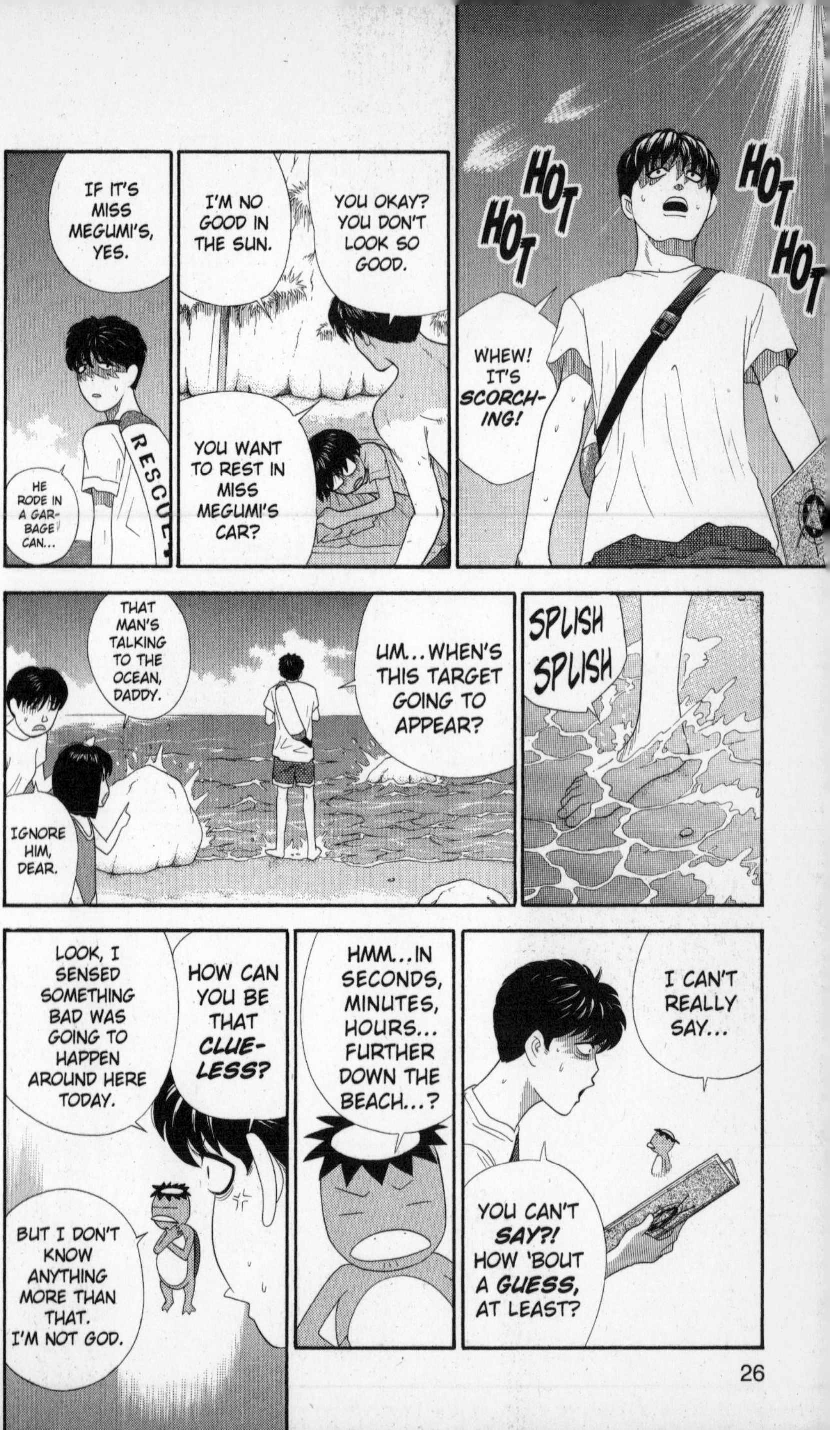
HOT HOT
HOT HOT
WHEW! IT'S SCORCHING!
YOU OKAY? YOU DON'T LOOK SO GOOD.
I'M NO GOOD IN THE SUN.
YOU WANT TO REST IN MISS MEGUMI'S CAR?
IF IT'S MISS MEGUMI'S, YES.
HE RODE IN A GARBAGE CAN...
RESCUE
SPLISH SPLISH
UM...WHEN'S THIS TARGET GOING TO APPEAR?
THAT MAN'S TALKING TO THE OCEAN, DADDY.
IGNORE HIM, DEAR.
I CAN'T REALLY SAY...
YOU CAN'T SAY?! HOW 'BOUT A GUESS, AT LEAST?
HMM...IN SECONDS, MINUTES, HOURS... FURTHER DOWN THE BEACH...?
HOW CAN YOU BE THAT CLUELESS?
LOOK, I SENSED SOMETHING BAD WAS GOING TO HAPPEN AROUND HERE TODAY.
BUT I DON'T KNOW ANYTHING MORE THAN THAT. I'M NOT GOD.

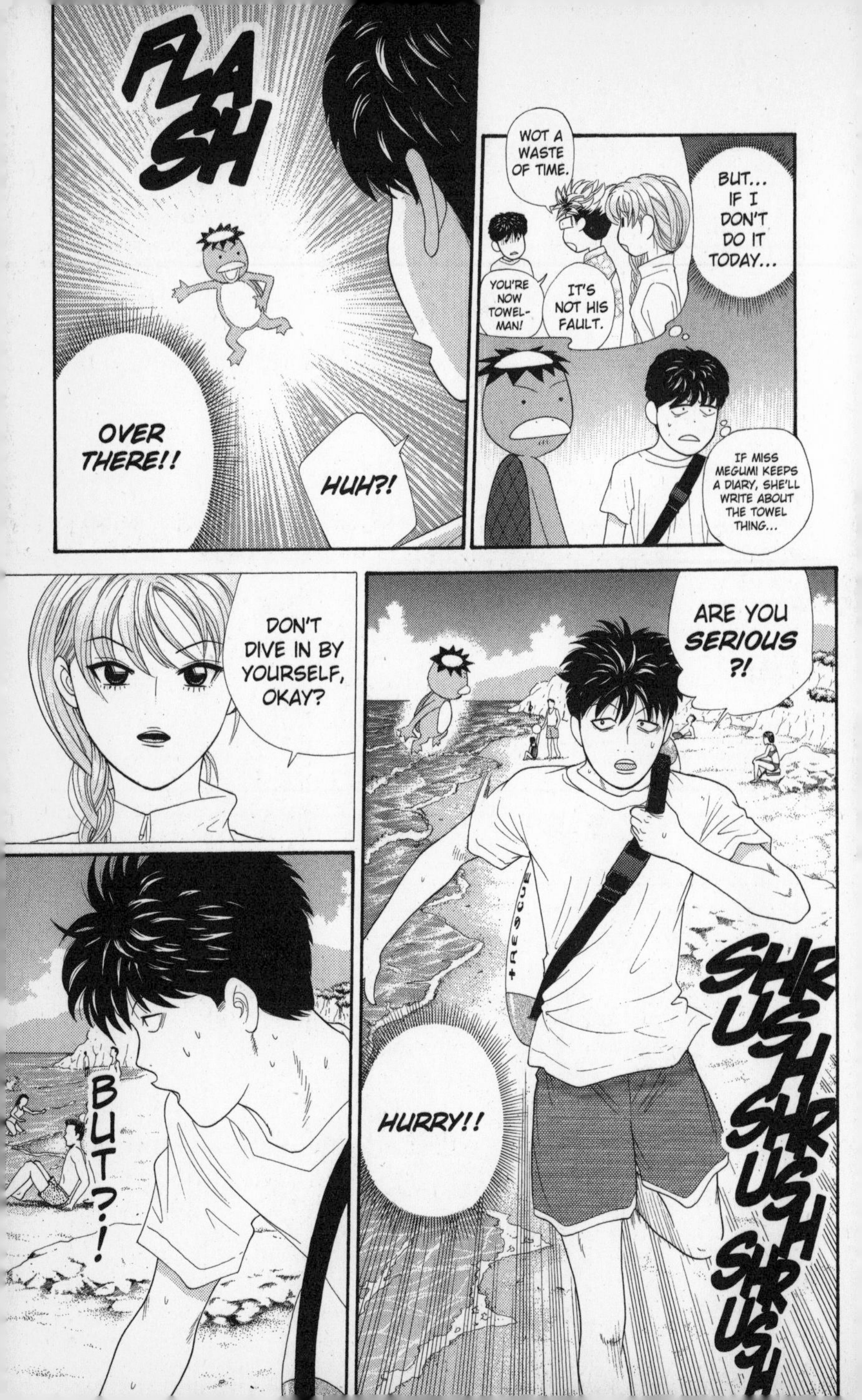
BUT... IF I DON'T DO IT TODAY...
WOT A WASTE OF TIME.
IT'S NOT HIS FAULT.
YOU'RE NOW TOWEL-MAN!
IF MISS MEGUMI KEEPS A DIARY, SHE'LL WRITE ABOUT THE TOWEL THING...
FLASH
OVER THERE!!
HUH?!
ARE YOU SERIOUS ?!
SHRUSH SHRUSH SHRUSH
RESCUE
HURRY!!
DON'T DIVE IN BY YOURSELF, OKAY?
BUT?!

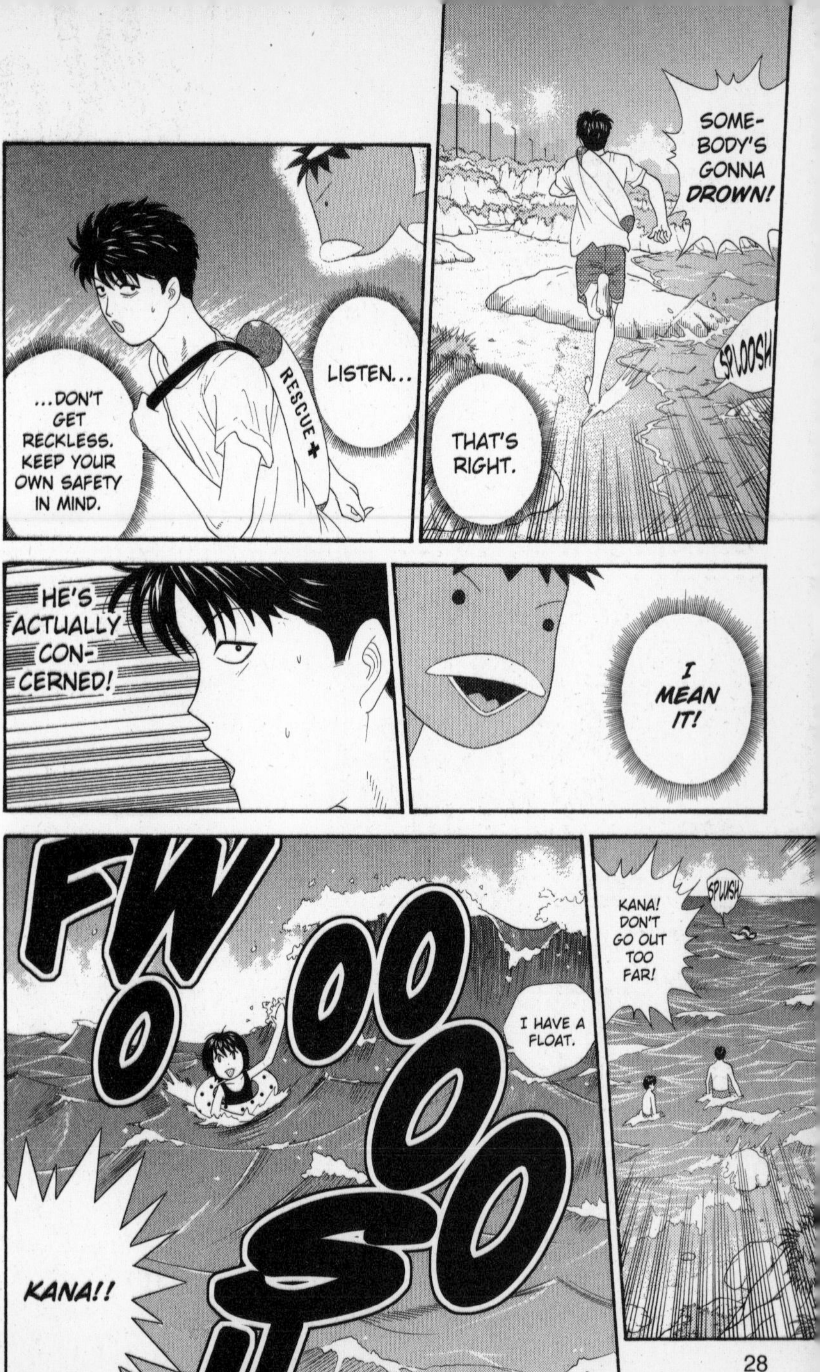
SOME-BODY'S GONNA DROWN!
SPLOOSH
THAT'S RIGHT.
LISTEN...
RESCUE
...DON'T GET RECKLESS. KEEP YOUR OWN SAFETY IN MIND.
I MEAN IT!
HE'S ACTUALLY CON-CERNED!
SPLUSH
KANA! DON'T GO OUT TOO FAR!
I HAVE A FLOAT.
FWOOOOOOSH
KANA!!

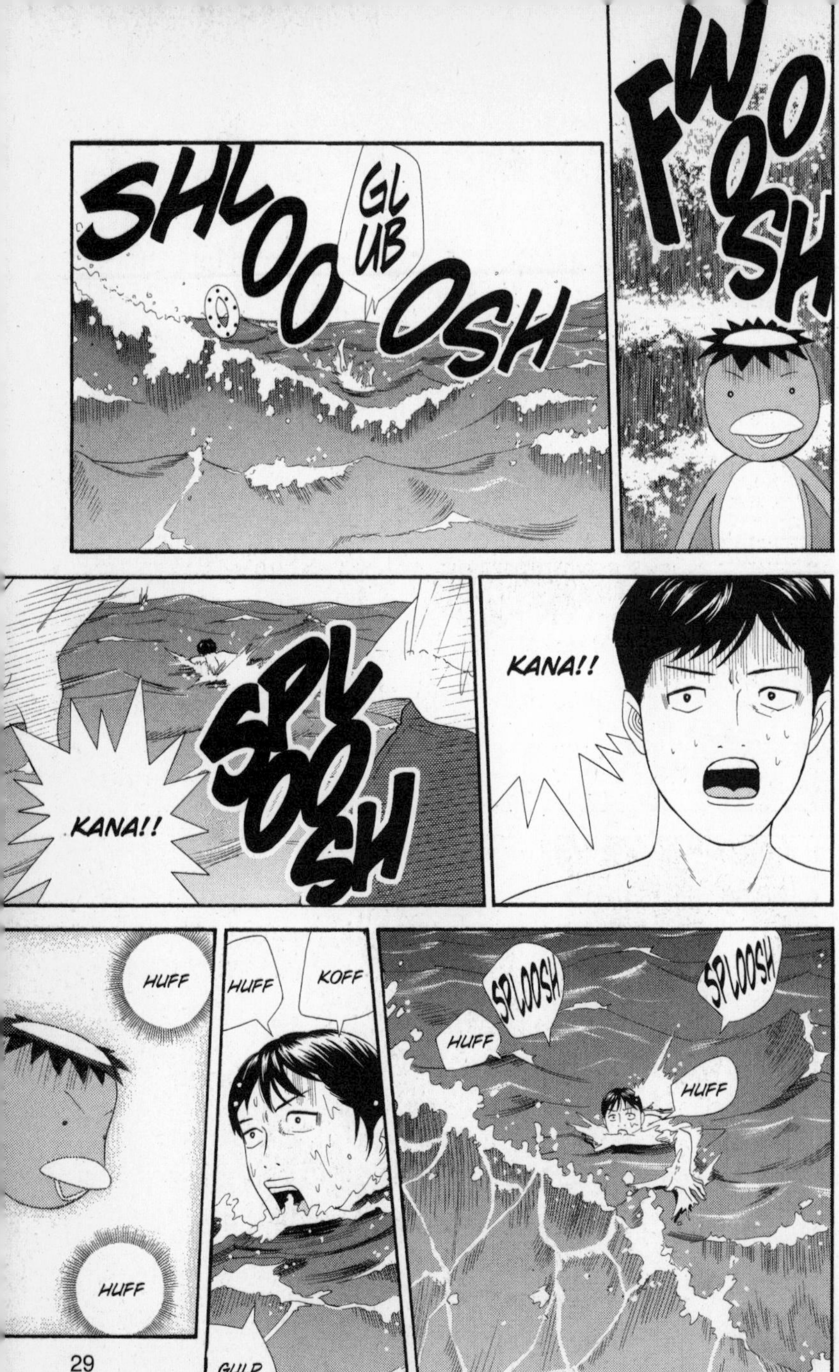
FWOOSH
SHLOOOSH
GLUB
KANA!!
SPLOOOSH
KANA!!
SPLOOSH
SPLOOSH
HUFF
HUFF
KOFF
HUFF
GULP
HUFF
HUFF

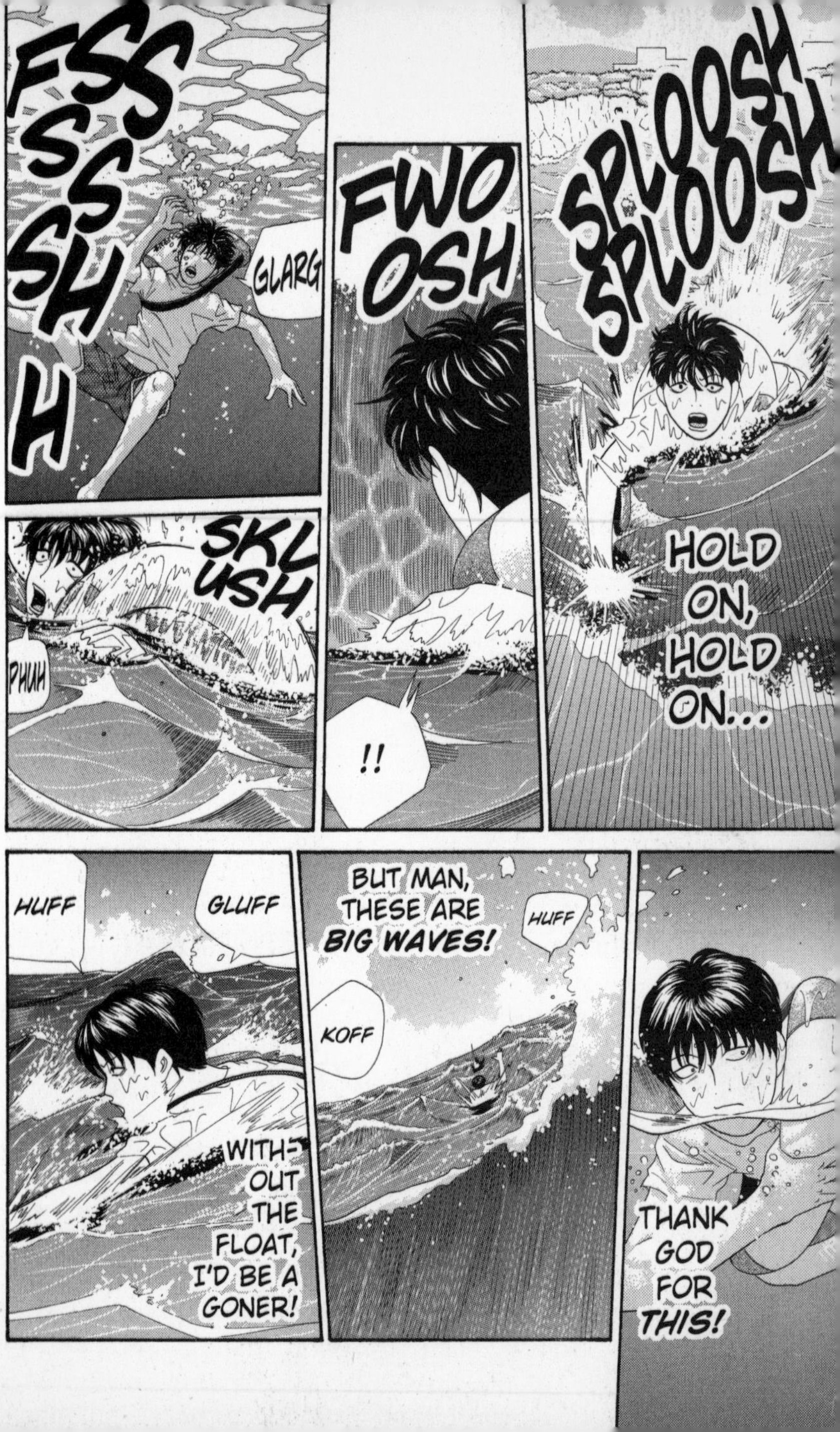
SPLOOSH
SPLOOSH
HOLD ON, HOLD ON...
FWOOSH
!!
FSSSSSHH
GLARG
SKLUSH
PHUH
THANK GOD FOR THIS!
BUT MAN, THESE ARE BIG WAVES!
HUFF
KOFF
GLUFF
HUFF
WITH-OUT THE FLOAT, I'D BE A GONER!

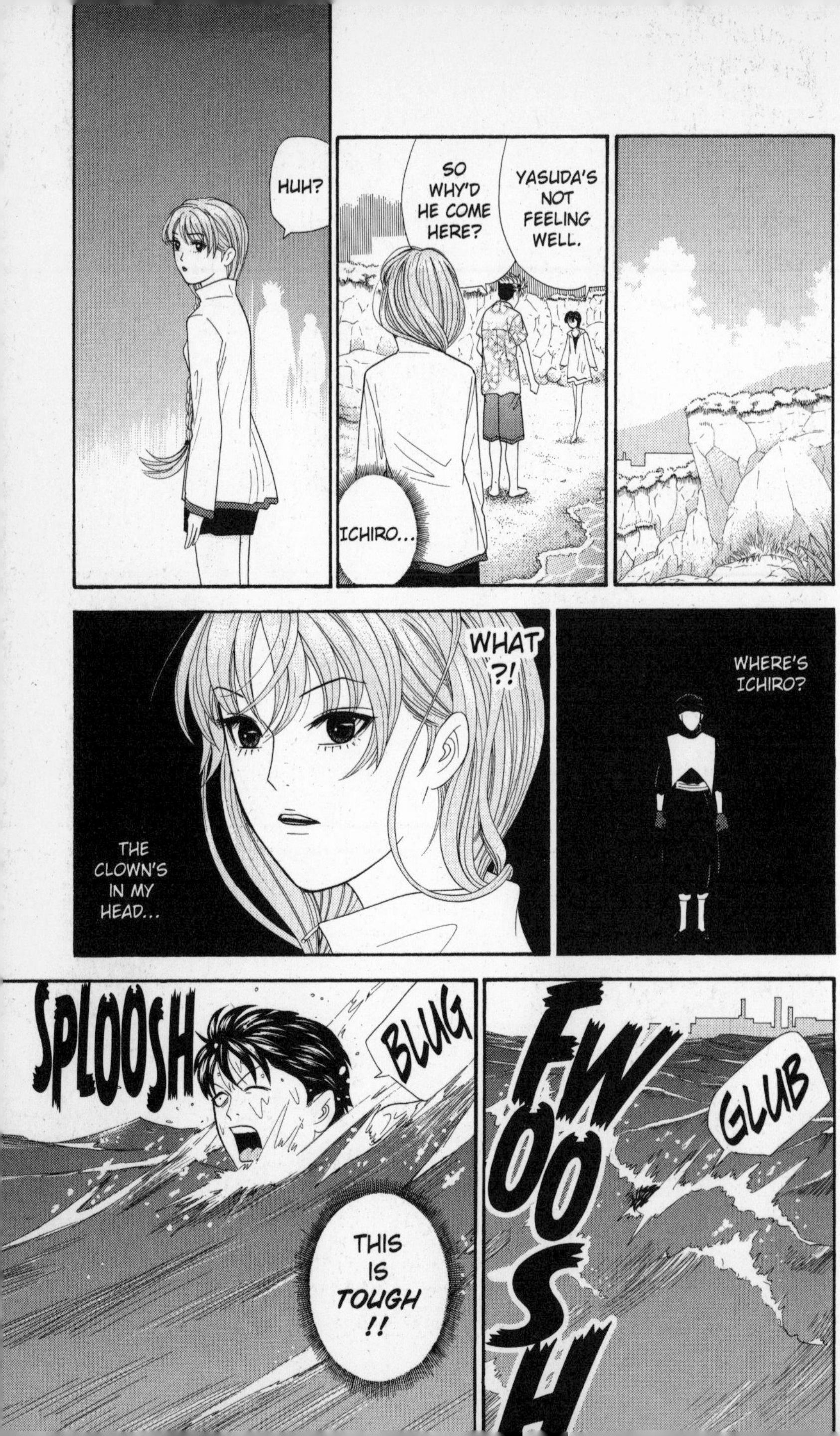
YASUDA'S NOT FEELING WELL.
SO WHY'D HE COME HERE?
ICHIRO...
HUH?
WHERE'S ICHIRO?
WHAT?!
THE CLOWN'S IN MY HEAD...
FWOOSH
GLUB
SPLOOSH
BLUG
THIS IS TOUGH!!

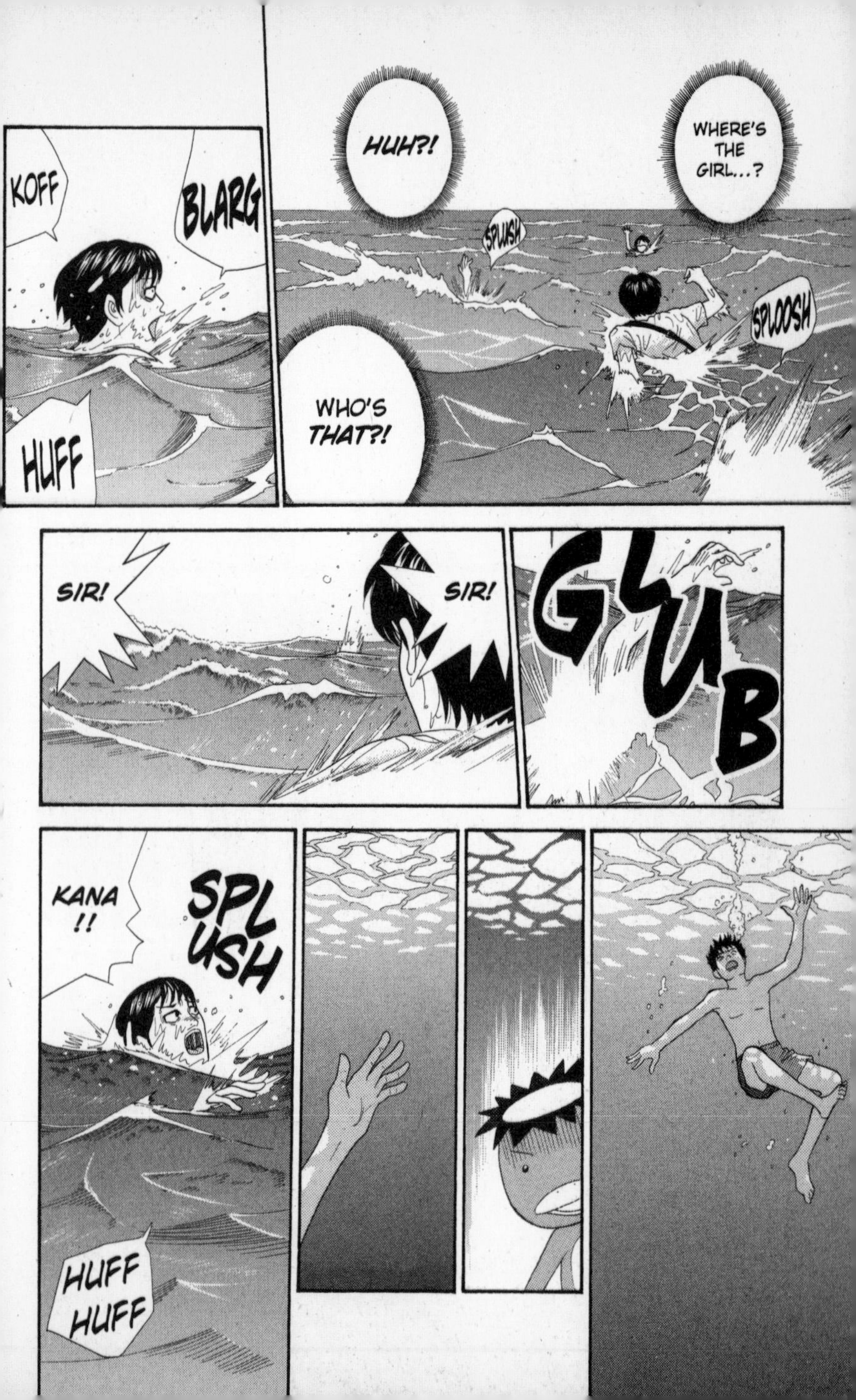
WHERE'S THE GIRL...?
HUH?!
SPLOOSH
SPLUSH
WHO'S THAT?!
BLARG
KOFF
HUFF
GLUB
SIR!
SIR!
SPLUSH
KANA!!
HUFF HUFF

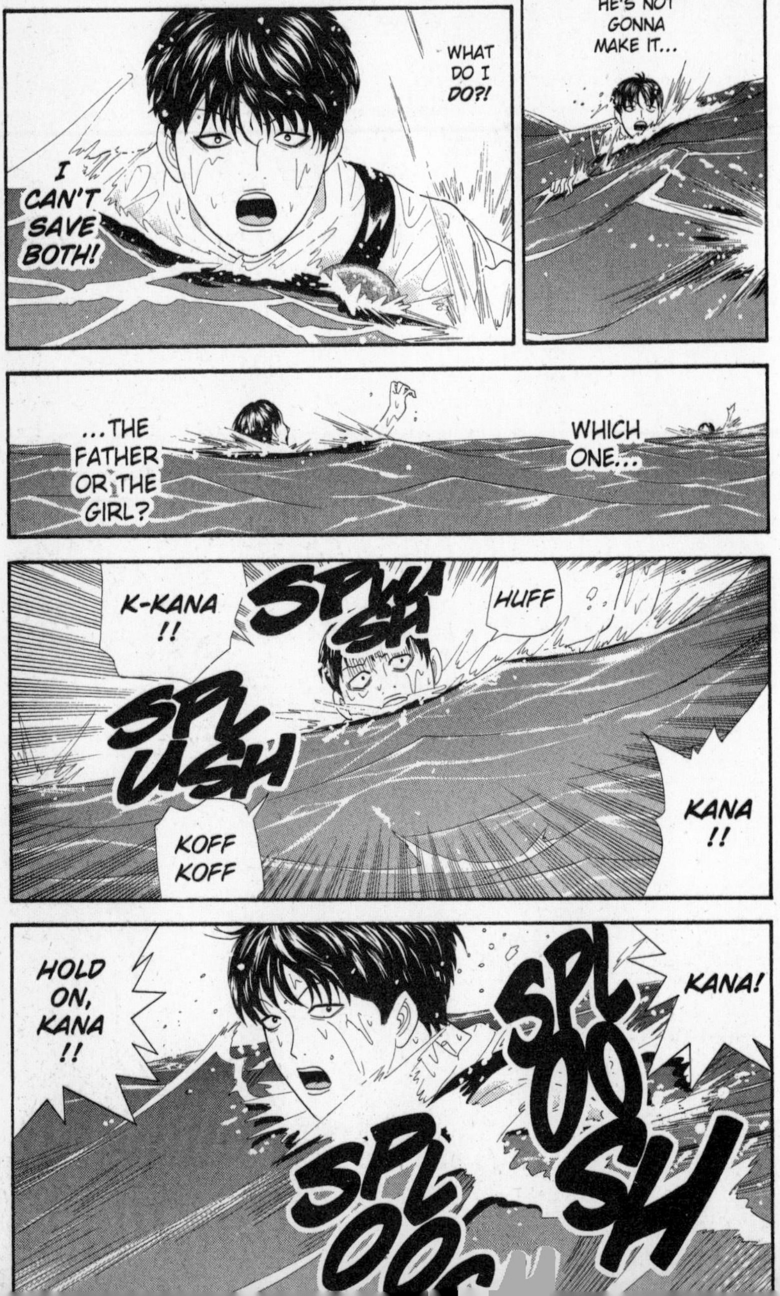
HE'S NOT GONNA MAKE IT...
WHAT DO I DO?!
I CAN'T SAVE BOTH!
WHICH ONE...
...THE FATHER OR THE GIRL?
KANA !!
HUFF
K-KANA !!
KOFF KOFF
KANA!
HOLD ON, KANA !!

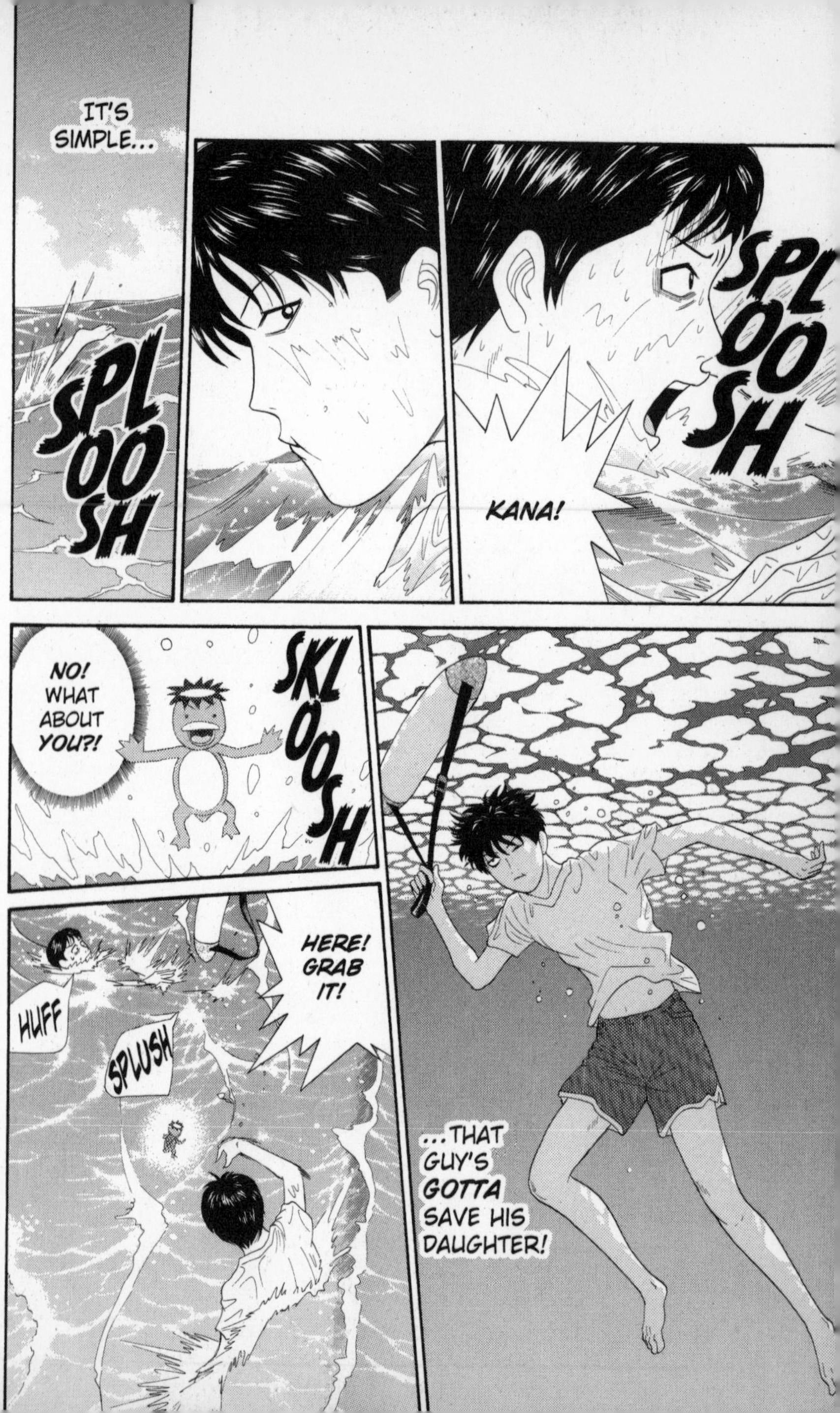
SPLOOSH
KANA!
IT'S SIMPLE...
SPLOOSH
...THAT GUY'S GOTTA SAVE HIS DAUGHTER!
NO! WHAT ABOUT YOU?!
SKLOOSH
HERE! GRAB IT!
HUFF
SPLUSH

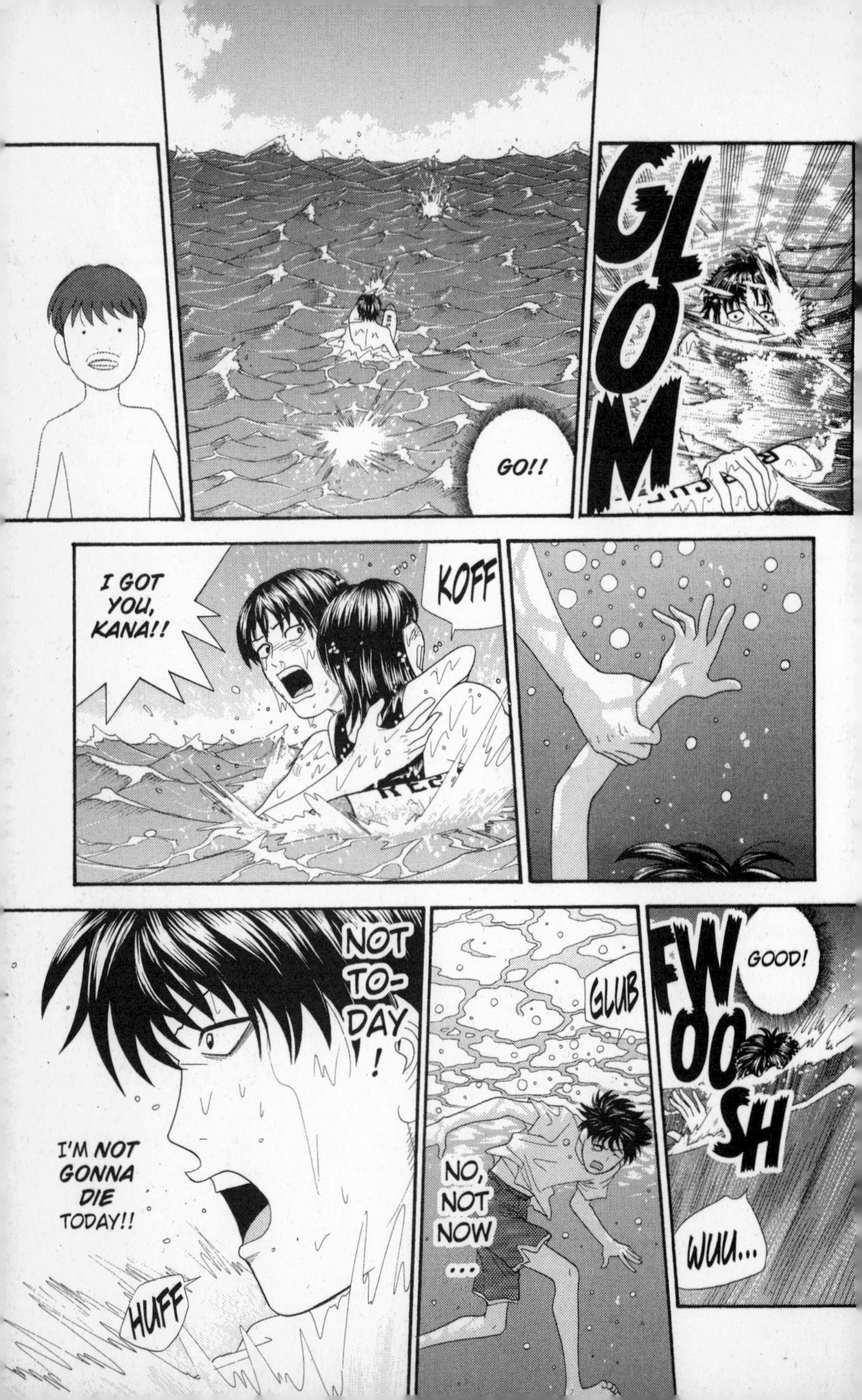
GLOM
GO!!
KOFF
I GOT YOU, KANA!!
GOOD!
FWOOSH
WUU...
GLUB
NO, NOT NOW ...
NOT TO-DAY!
I'M NOT GONNA DIE TODAY!!
HUFF

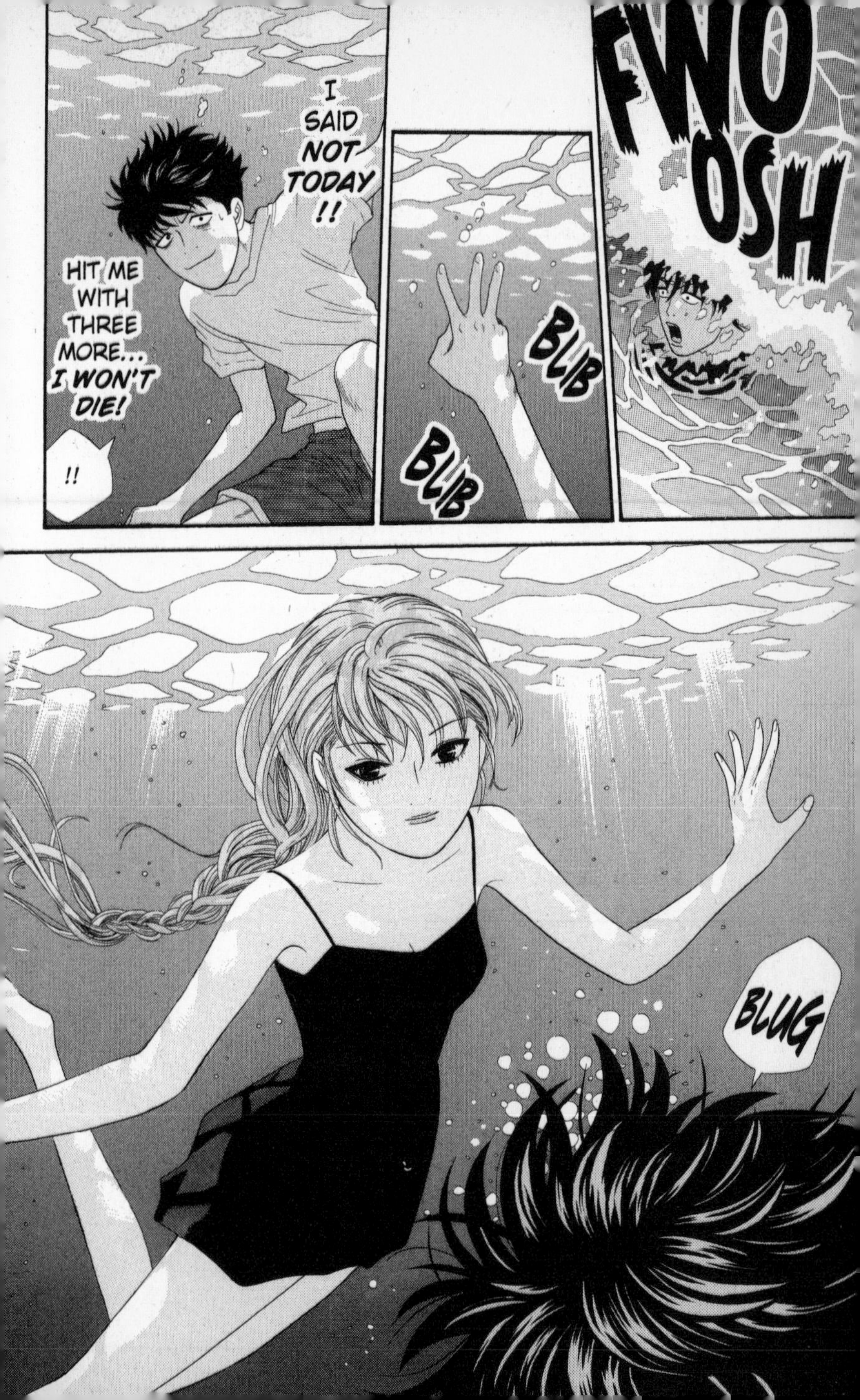
FWOOSH
BLUB
BLUB
I SAID NOT TODAY!!
HIT ME WITH THREE MORE... I WON'T DIE!
!!
BLUG

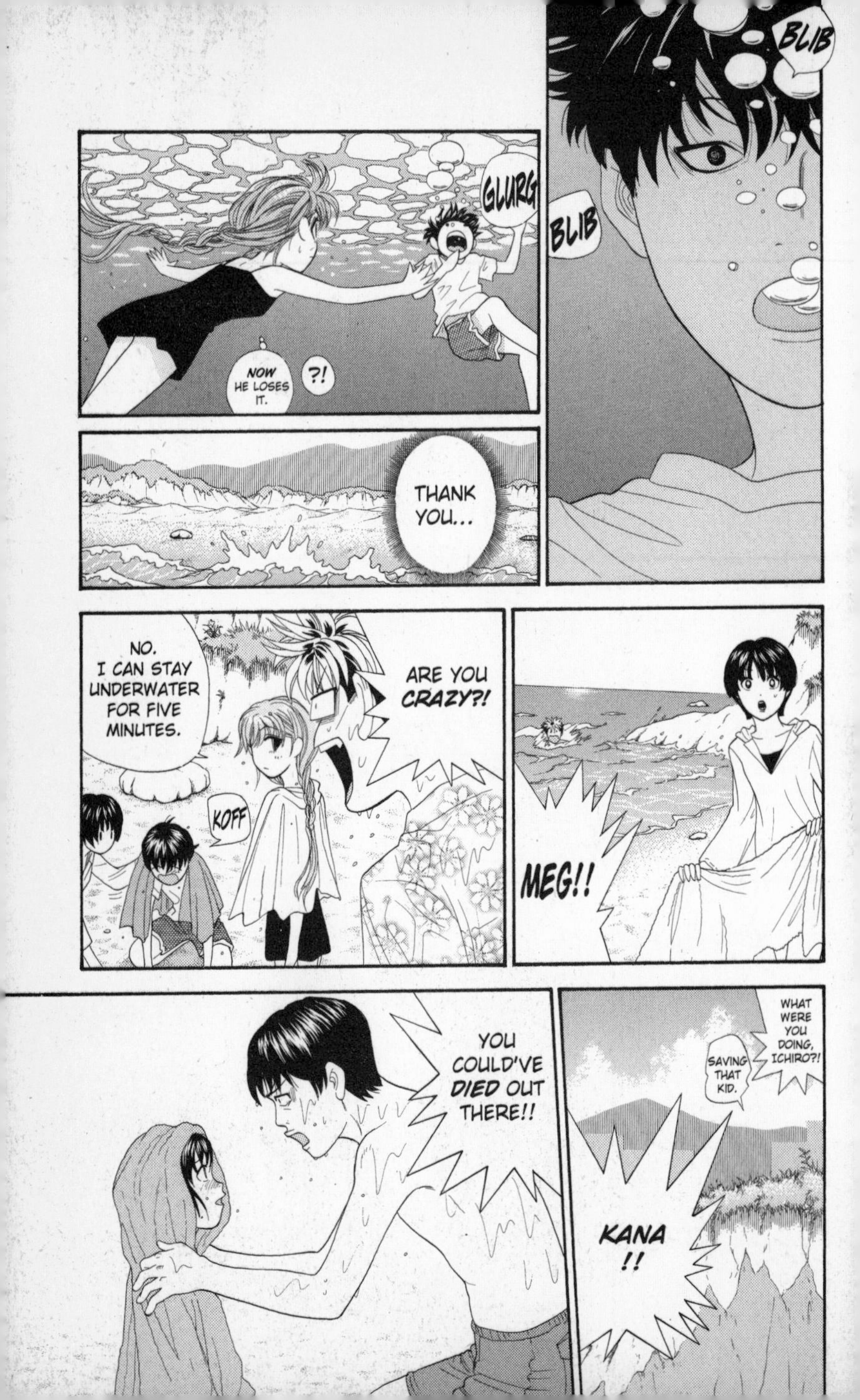
BLIB
BLIB
GLURG
?!
NOW HE LOSES IT.
THANK YOU...
MEG!!
ARE YOU CRAZY?!
NO. I CAN STAY UNDERWATER FOR FIVE MINUTES.
KOFF
WHAT WERE YOU DOING, ICHIRO?!
SAVING THAT KID.
KANA!!
YOU COULD'VE DIED OUT THERE!!

THANK YOU.

BWUH BWUH

I'M SORRY... SNIFF...

A GHOST ?!

WHO'S *THAT*?

THANK YOU, ICHIRO.

I WANTED TO SCOLD HER, TOO.

I CHOSE YOU BECAUSE YOU LOOK LIKE ME.

WEIRD HAIR...

WHO *IS* THAT GUY?

I THINK HE'S THE KAPPA.

SORTA.

IS IT REALLY *YOU?!*

YURI!!!

FATHER.

I'VE JUST BEEN WAITING...

FATHER, IT'S ALL RIGHT.

I'M SORRY.

I'M SO SORRY.

... FOR YOU TO FIND PEACE AND COME TO HEAVEN.

YOU TRIED YOUR HARDEST.

I'M SORRY I COULDN'T *SAVE* YOU.

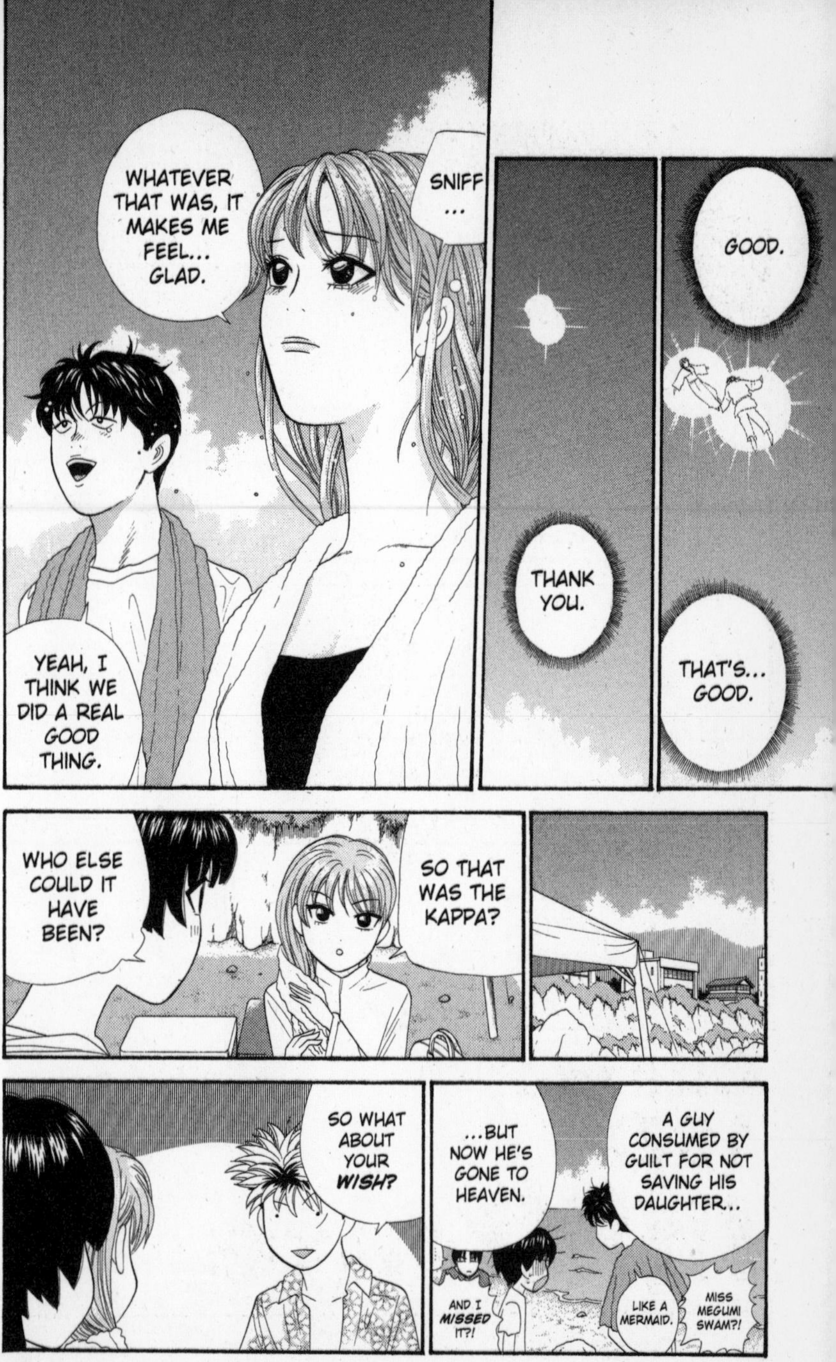
GOOD.
THAT'S... GOOD.
THANK YOU.
SNIFF ...
WHATEVER THAT WAS, IT MAKES ME FEEL... GLAD.
YEAH, I THINK WE DID A REAL GOOD THING.
SO THAT WAS THE KAPPA?
WHO ELSE COULD IT HAVE BEEN?
A GUY CONSUMED BY GUILT FOR NOT SAVING HIS DAUGHTER...
...BUT NOW HE'S GONE TO HEAVEN.
MISS MEGUMI SWAM?!
LIKE A MERMAID.
AND I *MISSED* IT?!
SO WHAT ABOUT YOUR *WISH?*

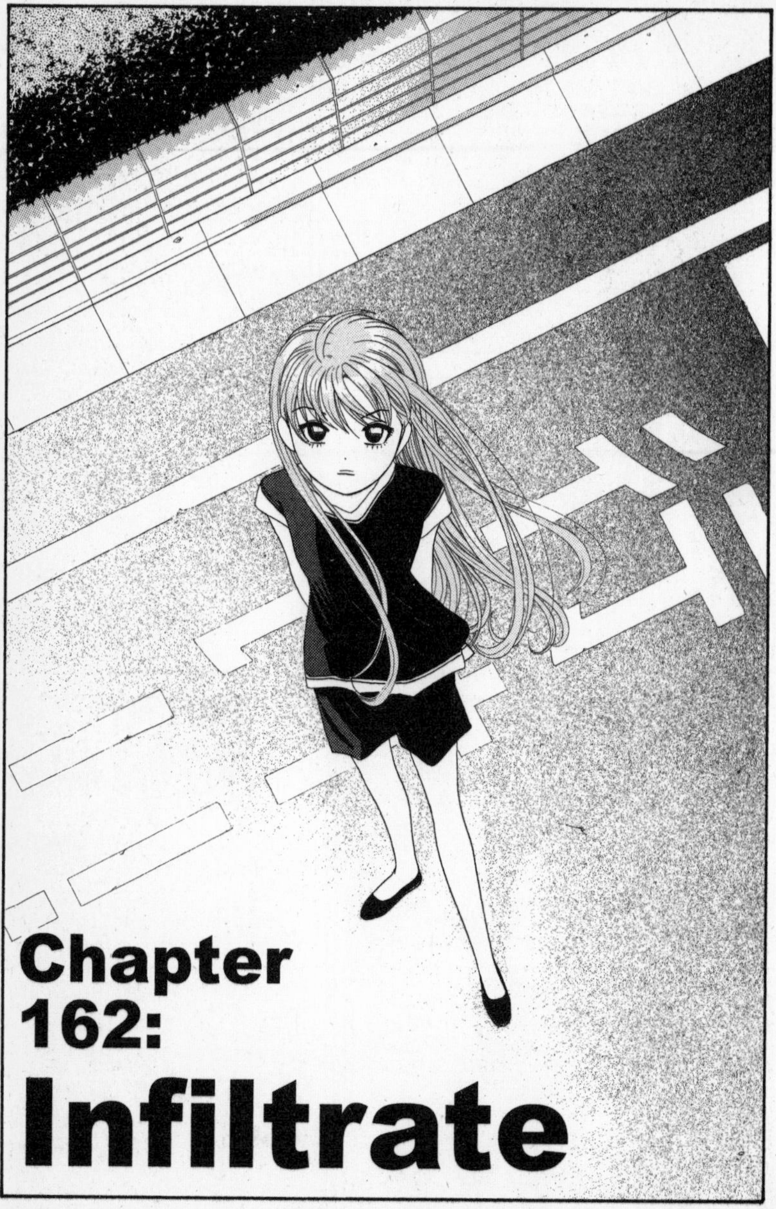

Chapter 162: Infiltrate

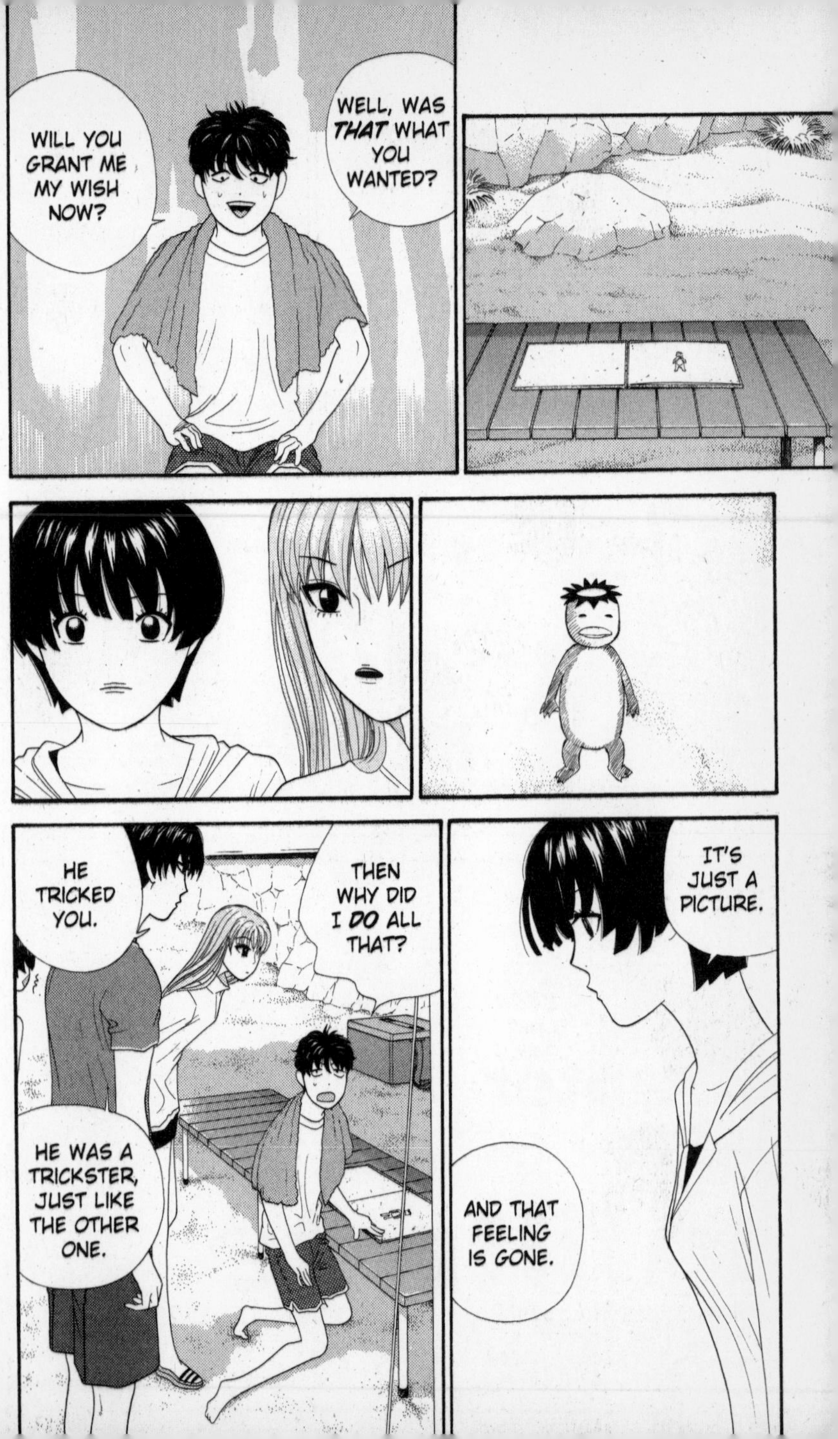
WELL, WAS *THAT* WHAT YOU WANTED?
WILL YOU GRANT ME MY WISH NOW?
IT'S JUST A PICTURE.
AND THAT FEELING IS GONE.
THEN WHY DID I *DO* ALL THAT?
HE TRICKED YOU.
HE WAS A TRICKSTER, JUST LIKE THE OTHER ONE.

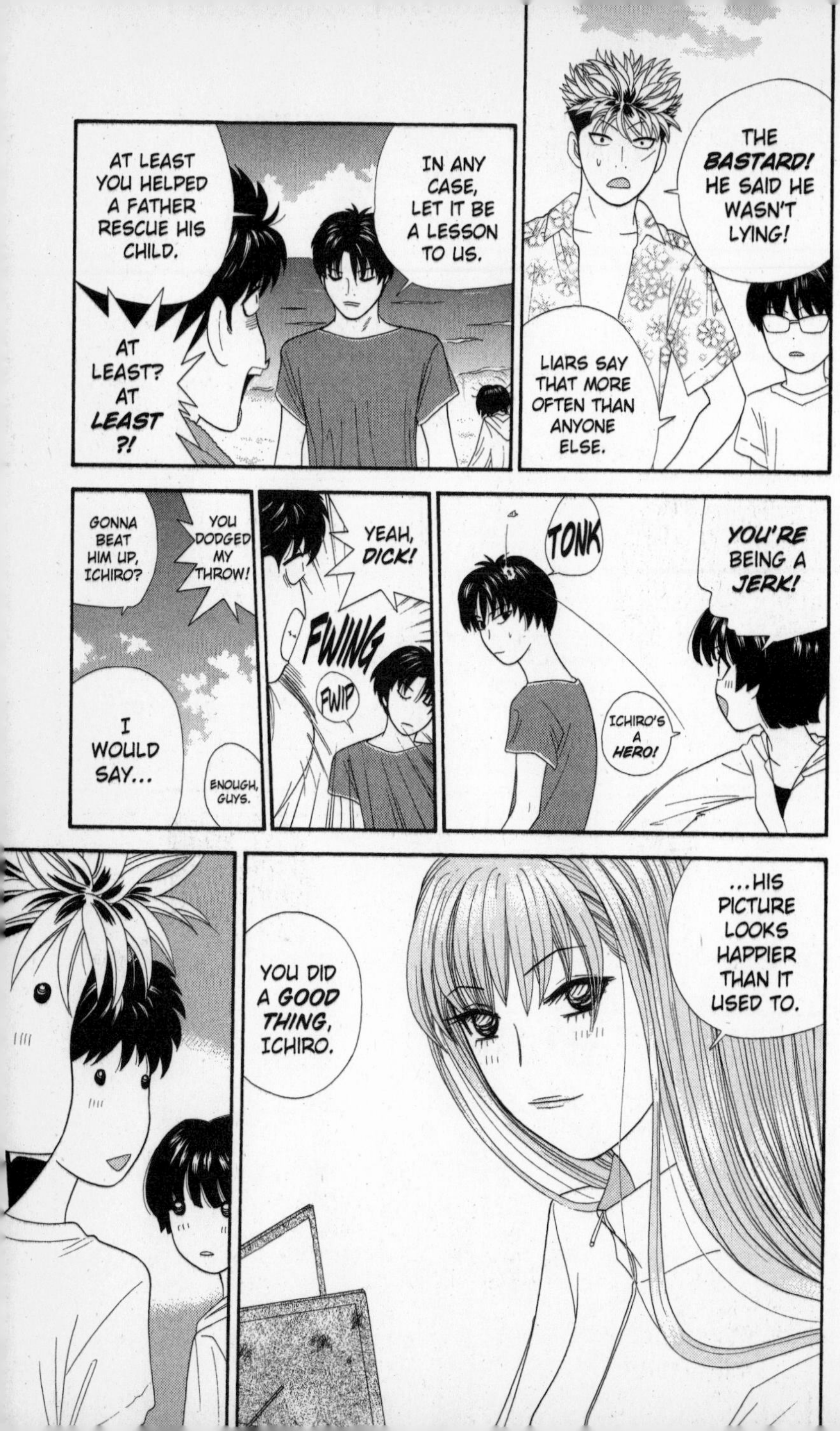
THE BASTARD! HE SAID HE WASN'T LYING!
LIARS SAY THAT MORE OFTEN THAN ANYONE ELSE.
IN ANY CASE, LET IT BE A LESSON TO US.
AT LEAST YOU HELPED A FATHER RESCUE HIS CHILD.
AT LEAST? AT LEAST?!
YOU'RE BEING A JERK!
TONK
ICHIRO'S A HERO!
YEAH, DICK!
FWING
FWIP
YOU DODGED MY THROW!
GONNA BEAT HIM UP, ICHIRO?
I WOULD SAY...
ENOUGH, GUYS.
...HIS PICTURE LOOKS HAPPIER THAN IT USED TO.
YOU DID A GOOD THING, ICHIRO.

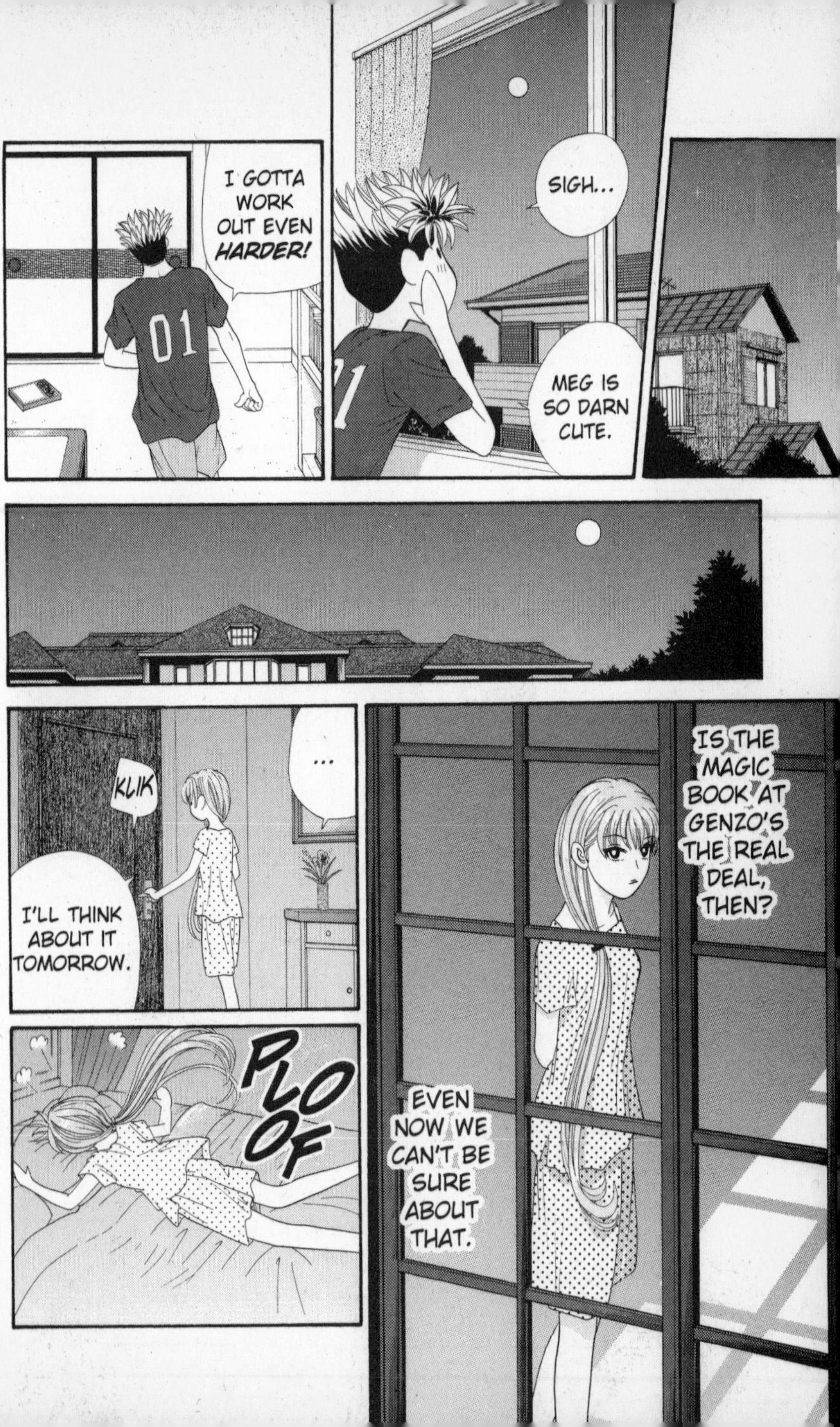
SIGH...
MEG IS SO DARN CUTE.
I GOTTA WORK OUT EVEN HARDER!
IS THE MAGIC BOOK AT GENZO'S THE REAL DEAL, THEN?
EVEN NOW WE CAN'T BE SURE ABOUT THAT.
KLIK
...
I'LL THINK ABOUT IT TOMORROW.
PLOOF

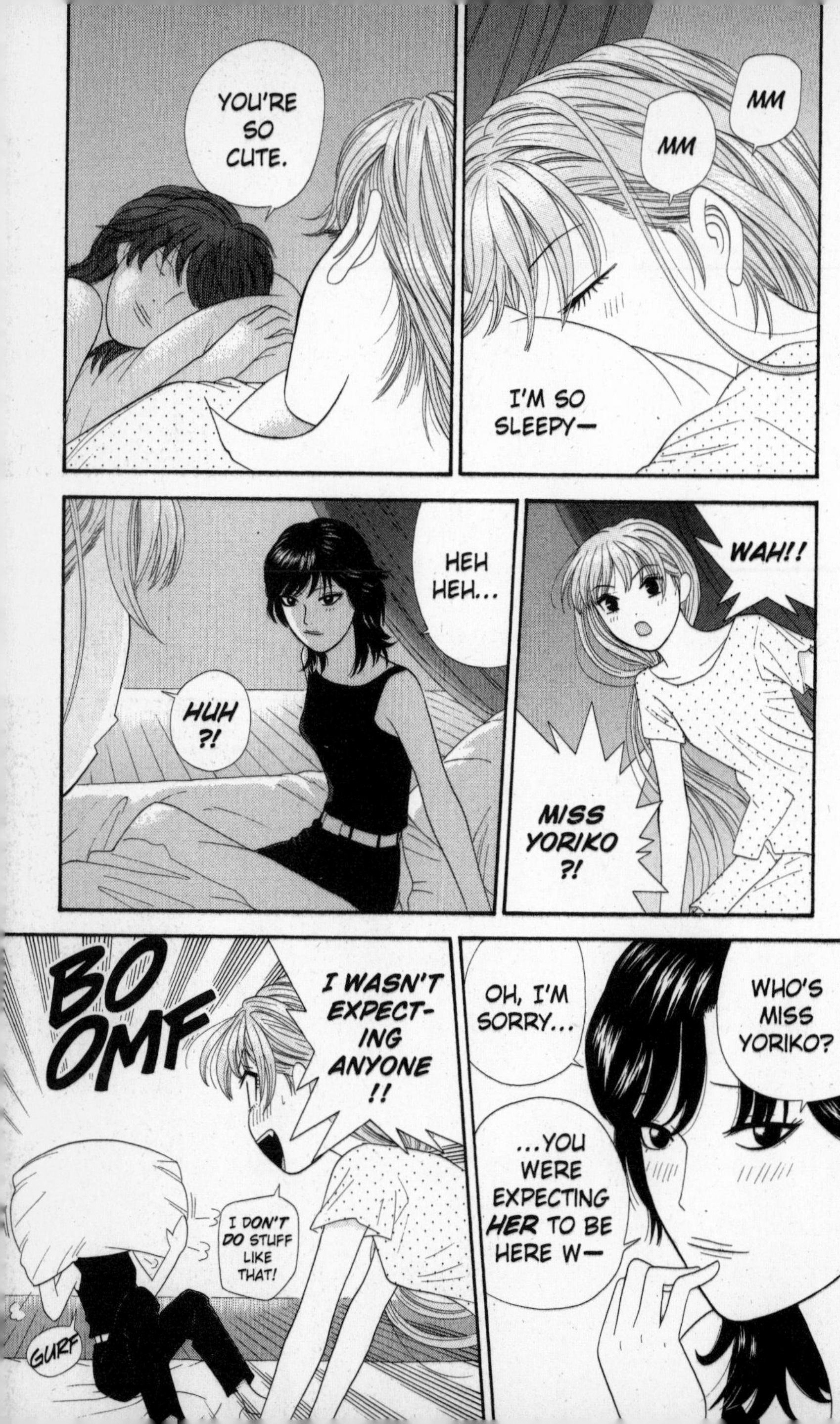
MM
MM
I'M SO SLEEPY—
YOU'RE SO CUTE.
WAH!!
MISS YORIKO ?!
HEH HEH...
HUH ?!
WHO'S MISS YORIKO?
OH, I'M SORRY...
...YOU WERE EXPECTING HER TO BE HERE W—
I WASN'T EXPECT-ING ANYONE !!
BOOMF
I DON'T DO STUFF LIKE THAT!
GURF

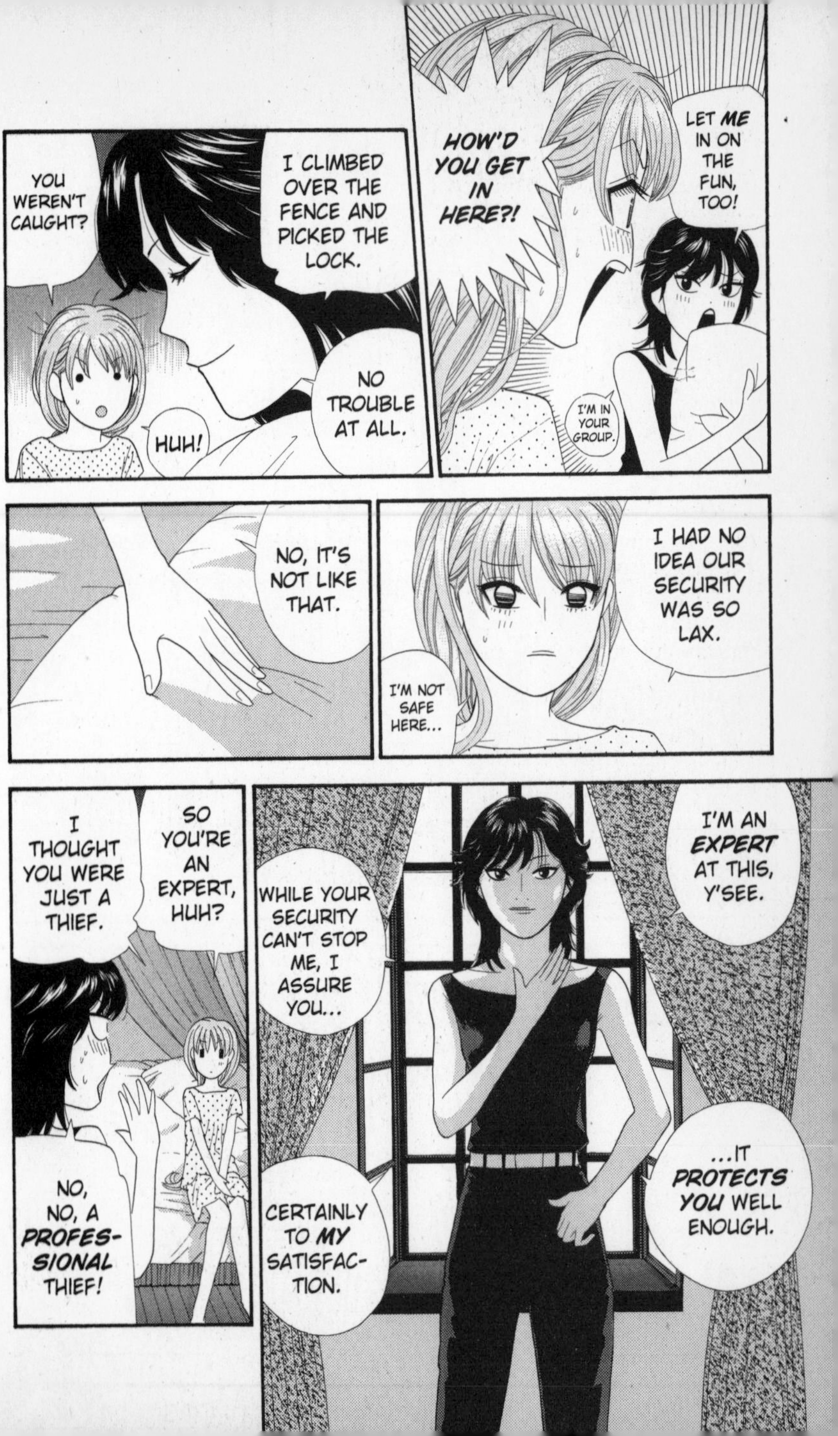
HOW'D YOU GET IN HERE?!
LET ME IN ON THE FUN, TOO!
I'M IN YOUR GROUP.
I CLIMBED OVER THE FENCE AND PICKED THE LOCK.
YOU WEREN'T CAUGHT?
NO TROUBLE AT ALL.
HUH!
I HAD NO IDEA OUR SECURITY WAS SO LAX.
I'M NOT SAFE HERE...
NO, IT'S NOT LIKE THAT.
I'M AN EXPERT AT THIS, Y'SEE.
WHILE YOUR SECURITY CAN'T STOP ME, I ASSURE YOU...
...IT PROTECTS YOU WELL ENOUGH.
CERTAINLY TO MY SATISFACTION.
SO YOU'RE AN EXPERT, HUH?
I THOUGHT YOU WERE JUST A THIEF.
NO, NO, A PROFESSIONAL THIEF!

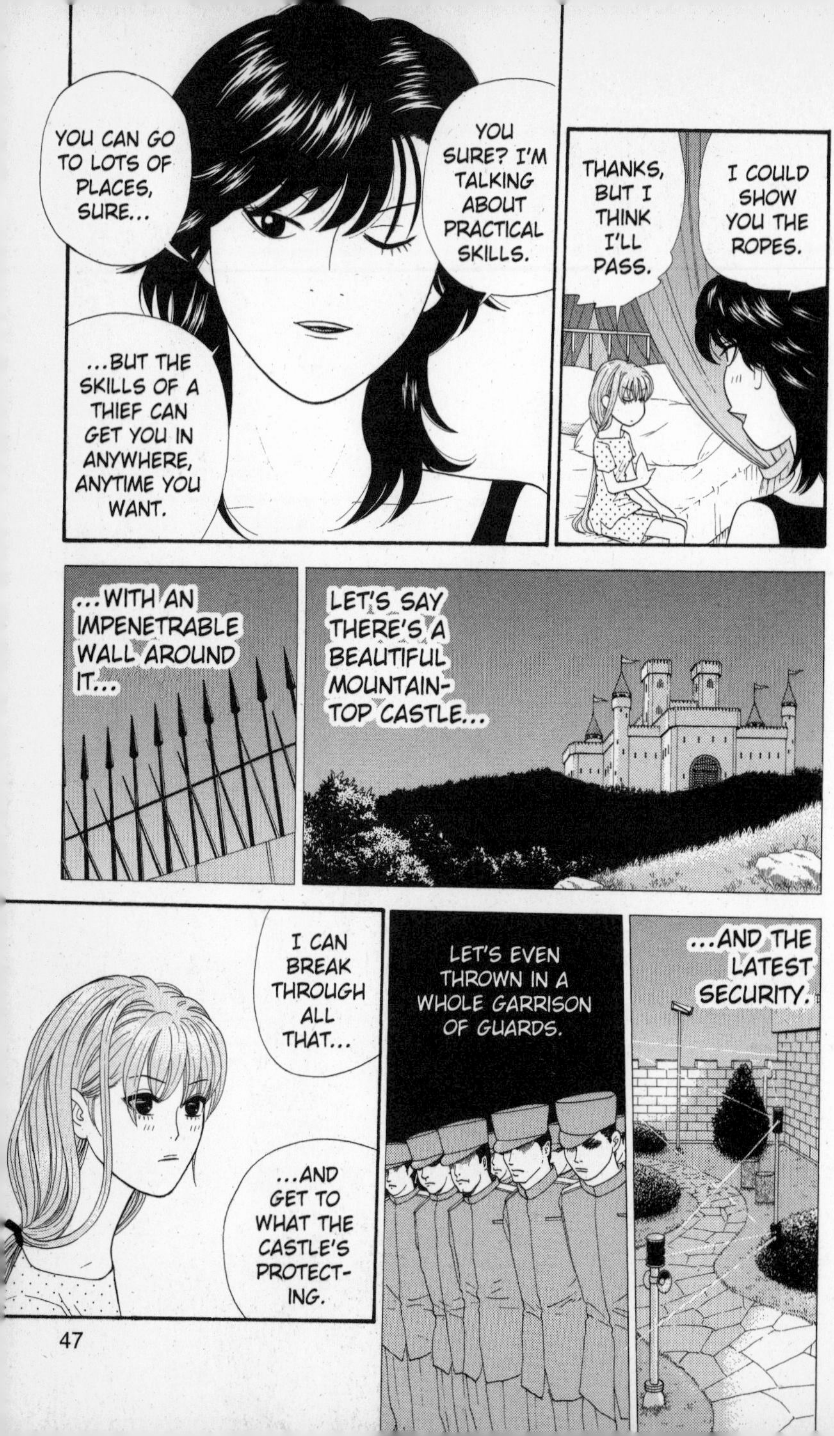
I COULD SHOW YOU THE ROPES.
THANKS, BUT I THINK I'LL PASS.
YOU SURE? I'M TALKING ABOUT PRACTICAL SKILLS.
YOU CAN GO TO LOTS OF PLACES, SURE...
...BUT THE SKILLS OF A THIEF CAN GET YOU IN ANYWHERE, ANYTIME YOU WANT.
LET'S SAY THERE'S A BEAUTIFUL MOUNTAIN-TOP CASTLE...
...WITH AN IMPENETRABLE WALL AROUND IT...
...AND THE LATEST SECURITY.
LET'S EVEN THROWN IN A WHOLE GARRISON OF GUARDS.
I CAN BREAK THROUGH ALL THAT...
...AND GET TO WHAT THE CASTLE'S PROTECTING.

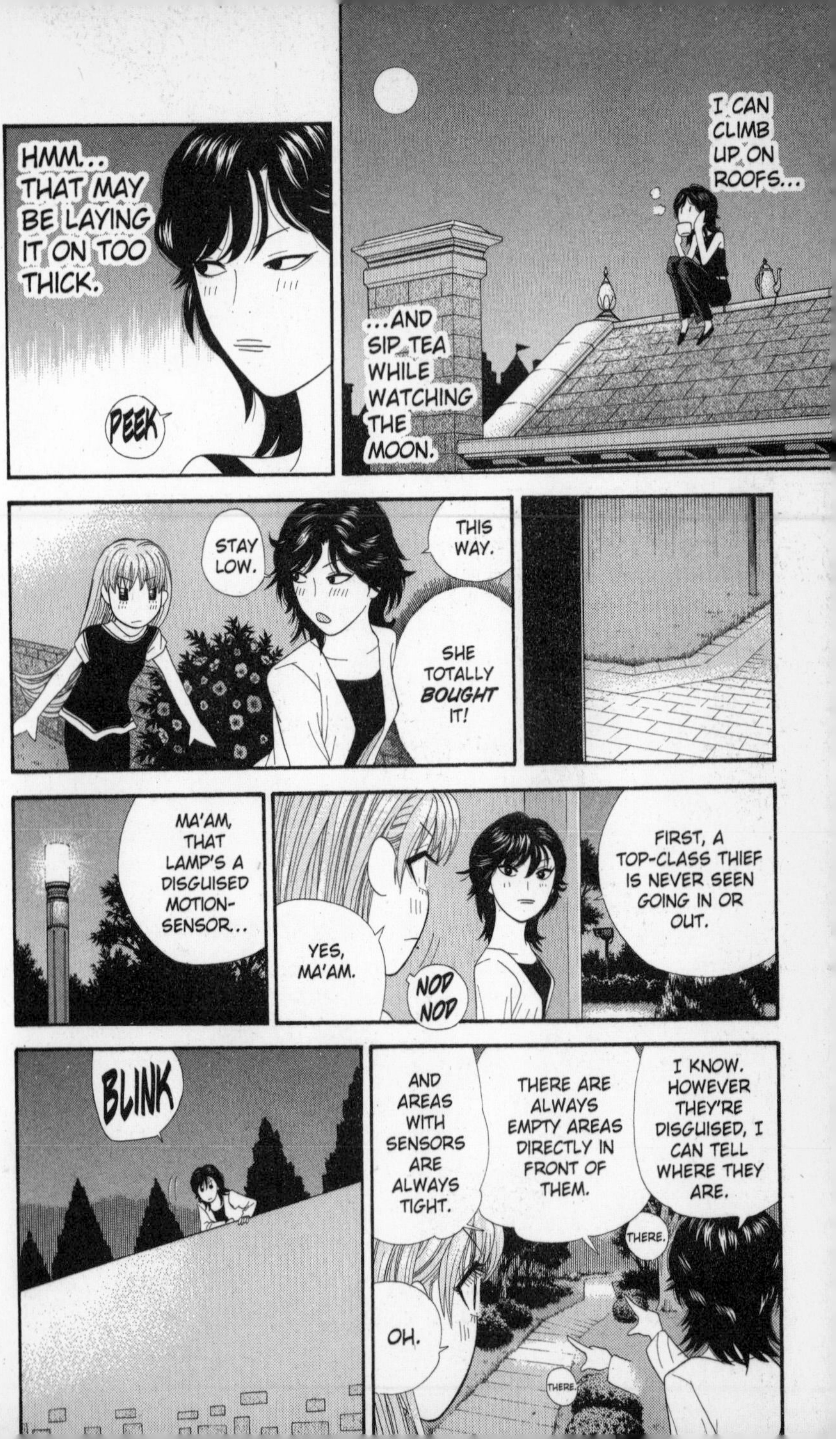
I CAN CLIMB UP ON ROOFS...
...AND SIP TEA WHILE WATCHING THE MOON.
HMM... THAT MAY BE LAYING IT ON TOO THICK.
PEEK
THIS WAY.
STAY LOW.
SHE TOTALLY *BOUGHT* IT!
FIRST, A TOP-CLASS THIEF IS NEVER SEEN GOING IN OR OUT.
YES, MA'AM.
NOD NOD
MA'AM, THAT LAMP'S A DISGUISED MOTION-SENSOR...
I KNOW. HOWEVER THEY'RE DISGUISED, I CAN TELL WHERE THEY ARE.
THERE ARE ALWAYS EMPTY AREAS DIRECTLY IN FRONT OF THEM.
AND AREAS WITH SENSORS ARE ALWAYS TIGHT.
THERE.
OH.
THERE.
BLINK

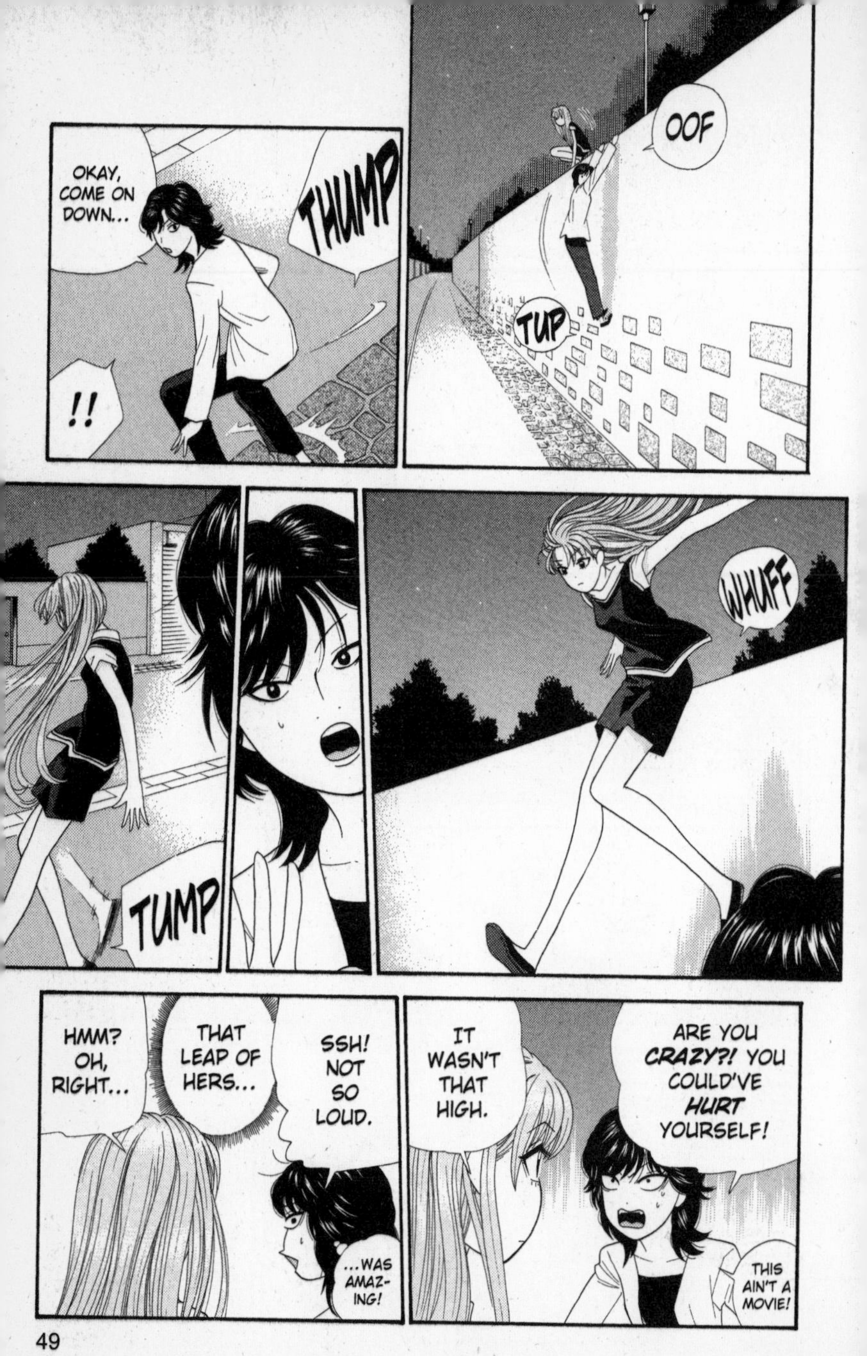
OOF
TUP
THUMP
OKAY, COME ON DOWN...
!!
WHUFF
TUMP
ARE YOU *CRAZY?!* YOU COULD'VE *HURT* YOURSELF!
THIS AIN'T A MOVIE!
IT WASN'T THAT HIGH.
SSH! NOT SO LOUD.
THAT LEAP OF HERS...
HMM? OH, RIGHT...
...WAS AMAZ-ING!

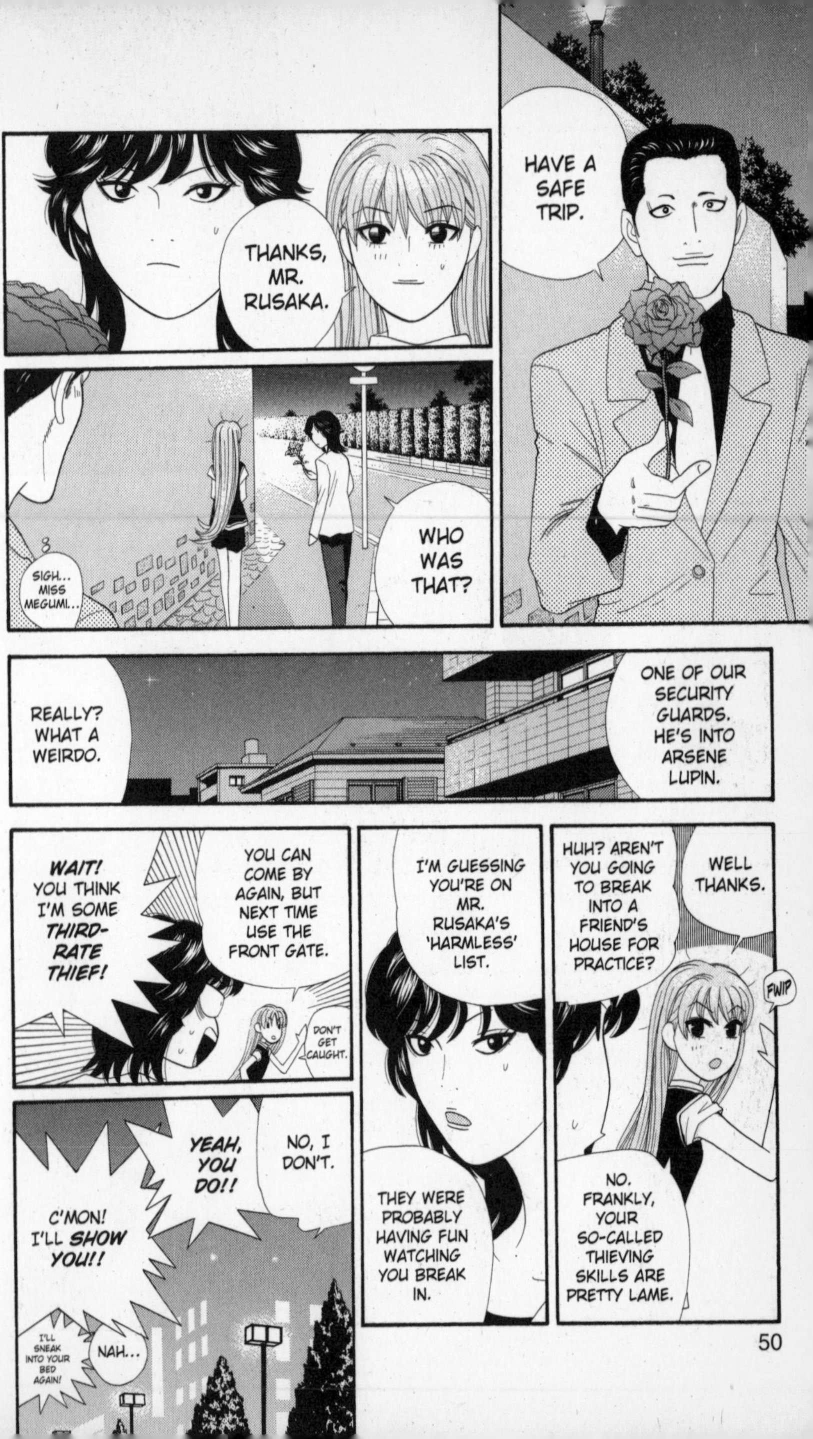
HAVE A SAFE TRIP.
THANKS, MR. RUSAKA.
WHO WAS THAT?
SIGH... MISS MEGUMI...
ONE OF OUR SECURITY GUARDS. HE'S INTO ARSENE LUPIN.
REALLY? WHAT A WEIRDO.
WELL THANKS.
FWIP
HUH? AREN'T YOU GOING TO BREAK INTO A FRIEND'S HOUSE FOR PRACTICE?
NO. FRANKLY, YOUR SO-CALLED THIEVING SKILLS ARE PRETTY LAME.
I'M GUESSING YOU'RE ON MR. RUSAKA'S 'HARMLESS' LIST.
THEY WERE PROBABLY HAVING FUN WATCHING YOU BREAK IN.
YOU CAN COME BY AGAIN, BUT NEXT TIME USE THE FRONT GATE.
WAIT! YOU THINK I'M SOME THIRD-RATE THIEF!
DON'T GET CAUGHT.
NO, I DON'T.
YEAH, YOU DO!!
C'MON! I'LL SHOW YOU!!
NAH...
I'LL SNEAK INTO YOUR BED AGAIN!

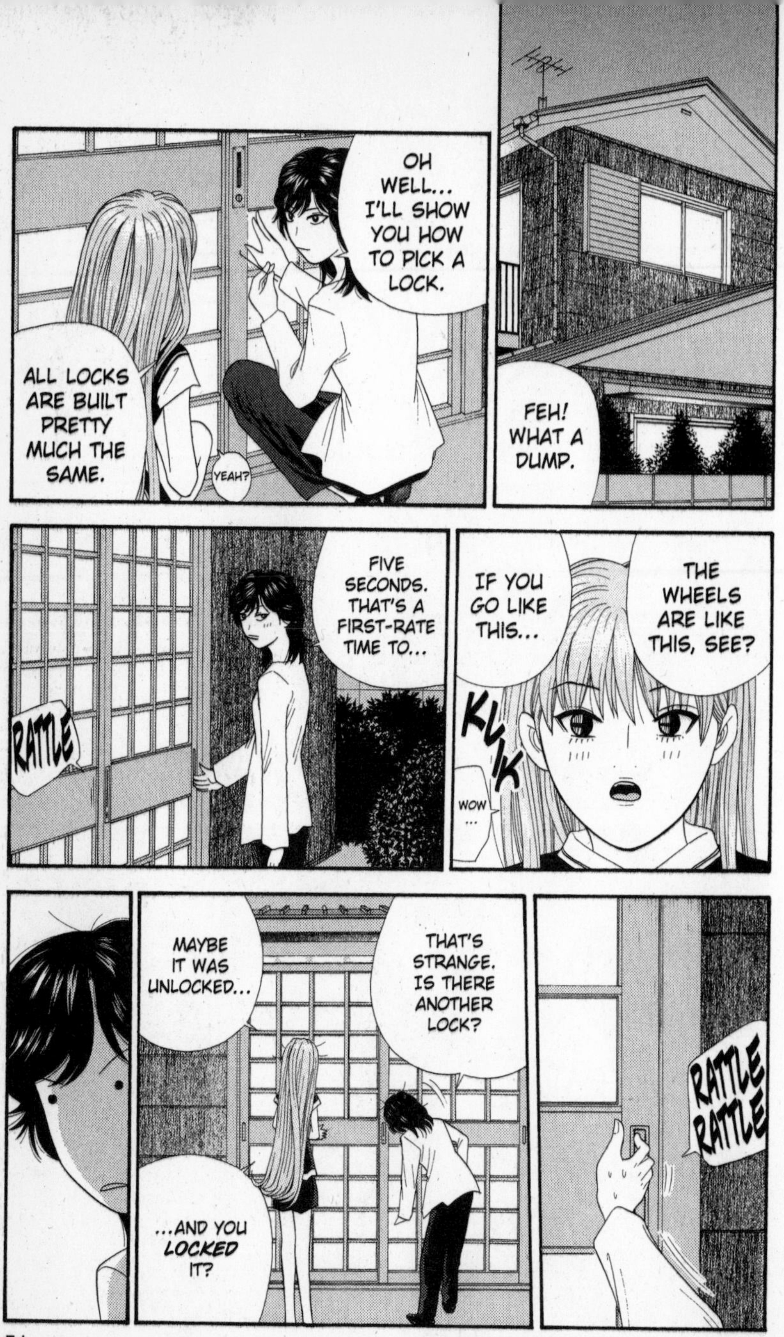
FEH! WHAT A DUMP.
OH WELL... I'LL SHOW YOU HOW TO PICK A LOCK.
ALL LOCKS ARE BUILT PRETTY MUCH THE SAME.
YEAH?
THE WHEELS ARE LIKE THIS, SEE?
IF YOU GO LIKE THIS...
KLIK
WOW...
FIVE SECONDS. THAT'S A FIRST-RATE TIME TO...
RATTLE
RATTLE RATTLE
THAT'S STRANGE. IS THERE ANOTHER LOCK?
MAYBE IT WAS UNLOCKED...
...AND YOU LOCKED IT?

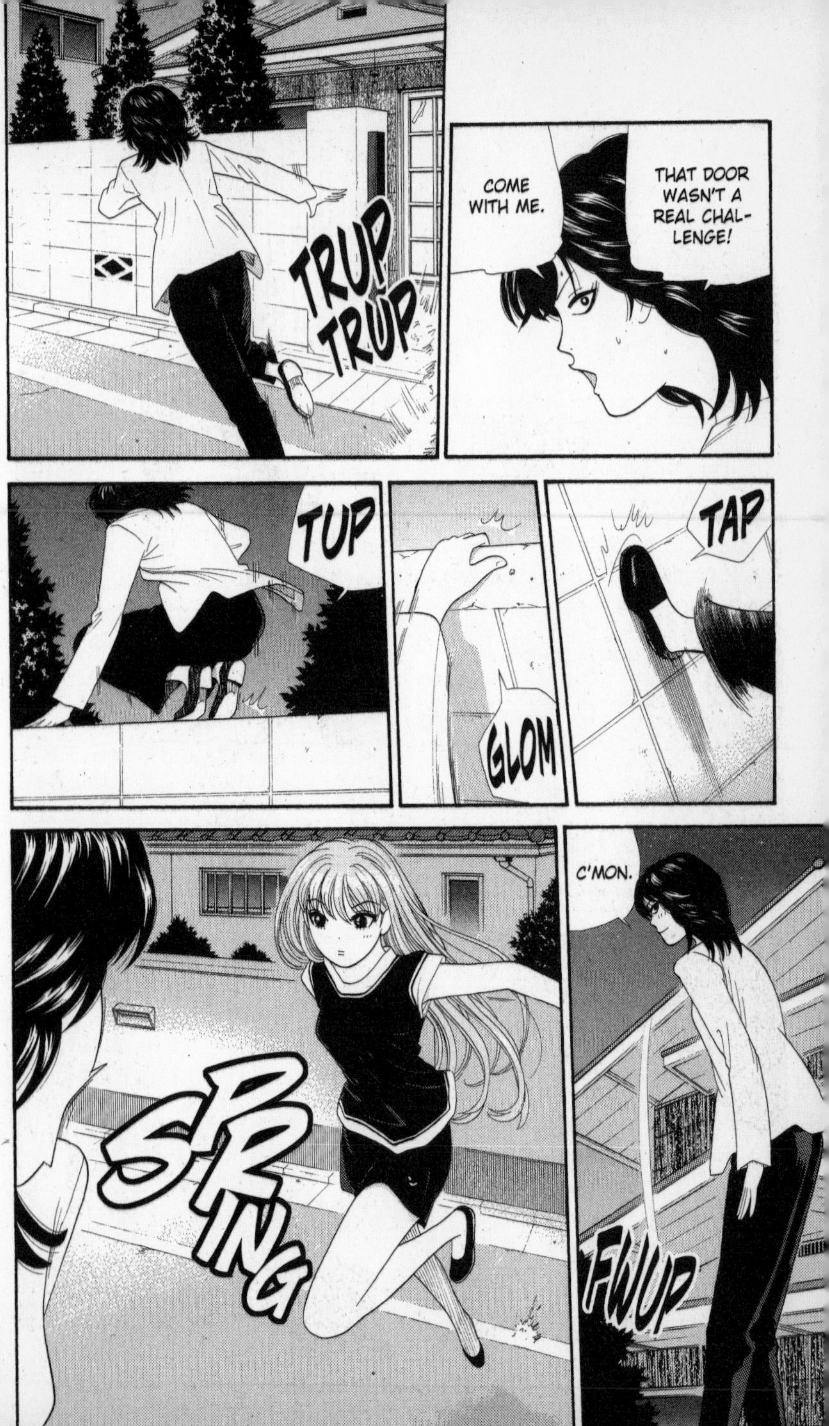
THAT DOOR WASN'T A REAL CHAL-LENGE!
COME WITH ME.
TRUP TRUP
TAP
GLOM
TUP
C'MON.
FWUP
SPRING

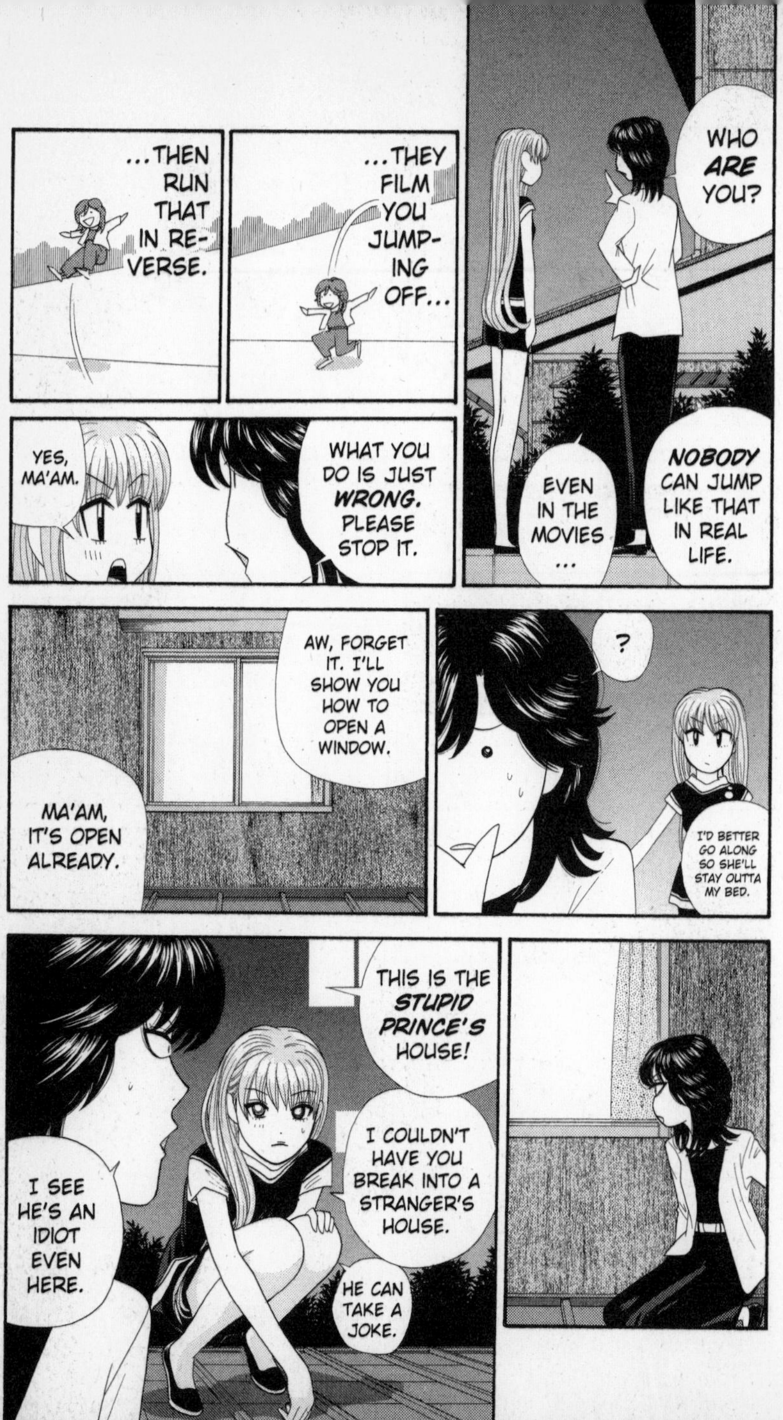
WHO **ARE** YOU?
NOBODY CAN JUMP LIKE THAT IN REAL LIFE.
EVEN IN THE MOVIES ...
...THEY FILM YOU JUMPING OFF...
...THEN RUN THAT IN REVERSE.
WHAT YOU DO IS JUST **WRONG.** PLEASE STOP IT.
YES, MA'AM.
?
I'D BETTER GO ALONG SO SHE'LL STAY OUTTA MY BED.
AW, FORGET IT. I'LL SHOW YOU HOW TO OPEN A WINDOW.
MA'AM, IT'S OPEN ALREADY.
THIS IS THE **STUPID PRINCE'S** HOUSE!
I COULDN'T HAVE YOU BREAK INTO A STRANGER'S HOUSE.
HE CAN TAKE A JOKE.
I SEE HE'S AN IDIOT EVEN HERE.

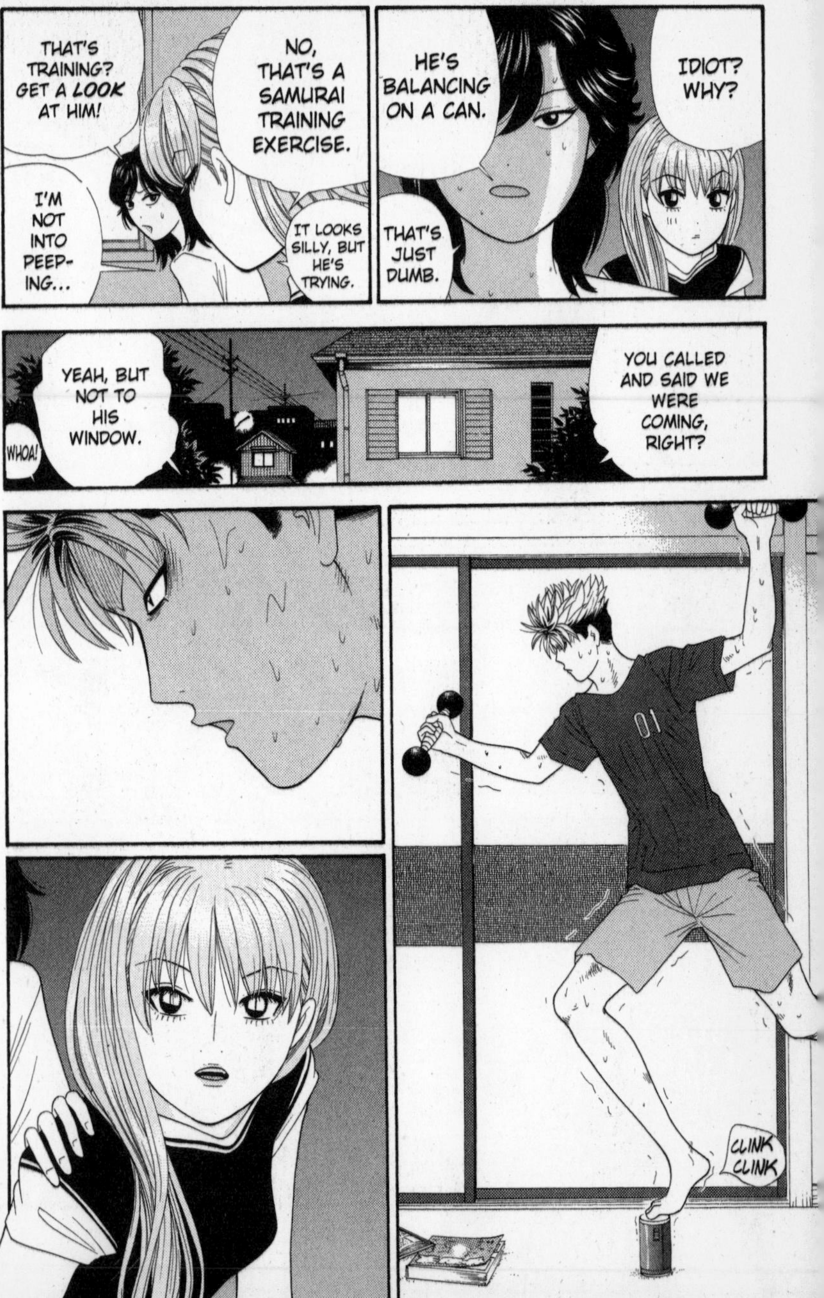
IDIOT? WHY?
HE'S BALANCING ON A CAN.
THAT'S JUST DUMB.
NO, THAT'S A SAMURAI TRAINING EXERCISE.
THAT'S TRAINING? GET A *LOOK* AT HIM!
IT LOOKS SILLY, BUT HE'S TRYING.
I'M NOT INTO PEEP-ING...
YOU CALLED AND SAID WE WERE COMING, RIGHT?
YEAH, BUT NOT TO HIS WINDOW.
WHOA!
CLINK CLINK

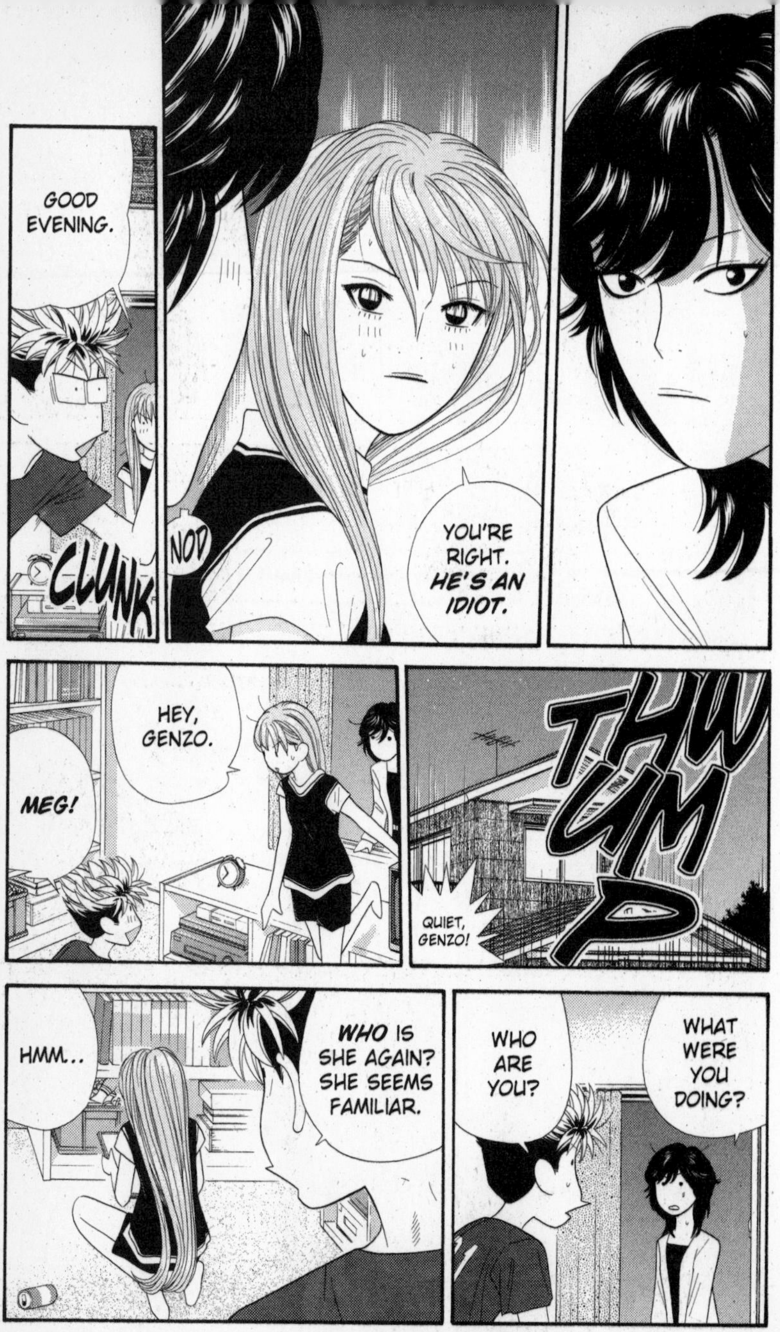
NOD
YOU'RE RIGHT. ***HE'S AN IDIOT.***
GOOD EVENING.
CLUNK
THWUMP
QUIET, GENZO!
HEY, GENZO.
MEG!
WHAT WERE YOU DOING?
WHO ARE YOU?
WHO IS SHE AGAIN? SHE SEEMS FAMILIAR.
HMM...

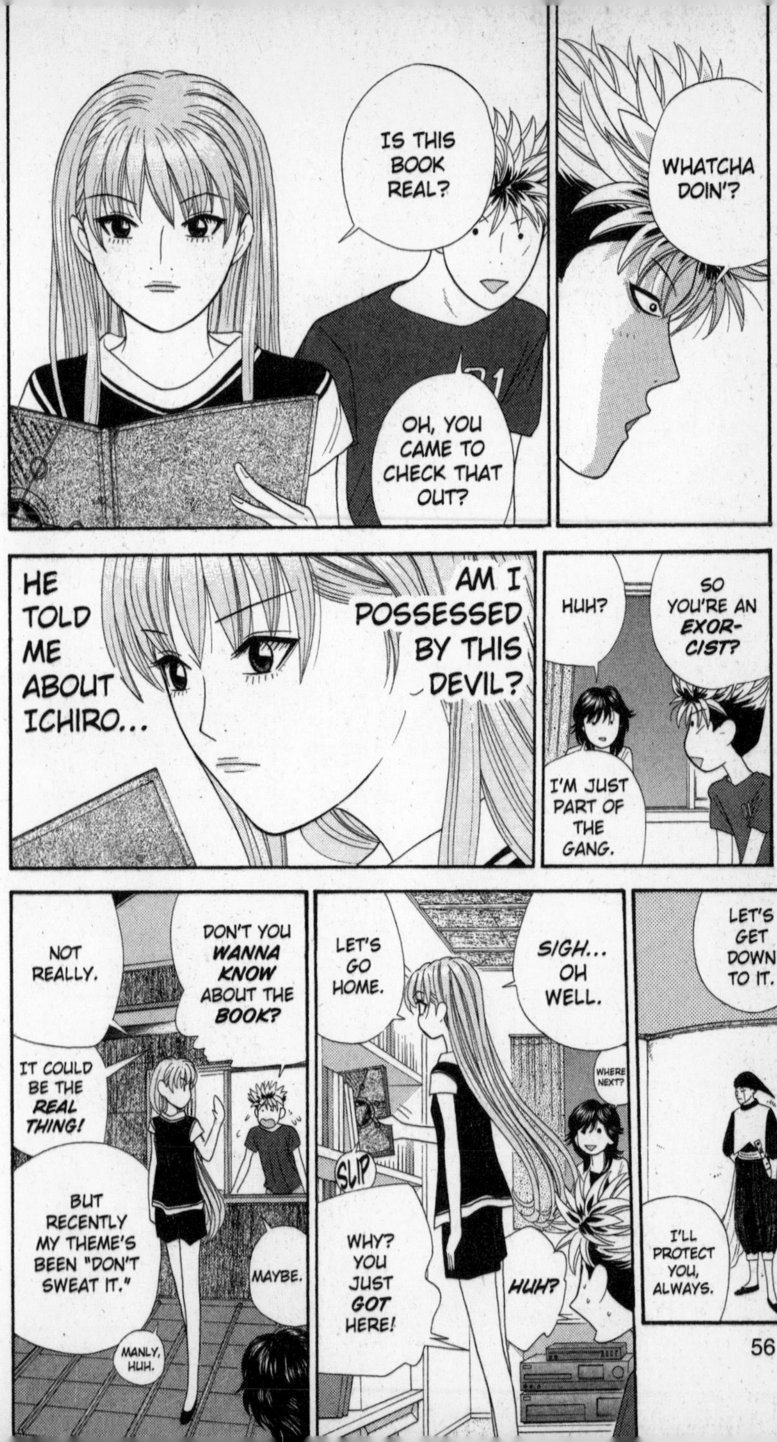
WHATCHA DOIN'?
IS THIS BOOK REAL?
OH, YOU CAME TO CHECK THAT OUT?
SO YOU'RE AN *EXORCIST?*
HUH?
I'M JUST PART OF THE GANG.
AM I POSSESSED BY THIS DEVIL?
HE TOLD ME ABOUT ICHIRO...
LET'S GET DOWN TO IT.
I'LL PROTECT YOU, ALWAYS.
SIGH... OH WELL.
WHERE NEXT?
LET'S GO HOME.
SLIP
HUH?
WHY? YOU JUST *GOT* HERE!
DON'T YOU *WANNA KNOW* ABOUT THE *BOOK?*
NOT REALLY.
IT COULD BE THE *REAL THING!*
MAYBE.
BUT RECENTLY MY THEME'S BEEN "DON'T SWEAT IT."
MANLY, HUH.

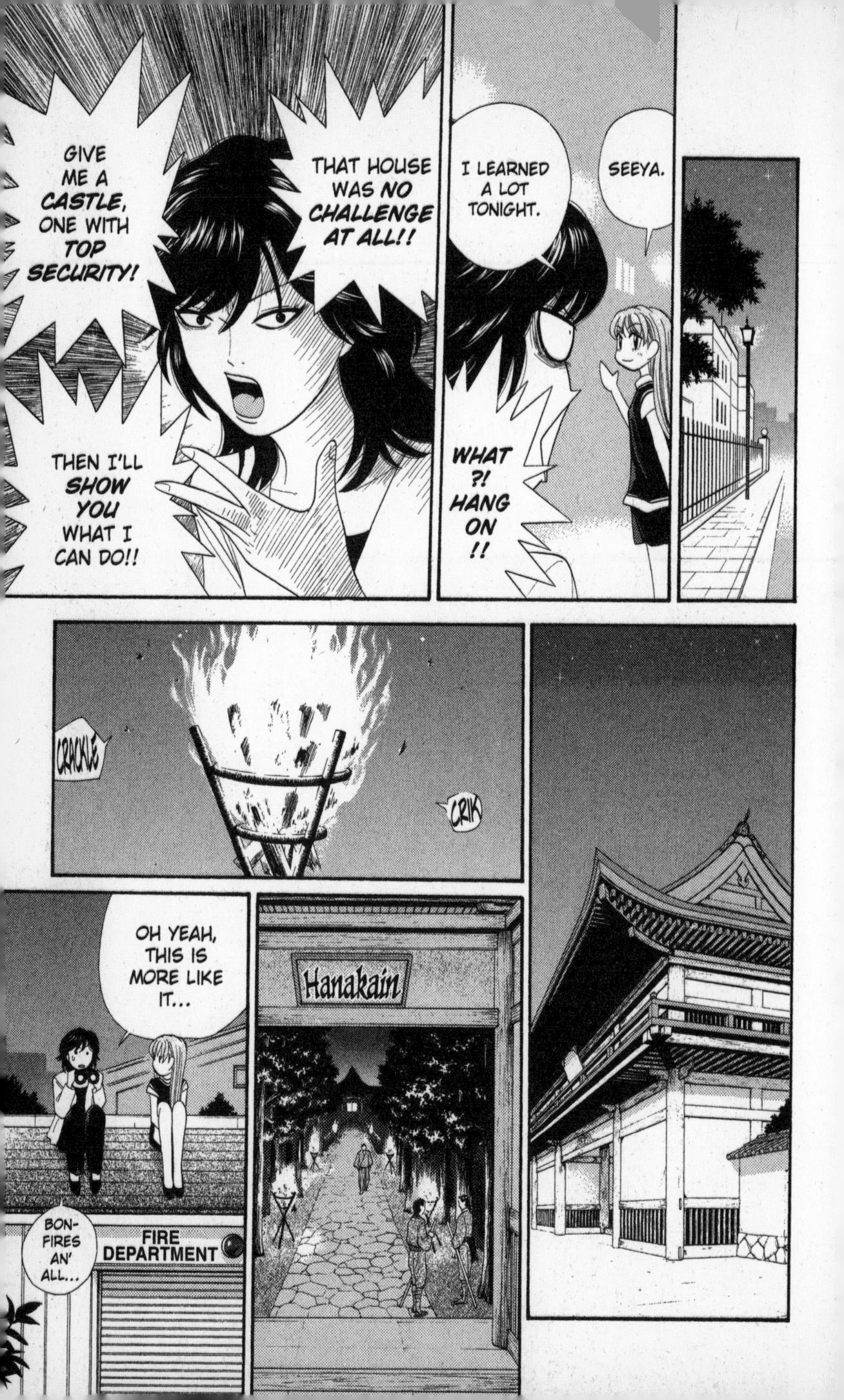
SEEYA.
I LEARNED A LOT TONIGHT.
WHAT?! HANG ON!!
THAT HOUSE WAS NO CHALLENGE AT ALL!!
GIVE ME A CASTLE, ONE WITH TOP SECURITY!
THEN I'LL SHOW YOU WHAT I CAN DO!!
CRIK
CRACKLE
Hanakain
OH YEAH, THIS IS MORE LIKE IT...
FIRE DEPARTMENT
BON-FIRES AN' ALL...

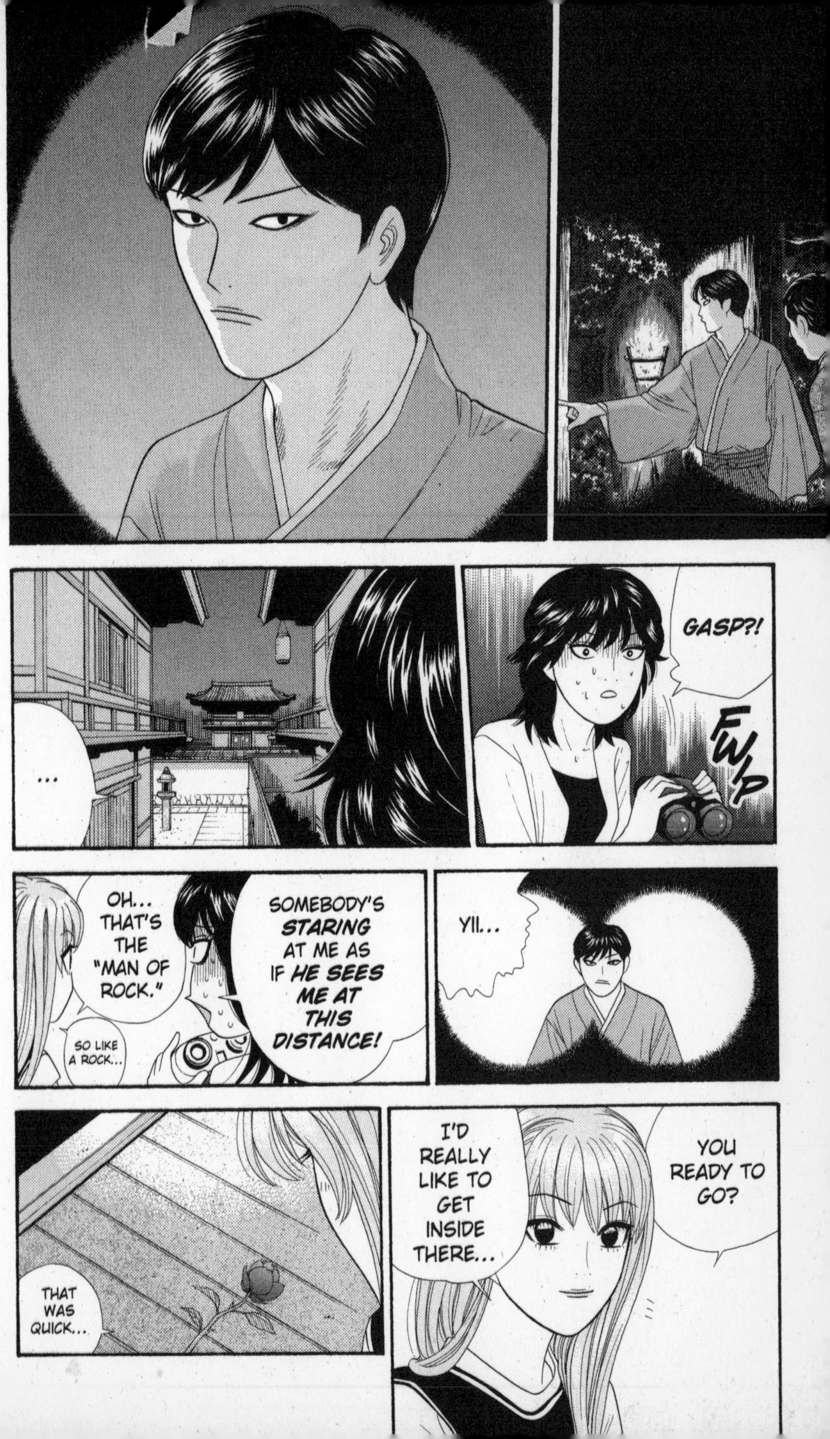
GASP?!
FWIP
...
YII...
SOMEBODY'S STARING AT ME AS IF HE SEES ME AT THIS DISTANCE!
OH... THAT'S THE "MAN OF ROCK."
SO LIKE A ROCK...
YOU READY TO GO?
I'D REALLY LIKE TO GET INSIDE THERE...
THAT WAS QUICK...

Chapter 163: 2nd Semester Starts!

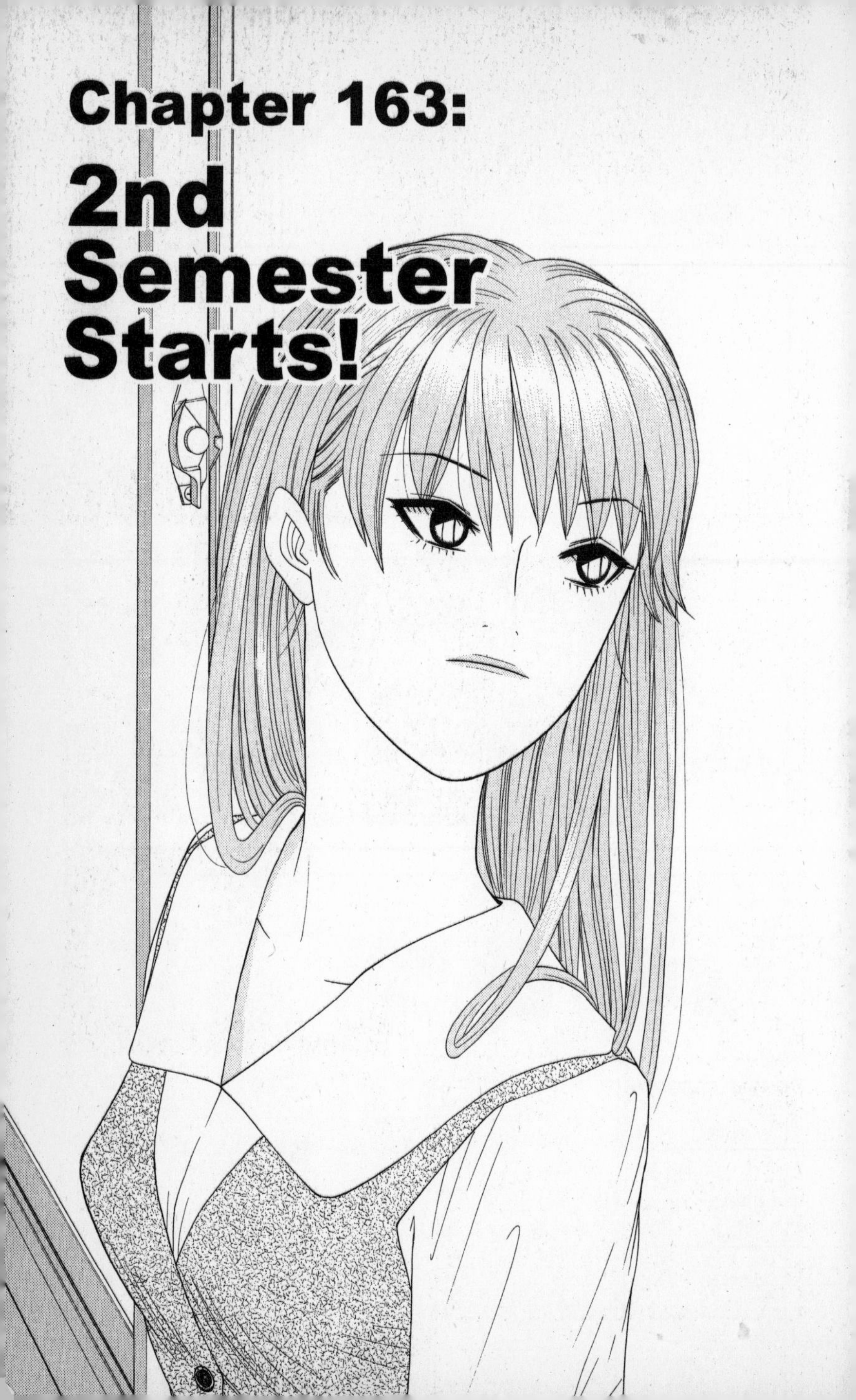

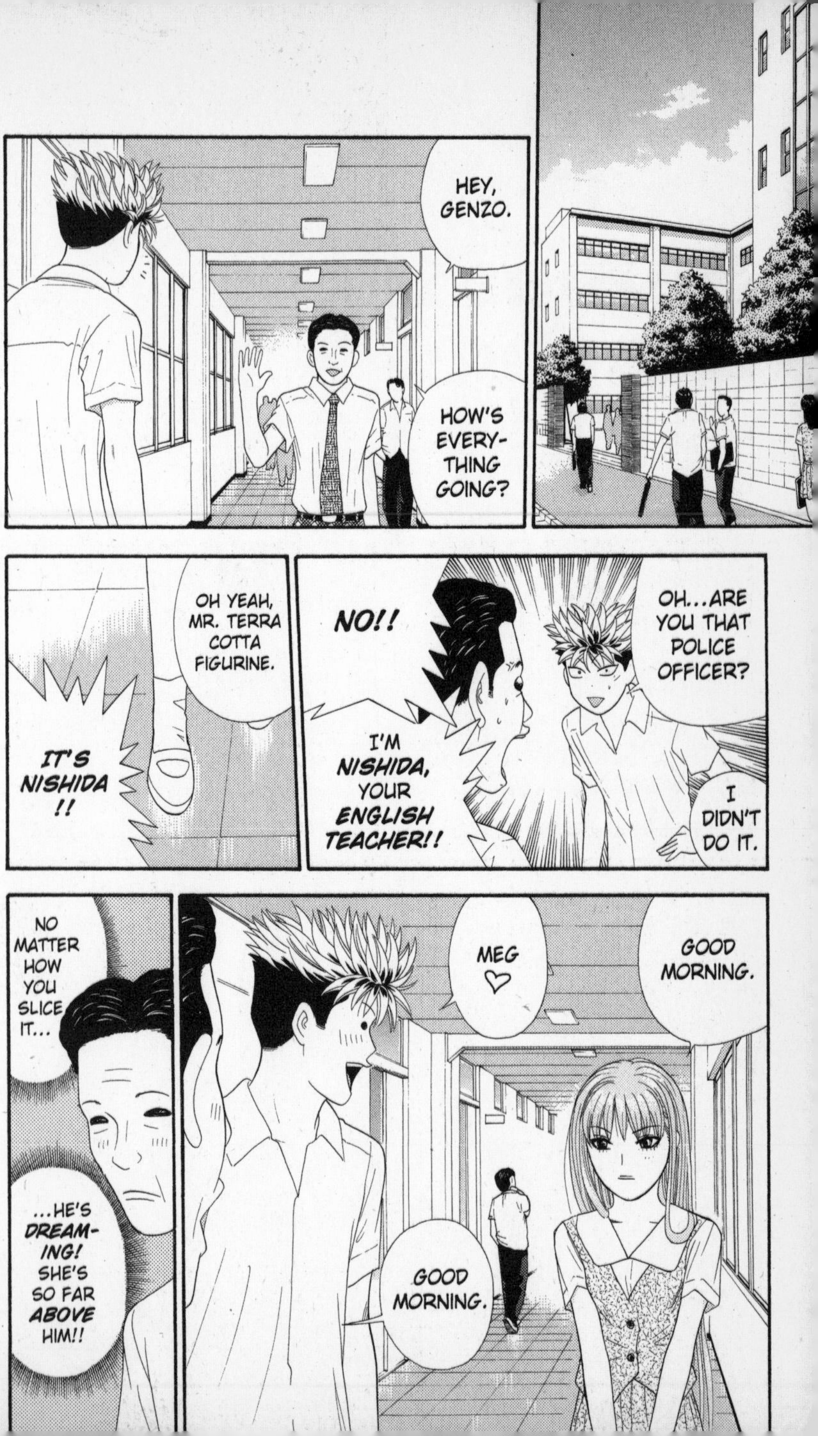
HEY, GENZO.
HOW'S EVERYTHING GOING?
OH...ARE YOU THAT POLICE OFFICER?
NO!!
I'M NISHIDA, YOUR ENGLISH TEACHER!!
I DIDN'T DO IT.
OH YEAH, MR. TERRA COTTA FIGURINE.
IT'S NISHIDA!!
GOOD MORNING.
MEG ♡
GOOD MORNING.
NO MATTER HOW YOU SLICE IT...
...HE'S DREAMING! SHE'S SO FAR ABOVE HIM!!

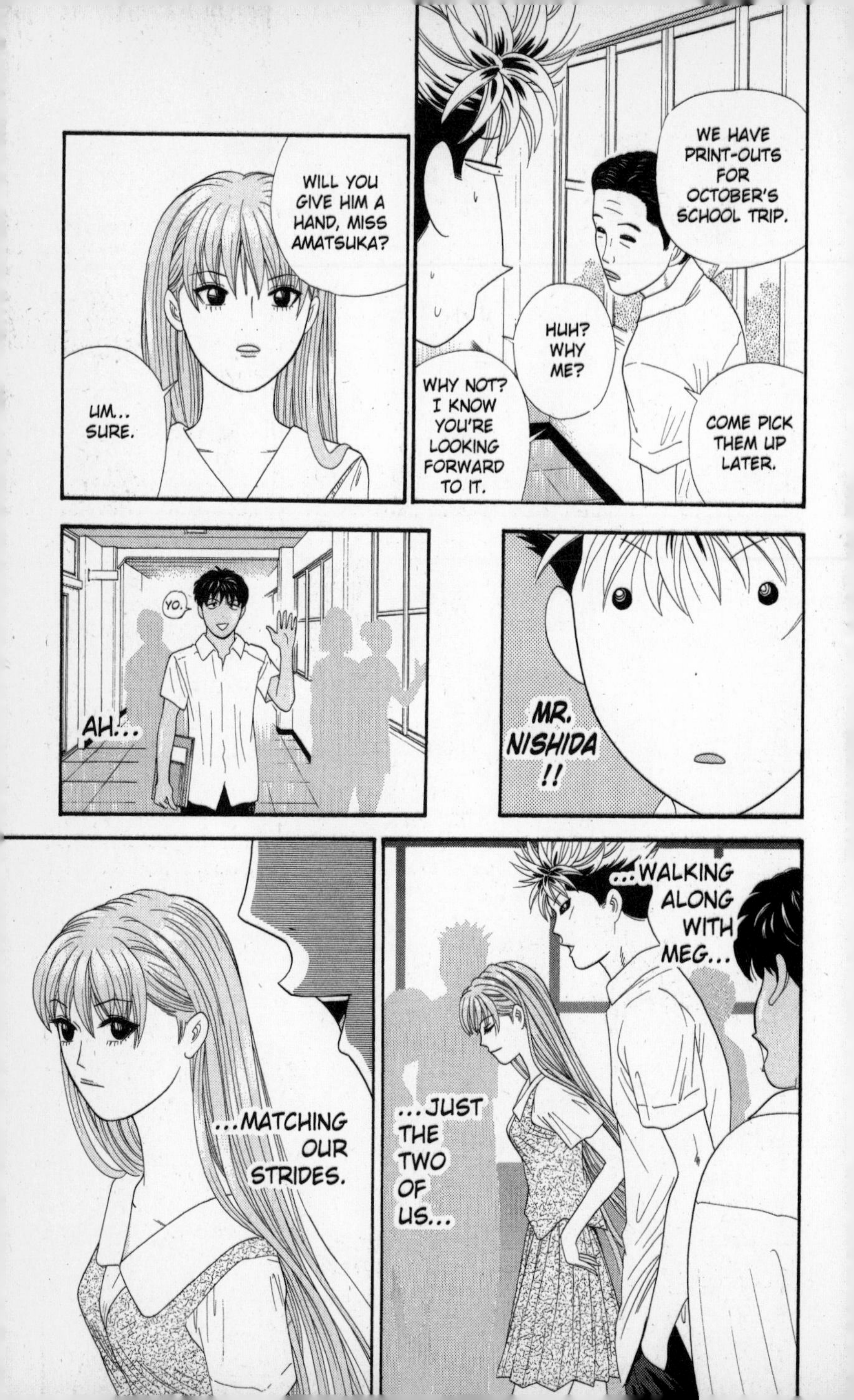
WE HAVE PRINT-OUTS FOR OCTOBER'S SCHOOL TRIP.
COME PICK THEM UP LATER.
HUH? WHY ME?
WHY NOT? I KNOW YOU'RE LOOKING FORWARD TO IT.
WILL YOU GIVE HIM A HAND, MISS AMATSUKA?
UM... SURE.
MR. NISHIDA !!
YO.
AH...
...WALKING ALONG WITH MEG...
...JUST THE TWO OF US...
...MATCHING OUR STRIDES.

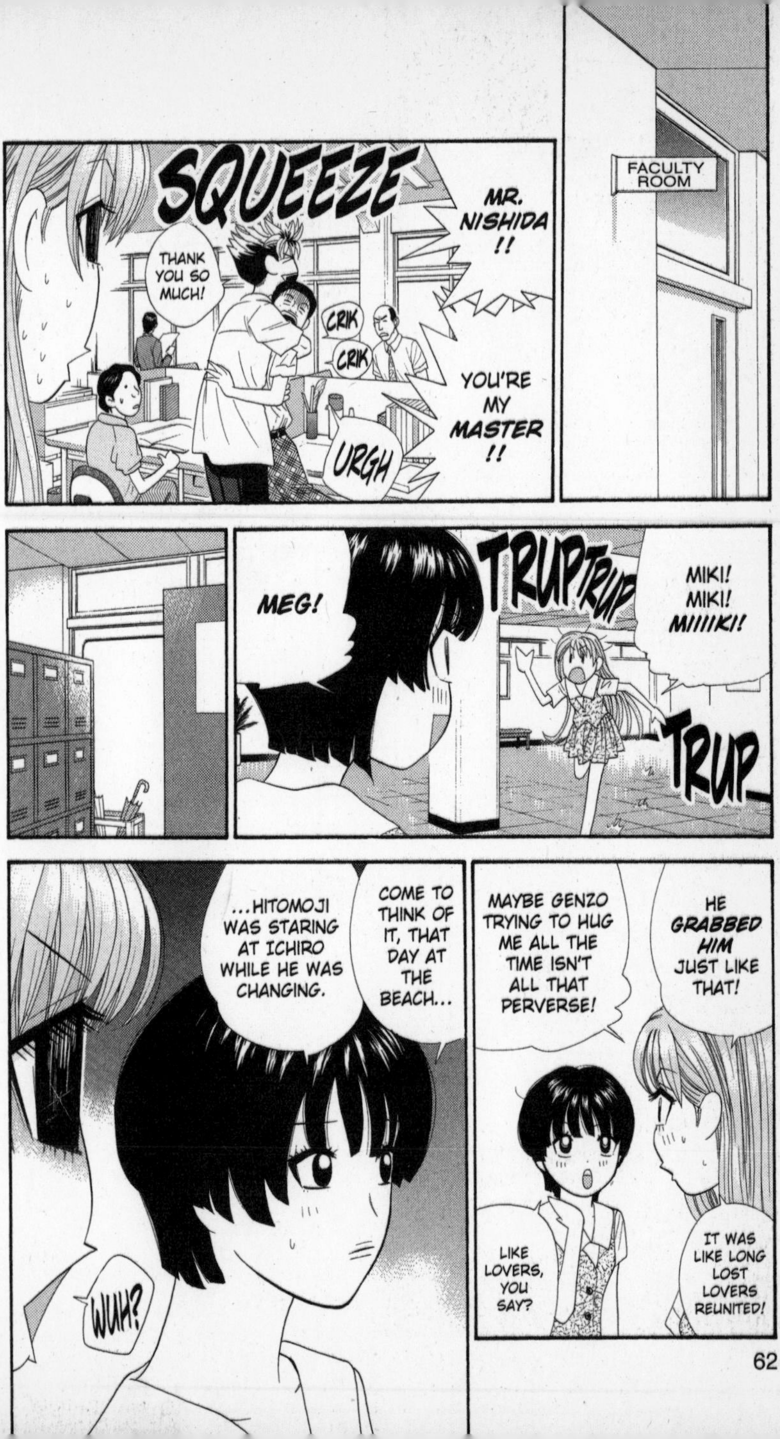
FACULTY ROOM
MR. NISHIDA !!
SQUEEZE
THANK YOU SO MUCH!
YOU'RE MY MASTER !!
CRIK
CRIK
URGH
MIKI! MIKI! MIIIIKI!
TRUP TRUP
TRUP
MEG!
HE GRABBED HIM JUST LIKE THAT!
IT WAS LIKE LONG LOST LOVERS REUNITED!
LIKE LOVERS, YOU SAY?
MAYBE GENZO TRYING TO HUG ME ALL THE TIME ISN'T ALL THAT PERVERSE!
COME TO THINK OF IT, THAT DAY AT THE BEACH...
...HITOMOJI WAS STARING AT ICHIRO WHILE HE WAS CHANGING.
WUH?

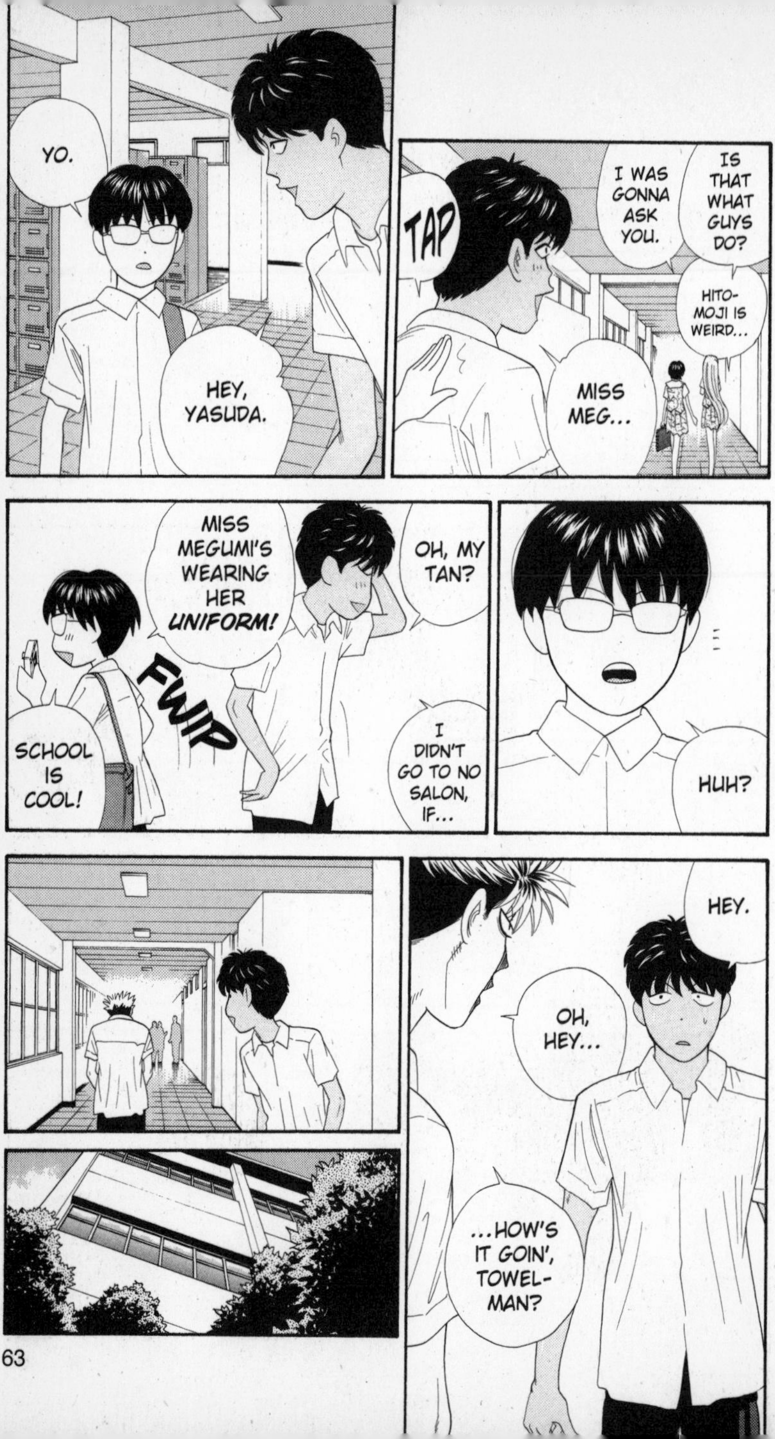
IS THAT WHAT GUYS DO?
I WAS GONNA ASK YOU.
HITO-MOJI IS WEIRD...
TAP
MISS MEG...
YO.
HEY, YASUDA.
HUH?
OH, MY TAN?
I DIDN'T GO TO NO SALON, IF...
MISS MEGUMI'S WEARING HER UNIFORM!
FWIP
SCHOOL IS COOL!
HEY.
OH, HEY...
...HOW'S IT GOIN', TOWEL-MAN?

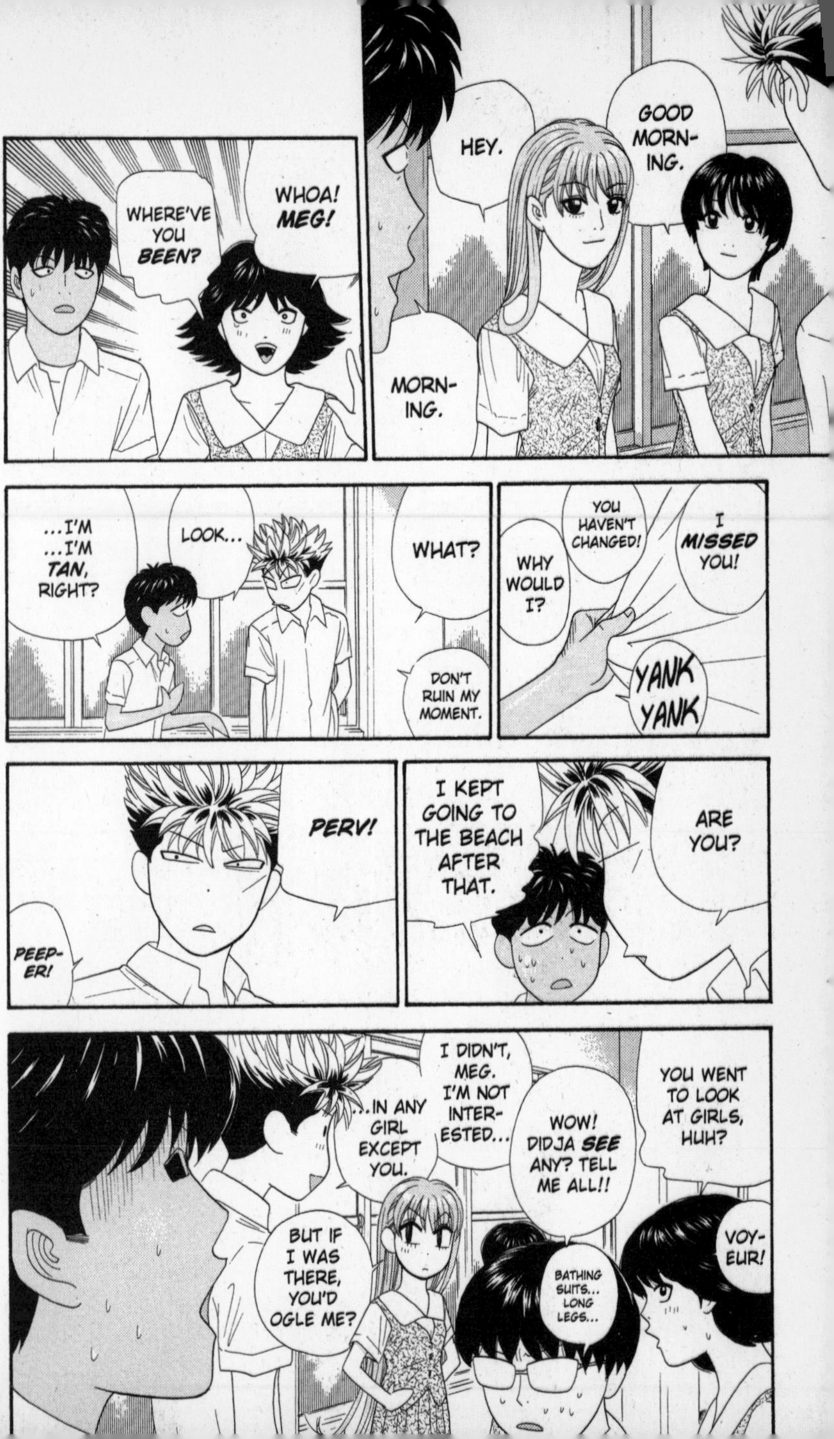
GOOD MORNING.
HEY.
MORNING.
WHOA! MEG!
WHERE'VE YOU BEEN?
I MISSED YOU!
YOU HAVEN'T CHANGED!
WHY WOULD I?
YANK YANK
WHAT?
DON'T RUIN MY MOMENT.
LOOK...
...I'M ...I'M TAN, RIGHT?
ARE YOU?
I KEPT GOING TO THE BEACH AFTER THAT.
PERV!
PEEPER!
YOU WENT TO LOOK AT GIRLS, HUH?
VOY-EUR!
WOW! DIDJA SEE ANY? TELL ME ALL!!
BATHING SUITS... LONG LEGS...
I DIDN'T, MEG. I'M NOT INTERESTED...
...IN ANY GIRL EXCEPT YOU.
BUT IF I WAS THERE, YOU'D OGLE ME?

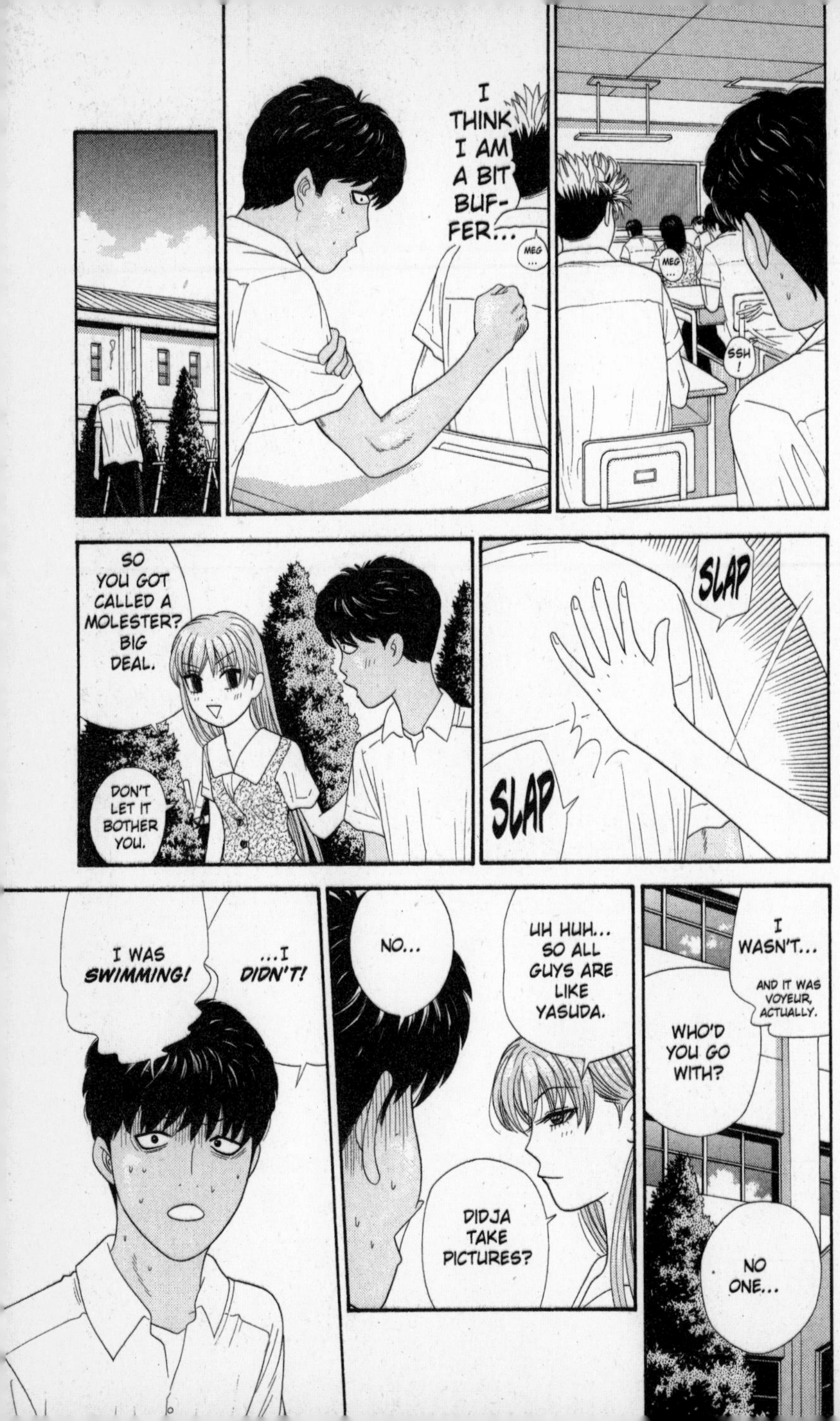
MEG...
SSH!
I THINK I AM A BIT BUFFER...
MEG...
SLAP
SLAP
SO YOU GOT CALLED A MOLESTER? BIG DEAL.
DON'T LET IT BOTHER YOU.
I WASN'T...
AND IT WAS VOYEUR, ACTUALLY.
WHO'D YOU GO WITH?
NO ONE...
UH HUH... SO ALL GUYS ARE LIKE YASUDA.
NO...
DIDJA TAKE PICTURES?
...I *DIDN'T!*
I WAS *SWIMMING!*

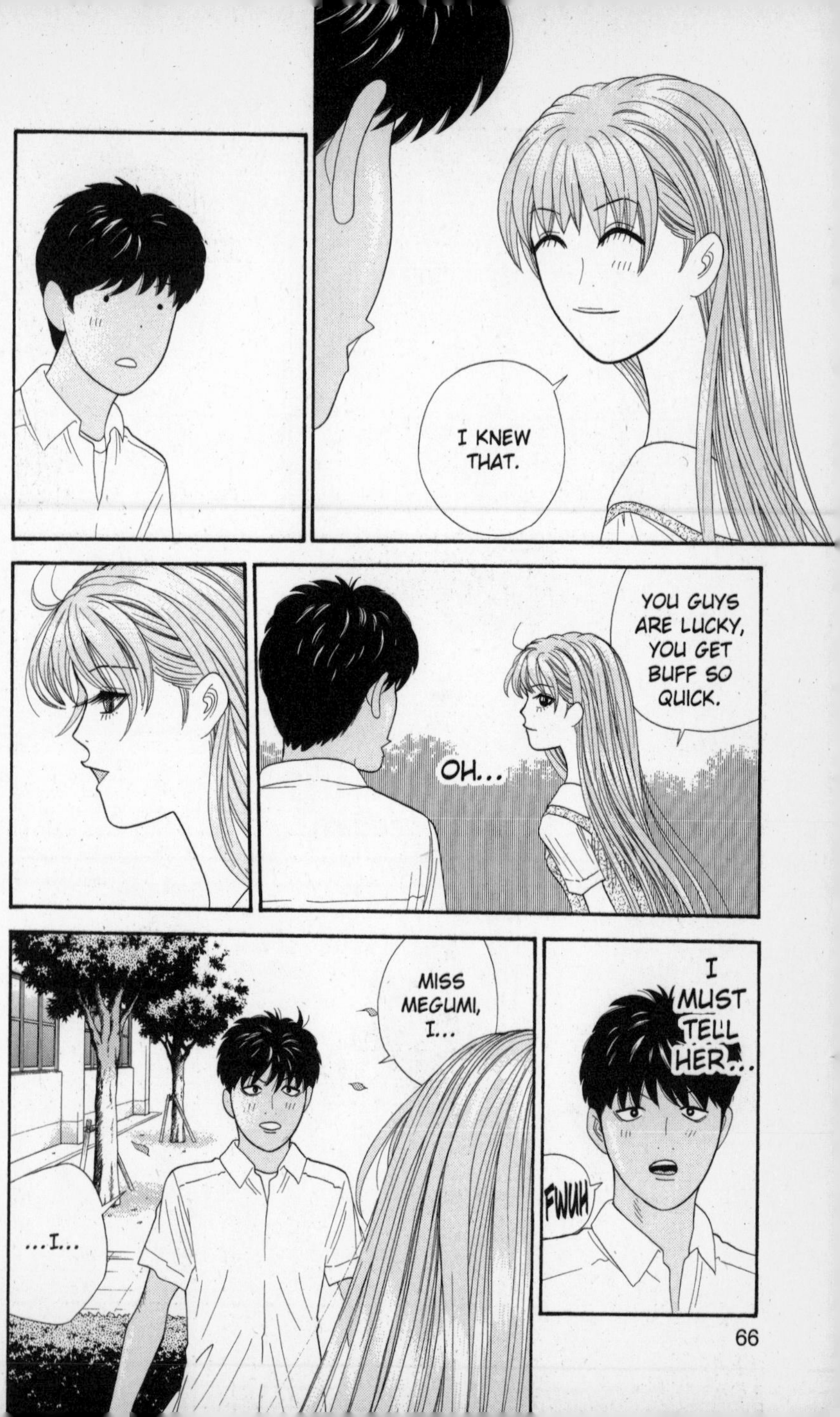
I KNEW THAT.
YOU GUYS ARE LUCKY, YOU GET BUFF SO QUICK.
OH...
I MUST TELL HER...
FWUH
MISS MEGUMI, I...
...I...

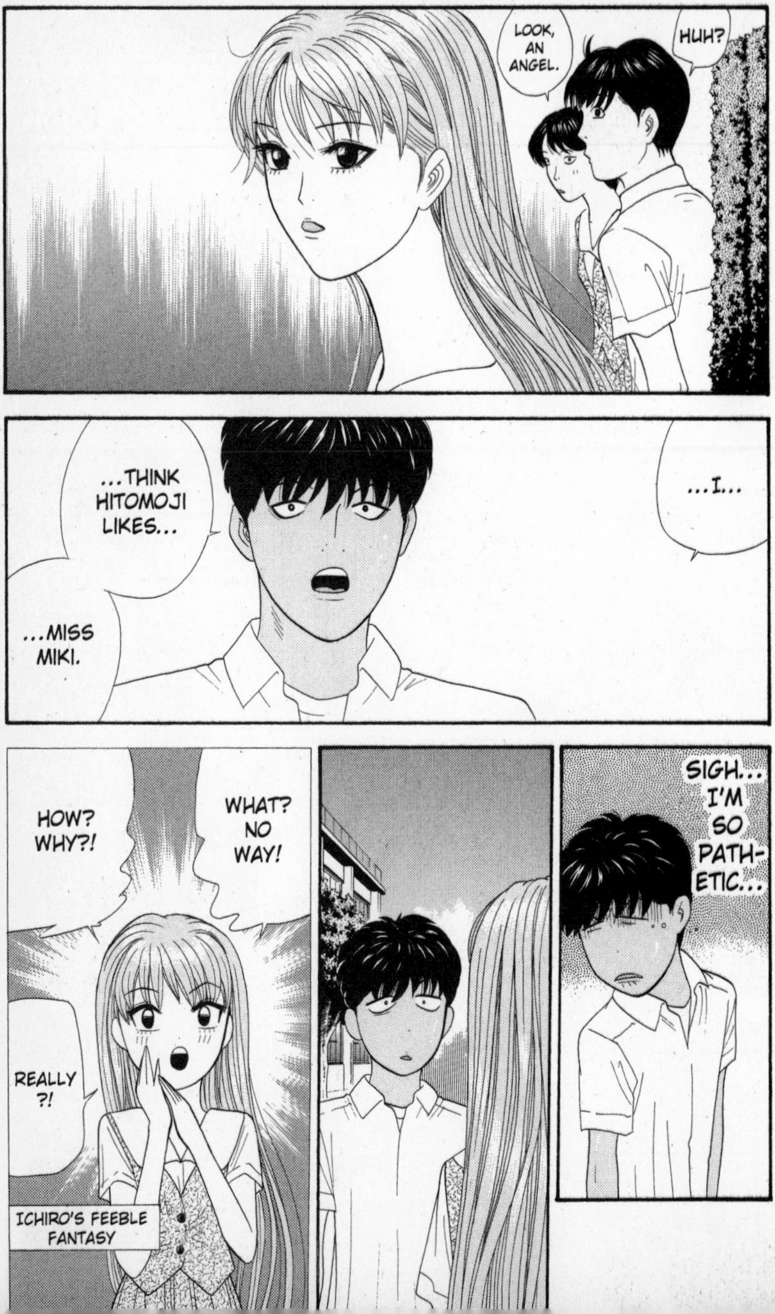
HUH?
LOOK, AN ANGEL.
...I...
...THINK HITOMOJI LIKES...
...MISS MIKI.
SIGH... I'M SO PATHETIC...
WHAT? NO WAY!
HOW? WHY?!
REALLY ?!
ICHIRO'S FEEBLE FANTASY

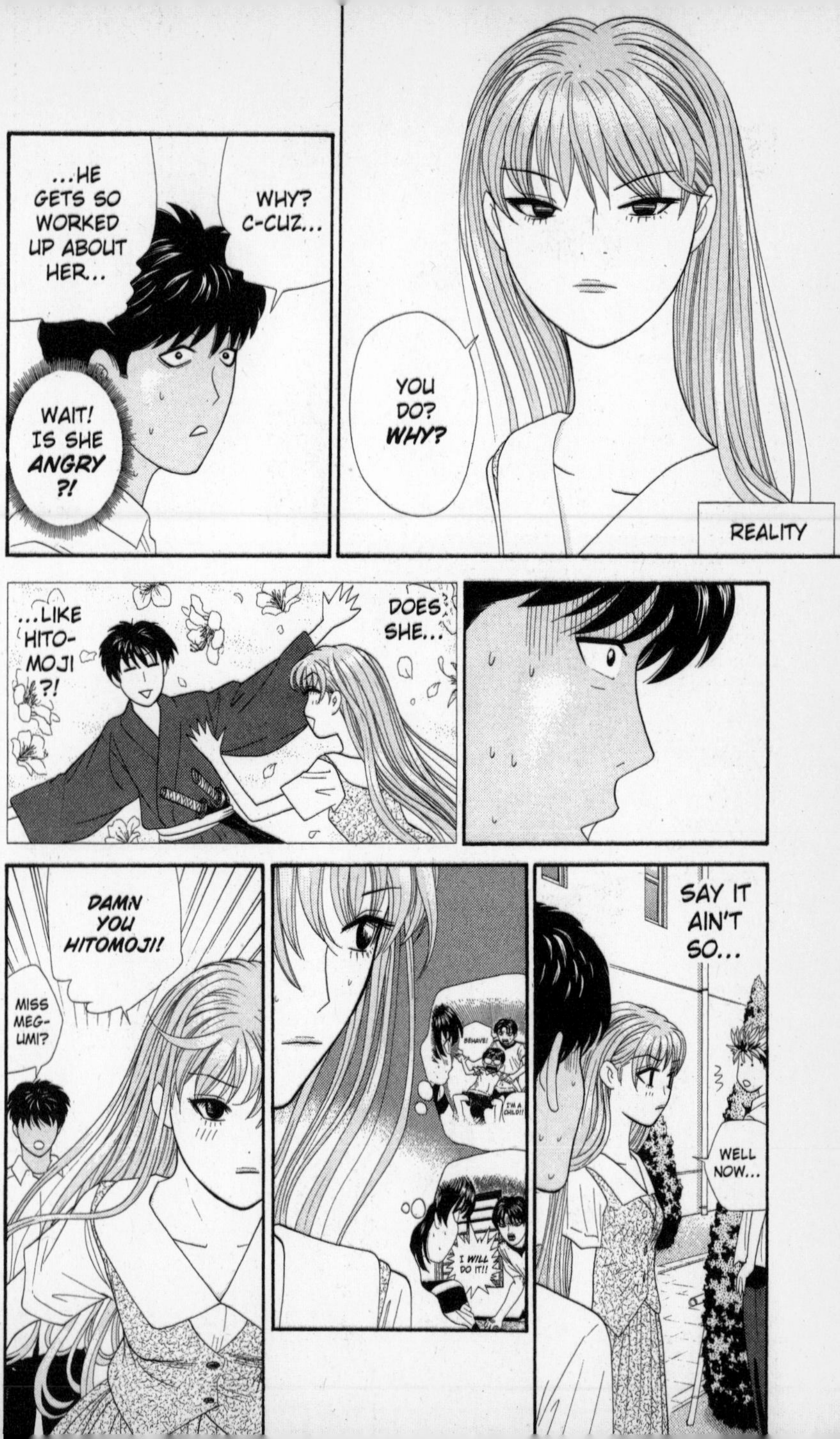

YOU DO? WHY?
REALITY
WHY? C-CUZ...
...HE GETS SO WORKED UP ABOUT HER...
WAIT! IS SHE ANGRY?!
DOES SHE...
...LIKE HITOMOJI?!
SAY IT AIN'T SO...
WELL NOW...
BEHAVE!
I'M A CHILD!!
I WILL DO IT!!
DAMN YOU HITOMOJI!
MISS MEGUMI?

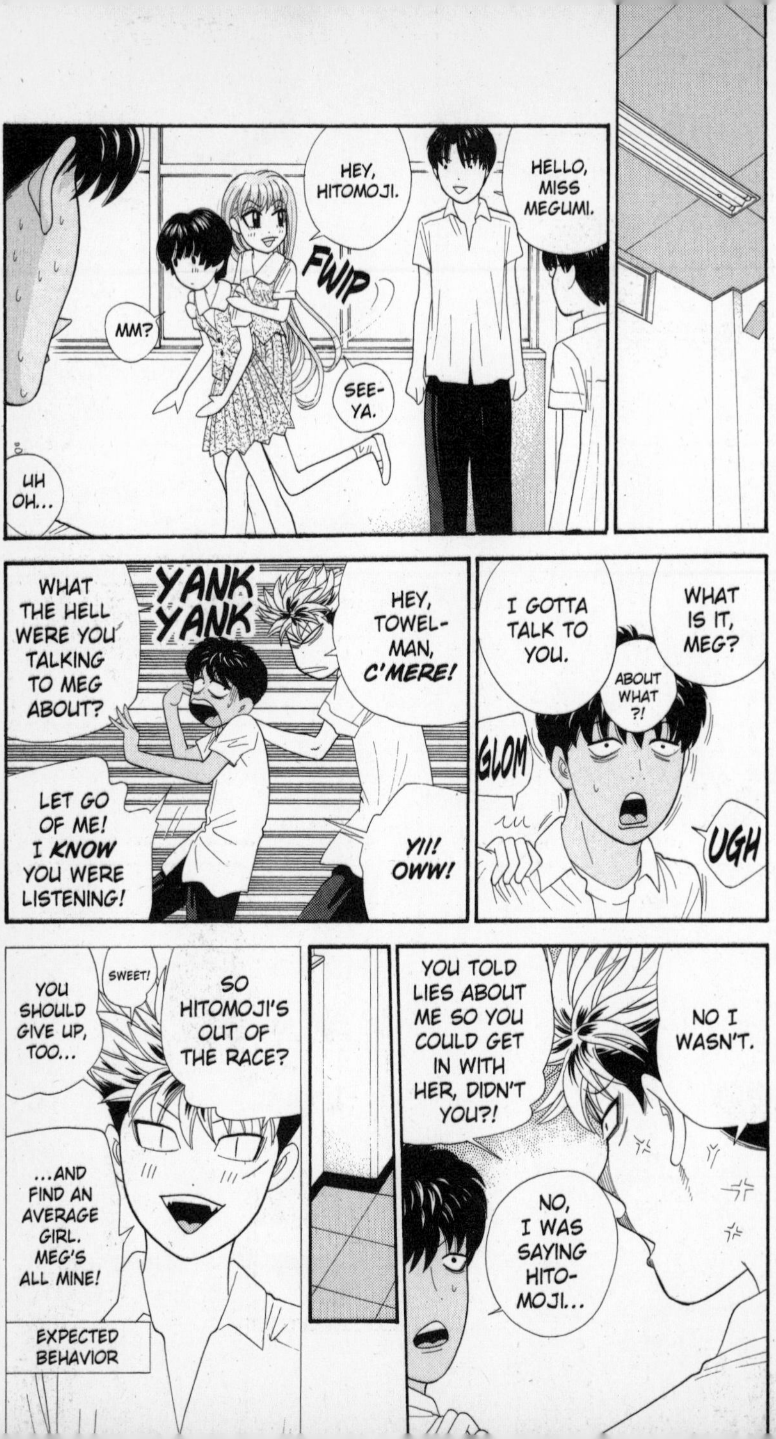
HELLO, MISS MEGUMI.
HEY, HITOMOJI.
FWIP
MM?
SEE-YA.
UH OH...
WHAT IS IT, MEG?
I GOTTA TALK TO YOU.
ABOUT WHAT ?!
GLOM
UGH
HEY, TOWEL-MAN, C'MERE!
YANK YANK
WHAT THE HELL WERE YOU TALKING TO MEG ABOUT?
YII! OWW!
LET GO OF ME! I KNOW YOU WERE LISTENING!
NO I WASN'T.
YOU TOLD LIES ABOUT ME SO YOU COULD GET IN WITH HER, DIDN'T YOU?!
NO, I WAS SAYING HITO-MOJI...
SO HITOMOJI'S OUT OF THE RACE?
SWEET!
YOU SHOULD GIVE UP, TOO...
...AND FIND AN AVERAGE GIRL. MEG'S ALL MINE!
EXPECTED BEHAVIOR

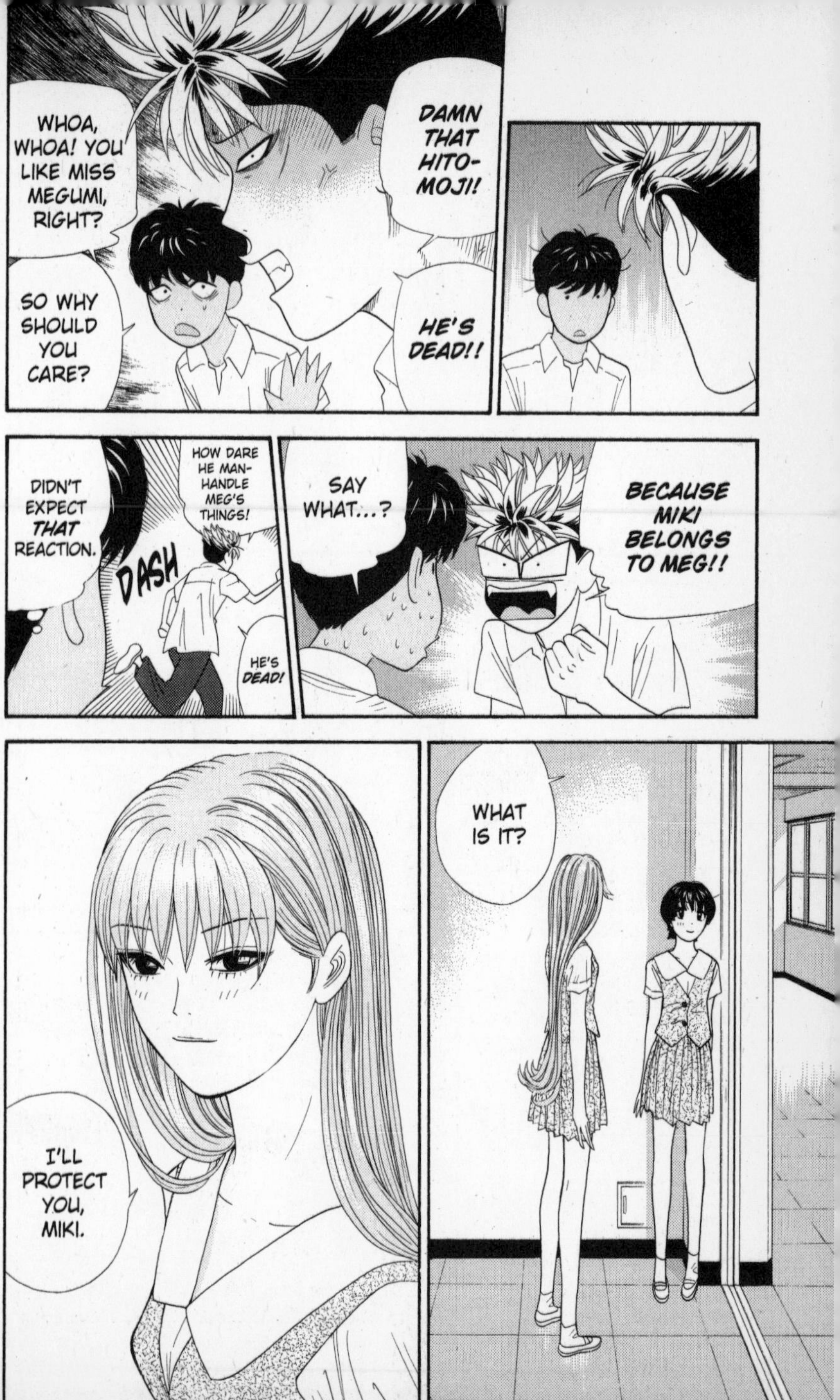
DAMN THAT HITO-MOJI!
HE'S DEAD!!
WHOA, WHOA! YOU LIKE MISS MEGUMI, RIGHT?
SO WHY SHOULD YOU CARE?
BECAUSE MIKI BELONGS TO MEG!!
SAY WHAT...?
HOW DARE HE MAN-HANDLE MEG'S THINGS!
DIDN'T EXPECT *THAT* REACTION.
DASH
HE'S DEAD!
WHAT IS IT?
I'LL PROTECT YOU, MIKI.

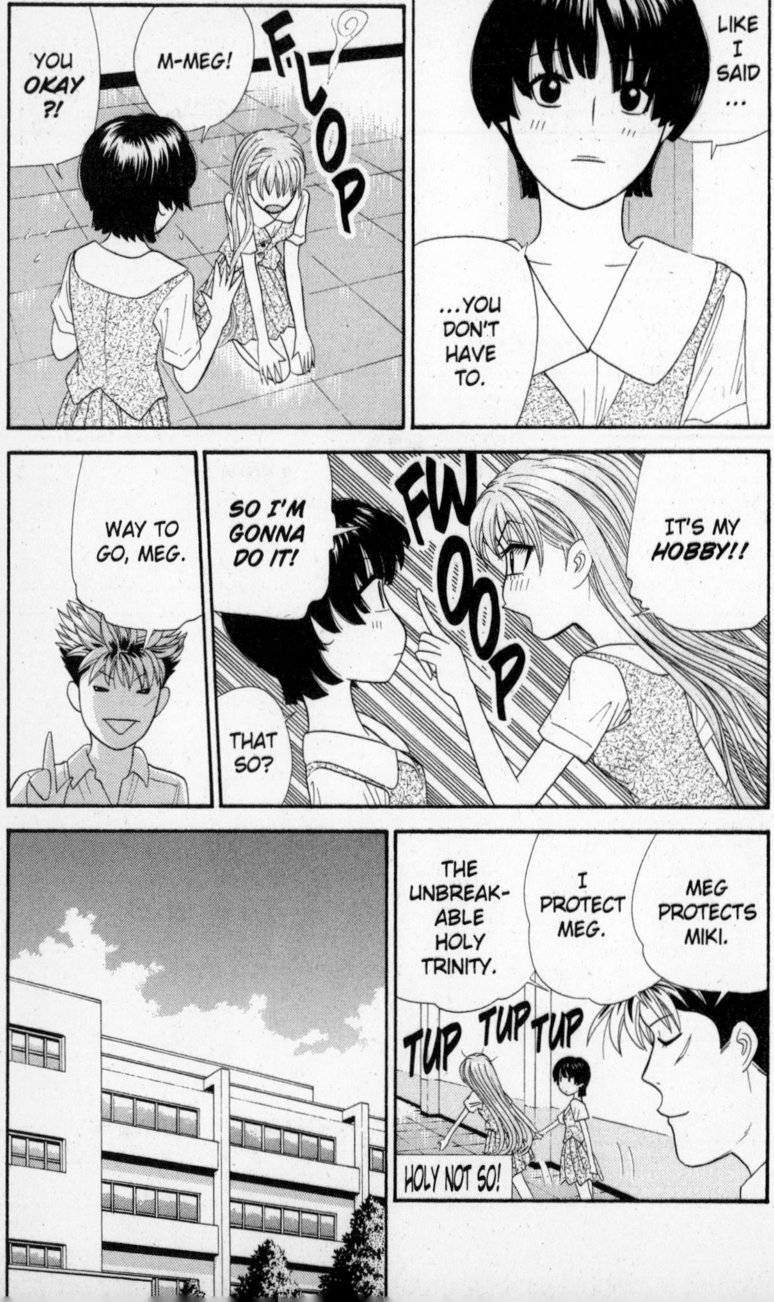
LIKE I SAID...
...YOU DON'T HAVE TO.
FLOP
M-MEG!
YOU OKAY?!
IT'S MY HOBBY!!
FWOOOP
SO I'M GONNA DO IT!
THAT SO?
WAY TO GO, MEG.
MEG PROTECTS MIKI.
I PROTECT MEG.
THE UNBREAK-ABLE HOLY TRINITY.
TUP TUP TUP
HOLY NOT SO!

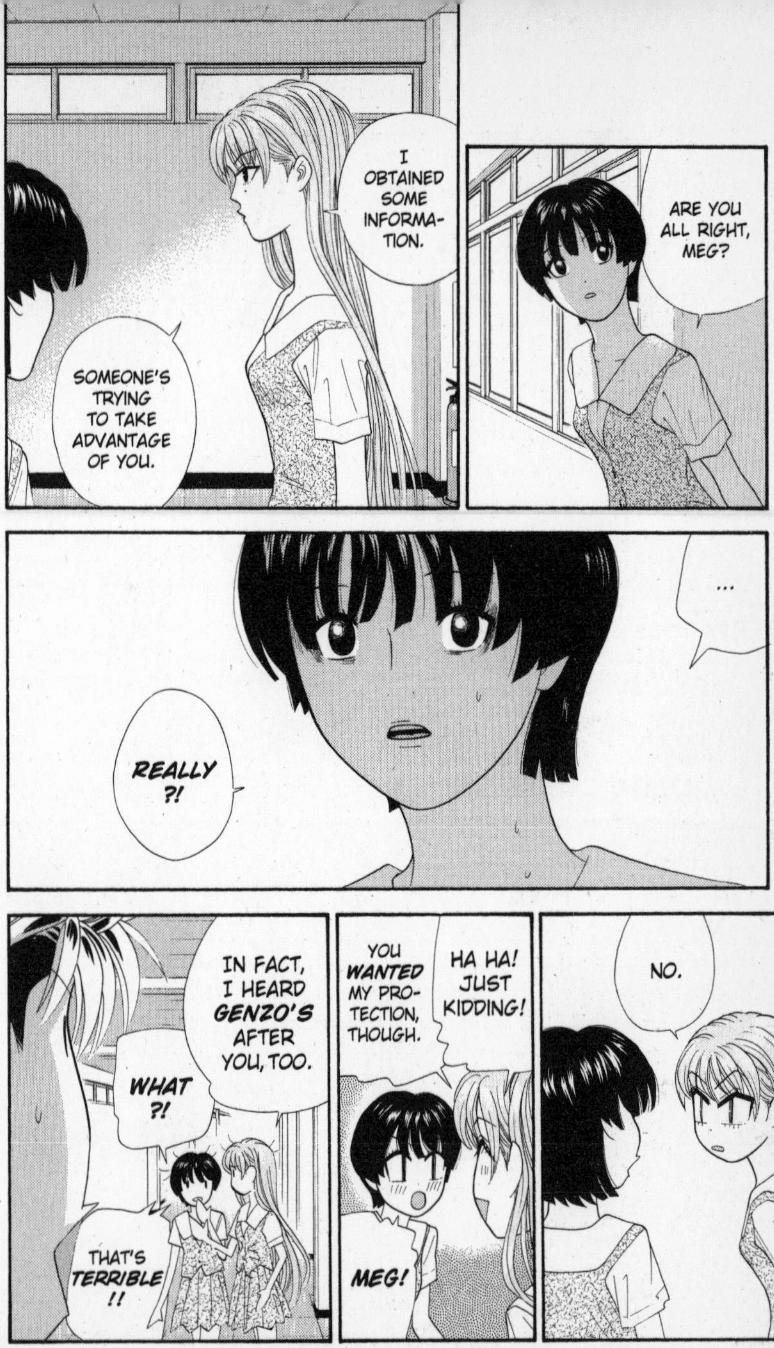
ARE YOU ALL RIGHT, MEG?
I OBTAINED SOME INFORMATION.
SOMEONE'S TRYING TO TAKE ADVANTAGE OF YOU.
...
REALLY ?!
NO.
HA HA! JUST KIDDING!
YOU WANTED MY PROTECTION, THOUGH.
MEG!
IN FACT, I HEARD GENZO'S AFTER YOU, TOO.
WHAT ?!
THAT'S TERRIBLE !!

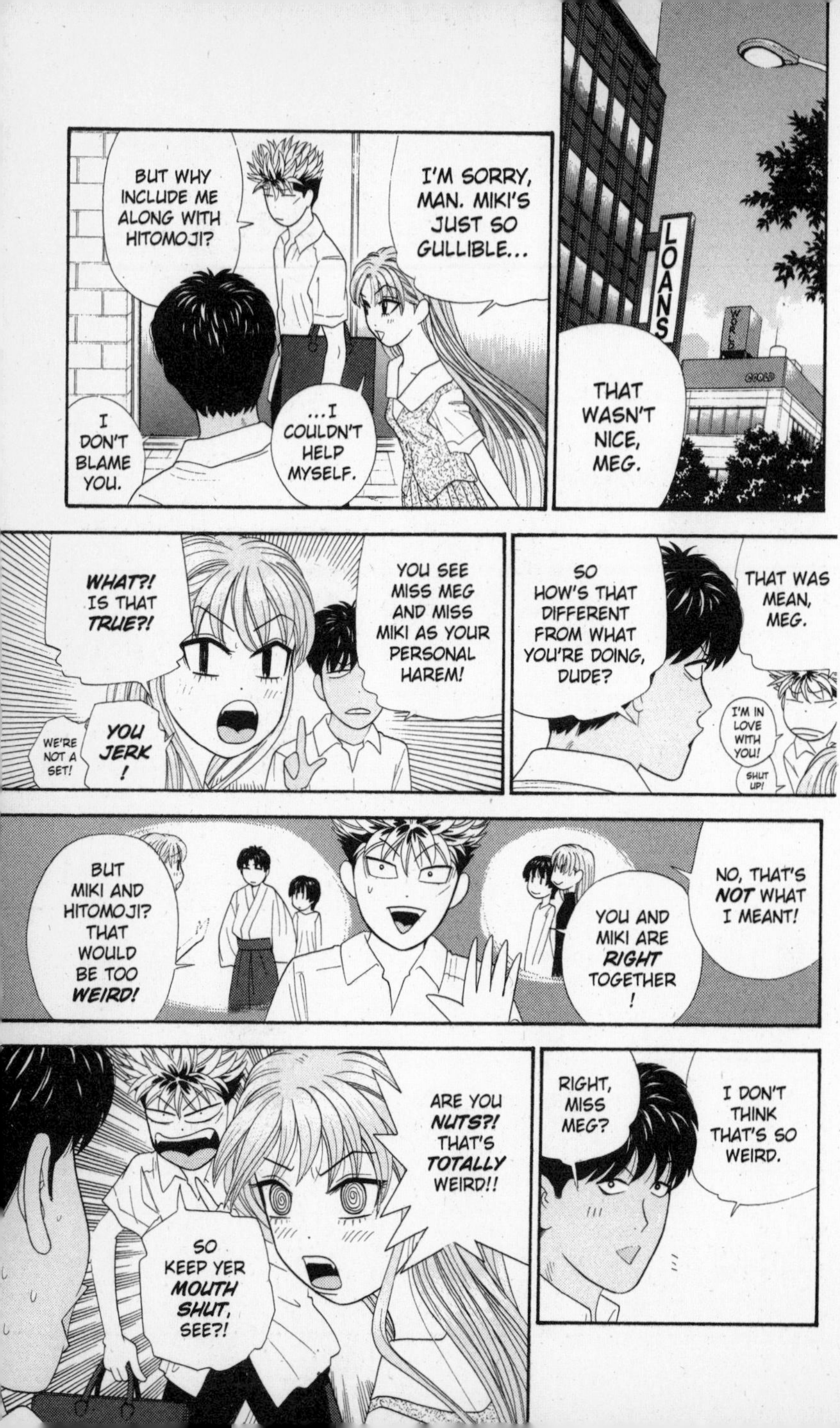
THAT WASN'T NICE, MEG.
I'M SORRY, MAN. MIKI'S JUST SO GULLIBLE...
BUT WHY INCLUDE ME ALONG WITH HITOMOJI?
...I COULDN'T HELP MYSELF.
I DON'T BLAME YOU.
THAT WAS MEAN, MEG.
SO HOW'S THAT DIFFERENT FROM WHAT YOU'RE DOING, DUDE?
I'M IN LOVE WITH YOU!
SHUT UP!
YOU SEE MISS MEG AND MISS MIKI AS YOUR PERSONAL HAREM!
WHAT?! IS THAT TRUE?!
YOU JERK!
WE'RE NOT A SET!
NO, THAT'S NOT WHAT I MEANT!
YOU AND MIKI ARE RIGHT TOGETHER!
BUT MIKI AND HITOMOJI? THAT WOULD BE TOO WEIRD!
I DON'T THINK THAT'S SO WEIRD.
RIGHT, MISS MEG?
ARE YOU NUTS?! THAT'S TOTALLY WEIRD!!
SO KEEP YER MOUTH SHUT, SEE?!

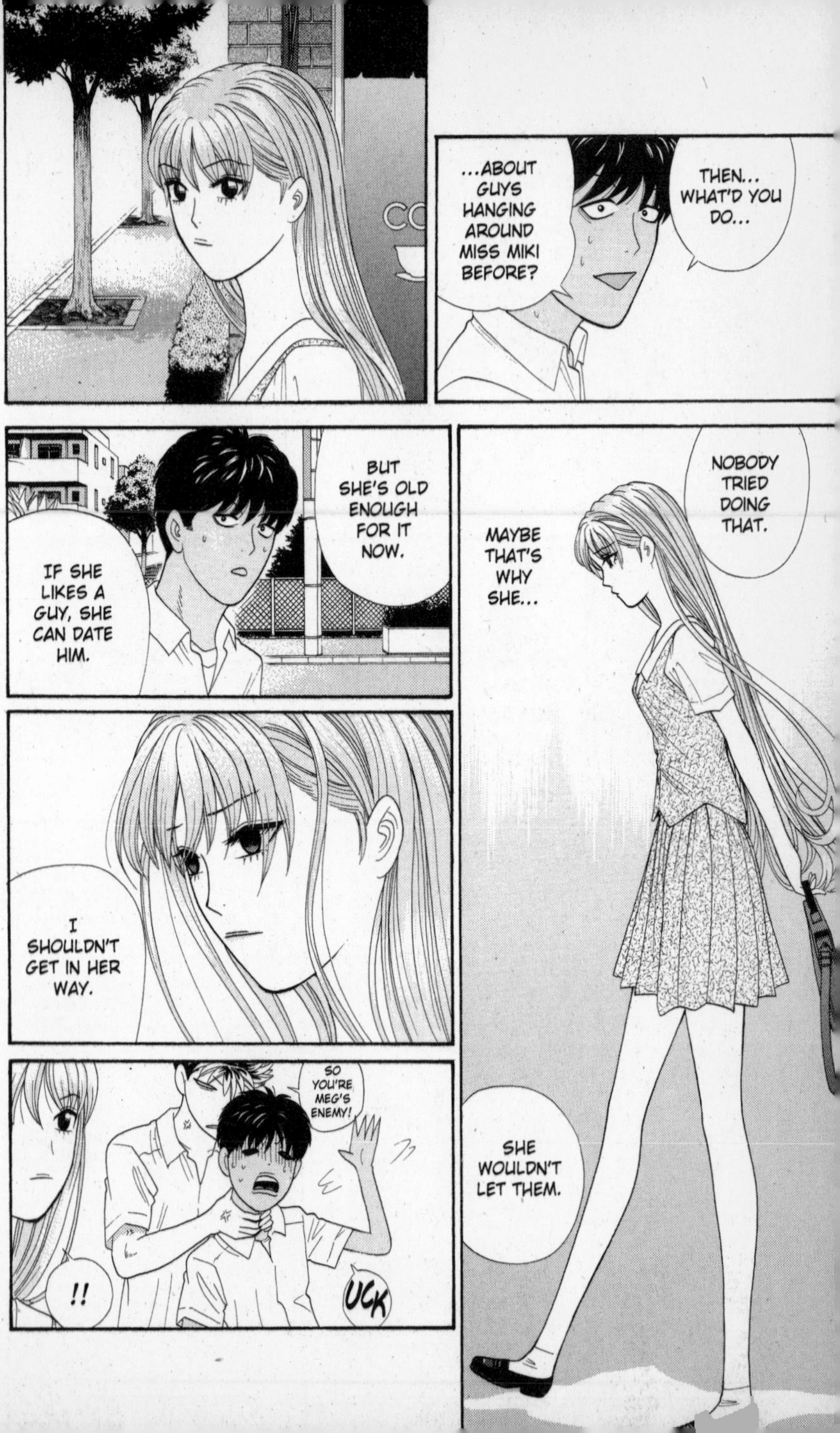
THEN... WHAT'D YOU DO...
...ABOUT GUYS HANGING AROUND MISS MIKI BEFORE?
NOBODY TRIED DOING THAT.
MAYBE THAT'S WHY SHE...
SHE WOULDN'T LET THEM.
BUT SHE'S OLD ENOUGH FOR IT NOW.
IF SHE LIKES A GUY, SHE CAN DATE HIM.
I SHOULDN'T GET IN HER WAY.
SO YOU'RE MEG'S ENEMY!
UCK
!!

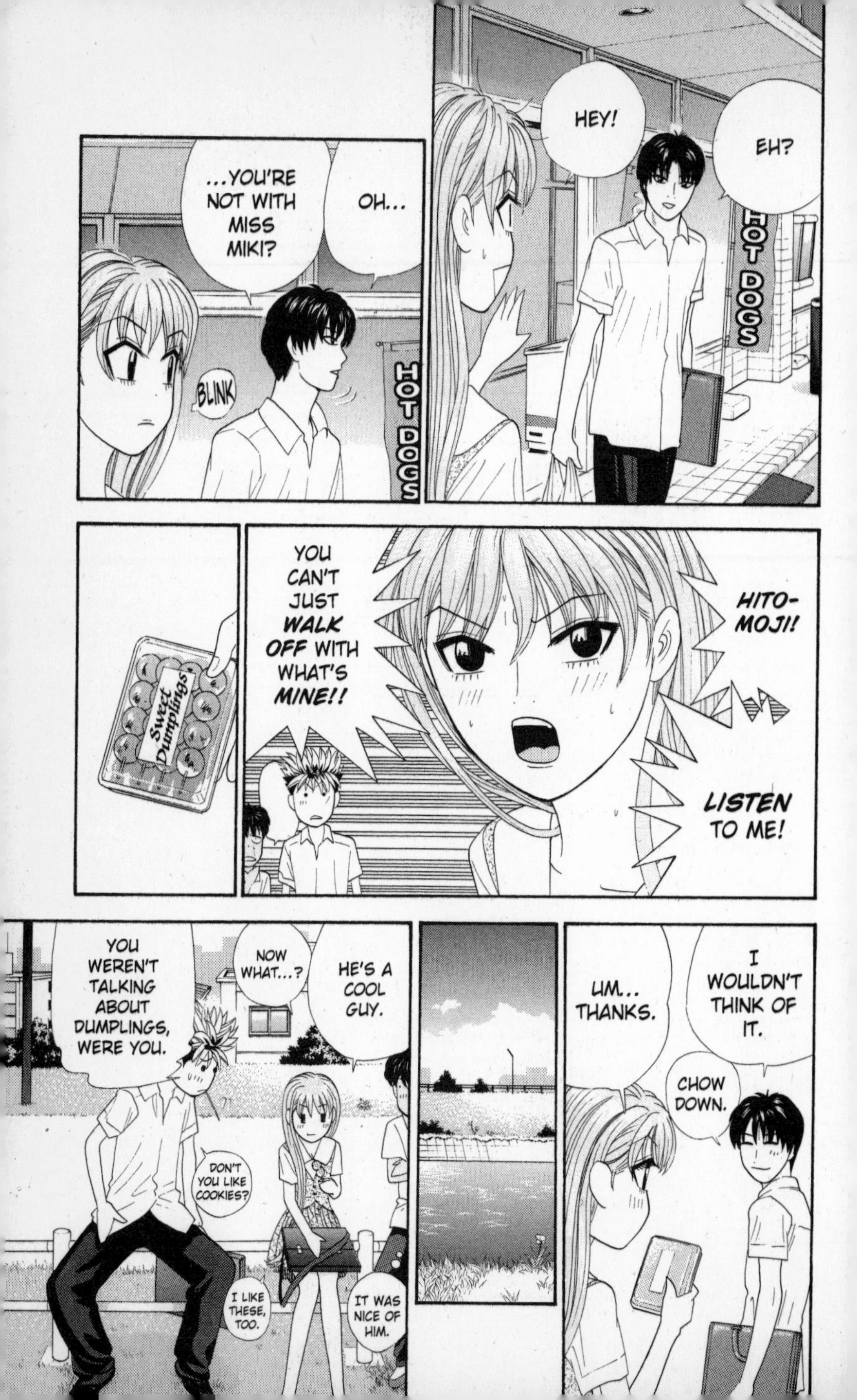
HEY!
EH?
HOT DOGS
OH...
...YOU'RE NOT WITH MISS MIKI?
BLINK
HOT DOGS
HITO-MOJI!
LISTEN TO ME!
YOU CAN'T JUST WALK OFF WITH WHAT'S MINE!!
Sweet Dumplings
I WOULDN'T THINK OF IT.
UM... THANKS.
CHOW DOWN.
HE'S A COOL GUY.
NOW WHAT...?
YOU WEREN'T TALKING ABOUT DUMPLINGS, WERE YOU.
DON'T YOU LIKE COOKIES?
IT WAS NICE OF HIM.
I LIKE THESE, TOO.

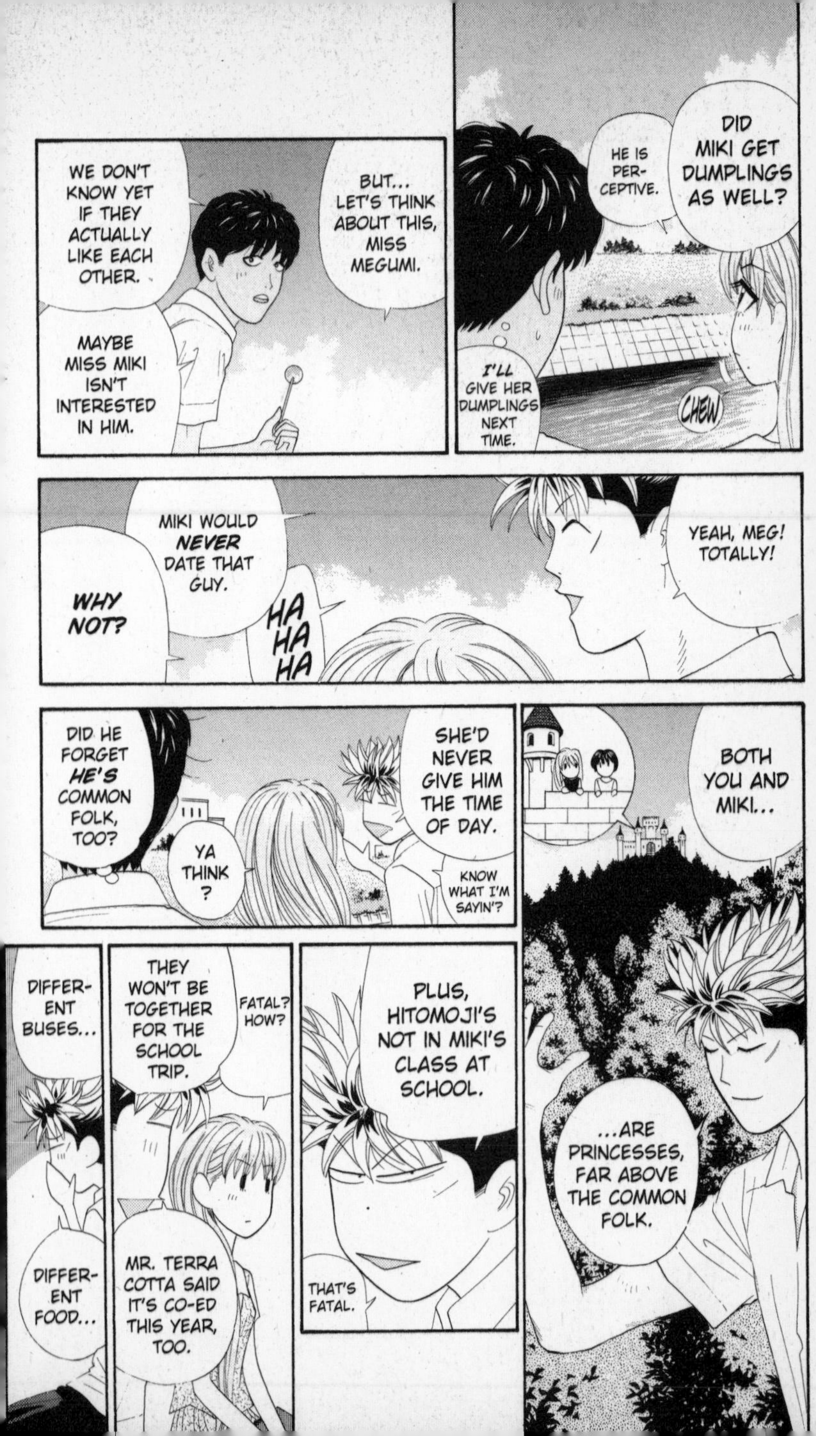
DID MIKI GET DUMPLINGS AS WELL?
HE IS PER-CEPTIVE.
I'LL GIVE HER DUMPLINGS NEXT TIME.
CHEW
BUT... LET'S THINK ABOUT THIS, MISS MEGUMI.
WE DON'T KNOW YET IF THEY ACTUALLY LIKE EACH OTHER.
MAYBE MISS MIKI ISN'T INTERESTED IN HIM.
YEAH, MEG! TOTALLY!
HA HA HA
MIKI WOULD NEVER DATE THAT GUY.
WHY NOT?
BOTH YOU AND MIKI...
...ARE PRINCESSES, FAR ABOVE THE COMMON FOLK.
SHE'D NEVER GIVE HIM THE TIME OF DAY.
KNOW WHAT I'M SAYIN'?
DID HE FORGET HE'S COMMON FOLK, TOO?
YA THINK?
PLUS, HITOMOJI'S NOT IN MIKI'S CLASS AT SCHOOL.
THAT'S FATAL.
FATAL? HOW?
THEY WON'T BE TOGETHER FOR THE SCHOOL TRIP.
MR. TERRA COTTA SAID IT'S CO-ED THIS YEAR, TOO.
DIFFER-ENT BUSES...
DIFFER-ENT FOOD...

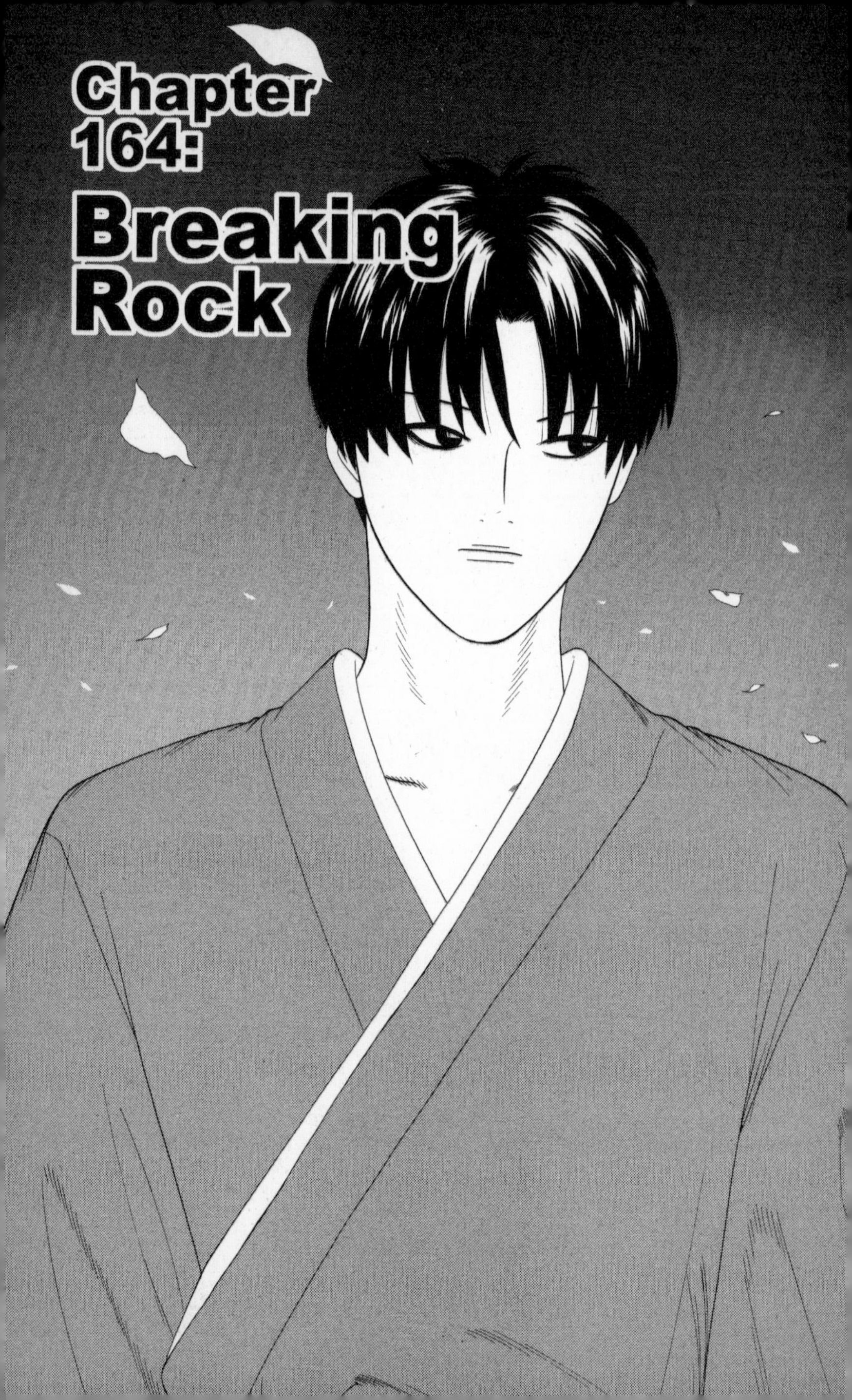
Chapter 164:
Breaking Rock

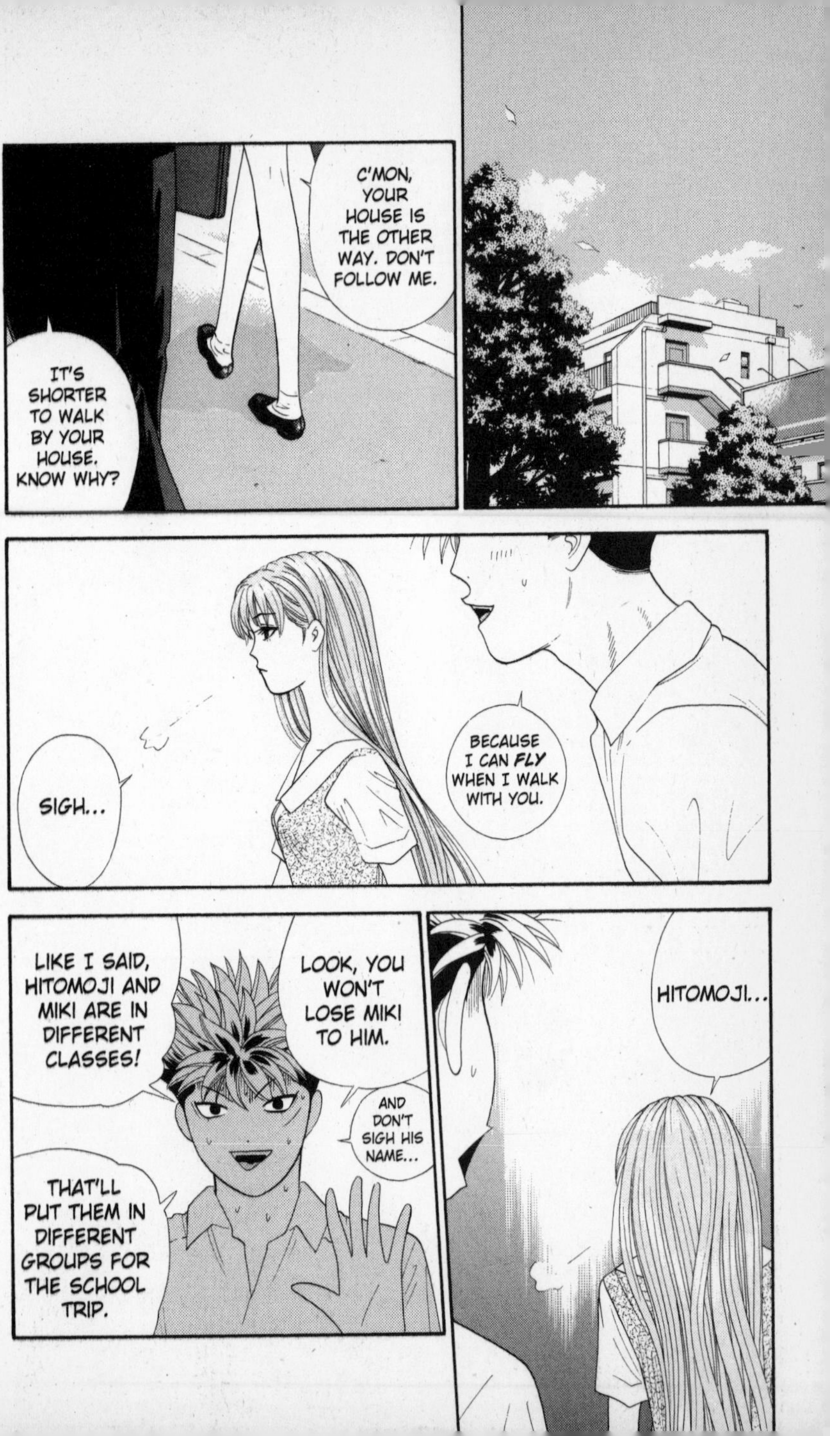
C'MON, YOUR HOUSE IS THE OTHER WAY. DON'T FOLLOW ME.
IT'S SHORTER TO WALK BY YOUR HOUSE. KNOW WHY?
BECAUSE I CAN *FLY* WHEN I WALK WITH YOU.
SIGH...
HITOMOJI...
LOOK, YOU WON'T LOSE MIKI TO HIM.
AND DON'T SIGH HIS NAME...
LIKE I SAID, HITOMOJI AND MIKI ARE IN DIFFERENT CLASSES!
THAT'LL PUT THEM IN DIFFERENT GROUPS FOR THE SCHOOL TRIP.

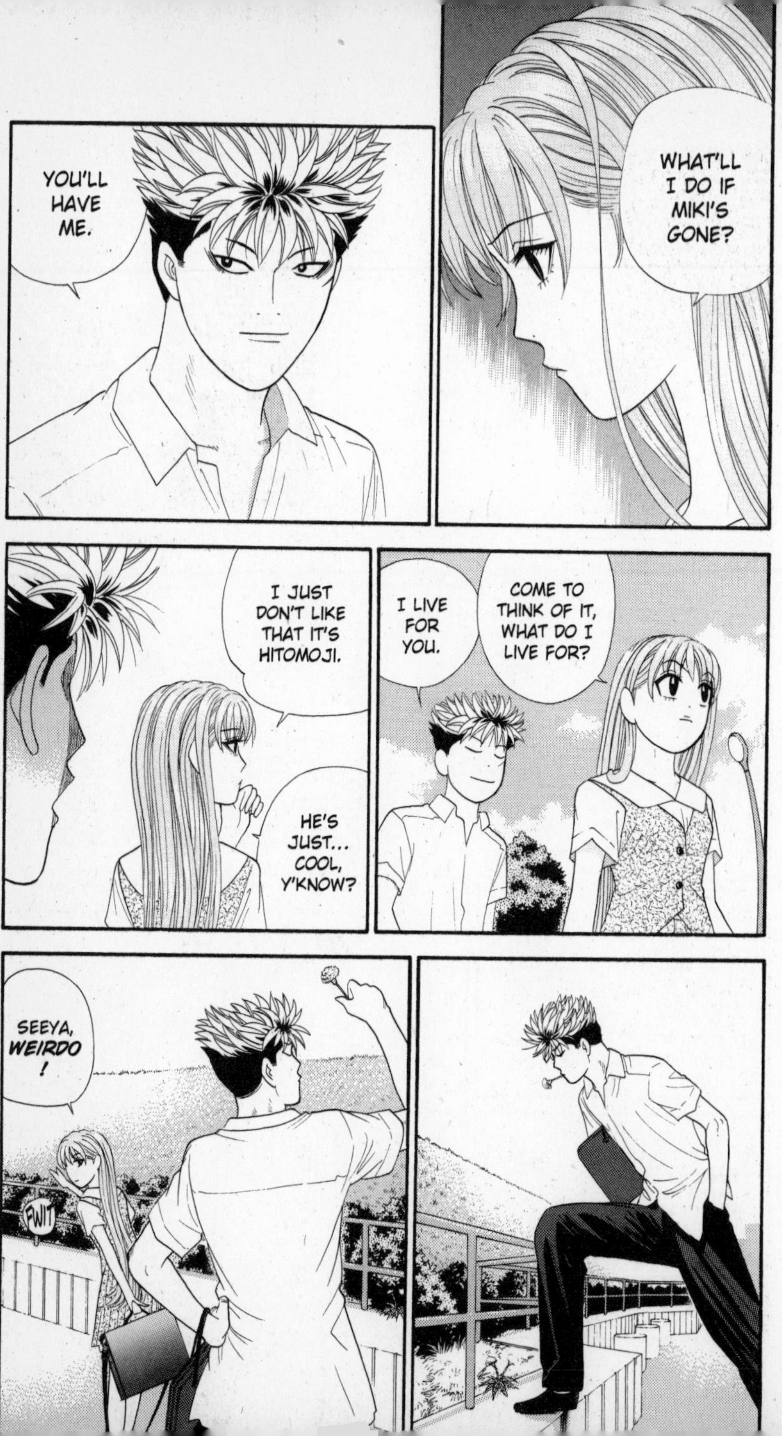
WHAT'LL I DO IF MIKI'S GONE?
YOU'LL HAVE ME.
COME TO THINK OF IT, WHAT DO I LIVE FOR?
I LIVE FOR YOU.
I JUST DON'T LIKE THAT IT'S HITOMOJI.
HE'S JUST... COOL, Y'KNOW?
SEEYA, WEIRDO!
FWIT

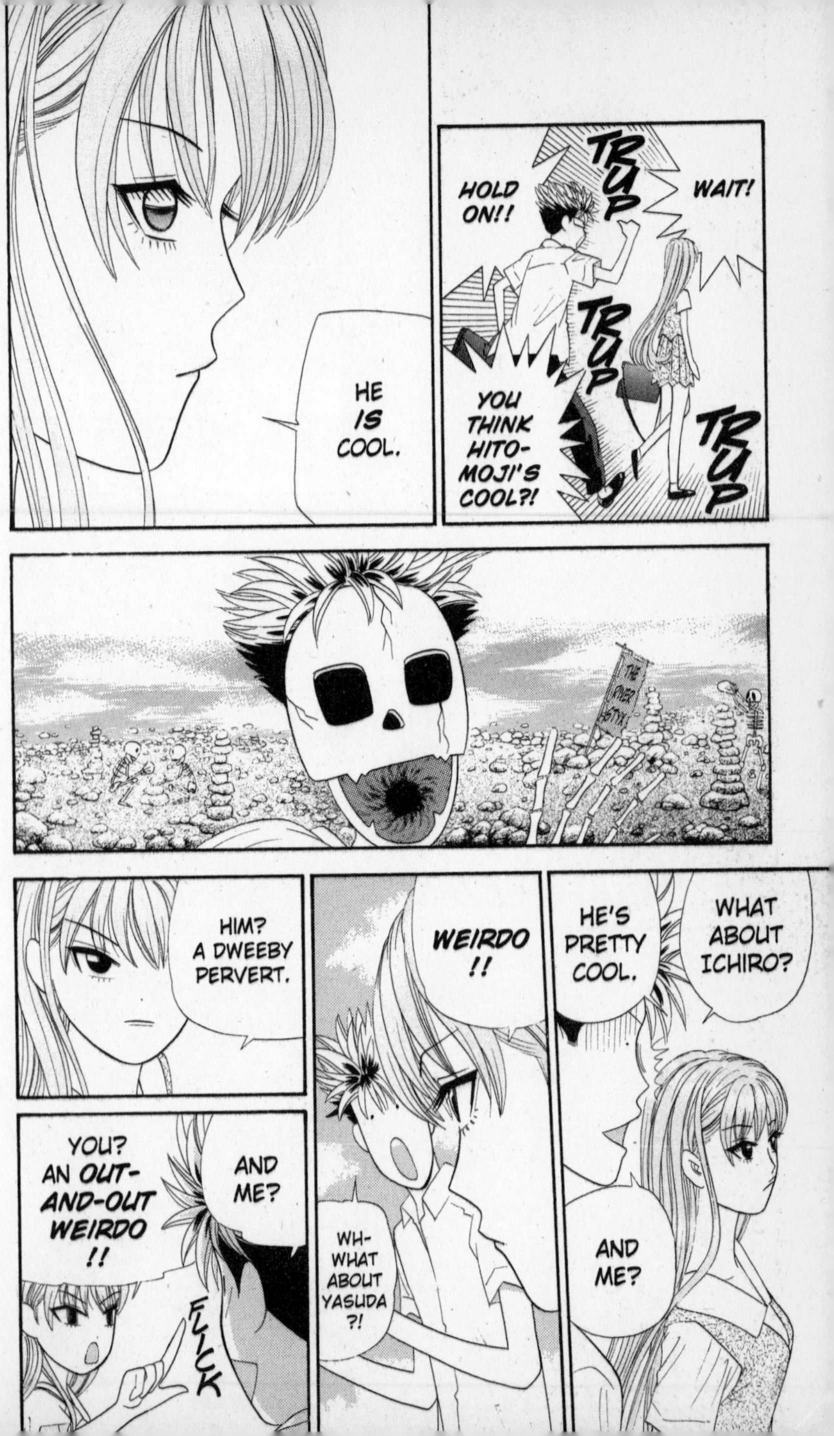
WAIT!
TRUP
HOLD ON!!
TRUP
TRUP
YOU THINK HITO-MOJI'S COOL?!
HE IS COOL.
THE RIVER STYX
WHAT ABOUT ICHIRO?
HE'S PRETTY COOL.
AND ME?
WEIRDO!!
WH-WHAT ABOUT YASUDA?!
HIM? A DWEEBY PERVERT.
AND ME?
YOU? AN OUT-AND-OUT WEIRDO!!
FLICK

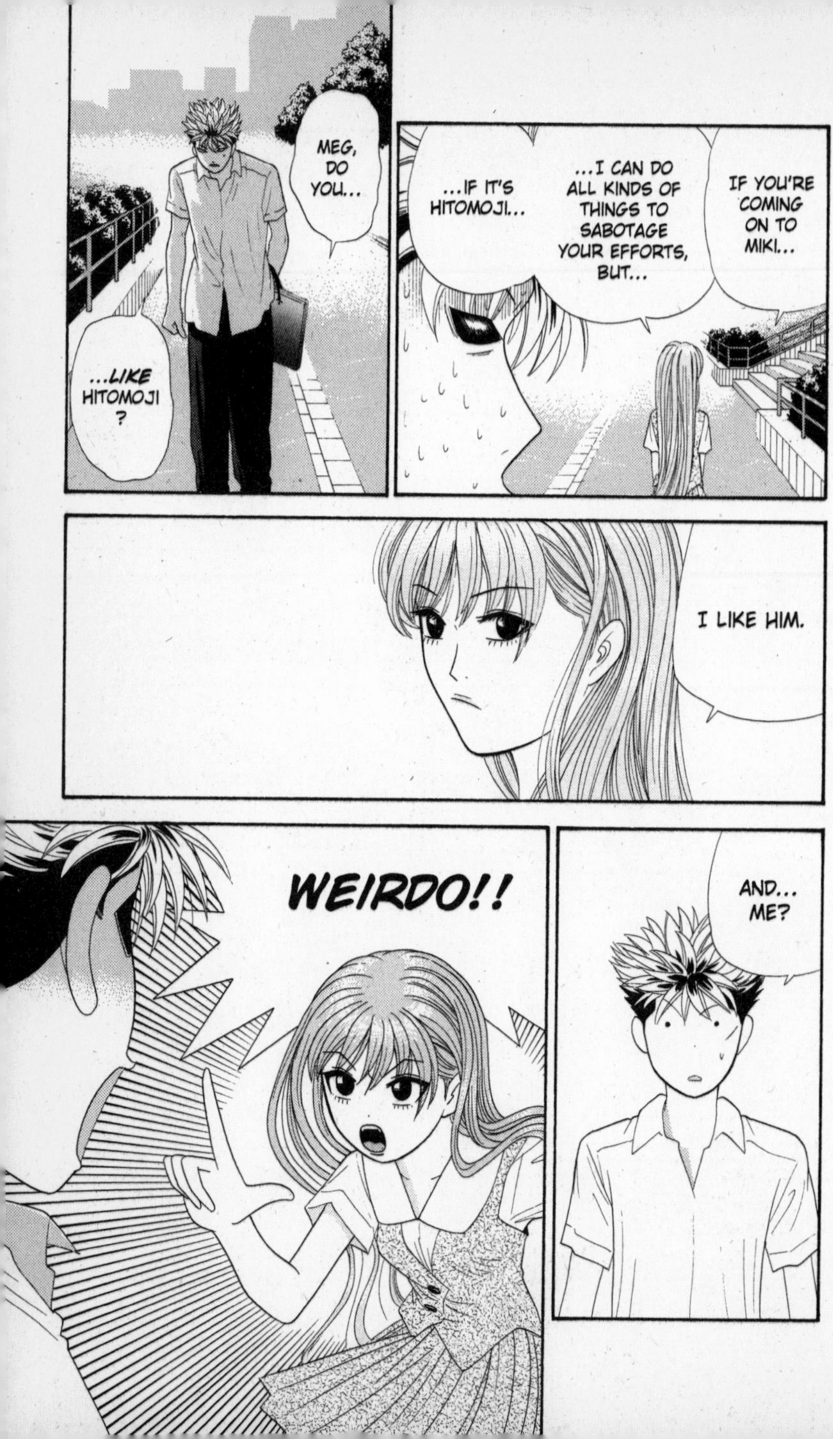
IF YOU'RE COMING ON TO MIKI...
...I CAN DO ALL KINDS OF THINGS TO SABOTAGE YOUR EFFORTS, BUT...
...IF IT'S HITOMOJI...
MEG, DO YOU...
...LIKE HITOMOJI?
I LIKE HIM.
AND... ME?
WEIRDO!!

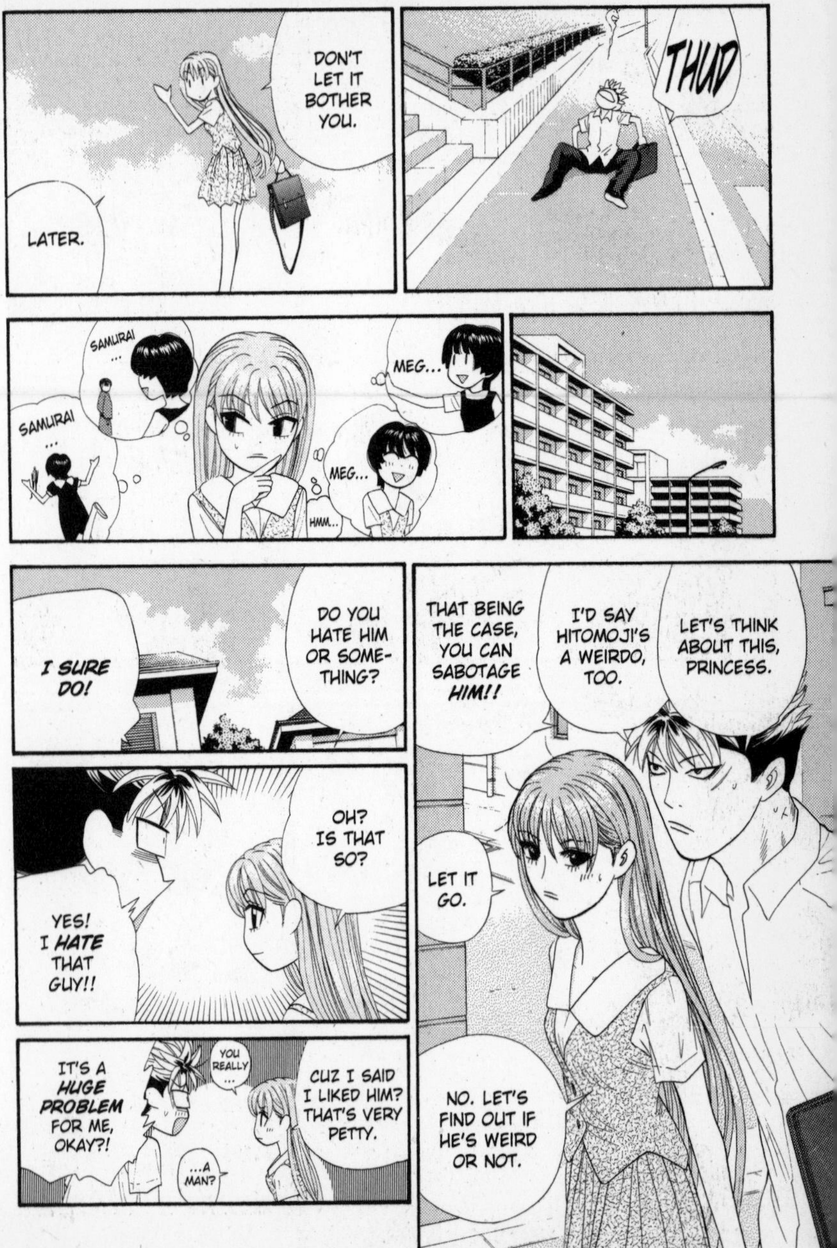
THUD
DON'T LET IT BOTHER YOU.
LATER.
MEG...
MEG...
HMM...
SAMURAI ...
SAMURAI ...
LET'S THINK ABOUT THIS, PRINCESS.
I'D SAY HITOMOJI'S A WEIRDO, TOO.
THAT BEING THE CASE, YOU CAN SABOTAGE *HIM!!*
LET IT GO.
NO. LET'S FIND OUT IF HE'S WEIRD OR NOT.
DO YOU HATE HIM OR SOME-THING?
I SURE DO!
OH? IS THAT SO?
YES! I *HATE* THAT GUY!!
CUZ I SAID I LIKED HIM? THAT'S VERY PETTY.
YOU REALLY ...
...A MAN?
IT'S A *HUGE PROBLEM* FOR ME, OKAY?!

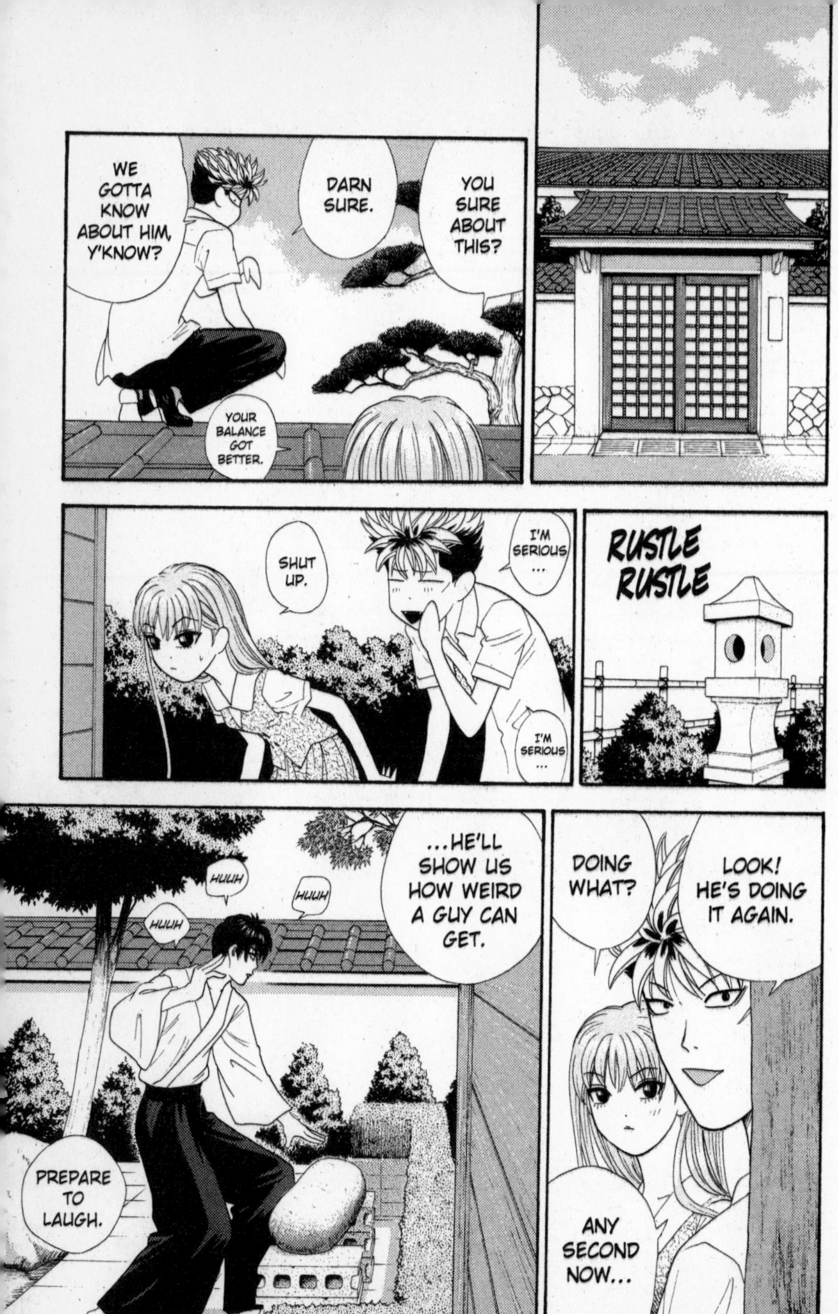
YOU SURE ABOUT THIS?
DARN SURE.
WE GOTTA KNOW ABOUT HIM, Y'KNOW?
YOUR BALANCE GOT BETTER.
RUSTLE RUSTLE
I'M SERIOUS...
SHUT UP.
I'M SERIOUS...
LOOK! HE'S DOING IT AGAIN.
DOING WHAT?
ANY SECOND NOW...
...HE'LL SHOW US HOW WEIRD A GUY CAN GET.
HUUH
HUUH
HUUH
PREPARE TO LAUGH.

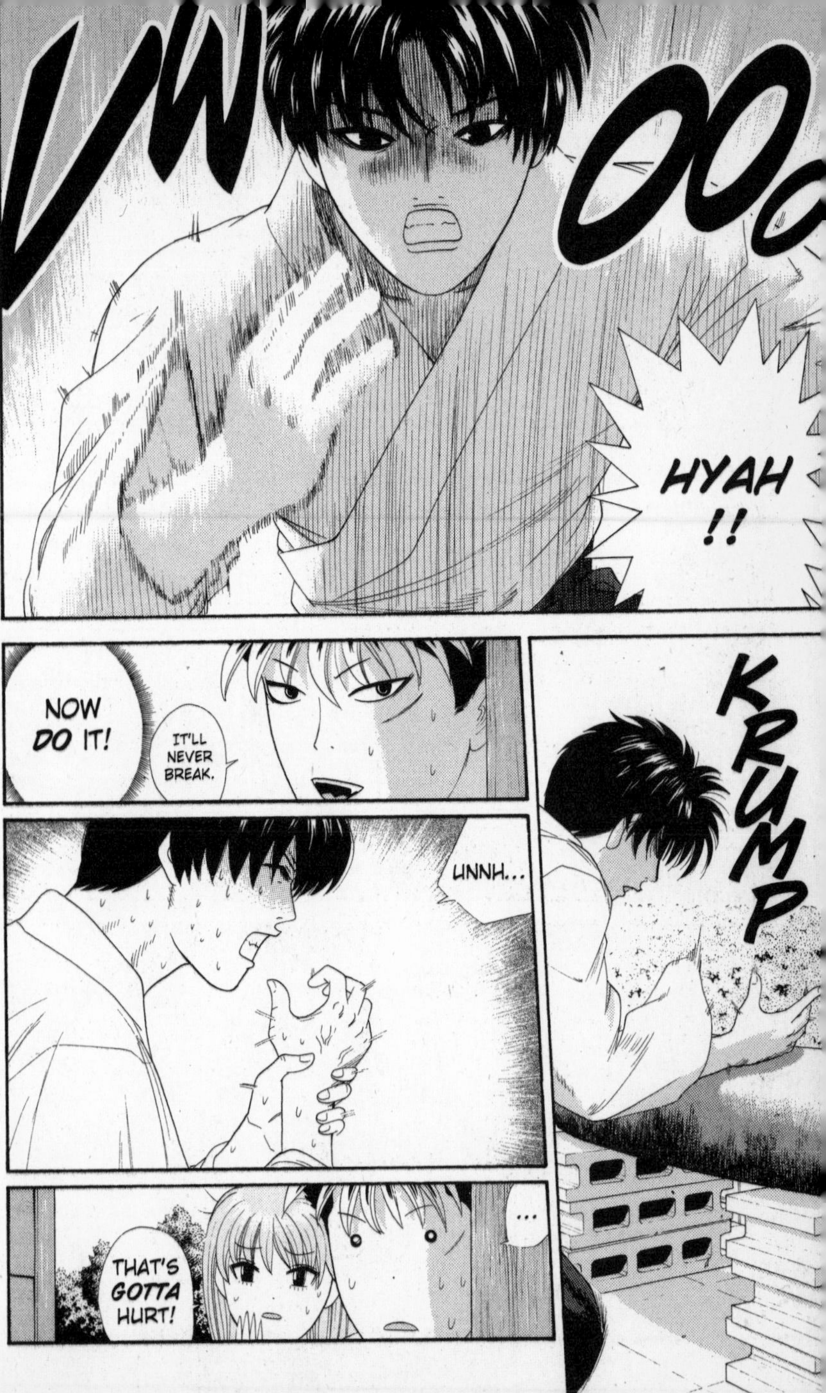
WOOO
HYAH!!
KRUMP
IT'LL NEVER BREAK.
NOW DO IT!
UNNH...
...
THAT'S GOTTA HURT!

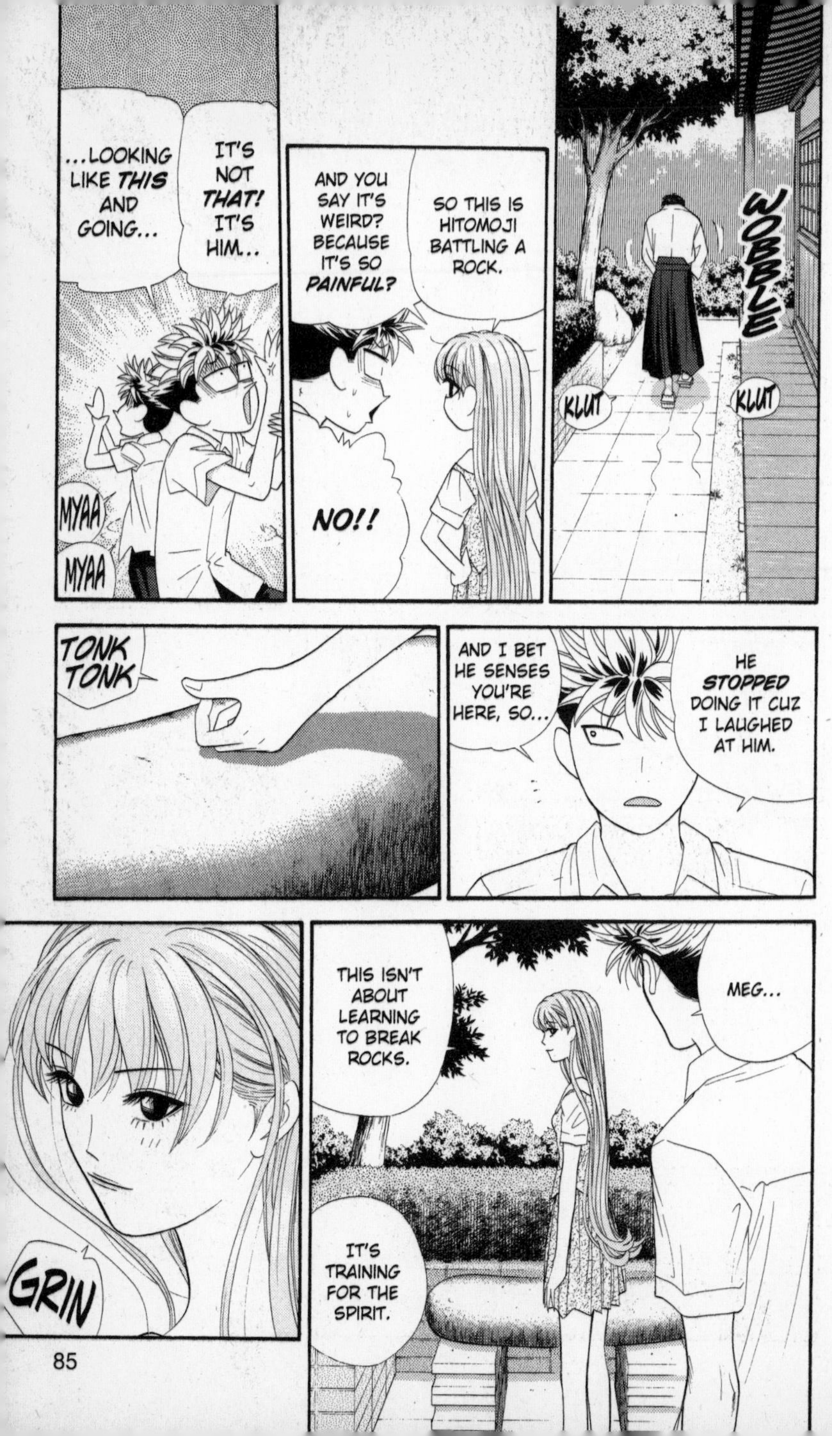
WOBBLE
KLUT
KLUT
SO THIS IS HITOMOJI BATTLING A ROCK.
AND YOU SAY IT'S WEIRD? BECAUSE IT'S SO *PAINFUL?*
NO!!
IT'S NOT *THAT!* IT'S HIM...
...LOOKING LIKE *THIS* AND GOING...
MYAA
MYAA
HE *STOPPED* DOING IT CUZ I LAUGHED AT HIM.
AND I BET HE SENSES YOU'RE HERE, SO...
TONK TONK
MEG...
THIS ISN'T ABOUT LEARNING TO BREAK ROCKS.
IT'S TRAINING FOR THE SPIRIT.
GRIN

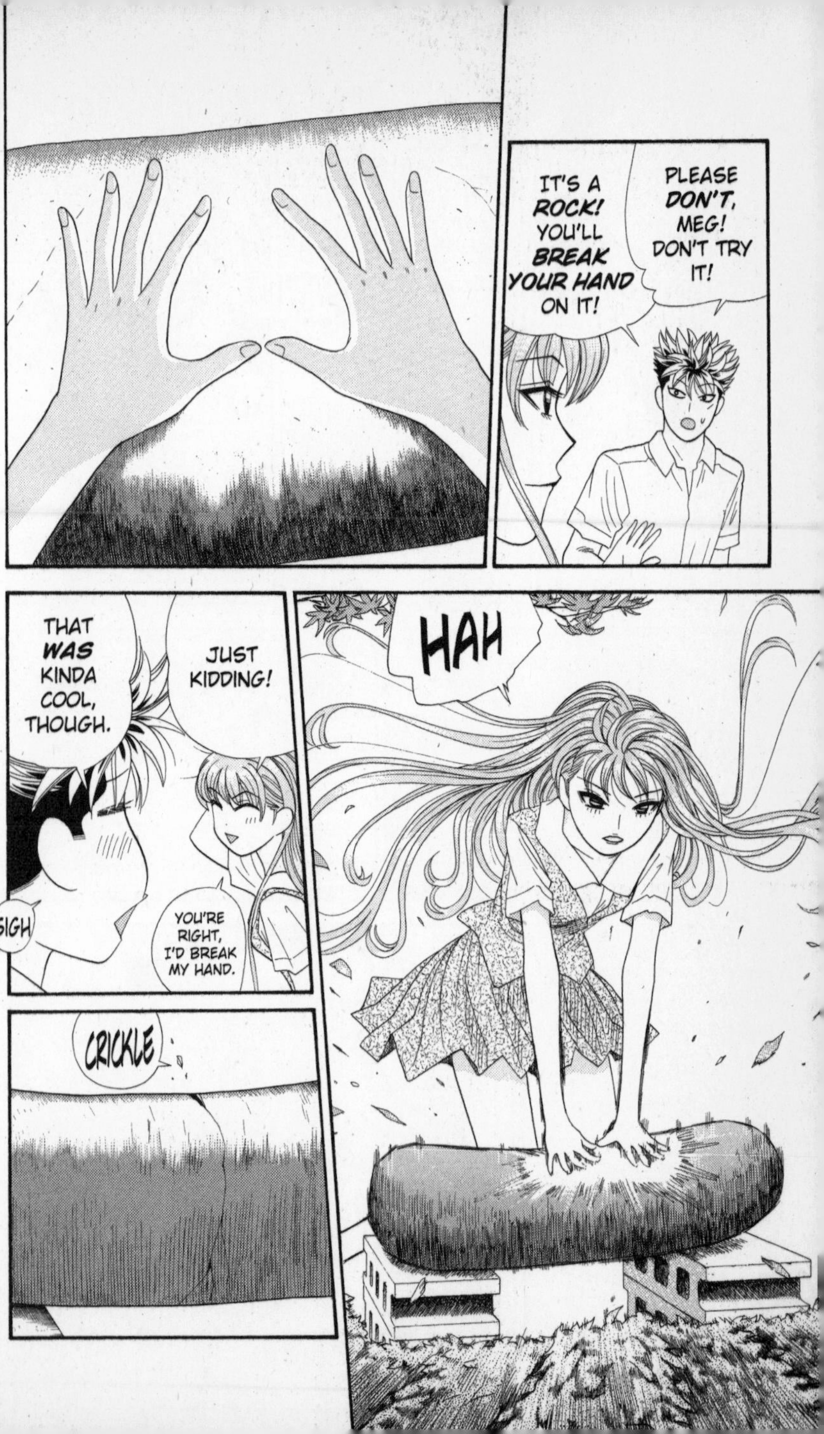
PLEASE DON'T, MEG! DON'T TRY IT!
IT'S A ROCK! YOU'LL BREAK YOUR HAND ON IT!
HAH
JUST KIDDING!
THAT WAS KINDA COOL, THOUGH.
YOU'RE RIGHT, I'D BREAK MY HAND.
SIGH
CRICKLE

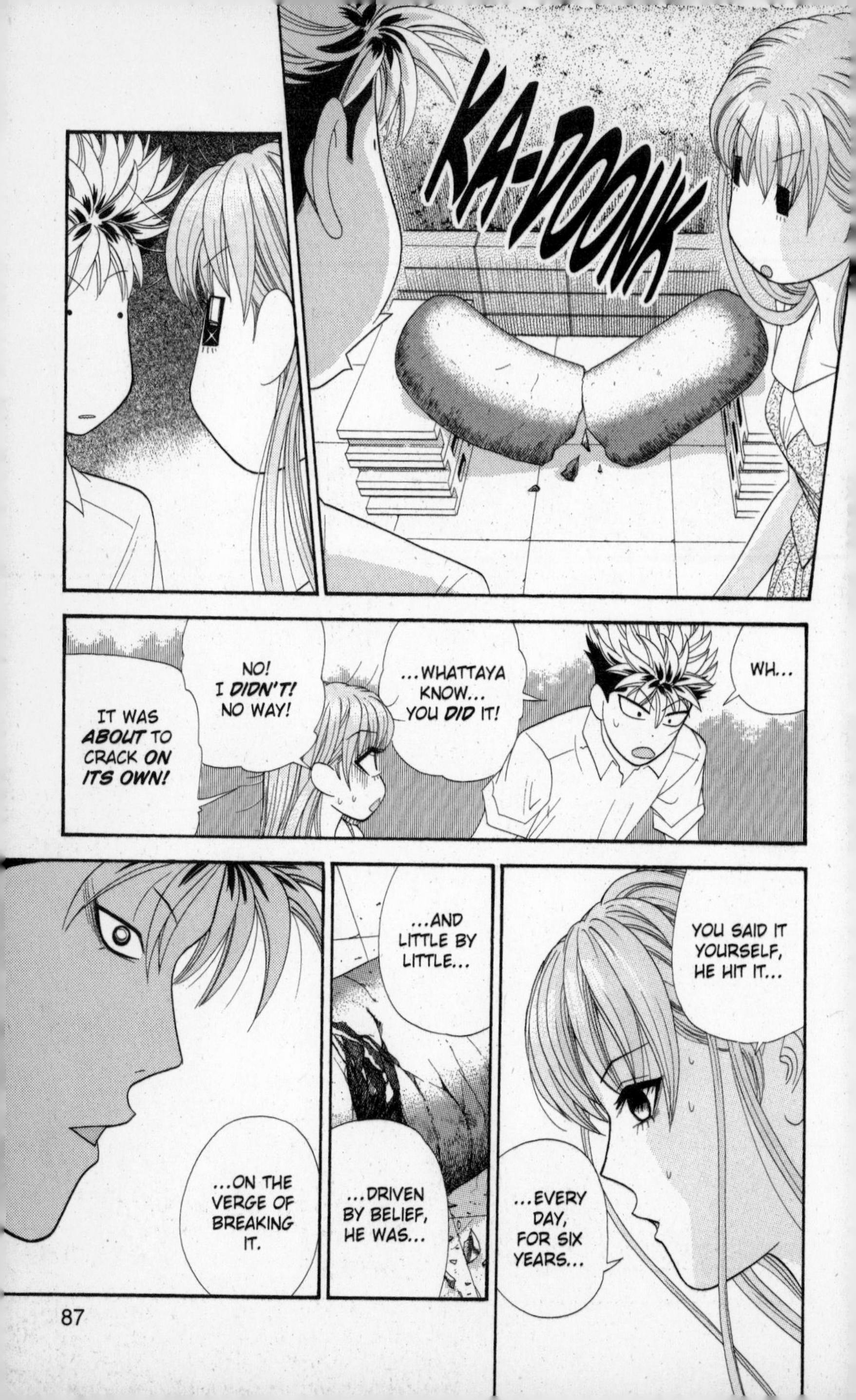
KA-DOONK
WH...
...WHATTAYA KNOW... YOU *DID* IT!
NO! I *DIDN'T!* NO WAY!
IT WAS *ABOUT* TO CRACK *ON ITS OWN!*
YOU SAID IT YOURSELF, HE HIT IT...
...EVERY DAY, FOR SIX YEARS...
...AND LITTLE BY LITTLE...
...DRIVEN BY BELIEF, HE WAS...
...ON THE VERGE OF BREAKING IT.

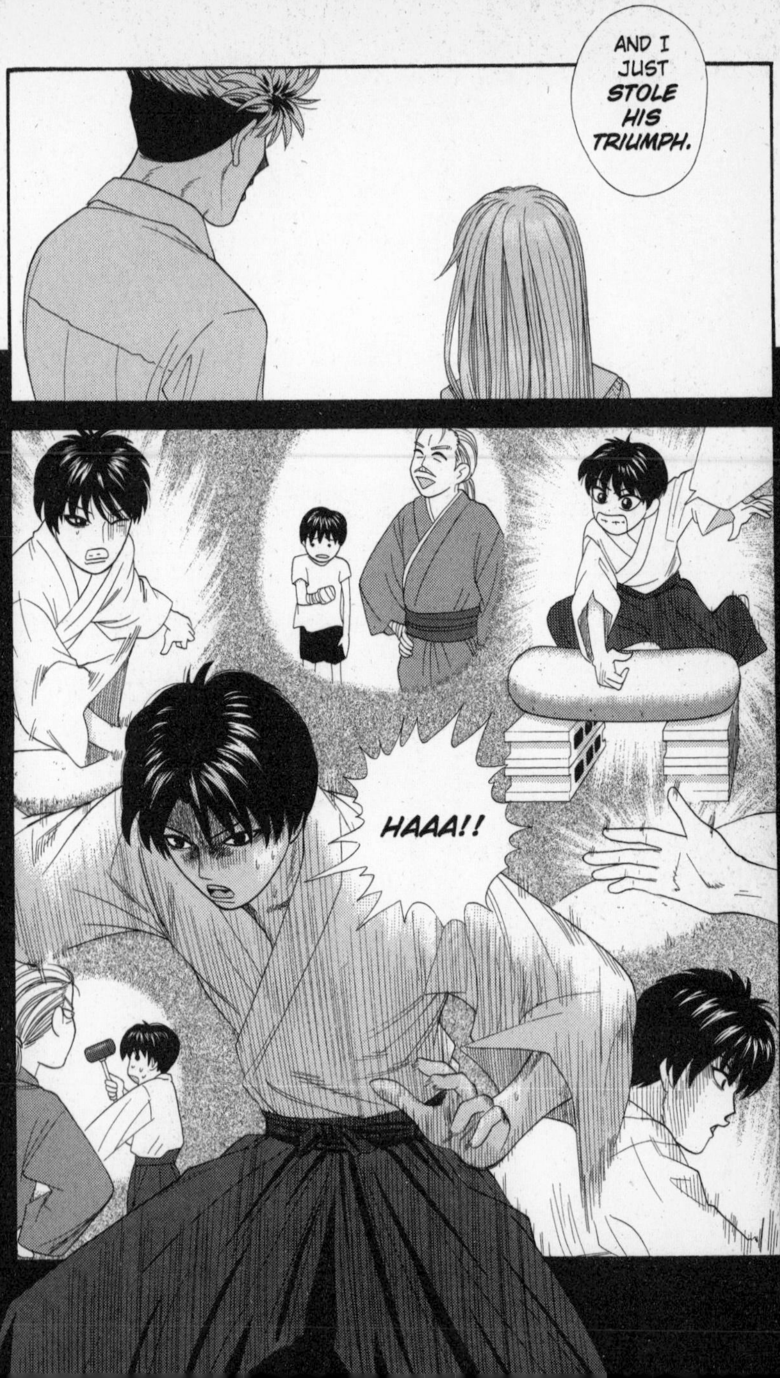
AND I JUST STOLE HIS TRIUMPH.
HAAA!!

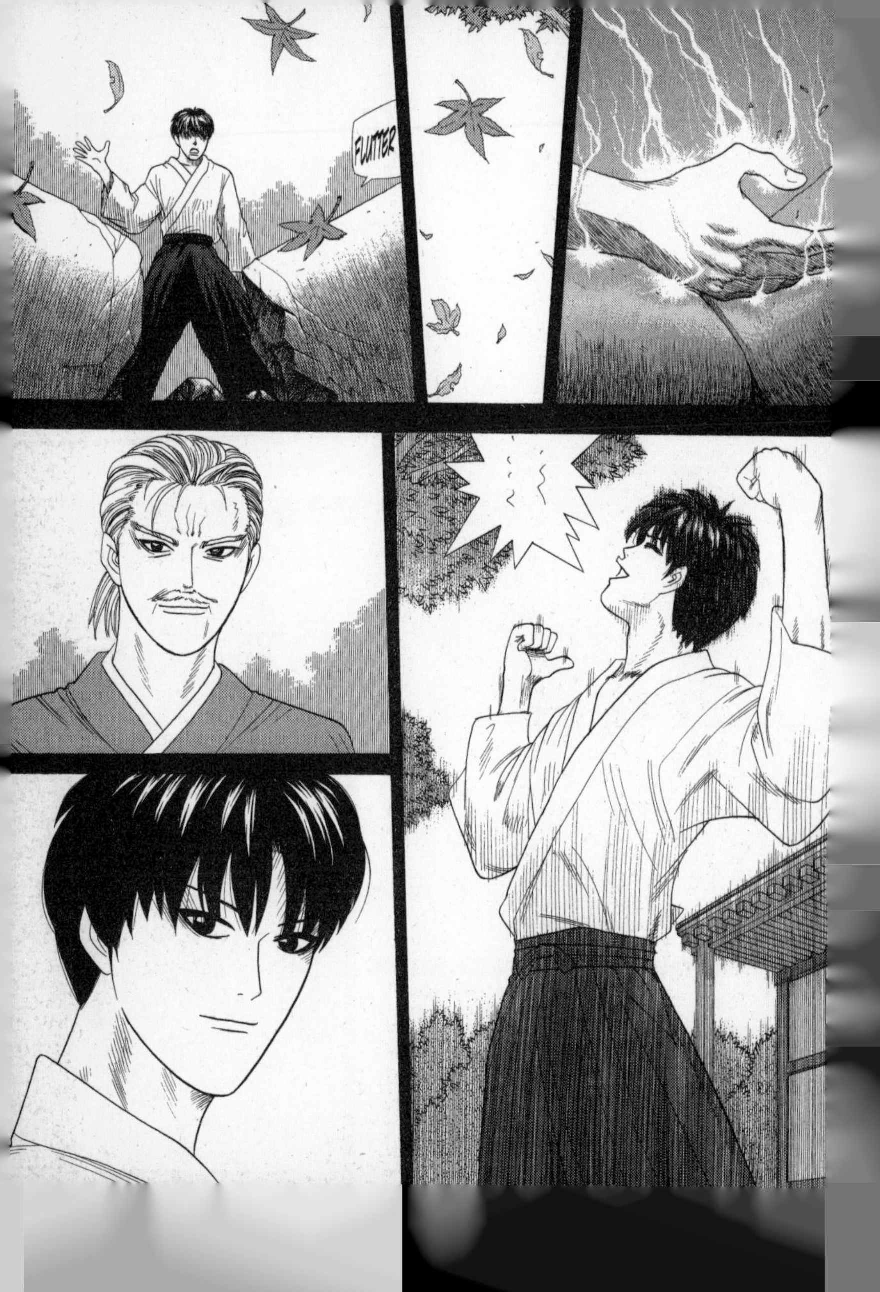
FLUTTER

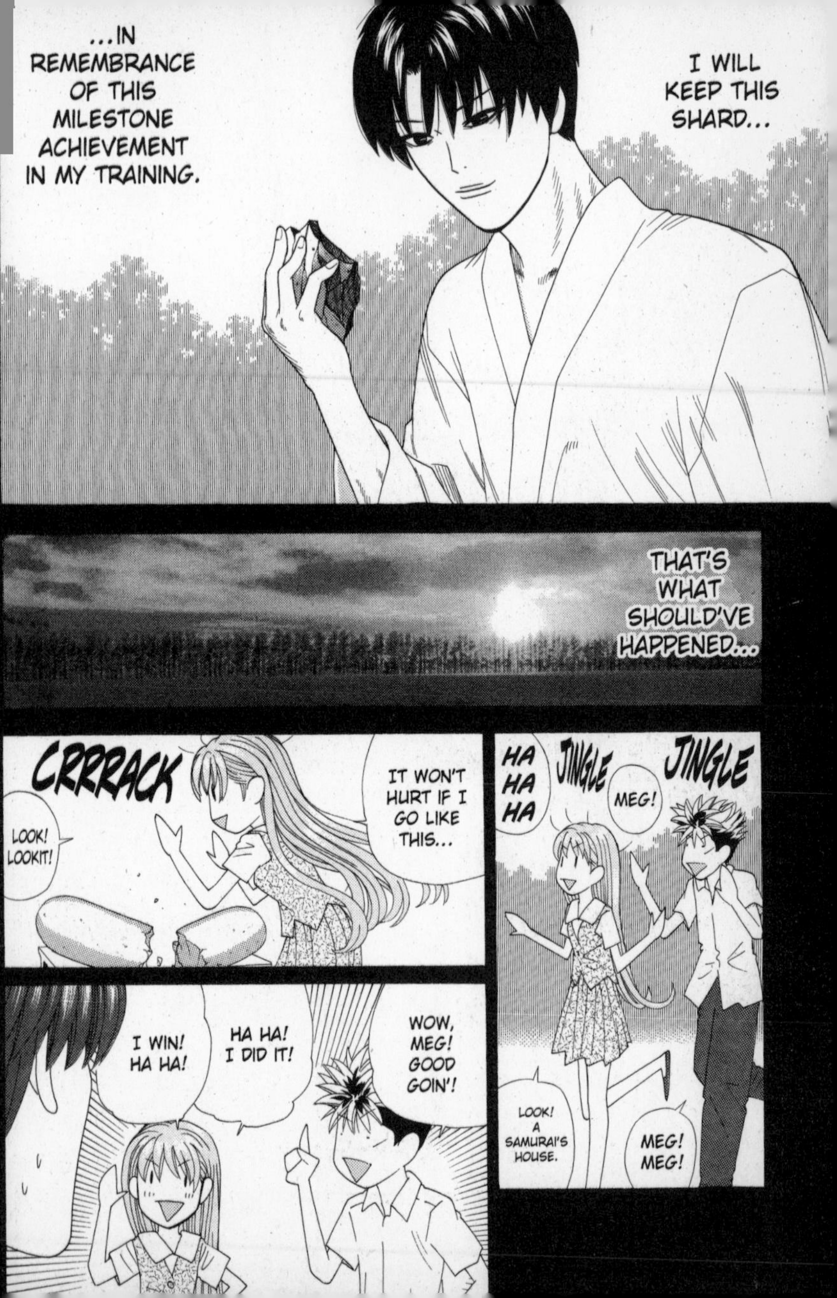
I WILL KEEP THIS SHARD...
...IN REMEMBRANCE OF THIS MILESTONE ACHIEVEMENT IN MY TRAINING.
THAT'S WHAT SHOULD'VE HAPPENED...
JINGLE
JINGLE
MEG!
HA HA HA
MEG! MEG!
LOOK! A SAMURAI'S HOUSE.
IT WON'T HURT IF I GO LIKE THIS...
CRRRACK
LOOK! LOOKIT!
WOW, MEG! GOOD GOIN'!
HA HA! I DID IT!
I WIN! HA HA!

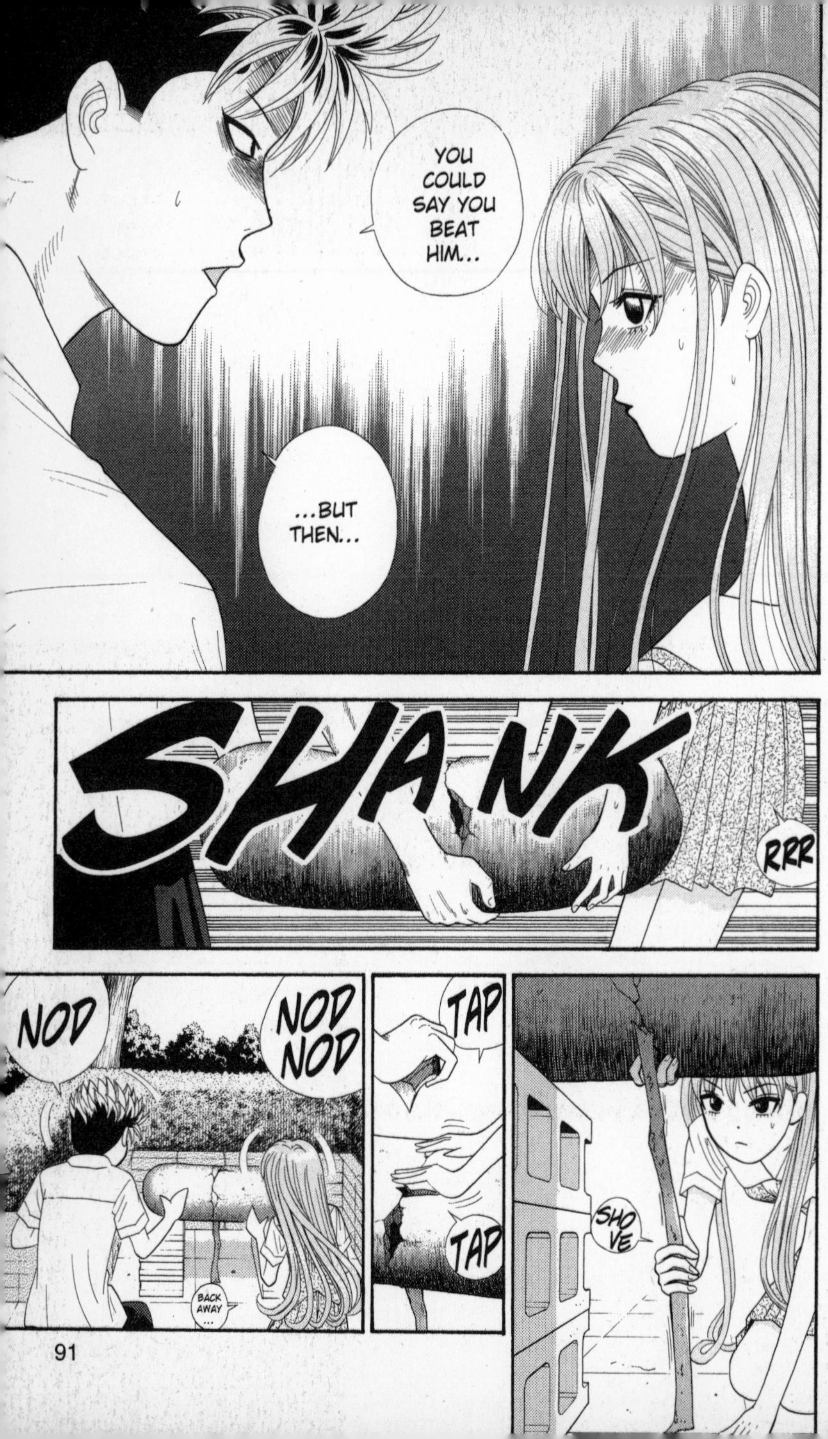
YOU COULD SAY YOU BEAT HIM...
...BUT THEN...
SHANK
RRR
SHOVE
TAP
TAP
NOD NOD
NOD
BACK AWAY ...

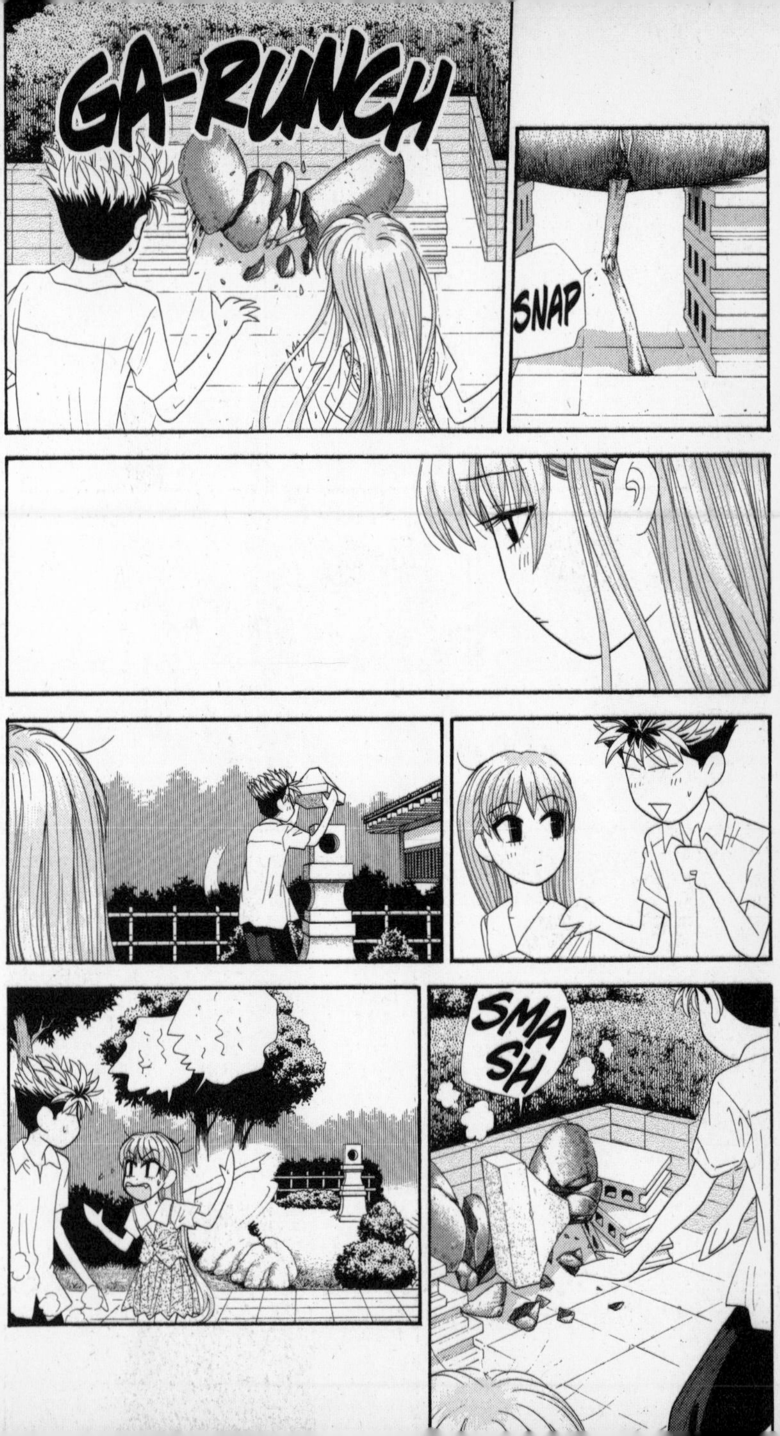
SNAP
GA-RUNCH
SMASH

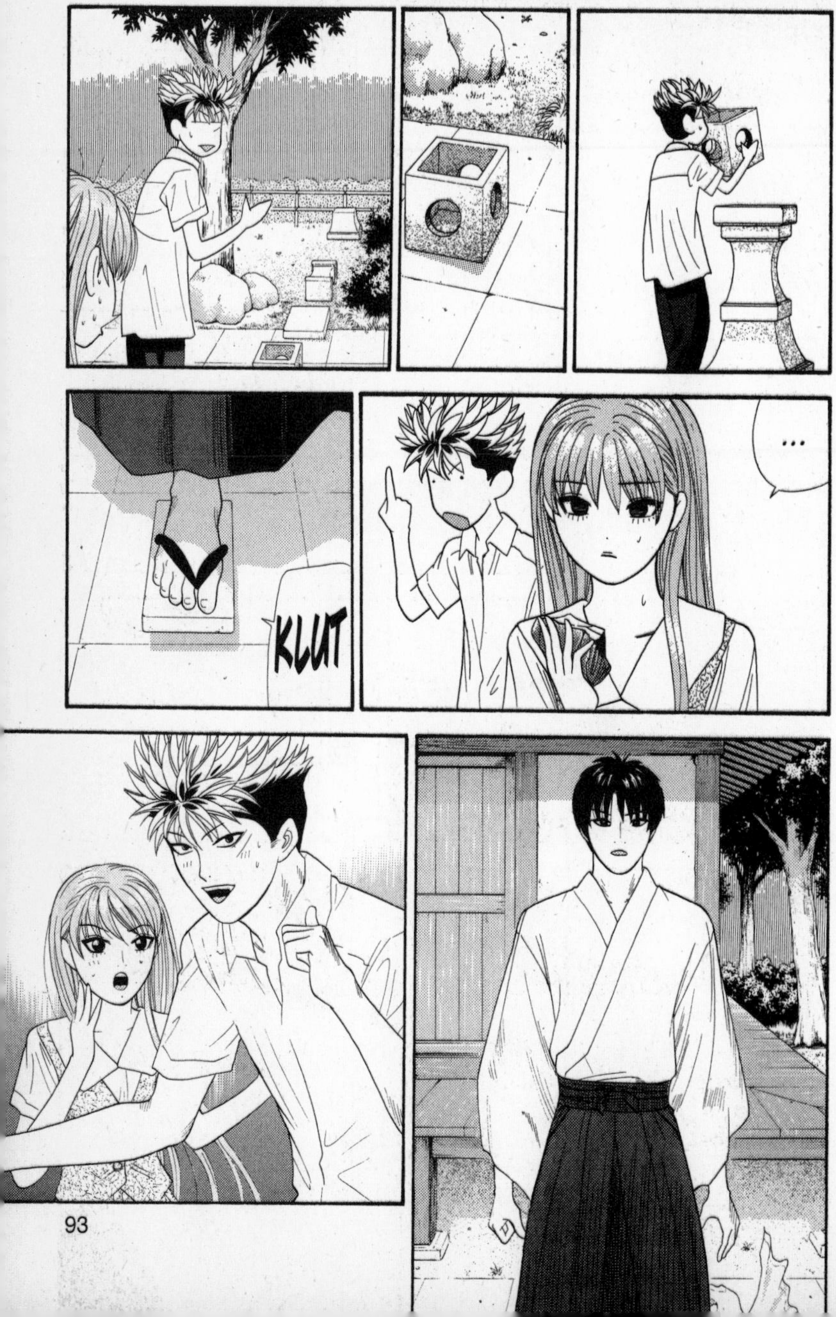
...
KLUT

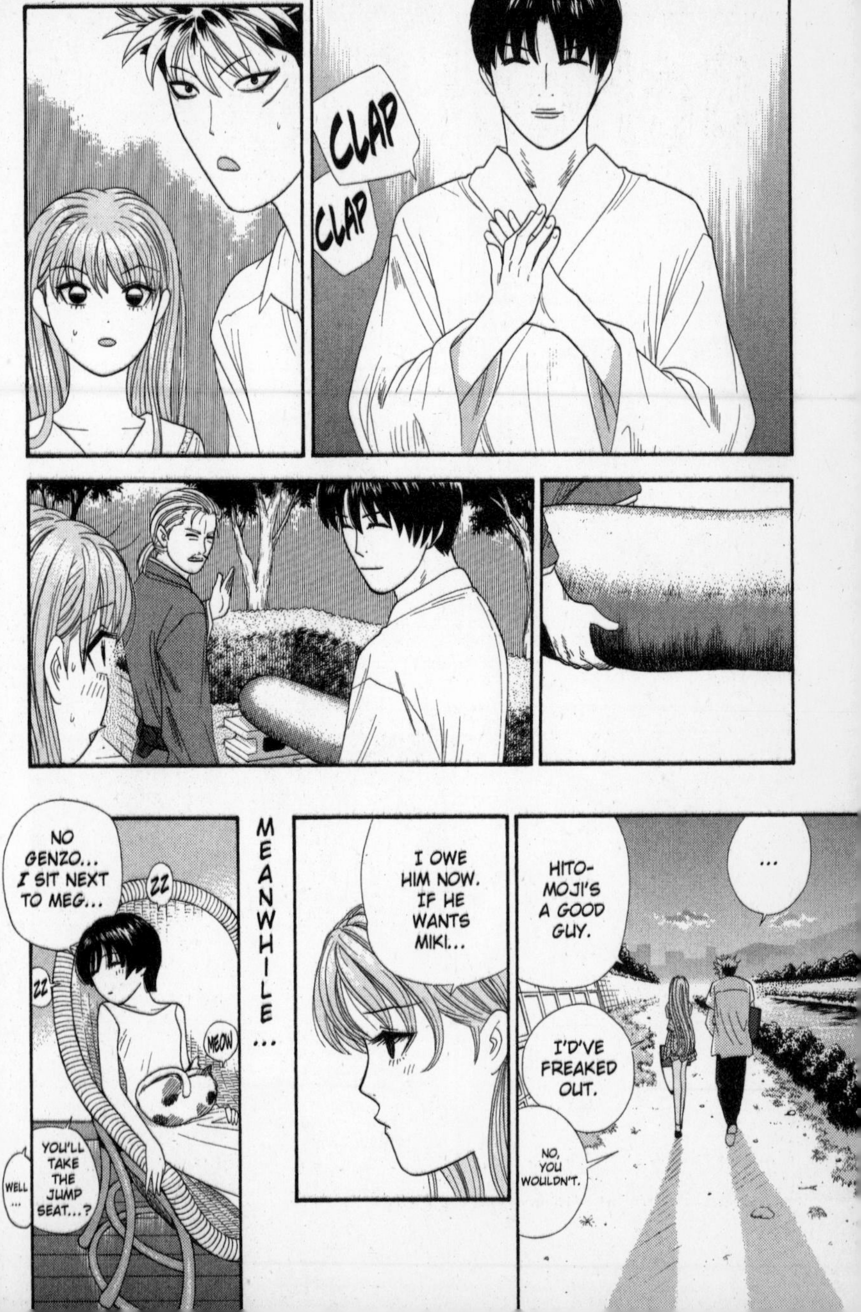
CLAP
CLAP
...
HITO-MOJI'S A GOOD GUY.
I'D'VE FREAKED OUT.
NO, YOU WOULDN'T.
I OWE HIM NOW. IF HE WANTS MIKI...
MEANWHILE...
ZZ
NO GENZO... I SIT NEXT TO MEG...
ZZ
MEOW
YOU'LL TAKE THE JUMP SEAT...?
WELL...

Chapter 165:

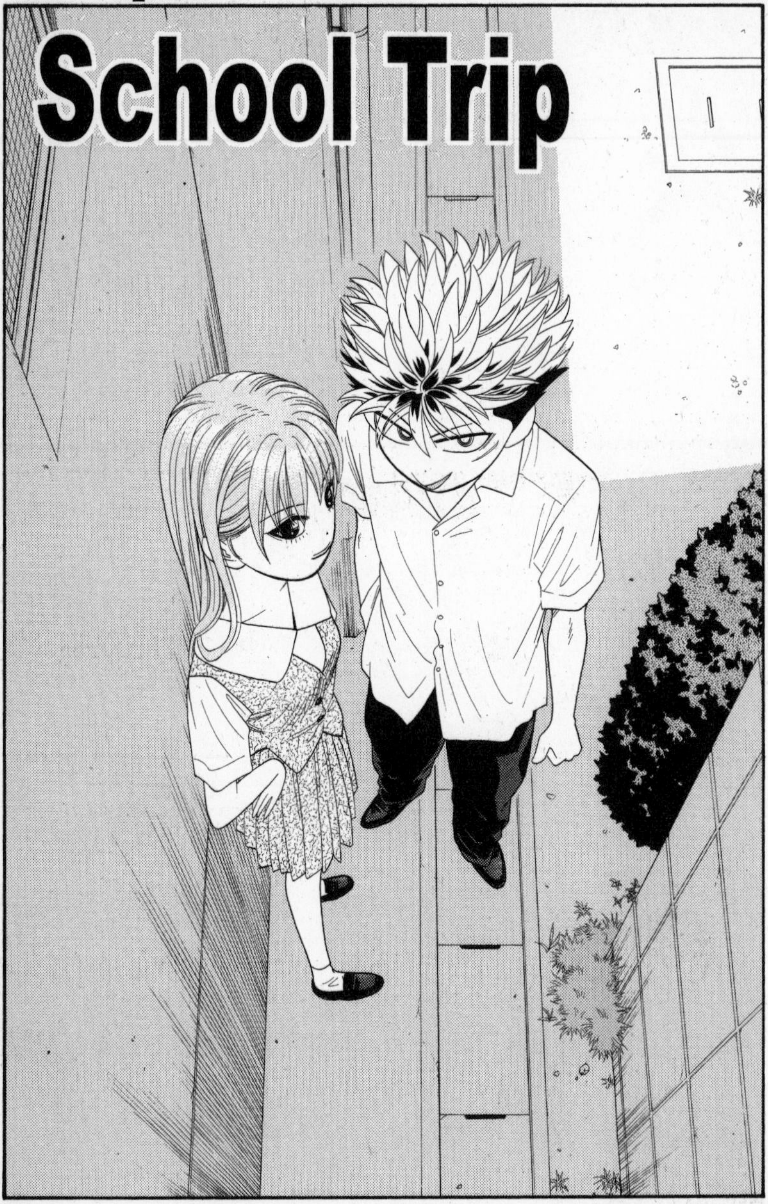
School Trip

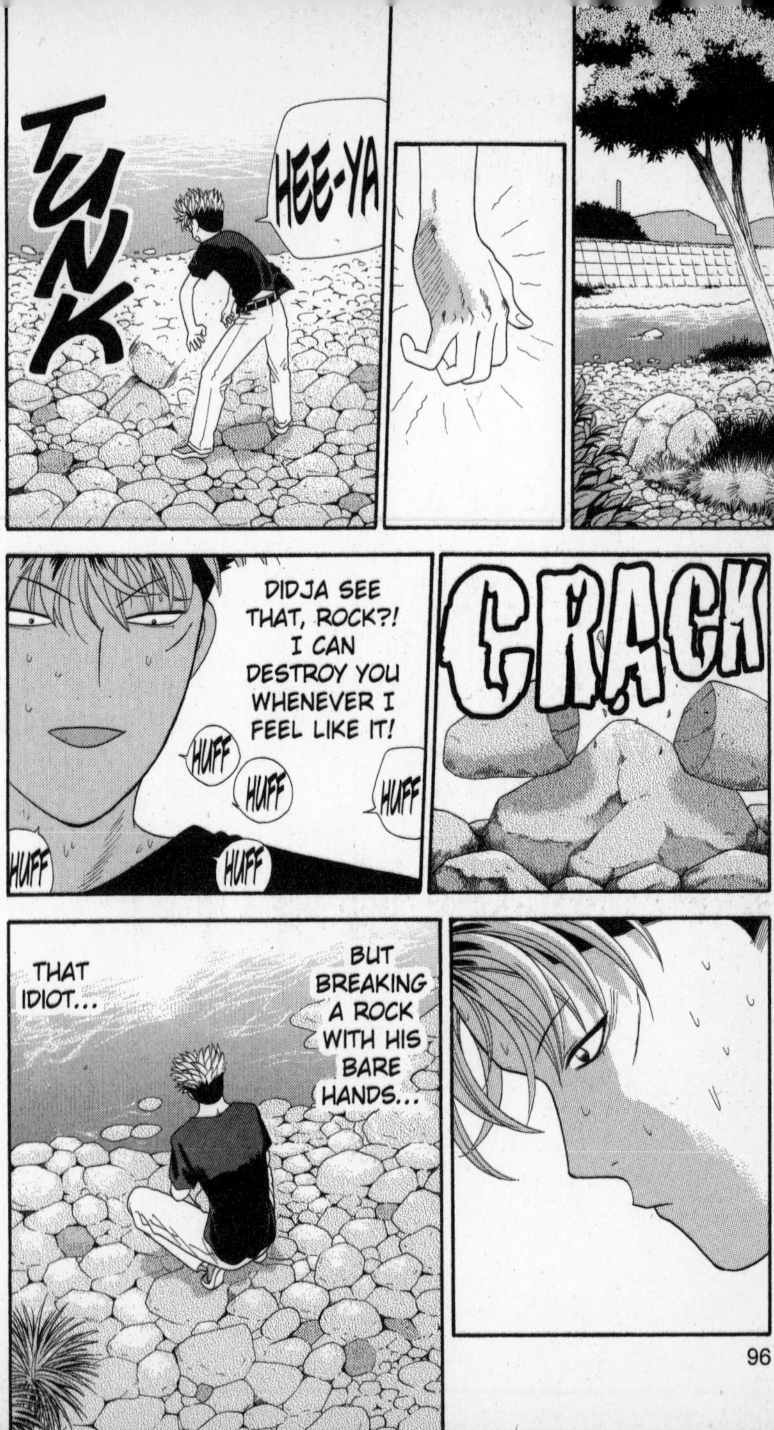
HEE-YA
TUNK
CRACK
DIDJA SEE THAT, ROCK?! I CAN DESTROY YOU WHENEVER I FEEL LIKE IT!
HUFF
HUFF
HUFF
HUFF
HUFF
THAT IDIOT...
BUT BREAKING A ROCK WITH HIS BARE HANDS...

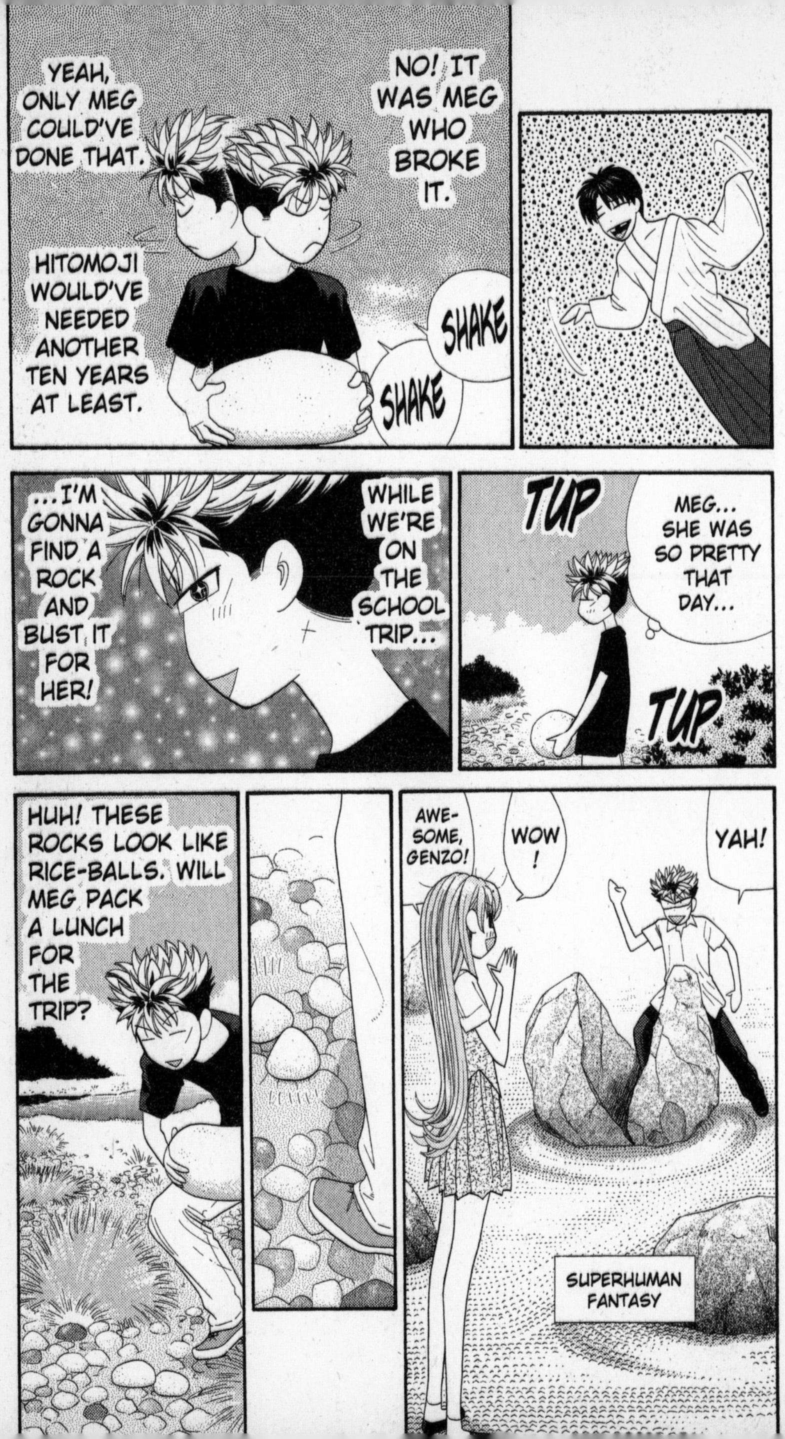
NO! IT WAS MEG WHO BROKE IT.
YEAH, ONLY MEG COULD'VE DONE THAT.
SHAKE
SHAKE
HITOMOJI WOULD'VE NEEDED ANOTHER TEN YEARS AT LEAST.
TUP
MEG... SHE WAS SO PRETTY THAT DAY...
TUP
WHILE WE'RE ON THE SCHOOL TRIP...
...I'M GONNA FIND A ROCK AND BUST IT FOR HER!
YAH!
WOW!
AWE-SOME, GENZO!
SUPERHUMAN FANTASY
HUH! THESE ROCKS LOOK LIKE RICE-BALLS. WILL MEG PACK A LUNCH FOR THE TRIP?

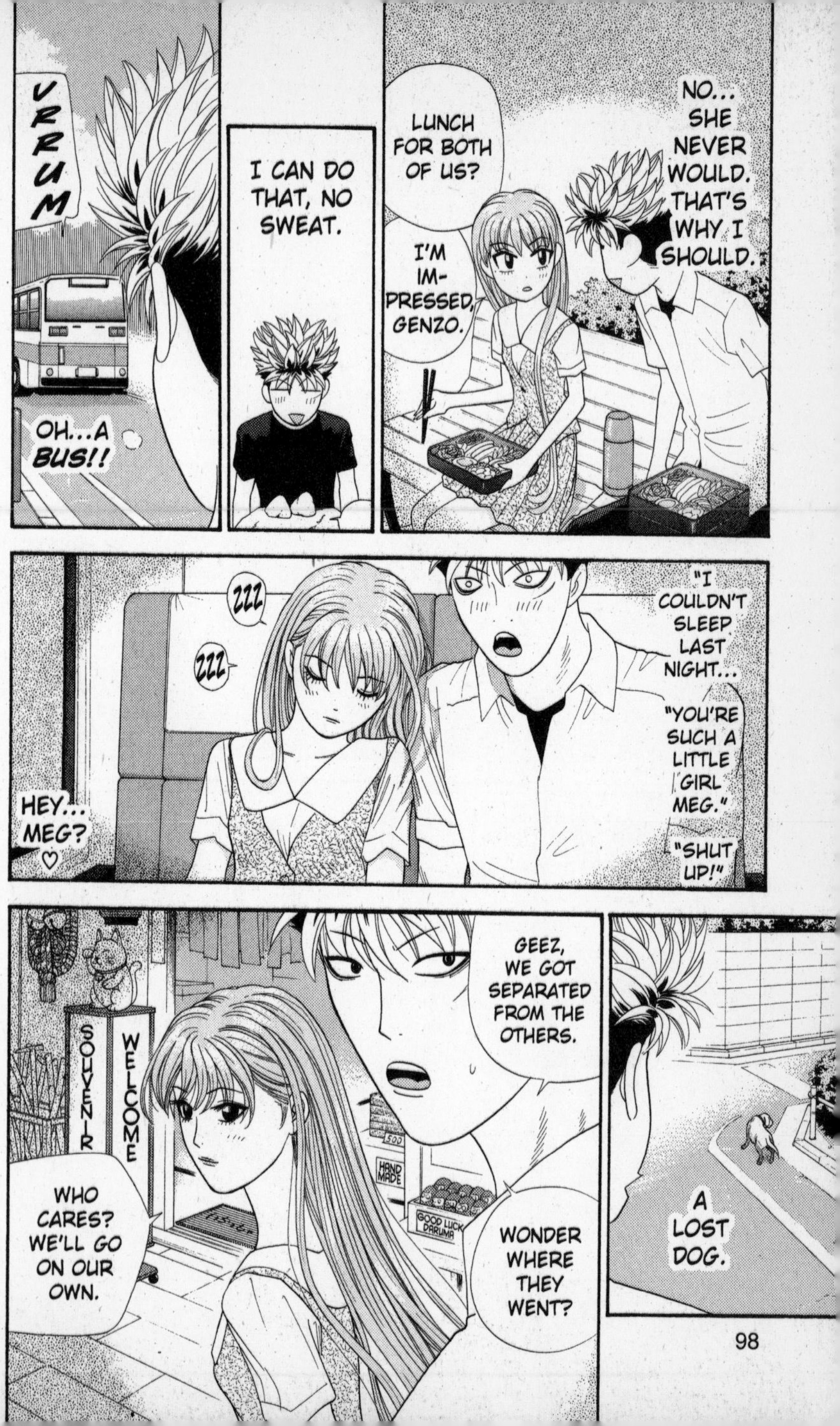
NO... SHE NEVER WOULD. THAT'S WHY I SHOULD.
LUNCH FOR BOTH OF US?
I'M IM-PRESSED, GENZO.
I CAN DO THAT, NO SWEAT.
URRUM
OH...A BUS!!
"I COULDN'T SLEEP LAST NIGHT...
"YOU'RE SUCH A LITTLE GIRL MEG."
"SHUT UP!"
ZZZ
ZZZ
HEY... MEG? ♡
A LOST DOG.
GEEZ, WE GOT SEPARATED FROM THE OTHERS.
WONDER WHERE THEY WENT?
WELCOME
SOUVENIR
500
HAND MADE
GOOD LUCK DARUMA
WHO CARES? WE'LL GO ON OUR OWN.

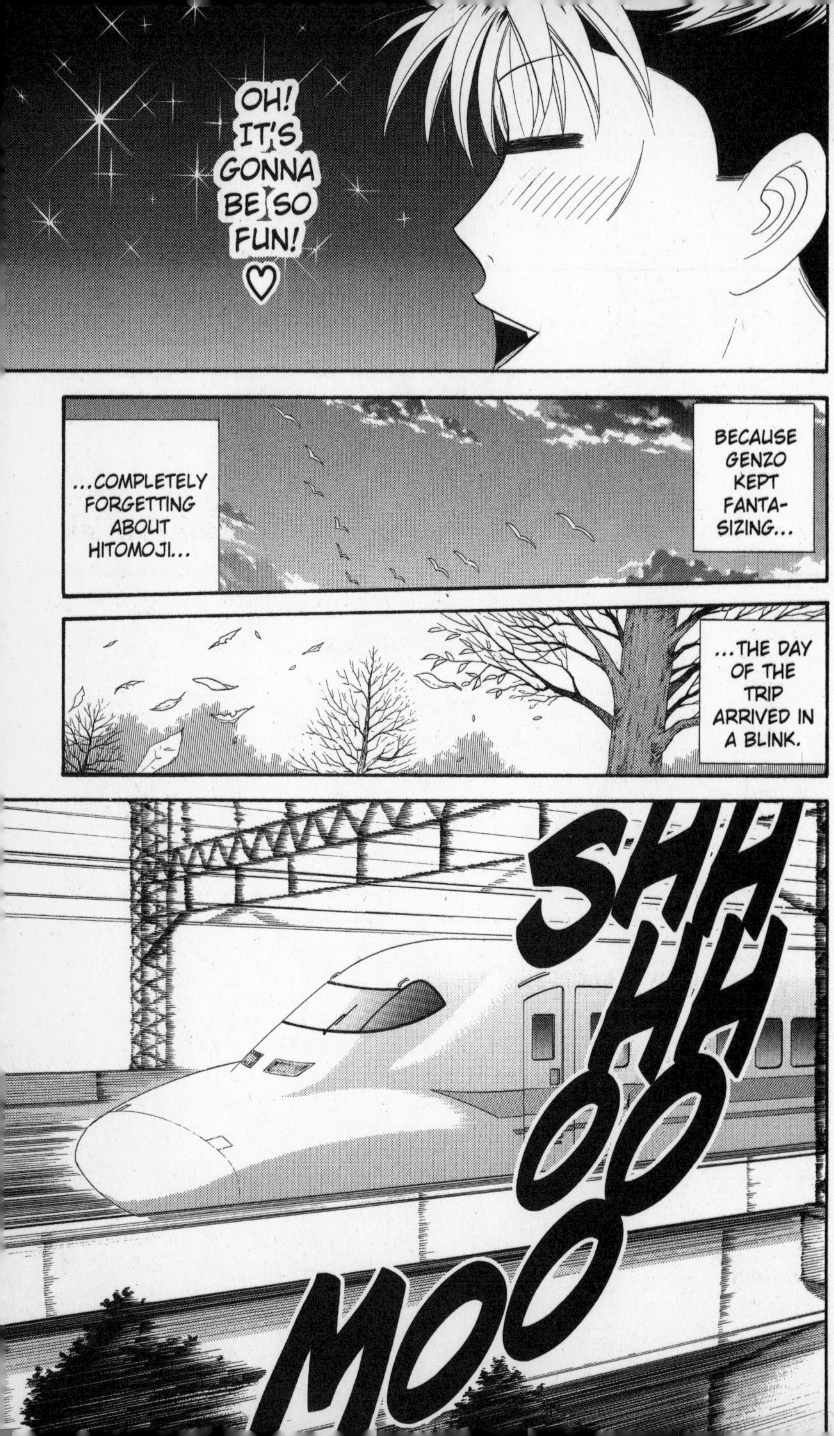
OH! IT'S GONNA BE SO FUN! ♡
BECAUSE GENZO KEPT FANTA-SIZING...
...COMPLETELY FORGETTING ABOUT HITOMOJI...
...THE DAY OF THE TRIP ARRIVED IN A BLINK.
SHHHOOOMOO

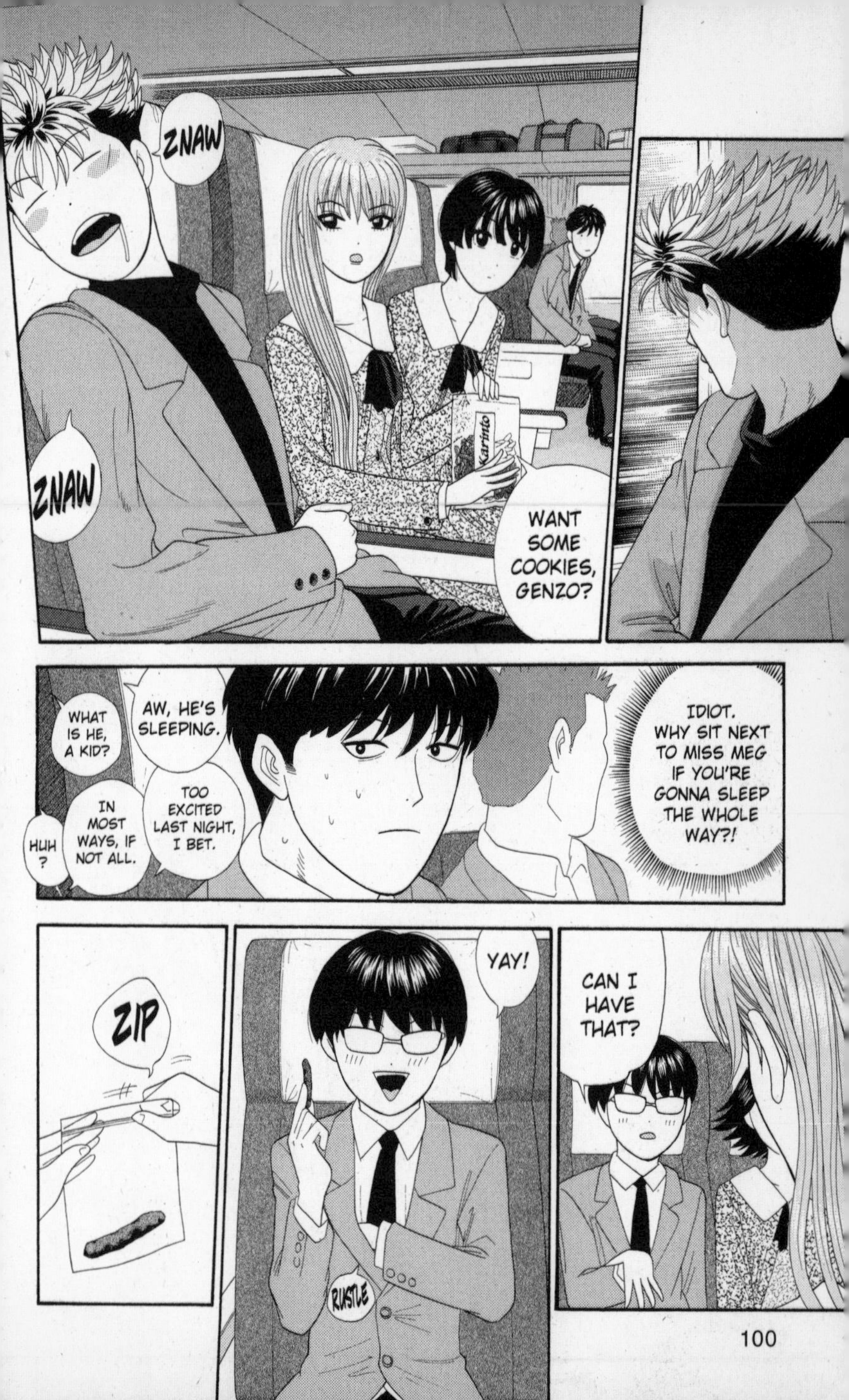
ZNAW
WANT SOME COOKIES, GENZO?
ZNAW
IDIOT. WHY SIT NEXT TO MISS MEG IF YOU'RE GONNA SLEEP THE WHOLE WAY?!
AW, HE'S SLEEPING.
TOO EXCITED LAST NIGHT, I BET.
WHAT IS HE, A KID?
IN MOST WAYS, IF NOT ALL.
HUH?
CAN I HAVE THAT?
YAY!
RUSTLE
ZIP

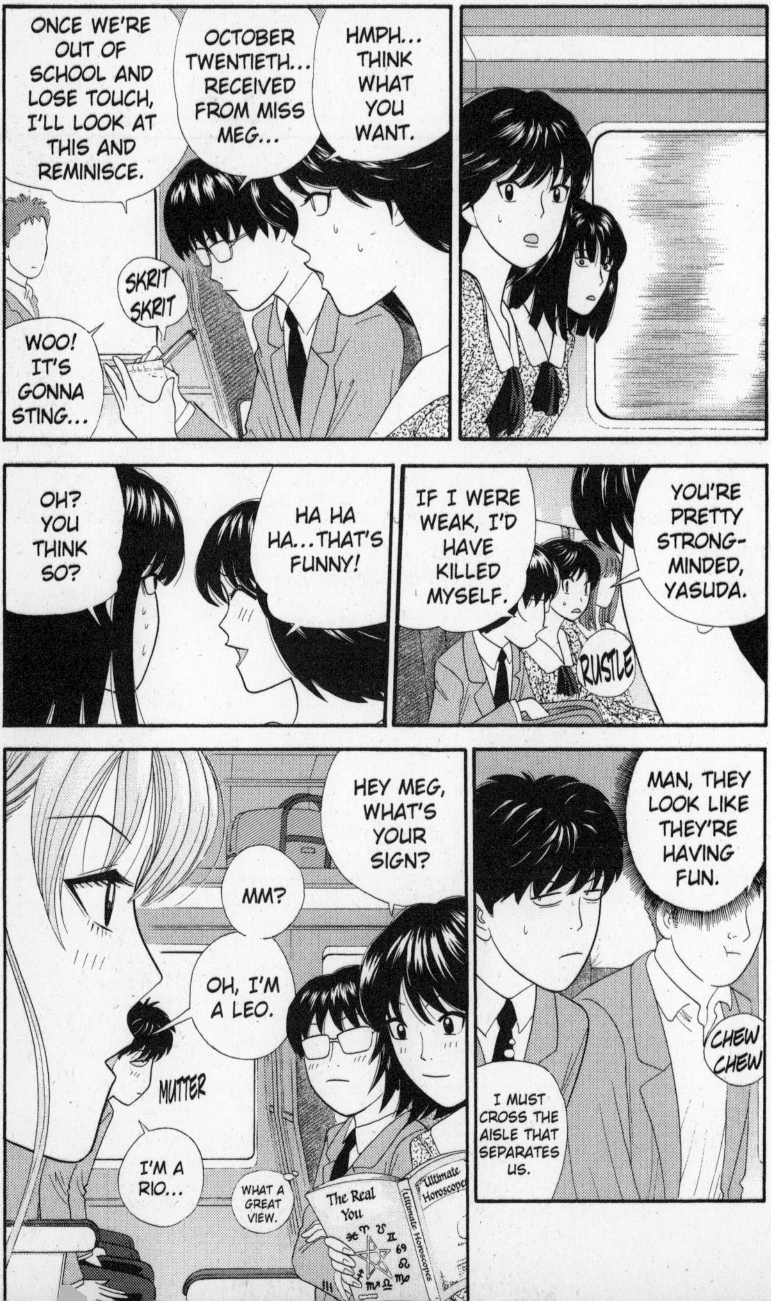
HMPH... THINK WHAT YOU WANT.
OCTOBER TWENTIETH... RECEIVED FROM MISS MEG...
ONCE WE'RE OUT OF SCHOOL AND LOSE TOUCH, I'LL LOOK AT THIS AND REMINISCE.
SKRIT SKRIT
WOO! IT'S GONNA STING...
YOU'RE PRETTY STRONG-MINDED, YASUDA.
IF I WERE WEAK, I'D HAVE KILLED MYSELF.
RUSTLE
HA HA HA...THAT'S FUNNY!
OH? YOU THINK SO?
MAN, THEY LOOK LIKE THEY'RE HAVING FUN.
CHEW CHEW
I MUST CROSS THE AISLE THAT SEPARATES US.
HEY MEG, WHAT'S YOUR SIGN?
MM?
OH, I'M A LEO.
MUTTER
I'M A RIO...
WHAT A GREAT VIEW.
Ultimate Horoscopes
The Real You
Ultimate Horoscopes

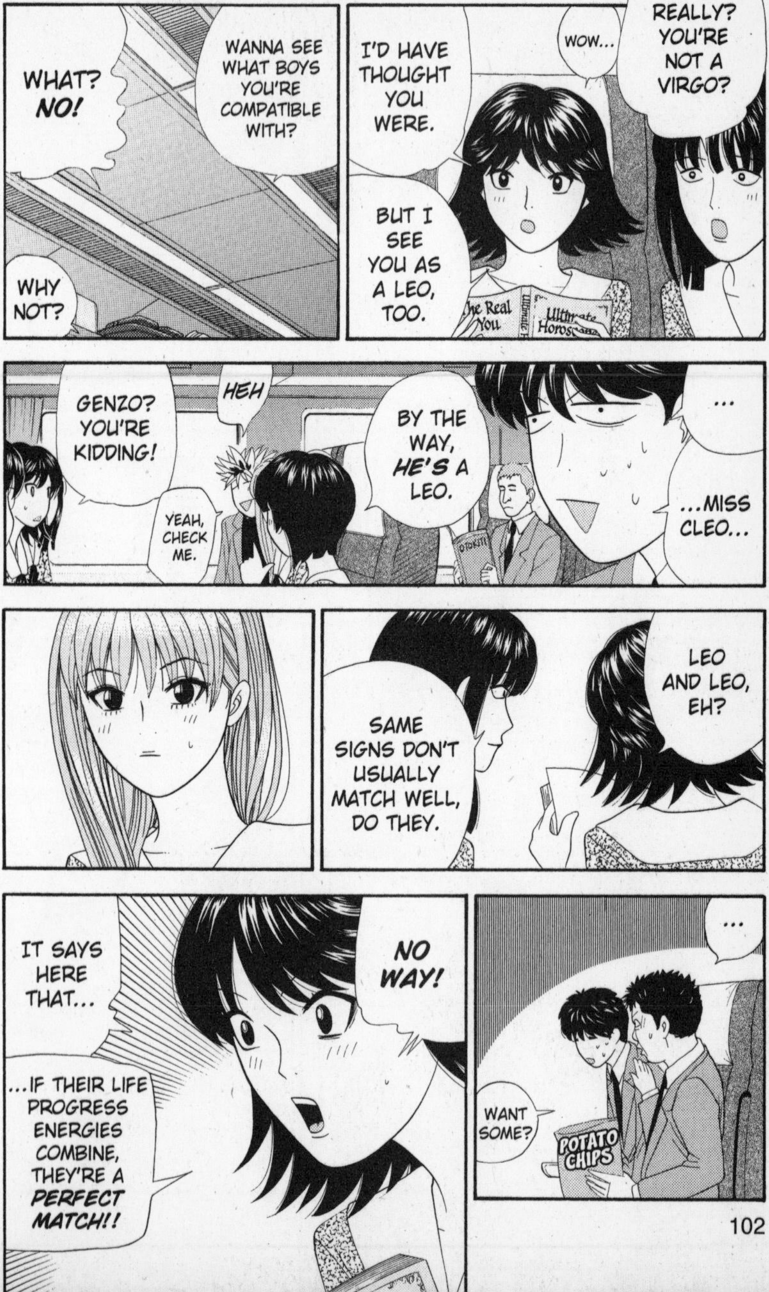
REALLY? YOU'RE NOT A VIRGO?
WOW...
I'D HAVE THOUGHT YOU WERE.
BUT I SEE YOU AS A LEO, TOO.
The Real You
WANNA SEE WHAT BOYS YOU'RE COMPATIBLE WITH?
WHAT? NO!
WHY NOT?
...
...MISS CLEO...
BY THE WAY, HE'S A LEO.
HEH
YEAH, CHECK ME.
GENZO? YOU'RE KIDDING!
LEO AND LEO, EH?
SAME SIGNS DON'T USUALLY MATCH WELL, DO THEY.
...
WANT SOME?
POTATO CHIPS
NO WAY!
IT SAYS HERE THAT...
...IF THEIR LIFE PROGRESS ENERGIES COMBINE, THEY'RE A PERFECT MATCH!!

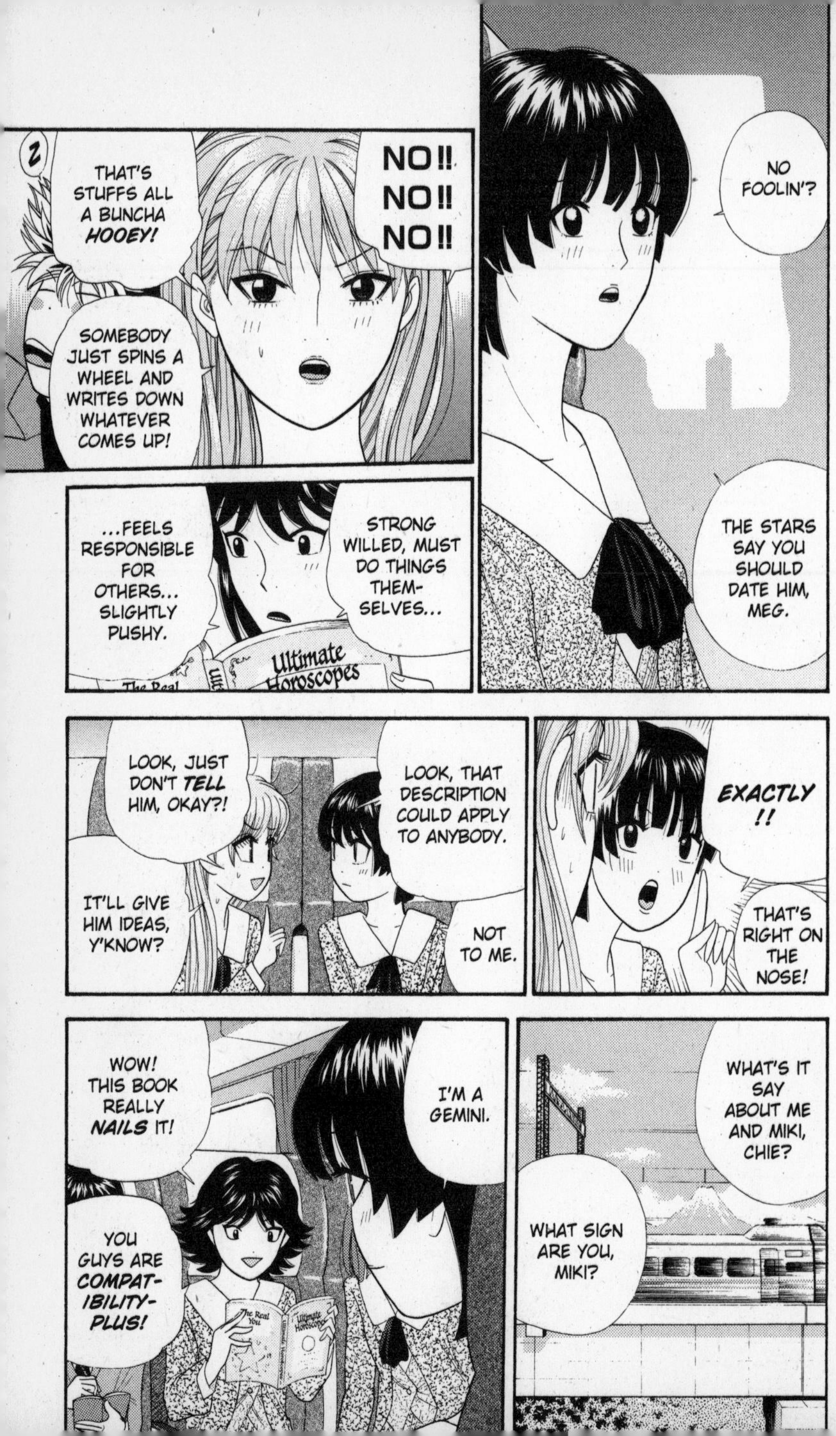
NO FOOLIN'?
THE STARS SAY YOU SHOULD DATE HIM, MEG.
NO!! NO!! NO!!
THAT'S STUFFS ALL A BUNCHA **HOOEY!**
SOMEBODY JUST SPINS A WHEEL AND WRITES DOWN WHATEVER COMES UP!
STRONG WILLED, MUST DO THINGS THEM-SELVES...
...FEELS RESPONSIBLE FOR OTHERS... SLIGHTLY PUSHY.
Ultimate Horoscopes
EXACTLY !!
THAT'S RIGHT ON THE NOSE!
LOOK, THAT DESCRIPTION COULD APPLY TO ANYBODY.
NOT TO ME.
LOOK, JUST DON'T ***TELL*** HIM, OKAY?!
IT'LL GIVE HIM IDEAS, Y'KNOW?
WHAT'S IT SAY ABOUT ME AND MIKI, CHIE?
WHAT SIGN ARE YOU, MIKI?
I'M A GEMINI.
WOW! THIS BOOK REALLY ***NAILS*** IT!
YOU GUYS ARE ***COMPAT-IBILITY-PLUS!***
The Real You
Ultimate Horoscopes

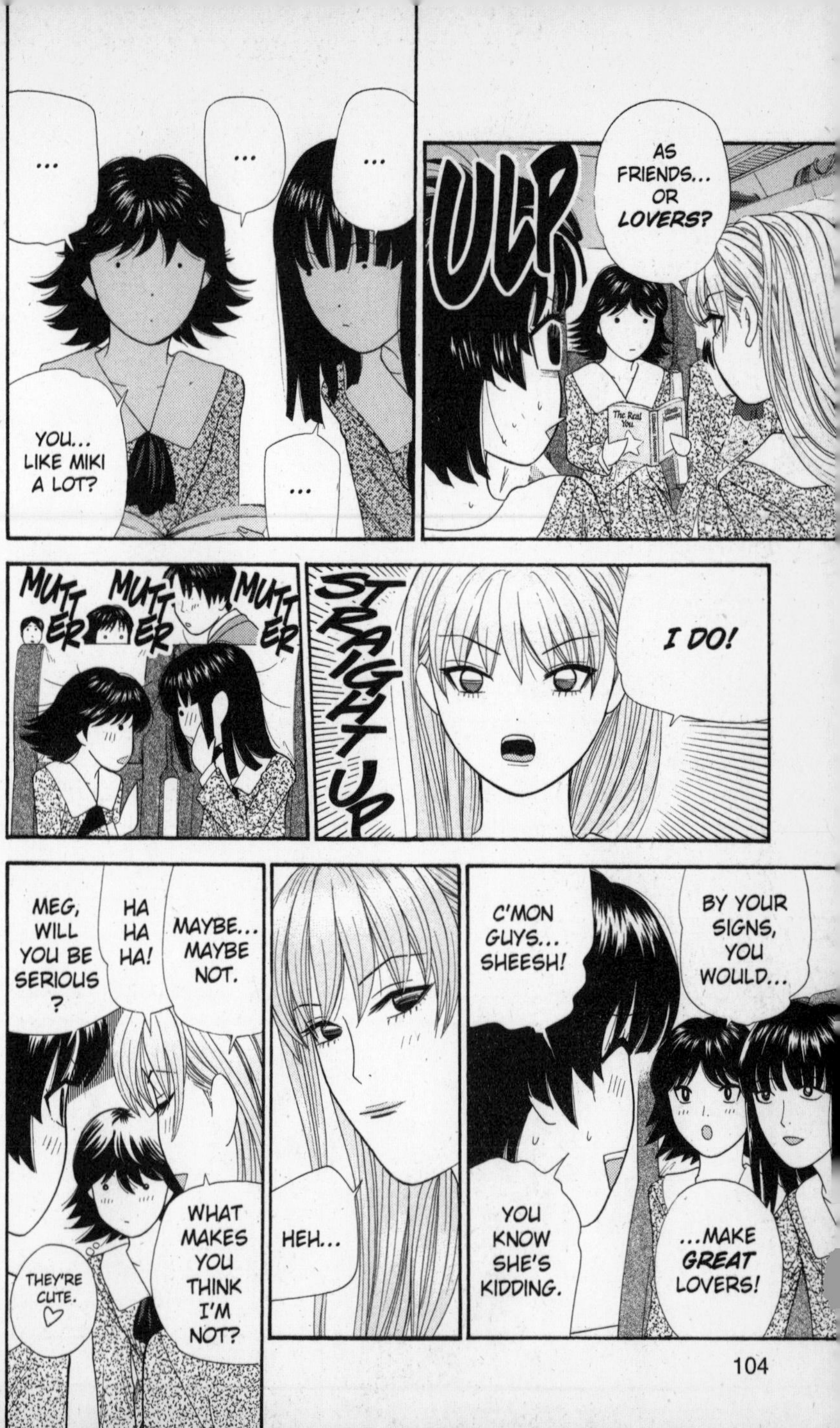
ULP
AS FRIENDS... OR LOVERS?
...
...
...
...
YOU... LIKE MIKI A LOT?
STRAIGHT UP
I DO!
MUTTER
MUTTER
MUTTER
BY YOUR SIGNS, YOU WOULD...
C'MON GUYS... SHEESH!
...MAKE GREAT LOVERS!
YOU KNOW SHE'S KIDDING.
HEH...
MAYBE... MAYBE NOT.
HA HA HA!
MEG, WILL YOU BE SERIOUS?
WHAT MAKES YOU THINK I'M NOT?
THEY'RE CUTE. ♡

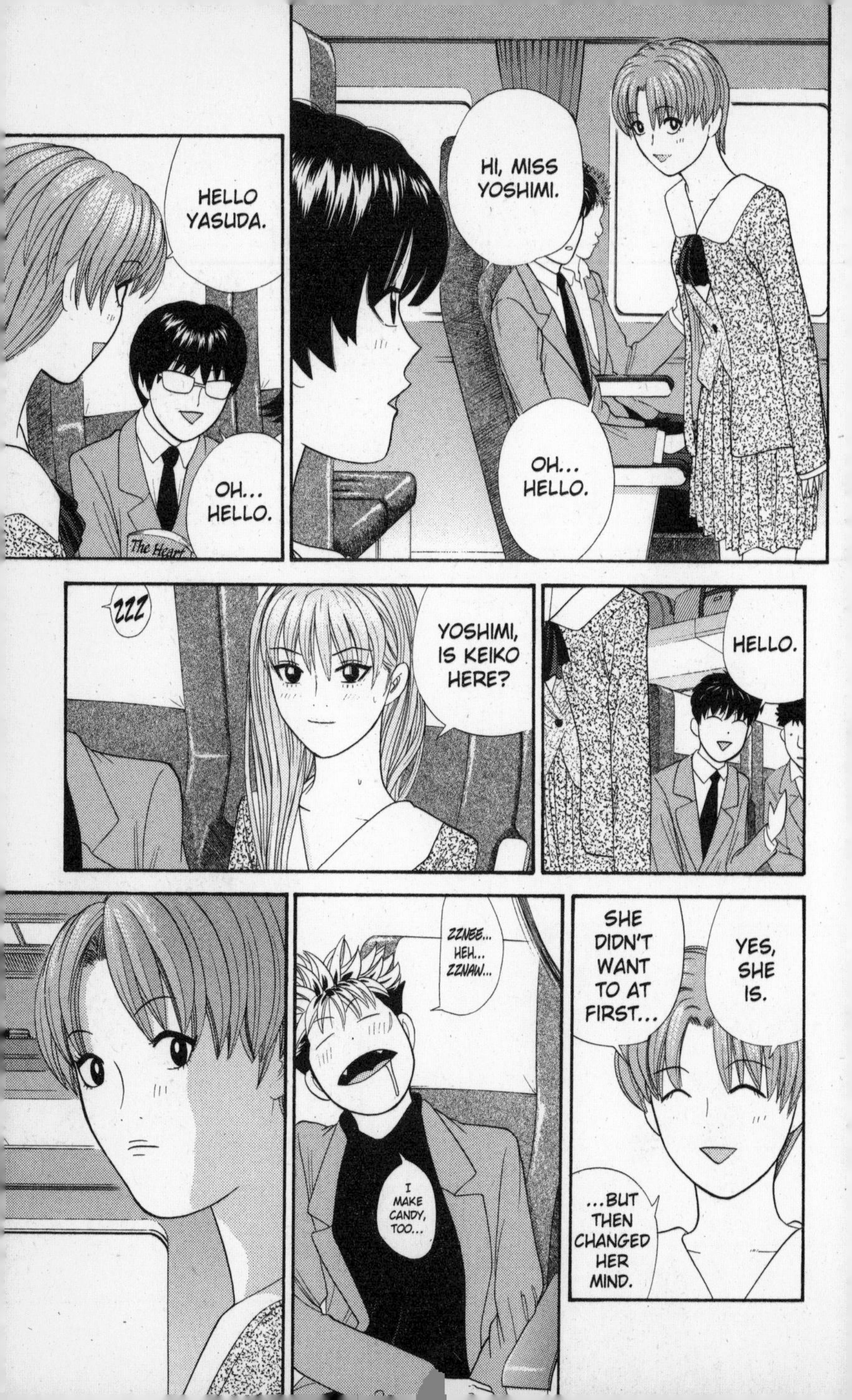
HI, MISS YOSHIMI.
OH... HELLO.
HELLO YASUDA.
OH... HELLO.
The Heart
HELLO.
YOSHIMI, IS KEIKO HERE?
ZZZ
YES, SHE IS.
SHE DIDN'T WANT TO AT FIRST...
...BUT THEN CHANGED HER MIND.
ZZNEE... HEH... ZZNAW...
I MAKE CANDY, TOO...

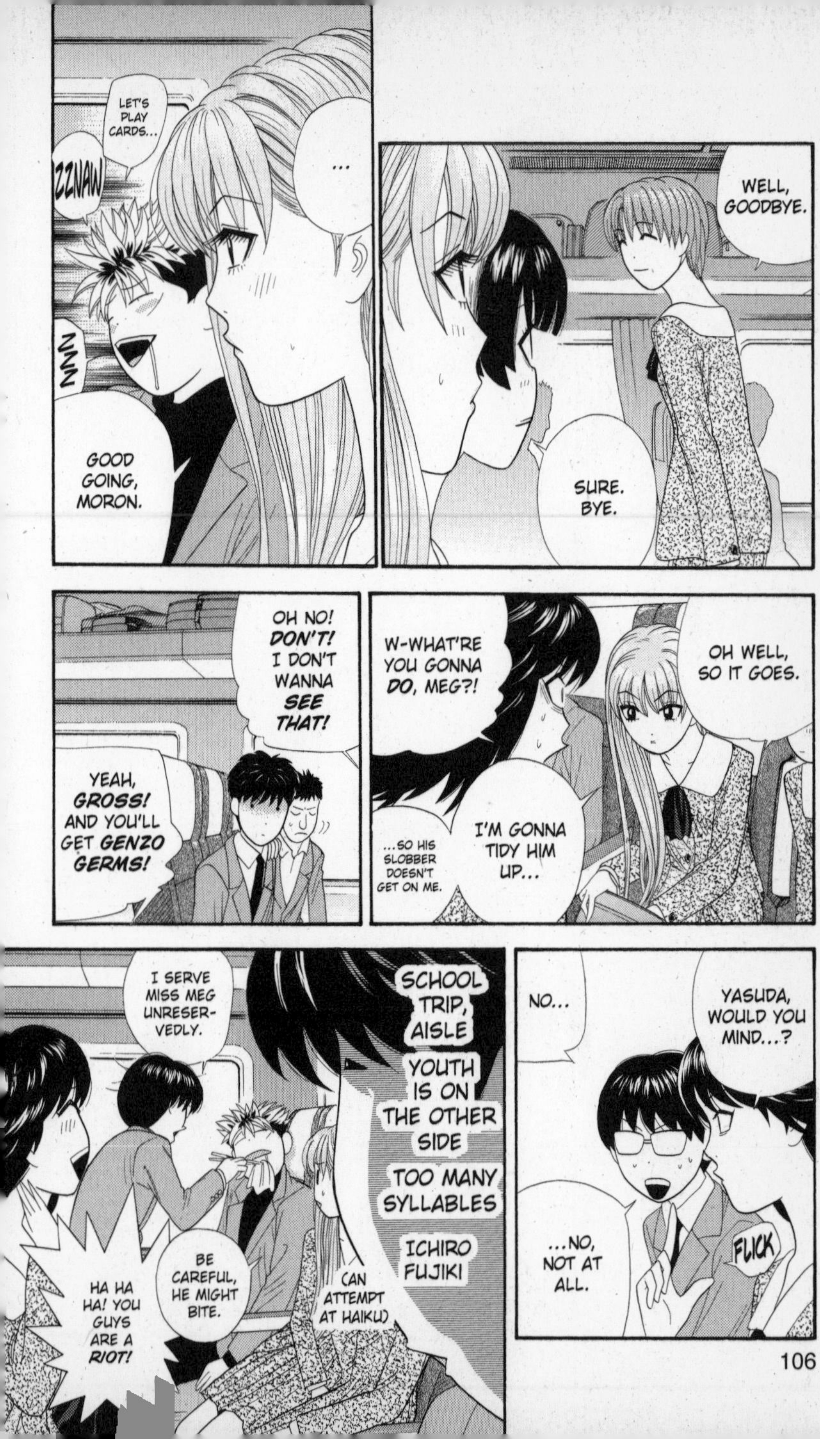
WELL, GOODBYE.
SURE. BYE.
...
LET'S PLAY CARDS...
ZZNAW
ZZZ
GOOD GOING, MORON.
OH WELL, SO IT GOES.
W-WHAT'RE YOU GONNA DO, MEG?!
I'M GONNA TIDY HIM UP...
...SO HIS SLOBBER DOESN'T GET ON ME.
OH NO! DON'T! I DON'T WANNA SEE THAT!
YEAH, GROSS! AND YOU'LL GET GENZO GERMS!
YASUDA, WOULD YOU MIND...?
NO...
FLICK
...NO, NOT AT ALL.
SCHOOL TRIP, AISLE
YOUTH IS ON THE OTHER SIDE
TOO MANY SYLLABLES
ICHIRO FUJIKI
I SERVE MISS MEG UNRESER-VEDLY.
(CAN ATTEMPT AT HAIKU)
BE CAREFUL, HE MIGHT BITE.
HA HA HA! YOU GUYS ARE A RIOT!

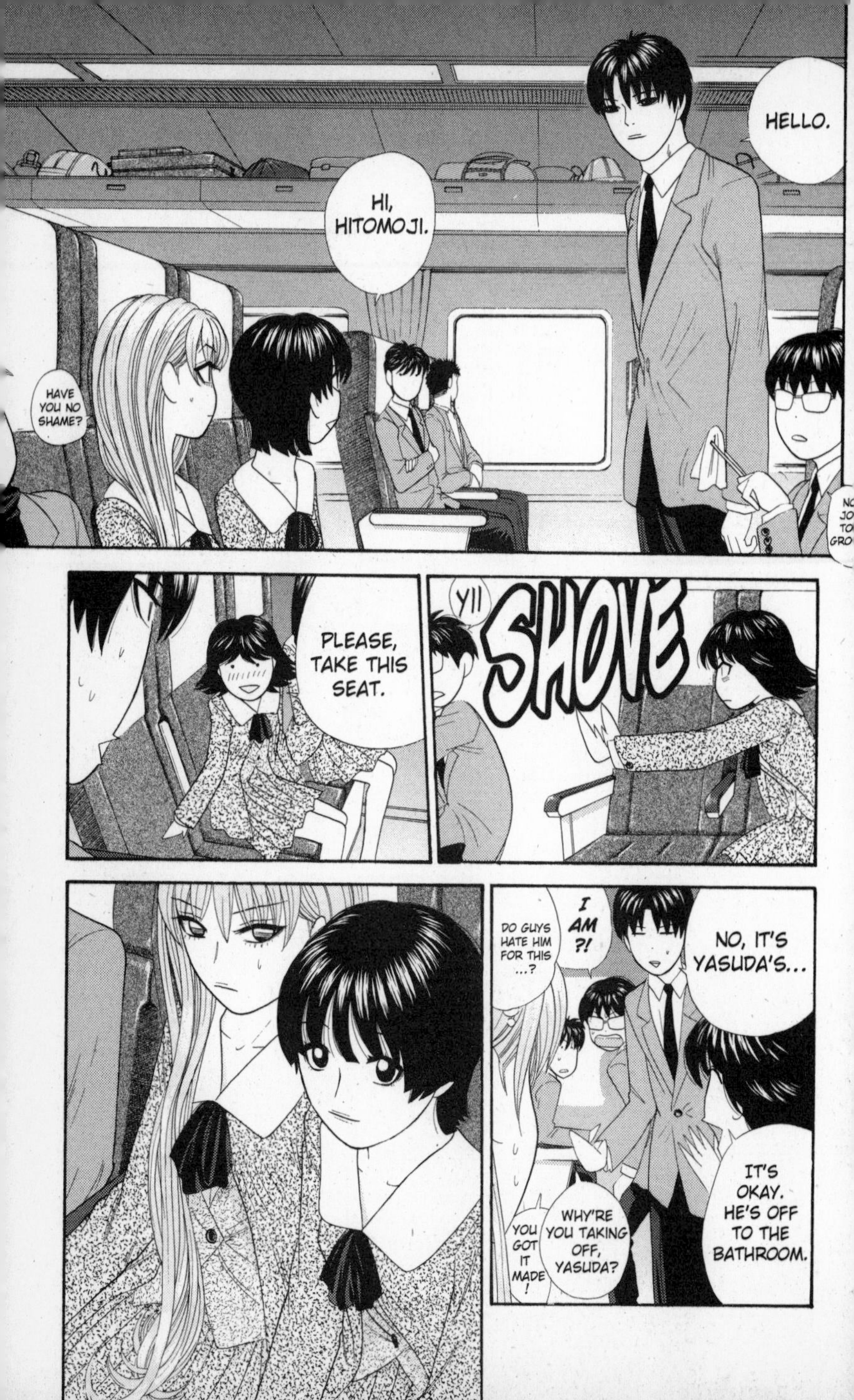
HELLO.
HI, HITOMOJI.
HAVE YOU NO SHAME?
YII
SHOVE
PLEASE, TAKE THIS SEAT.
NO, IT'S YASUDA'S...
I AM?!
DO GUYS HATE HIM FOR THIS ...?
IT'S OKAY. HE'S OFF TO THE BATHROOM.
WHY'RE YOU TAKING OFF, YASUDA?
YOU GOT IT MADE!

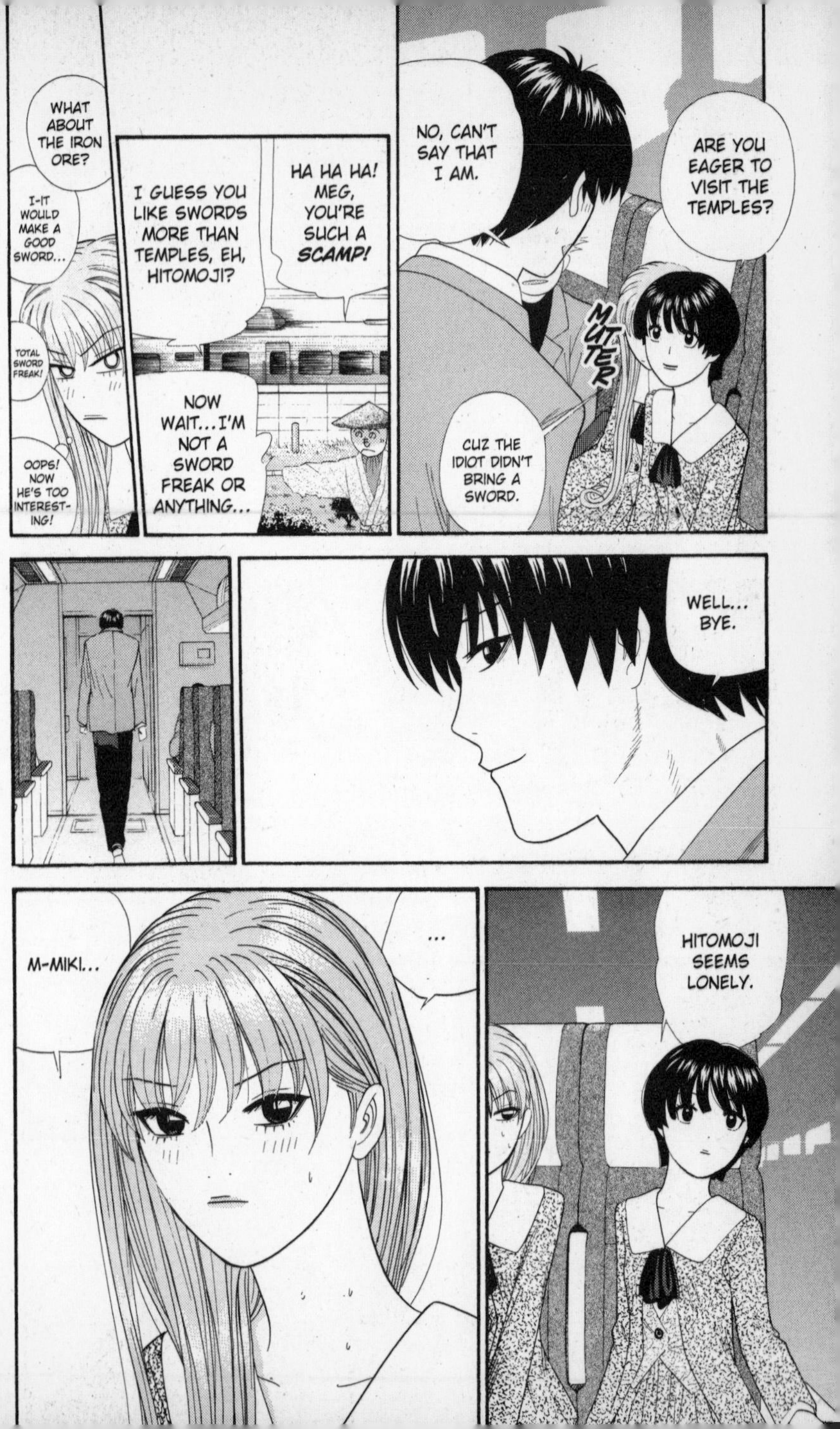
ARE YOU EAGER TO VISIT THE TEMPLES?
NO, CAN'T SAY THAT I AM.
MUTTER
CUZ THE IDIOT DIDN'T BRING A SWORD.
HA HA HA! MEG, YOU'RE SUCH A SCAMP!
I GUESS YOU LIKE SWORDS MORE THAN TEMPLES, EH, HITOMOJI?
NOW WAIT...I'M NOT A SWORD FREAK OR ANYTHING...
WHAT ABOUT THE IRON ORE?
I-IT WOULD MAKE A GOOD SWORD...
TOTAL SWORD FREAK!
OOPS! NOW HE'S TOO INTERESTING!
WELL... BYE.
HITOMOJI SEEMS LONELY.
...
M-MIKI...

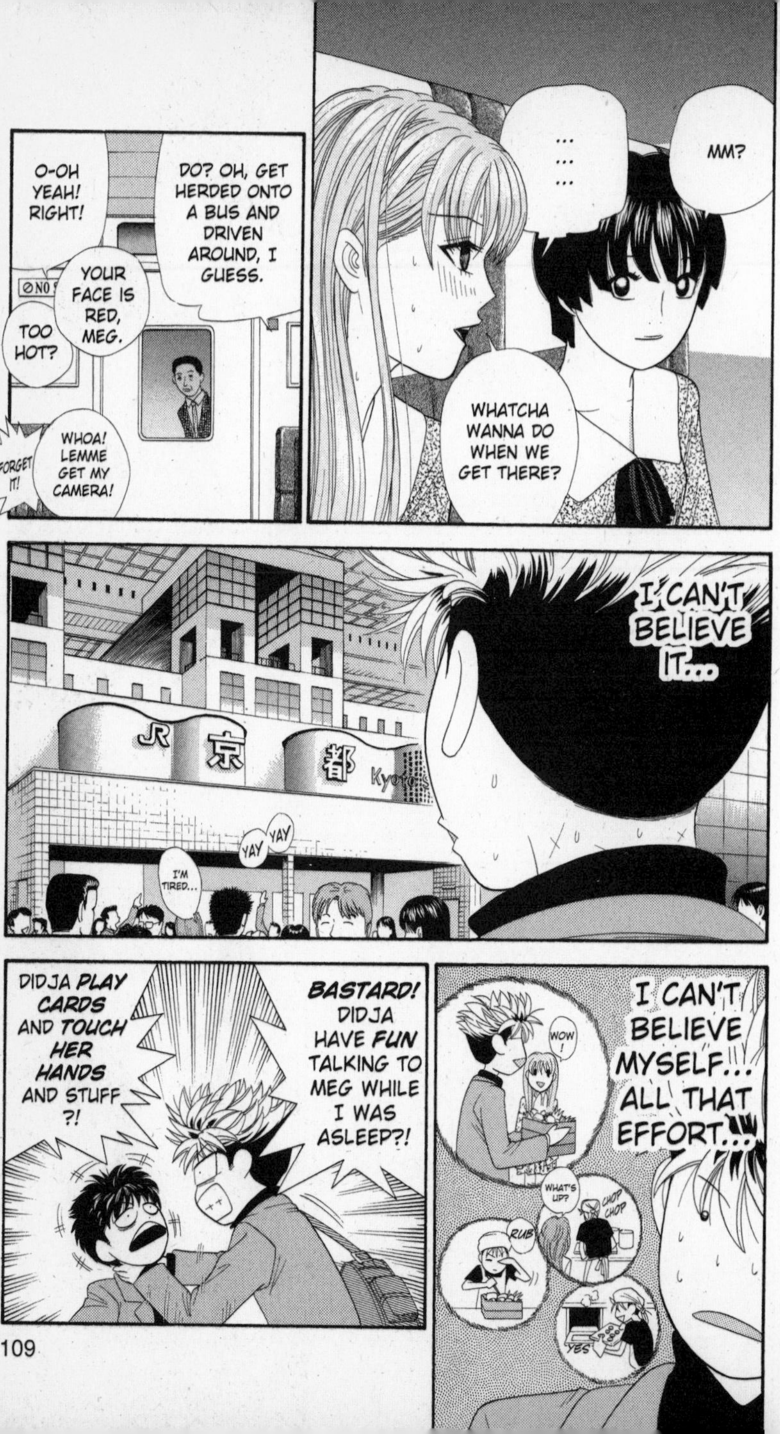
MM?
...
...
...
WHATCHA WANNA DO WHEN WE GET THERE?
DO? OH, GET HERDED ONTO A BUS AND DRIVEN AROUND, I GUESS.
O-OH YEAH! RIGHT!
YOUR FACE IS RED, MEG.
TOO HOT?
WHOA! LEMME GET MY CAMERA!
FORGET IT!
I CAN'T BELIEVE IT...
JR 京都 Kyoto
YAY
YAY
I'M TIRED...
I CAN'T BELIEVE MYSELF... ALL THAT EFFORT...
WOW!
CHOP CHOP
WHAT'S UP?
RUB
YES
BASTARD! DIDJA HAVE FUN TALKING TO MEG WHILE I WAS ASLEEP?!
DIDJA PLAY CARDS AND TOUCH HER HANDS AND STUFF?!

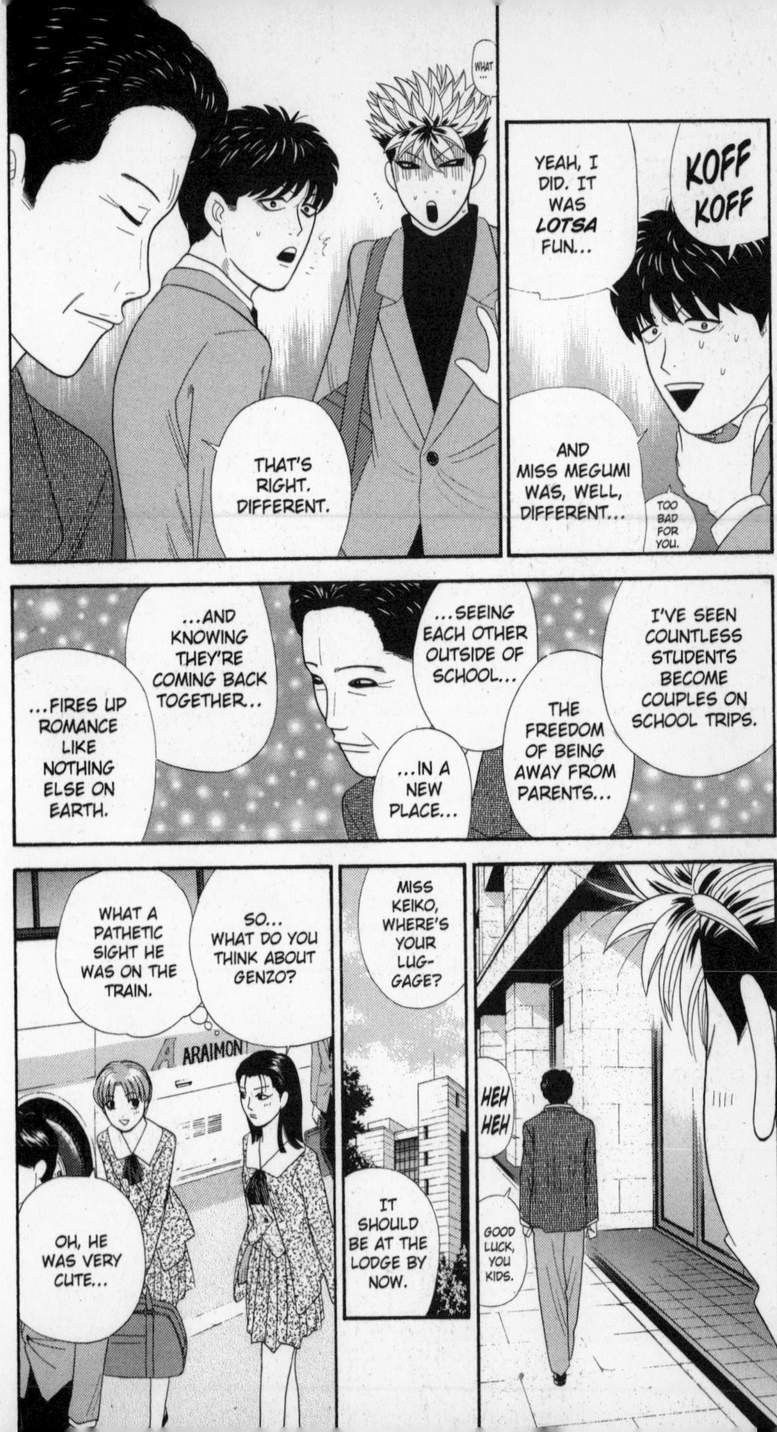
KOFF KOFF
YEAH, I DID. IT WAS LOTSA FUN...
AND MISS MEGUMI WAS, WELL, DIFFERENT...
TOO BAD FOR YOU.
WHAT...
THAT'S RIGHT. DIFFERENT.
I'VE SEEN COUNTLESS STUDENTS BECOME COUPLES ON SCHOOL TRIPS.
THE FREEDOM OF BEING AWAY FROM PARENTS...
...SEEING EACH OTHER OUTSIDE OF SCHOOL...
...IN A NEW PLACE...
...AND KNOWING THEY'RE COMING BACK TOGETHER...
...FIRES UP ROMANCE LIKE NOTHING ELSE ON EARTH.
HEH HEH
GOOD LUCK, YOU KIDS.
MISS KEIKO, WHERE'S YOUR LUG-GAGE?
IT SHOULD BE AT THE LODGE BY NOW.
SO... WHAT DO YOU THINK ABOUT GENZO?
WHAT A PATHETIC SIGHT HE WAS ON THE TRAIN.
ARAIMON
OH, HE WAS VERY CUTE...

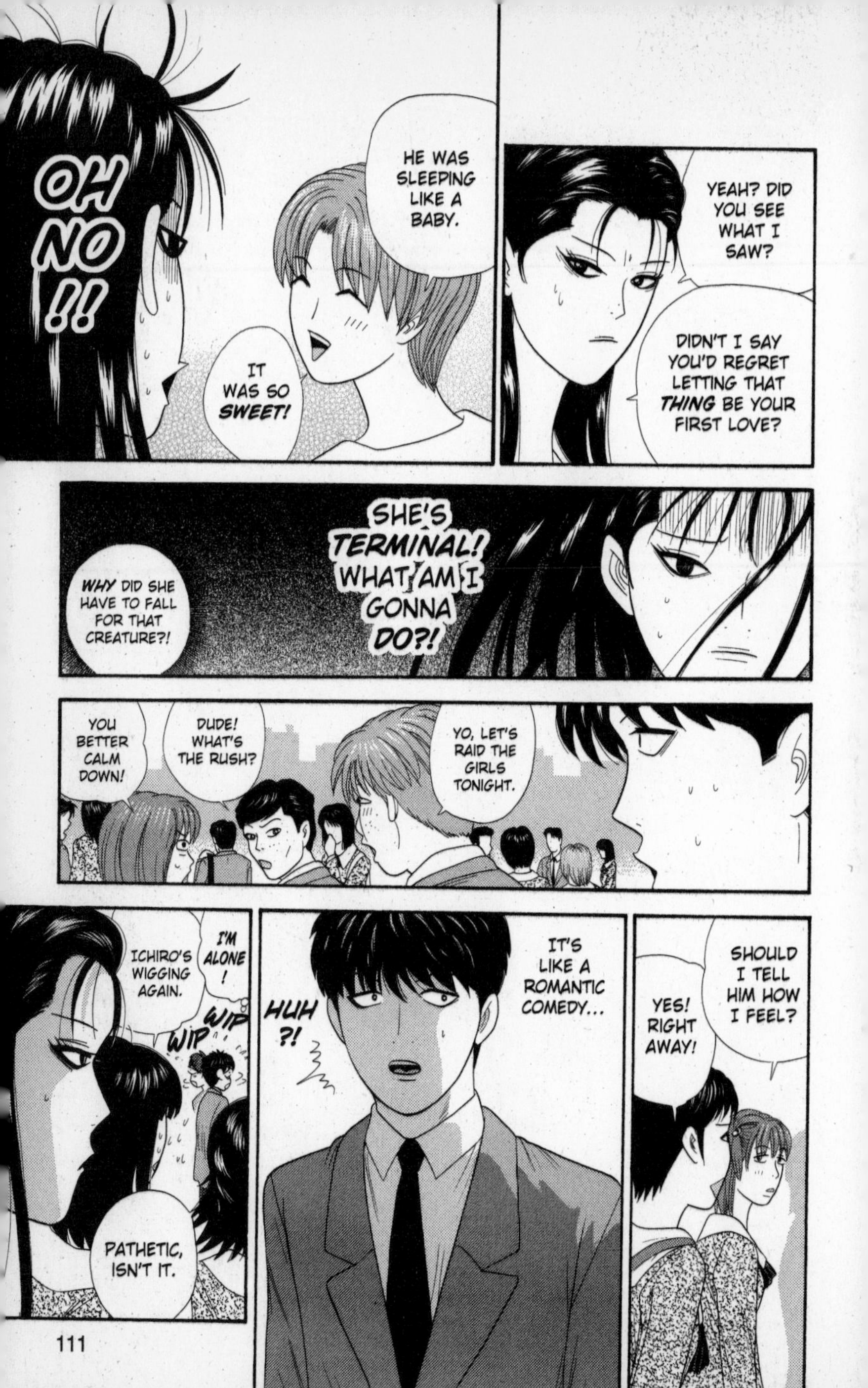
YEAH? DID YOU SEE WHAT I SAW?
DIDN'T I SAY YOU'D REGRET LETTING THAT *THING* BE YOUR FIRST LOVE?
HE WAS SLEEPING LIKE A BABY.
IT WAS SO **SWEET!**
OH NO!!
SHE'S *TERMINAL!* WHAT AM I GONNA *DO?!*
WHY DID SHE HAVE TO FALL FOR THAT CREATURE?!
YO, LET'S RAID THE GIRLS TONIGHT.
DUDE! WHAT'S THE RUSH?
YOU BETTER CALM DOWN!
SHOULD I TELL HIM HOW I FEEL?
YES! RIGHT AWAY!
IT'S LIKE A ROMANTIC COMEDY...
HUH?!
I'M ALONE!
ICHIRO'S WIGGING AGAIN.
WIP WIP
PATHETIC, ISN'T IT.

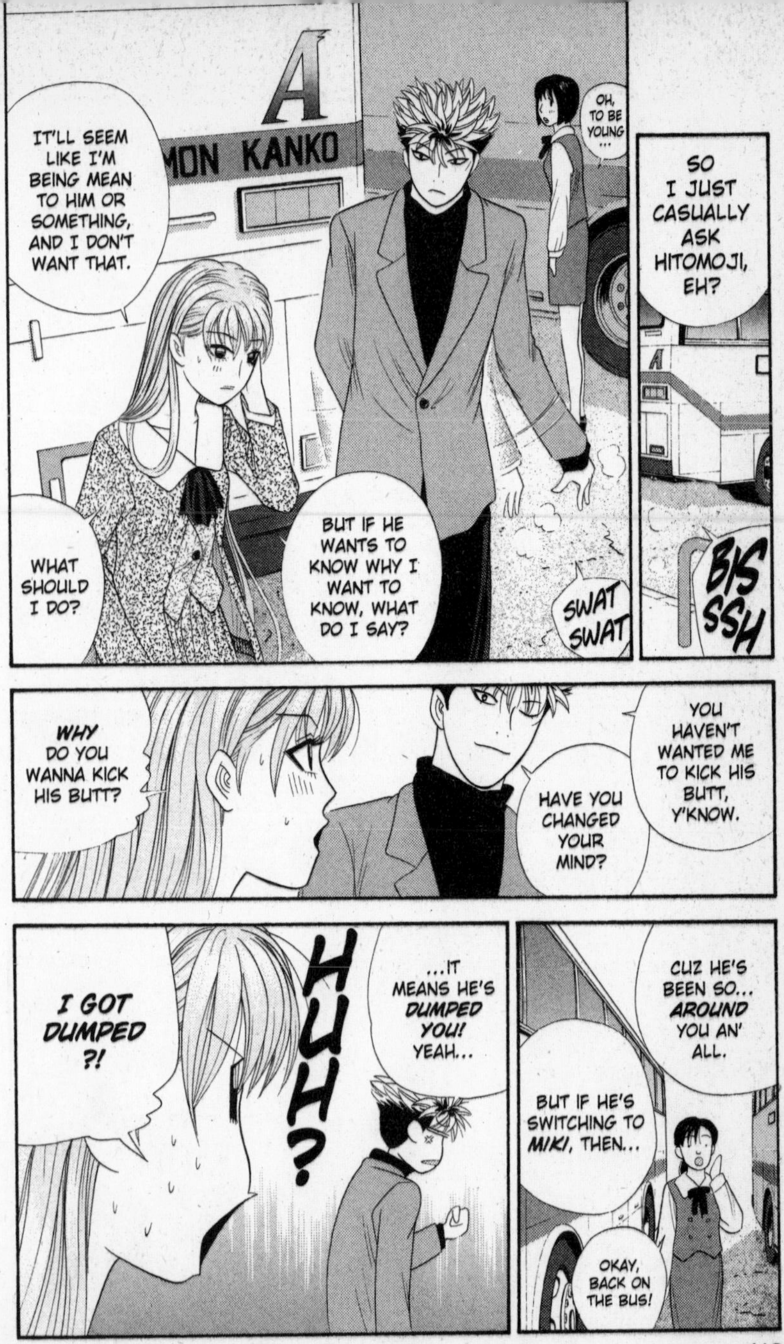
SO I JUST CASUALLY ASK HITOMOJI, EH?
BISSSH
OH, TO BE YOUNG...
IT'LL SEEM LIKE I'M BEING MEAN TO HIM OR SOMETHING, AND I DON'T WANT THAT.
MON KANKO
SWAT SWAT
BUT IF HE WANTS TO KNOW WHY I WANT TO KNOW, WHAT DO I SAY?
WHAT SHOULD I DO?
YOU HAVEN'T WANTED ME TO KICK HIS BUTT, Y'KNOW.
HAVE YOU CHANGED YOUR MIND?
WHY DO YOU WANNA KICK HIS BUTT?
CUZ HE'S BEEN SO... *AROUND* YOU AN' ALL.
BUT IF HE'S SWITCHING TO *MIKI*, THEN...
OKAY, BACK ON THE BUS!
...IT MEANS HE'S *DUMPED YOU!* YEAH...
HUH?
I GOT DUMPED?!

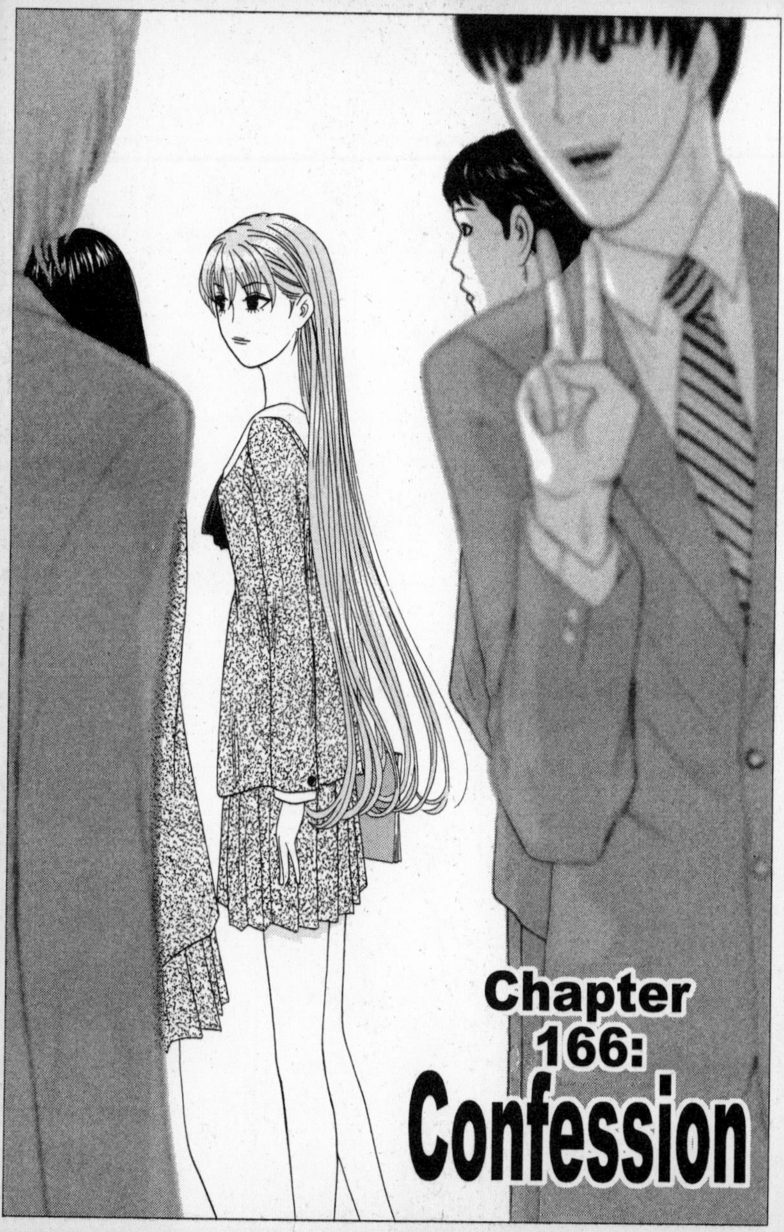
Chapter 166:
Confession

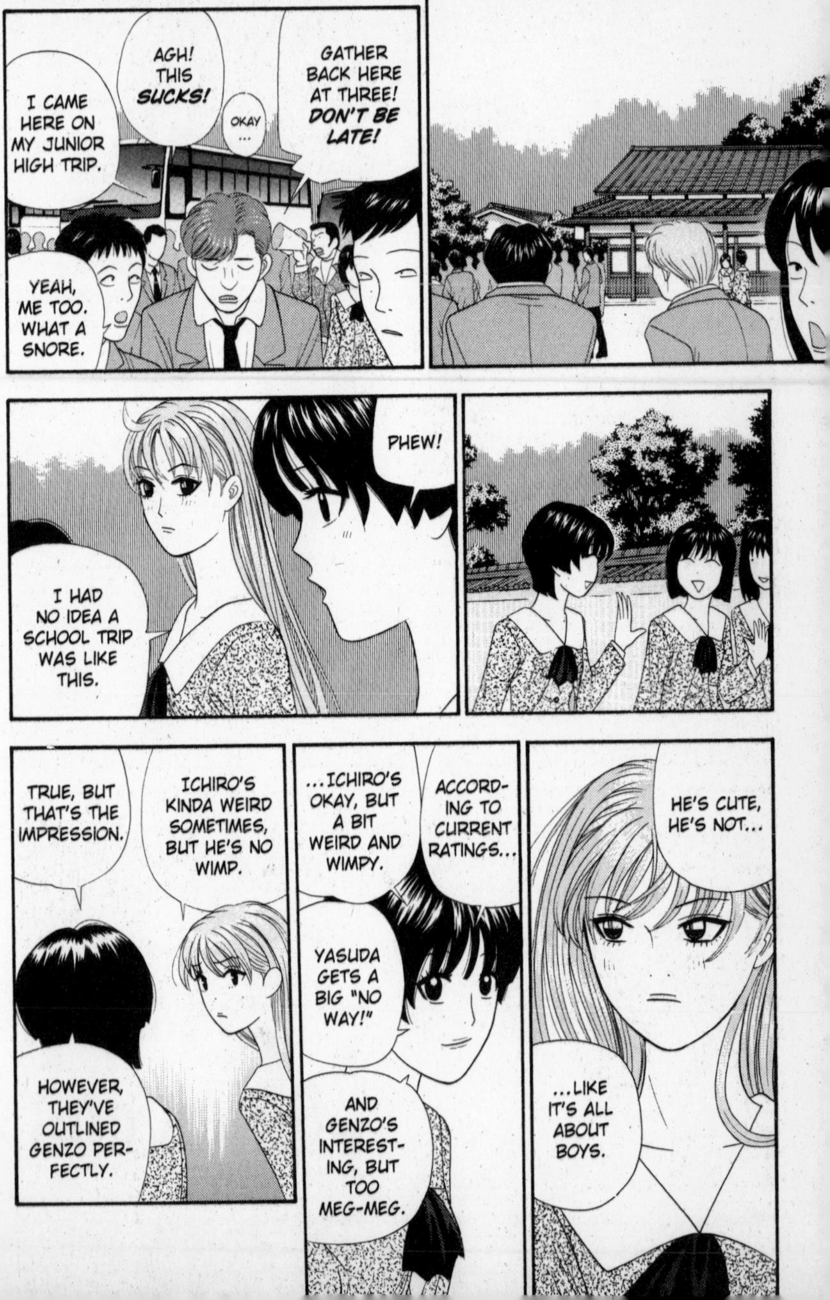
GATHER BACK HERE AT THREE! DON'T BE LATE!
OKAY...
AGH! THIS SUCKS!
I CAME HERE ON MY JUNIOR HIGH TRIP.
YEAH, ME TOO. WHAT A SNORE.
PHEW!
I HAD NO IDEA A SCHOOL TRIP WAS LIKE THIS.
HE'S CUTE, HE'S NOT...
...LIKE IT'S ALL ABOUT BOYS.
ACCORDING TO CURRENT RATINGS...
...ICHIRO'S OKAY, BUT A BIT WEIRD AND WIMPY.
YASUDA GETS A BIG "NO WAY!"
AND GENZO'S INTERESTING, BUT TOO MEG-MEG.
ICHIRO'S KINDA WEIRD SOMETIMES, BUT HE'S NO WIMP.
TRUE, BUT THAT'S THE IMPRESSION.
HOWEVER, THEY'VE OUTLINED GENZO PERFECTLY.

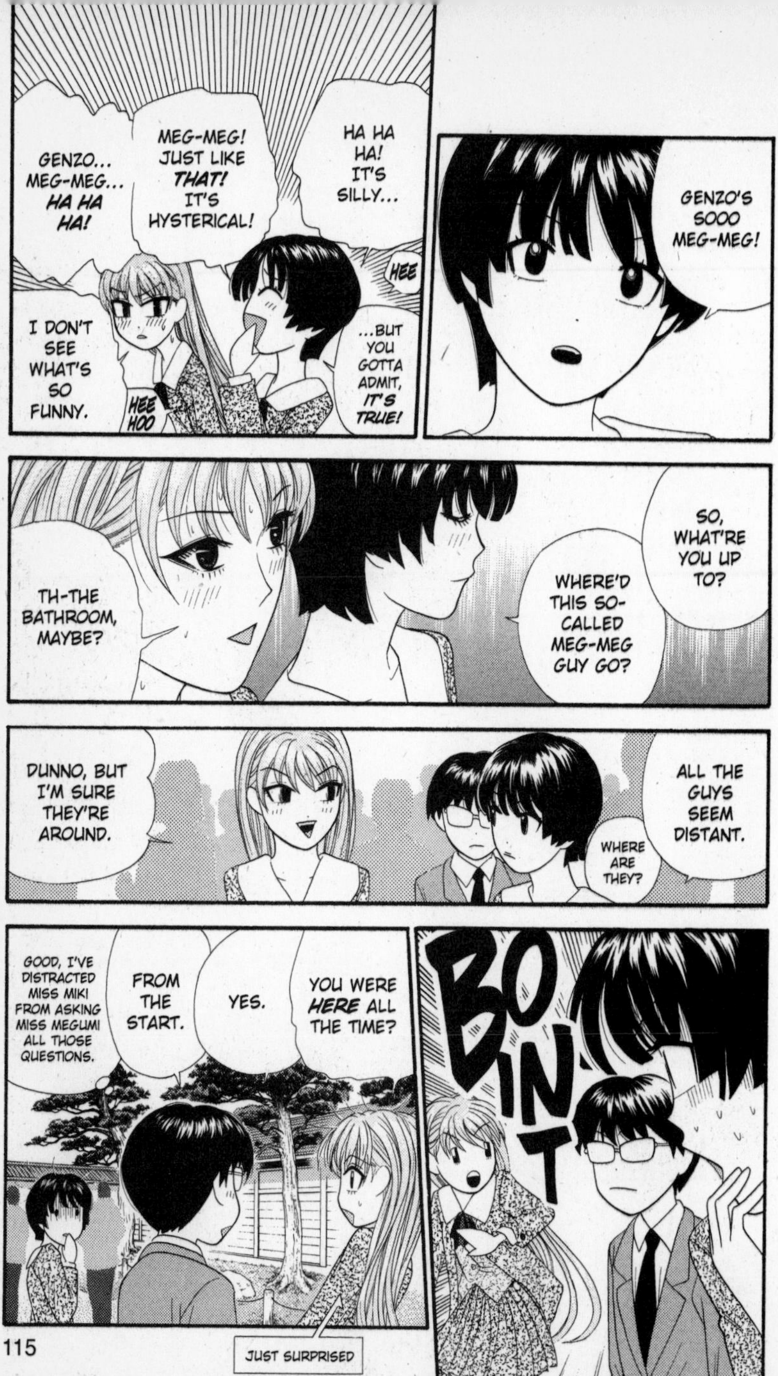
GENZO'S SOOO MEG-MEG!
HA HA HA! IT'S SILLY...
HEE
MEG-MEG! JUST LIKE THAT! IT'S HYSTERICAL!
GENZO... MEG-MEG... HA HA HA!
...BUT YOU GOTTA ADMIT, IT'S TRUE!
HEE HOO
I DON'T SEE WHAT'S SO FUNNY.
SO, WHAT'RE YOU UP TO?
WHERE'D THIS SO-CALLED MEG-MEG GUY GO?
TH-THE BATHROOM, MAYBE?
ALL THE GUYS SEEM DISTANT.
WHERE ARE THEY?
DUNNO, BUT I'M SURE THEY'RE AROUND.
BOINT
YOU WERE HERE ALL THE TIME?
YES.
FROM THE START.
GOOD, I'VE DISTRACTED MISS MIKI FROM ASKING MISS MEGUMI ALL THOSE QUESTIONS.
JUST SURPRISED

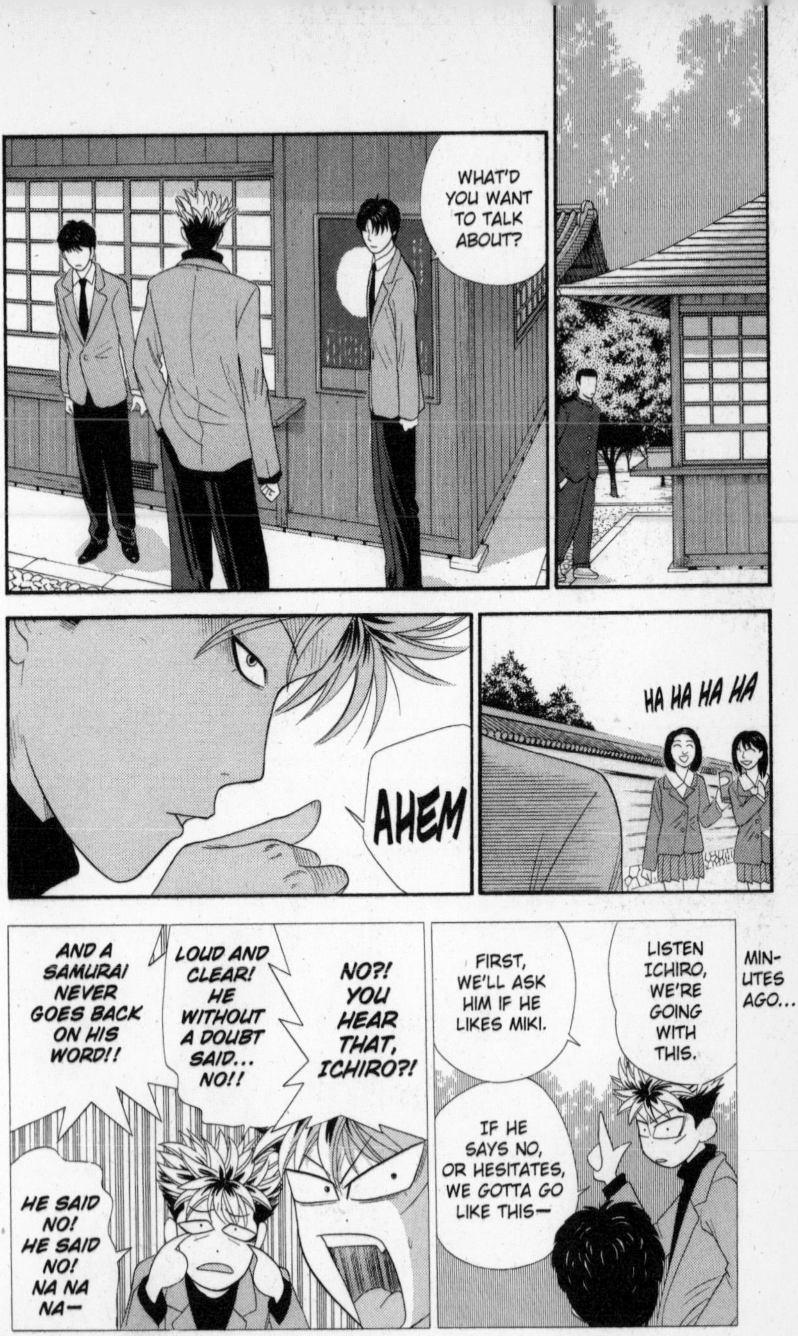
WHAT'D YOU WANT TO TALK ABOUT?
HA HA HA HA
AHEM
MIN-UTES AGO...
LISTEN ICHIRO, WE'RE GOING WITH THIS.
FIRST, WE'LL ASK HIM IF HE LIKES MIKI.
IF HE SAYS NO, OR HESITATES, WE GOTTA GO LIKE THIS—
NO?! YOU HEAR THAT, ICHIRO?!
LOUD AND CLEAR! HE WITHOUT A DOUBT SAID... NO!!
AND A SAMURAI NEVER GOES BACK ON HIS WORD!!
HE SAID NO! HE SAID NO! NA NA NA—

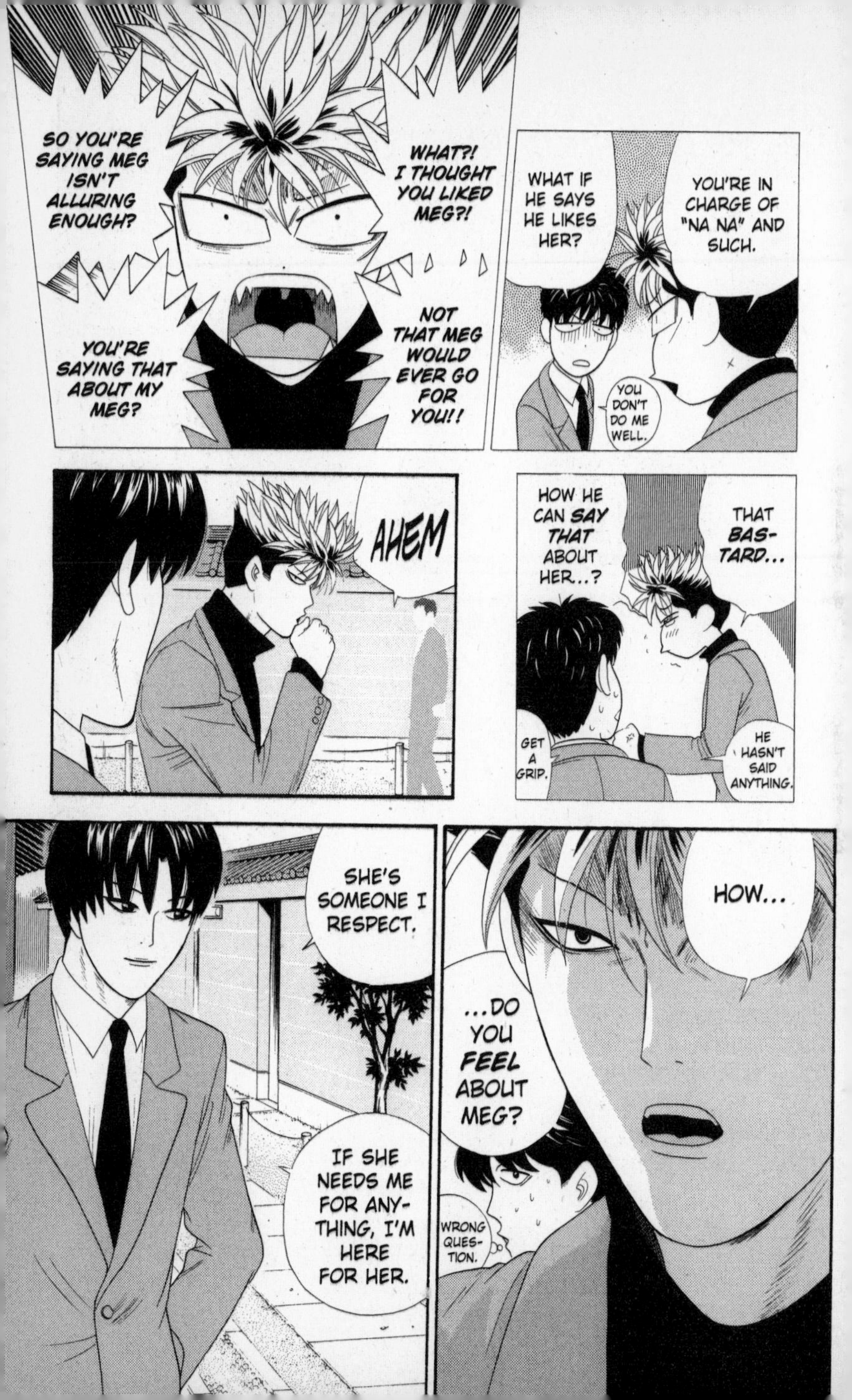

YOU'RE IN CHARGE OF "NA NA" AND SUCH.
WHAT IF HE SAYS HE LIKES HER?
YOU DON'T DO ME WELL.
WHAT?! I THOUGHT YOU LIKED MEG?!
SO YOU'RE SAYING MEG ISN'T ALLURING ENOUGH?
NOT THAT MEG WOULD EVER GO FOR YOU!!
YOU'RE SAYING THAT ABOUT MY MEG?
THAT BAS-TARD...
HOW HE CAN SAY THAT ABOUT HER...?
HE HASN'T SAID ANYTHING.
GET A GRIP.
AHEM
HOW...
...DO YOU FEEL ABOUT MEG?
WRONG QUES-TION.
SHE'S SOMEONE I RESPECT.
IF SHE NEEDS ME FOR ANY-THING, I'M HERE FOR HER.

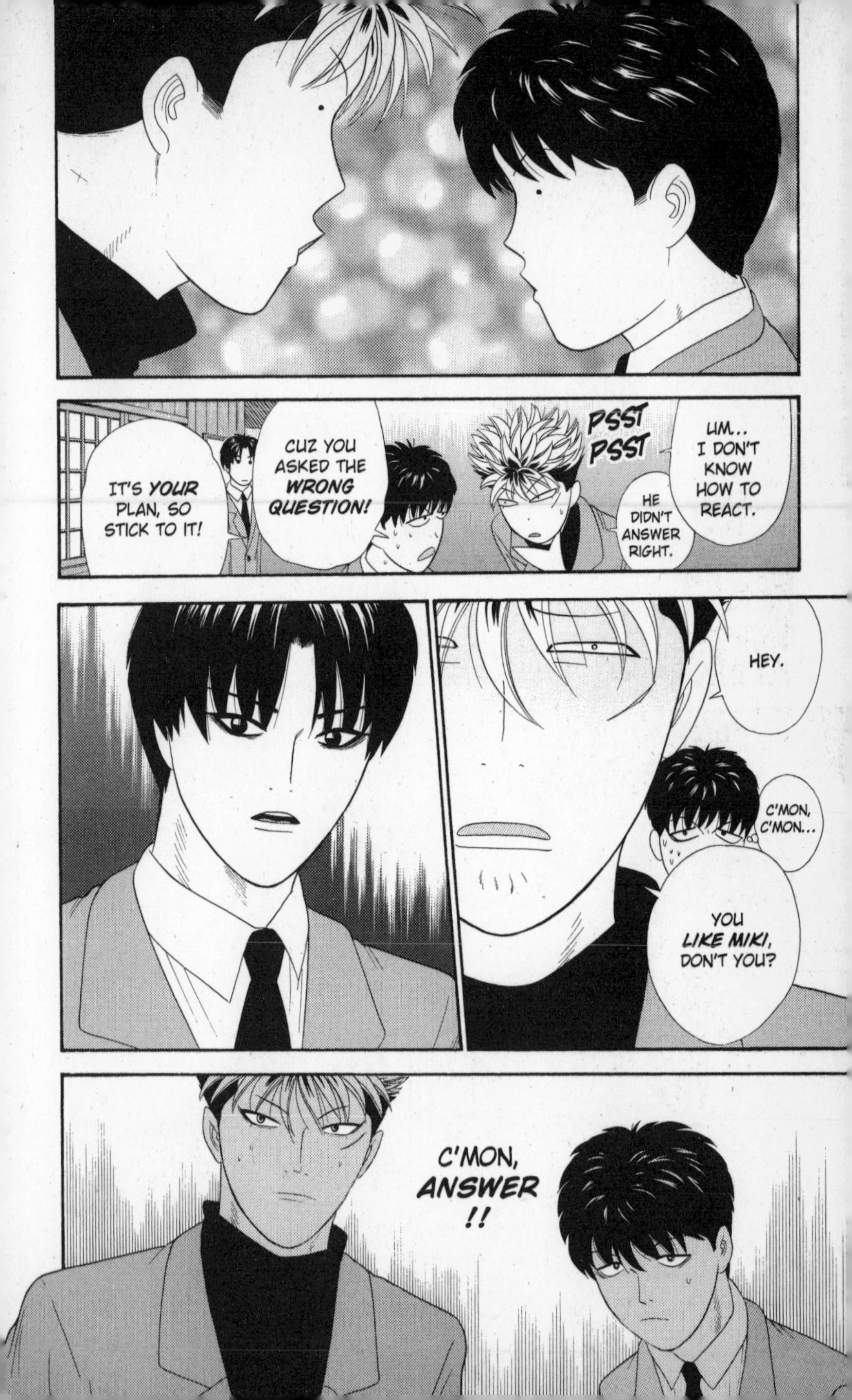
PSST PSST
UM... I DON'T KNOW HOW TO REACT.
HE DIDN'T ANSWER RIGHT.
CUZ YOU ASKED THE WRONG QUESTION!
IT'S YOUR PLAN, SO STICK TO IT!
HEY.
C'MON, C'MON...
YOU LIKE MIKI, DON'T YOU?
C'MON, ANSWER!!

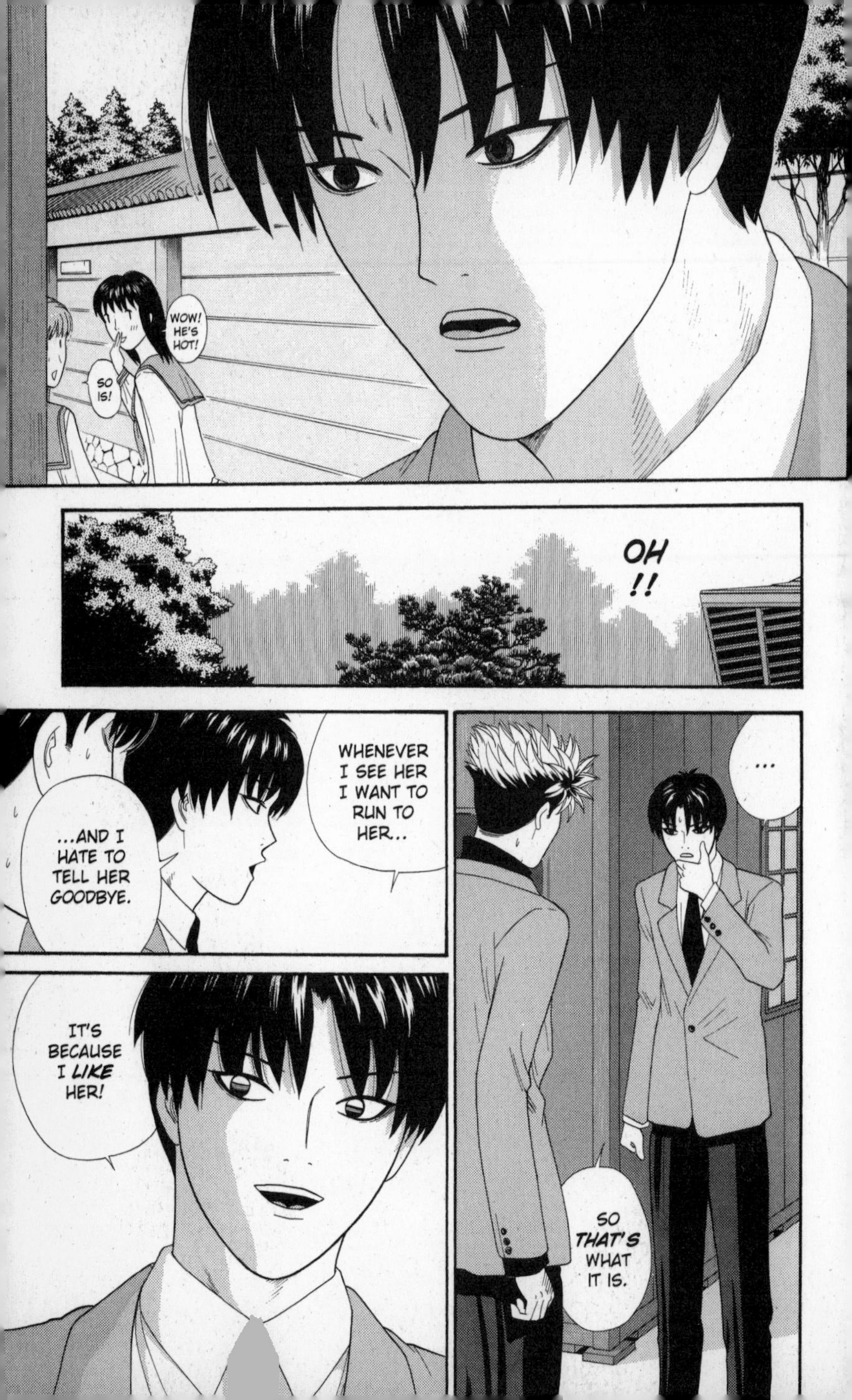
WOW! HE'S HOT!
SO IS!
OH !!
...
SO *THAT'S* WHAT IT IS.
WHENEVER I SEE HER I WANT TO RUN TO HER...
...AND I HATE TO TELL HER GOODBYE.
IT'S BECAUSE I *LIKE* HER!

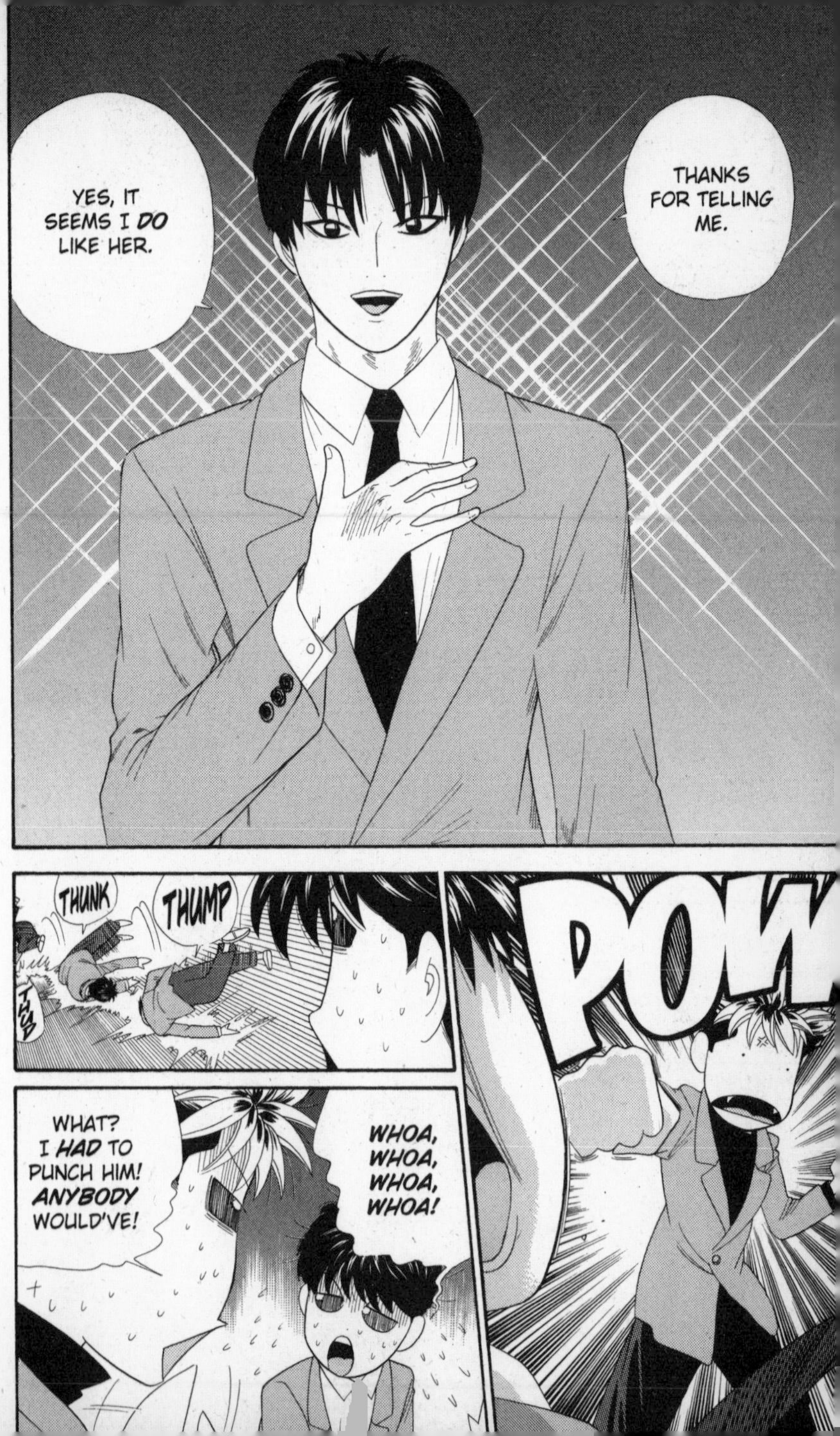
THANKS FOR TELLING ME.
YES, IT SEEMS I *DO* LIKE HER.
POW
THUMP
THUNK
THUD
WHOA, WHOA, WHOA, WHOA!
WHAT? I *HAD* TO PUNCH HIM! ***ANYBODY*** WOULD'VE!

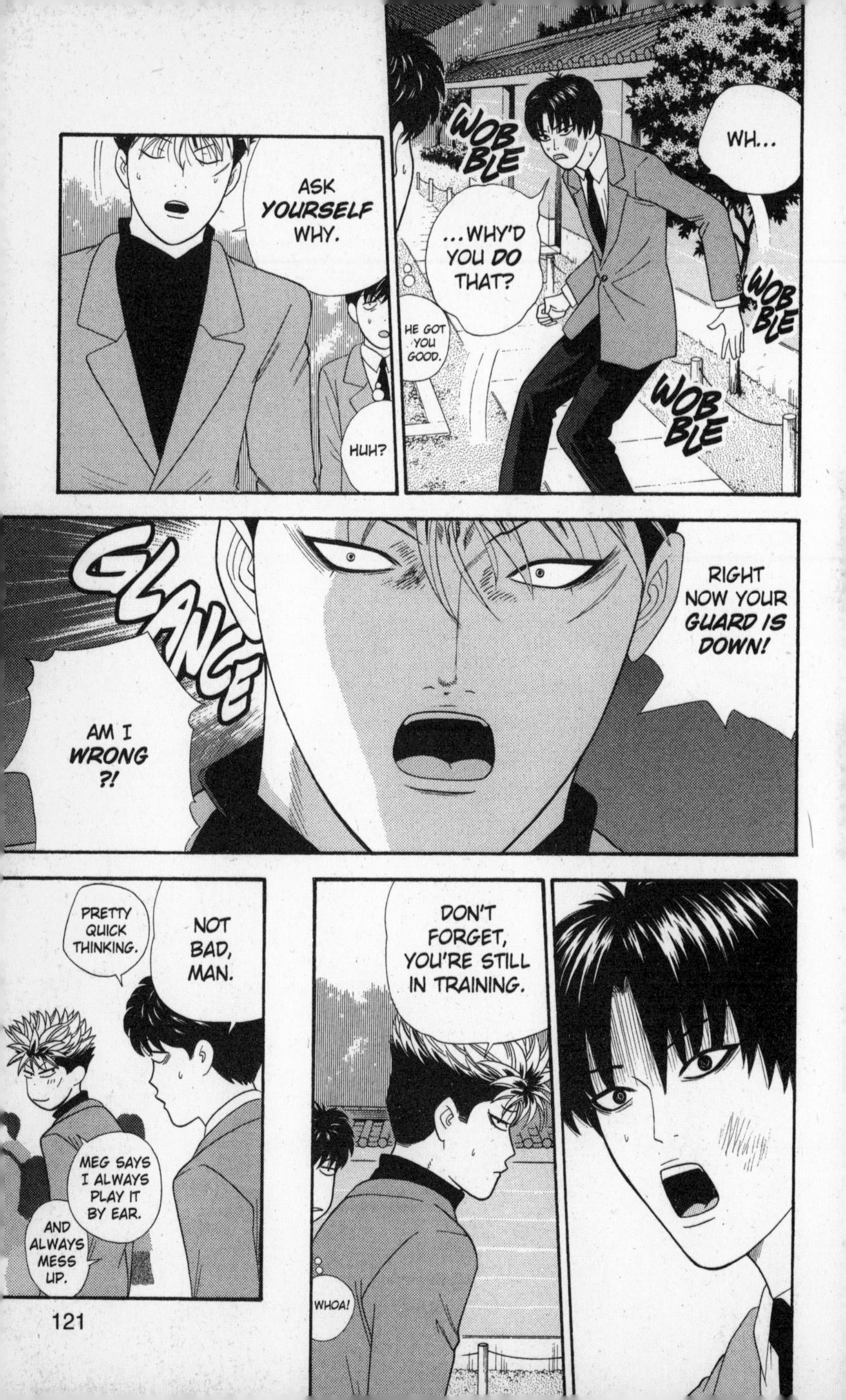
WH...
WOBBLE
...WHY'D YOU DO THAT?
HE GOT YOU GOOD.
WOBBLE
WOBBLE
ASK YOURSELF WHY.
HUH?
RIGHT NOW YOUR GUARD IS DOWN!
GLANCE
AM I WRONG?!
DON'T FORGET, YOU'RE STILL IN TRAINING.
WHOA!
NOT BAD, MAN.
PRETTY QUICK THINKING.
MEG SAYS I ALWAYS PLAY IT BY EAR.
AND ALWAYS MESS UP.

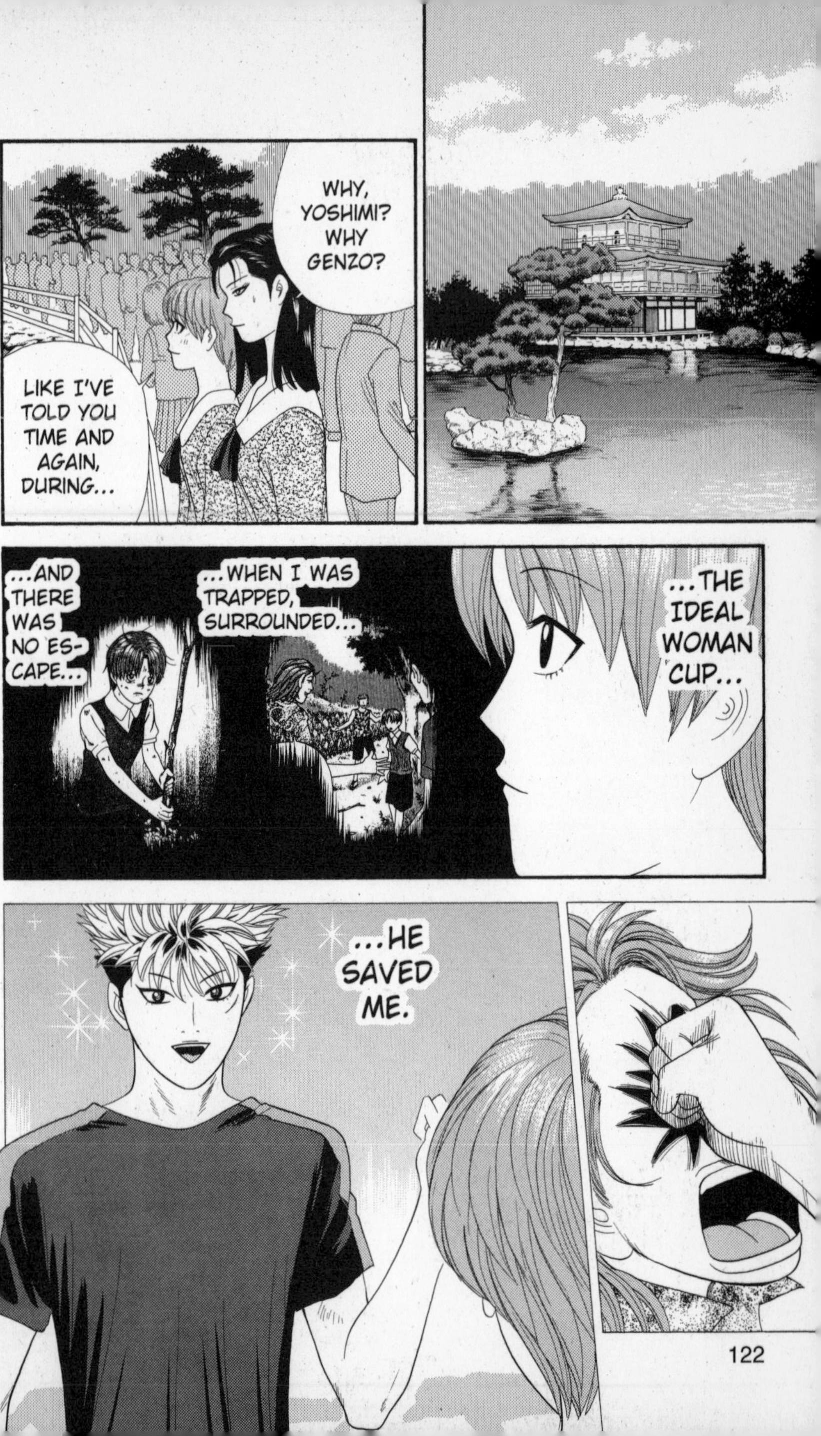
WHY, YOSHIMI? WHY GENZO?
LIKE I'VE TOLD YOU TIME AND AGAIN, DURING...
...THE IDEAL WOMAN CUP...
...WHEN I WAS TRAPPED, SURROUNDED...
...AND THERE WAS NO ES-CAPE...
...HE SAVED ME.

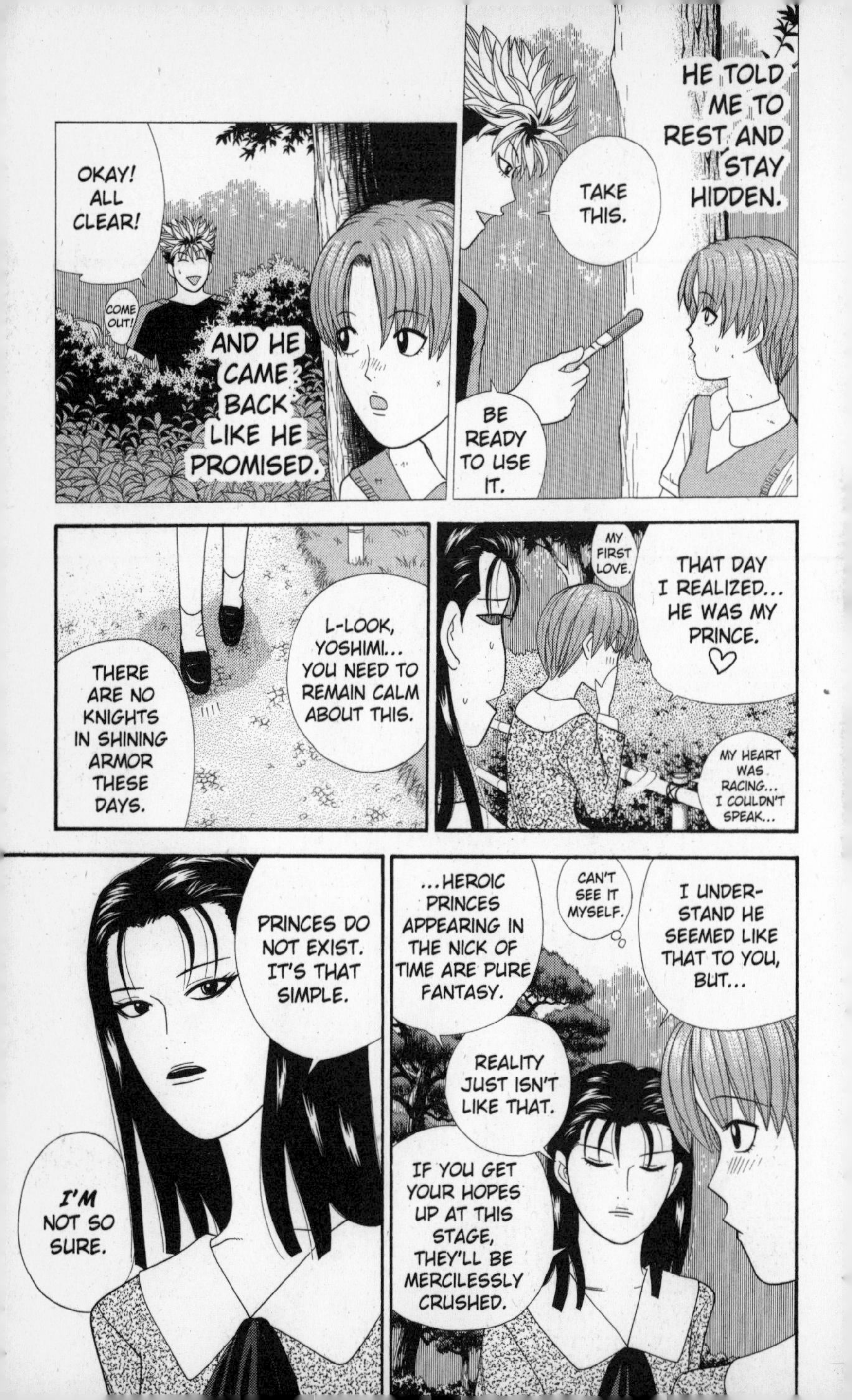
HE TOLD ME TO REST AND STAY HIDDEN.
TAKE THIS.
BE READY TO USE IT.
OKAY! ALL CLEAR!
COME OUT!
AND HE CAME BACK LIKE HE PROMISED.
THAT DAY I REALIZED... HE WAS MY PRINCE. ♡
MY FIRST LOVE.
MY HEART WAS RACING... I COULDN'T SPEAK...
L-LOOK, YOSHIMI... YOU NEED TO REMAIN CALM ABOUT THIS.
THERE ARE NO KNIGHTS IN SHINING ARMOR THESE DAYS.
I UNDER-STAND HE SEEMED LIKE THAT TO YOU, BUT...
CAN'T SEE IT MYSELF.
...HEROIC PRINCES APPEARING IN THE NICK OF TIME ARE PURE FANTASY.
REALITY JUST ISN'T LIKE THAT.
IF YOU GET YOUR HOPES UP AT THIS STAGE, THEY'LL BE MERCILESSLY CRUSHED.
PRINCES DO NOT EXIST. IT'S THAT SIMPLE.
I'M NOT SO SURE.

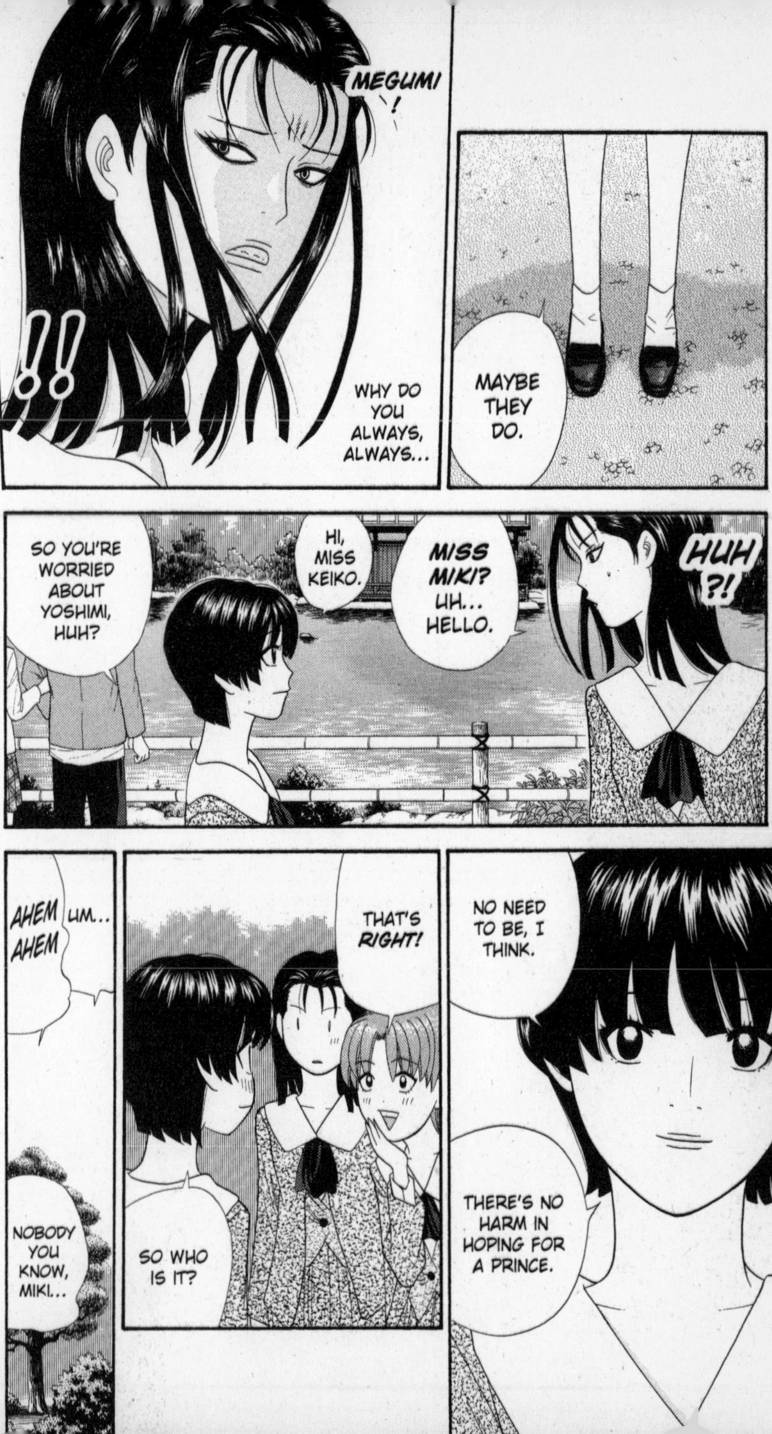
MAYBE THEY DO.
MEGUMI!
WHY DO YOU ALWAYS, ALWAYS...
!!
HUH?!
MISS MIKI? UH... HELLO.
HI, MISS KEIKO.
SO YOU'RE WORRIED ABOUT YOSHIMI, HUH?
NO NEED TO BE, I THINK.
THERE'S NO HARM IN HOPING FOR A PRINCE.
THAT'S RIGHT!
SO WHO IS IT?
UM...
AHEM AHEM
NOBODY YOU KNOW, MIKI...

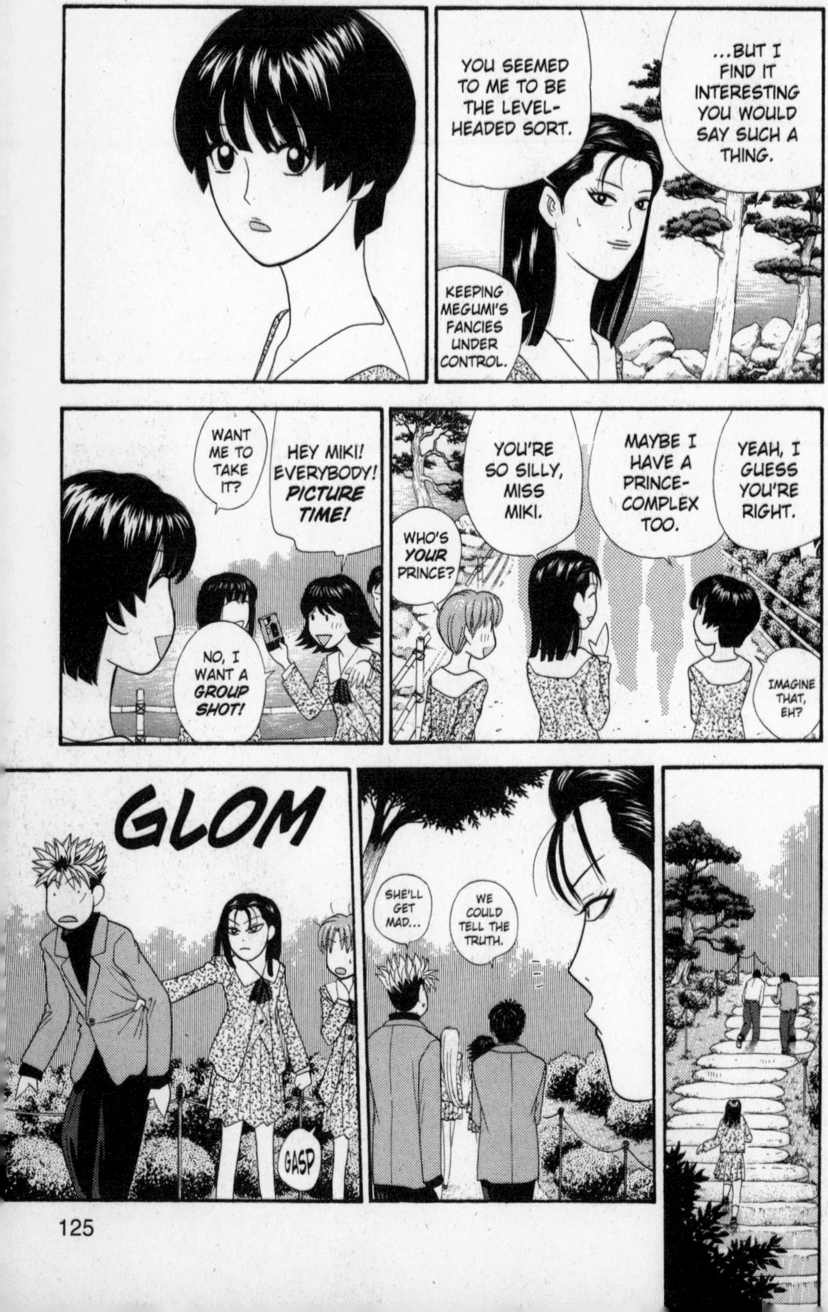
...BUT I FIND IT INTERESTING YOU WOULD SAY SUCH A THING.
YOU SEEMED TO ME TO BE THE LEVEL-HEADED SORT.
KEEPING MEGUMI'S FANCIES UNDER CONTROL.
YEAH, I GUESS YOU'RE RIGHT.
MAYBE I HAVE A PRINCE-COMPLEX TOO.
YOU'RE SO SILLY, MISS MIKI.
WHO'S *YOUR* PRINCE?
IMAGINE THAT, EH?
HEY MIKI! EVERYBODY! *PICTURE TIME!*
WANT ME TO TAKE IT?
NO, I WANT A *GROUP SHOT!*
WE COULD TELL THE TRUTH.
SHE'LL GET MAD...
GLOM
GASP

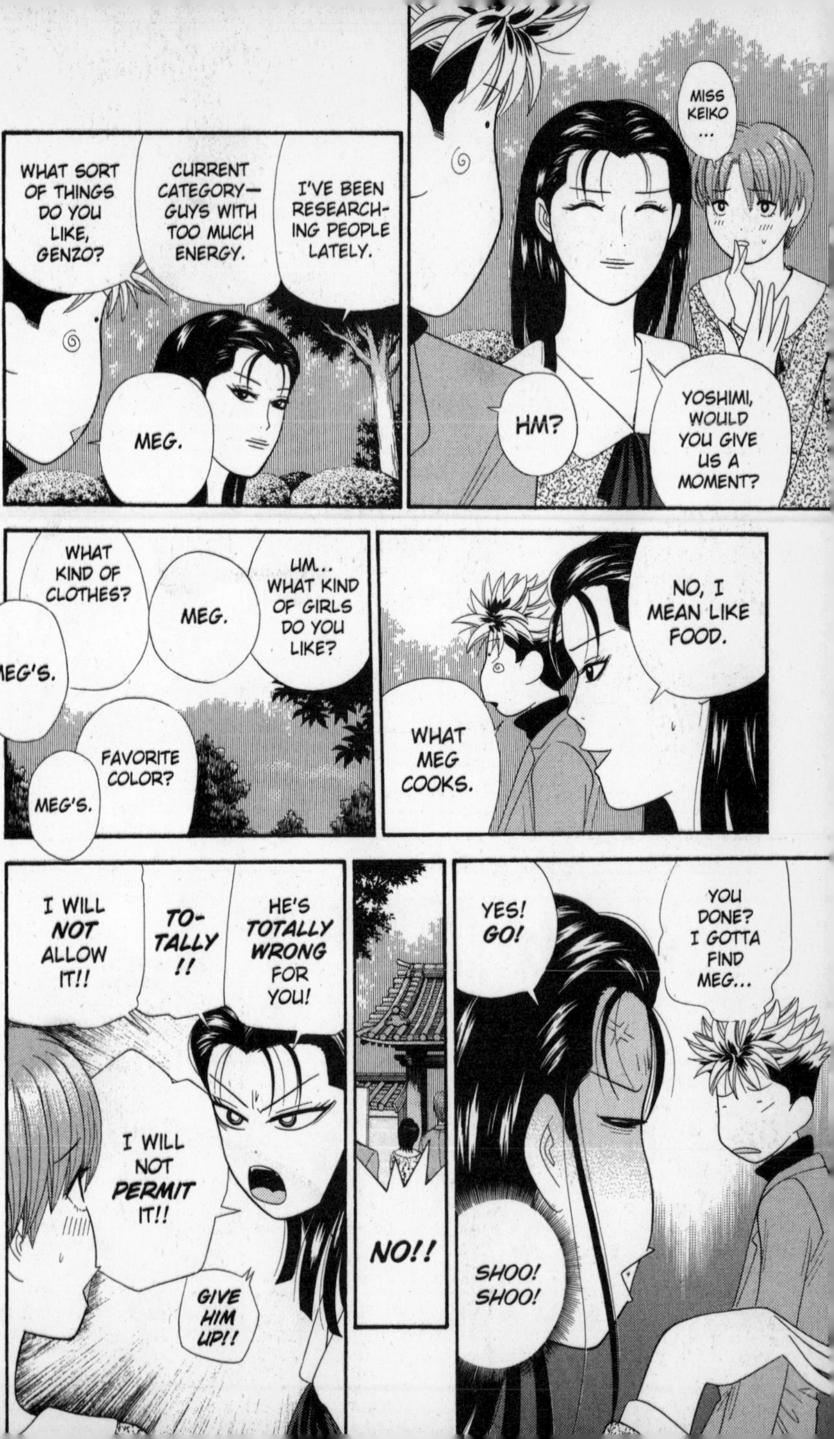
MISS KEIKO ...
YOSHIMI, WOULD YOU GIVE US A MOMENT?
HM?
I'VE BEEN RESEARCHING PEOPLE LATELY.
CURRENT CATEGORY—GUYS WITH TOO MUCH ENERGY.
WHAT SORT OF THINGS DO YOU LIKE, GENZO?
MEG.
NO, I MEAN LIKE FOOD.
WHAT MEG COOKS.
UM.. WHAT KIND OF GIRLS DO YOU LIKE?
MEG.
WHAT KIND OF CLOTHES?
MEG'S.
FAVORITE COLOR?
MEG'S.
YOU DONE? I GOTTA FIND MEG...
YES! GO!
SHOO! SHOO!
NO!!
HE'S TOTALLY WRONG FOR YOU!
TO-TALLY!!
I WILL NOT ALLOW IT!!
I WILL NOT PERMIT IT!!
GIVE HIM UP!!

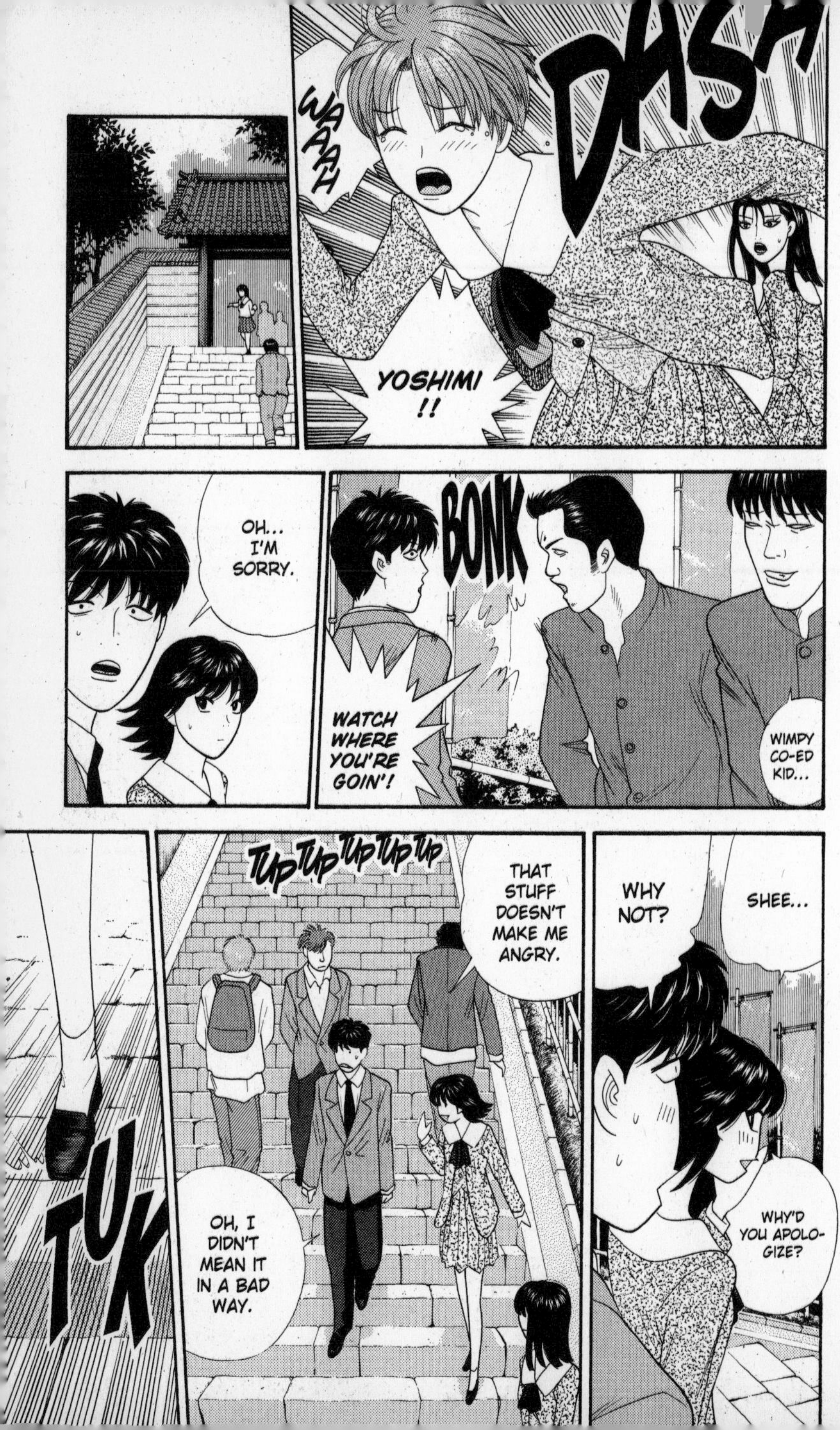
DASH
WAAAH
YOSHIMI !!
OH... I'M SORRY.
BONK
WIMPY CO-ED KID...
WATCH WHERE YOU'RE GOIN'!
SHEE...
WHY NOT?
WHY'D YOU APOLOGIZE?
THAT STUFF DOESN'T MAKE ME ANGRY.
TUPTUPTUPTUPTUP
OH, I DIDN'T MEAN IT IN A BAD WAY.
TUK

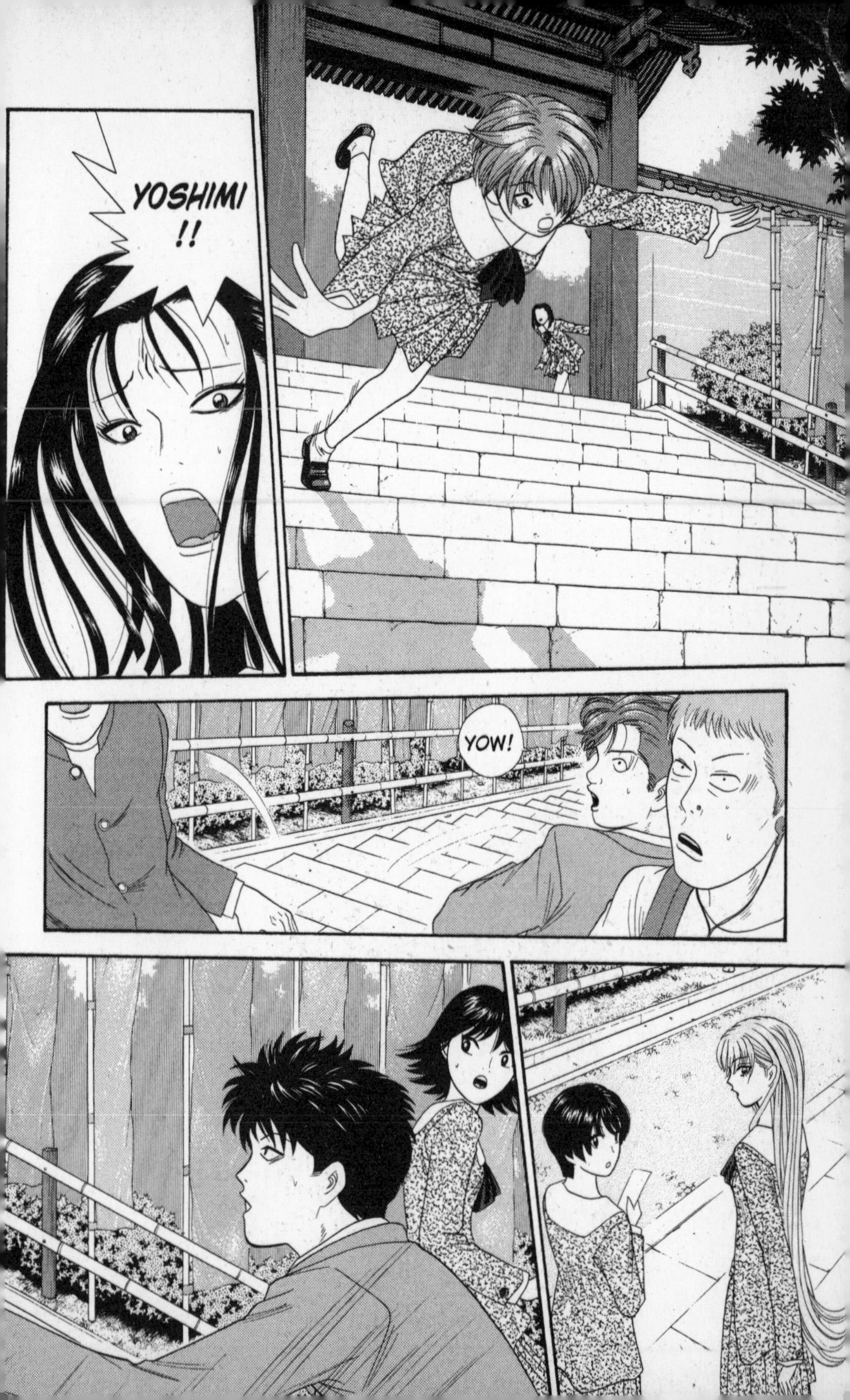
YOSHIMI !!
YOW!

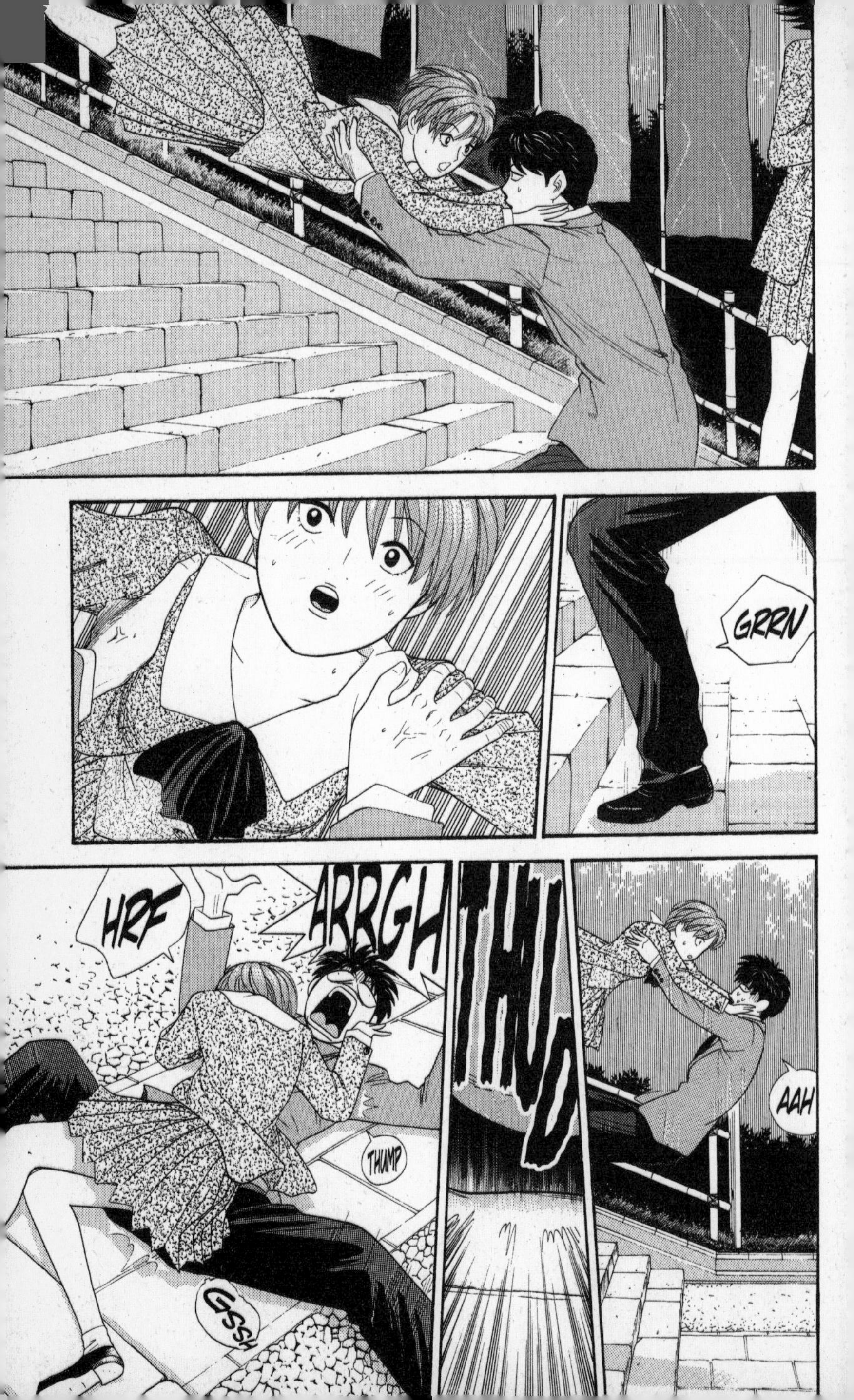
GRRN
AAH
THU
ARRGH
HRF
THUMP
GSSH

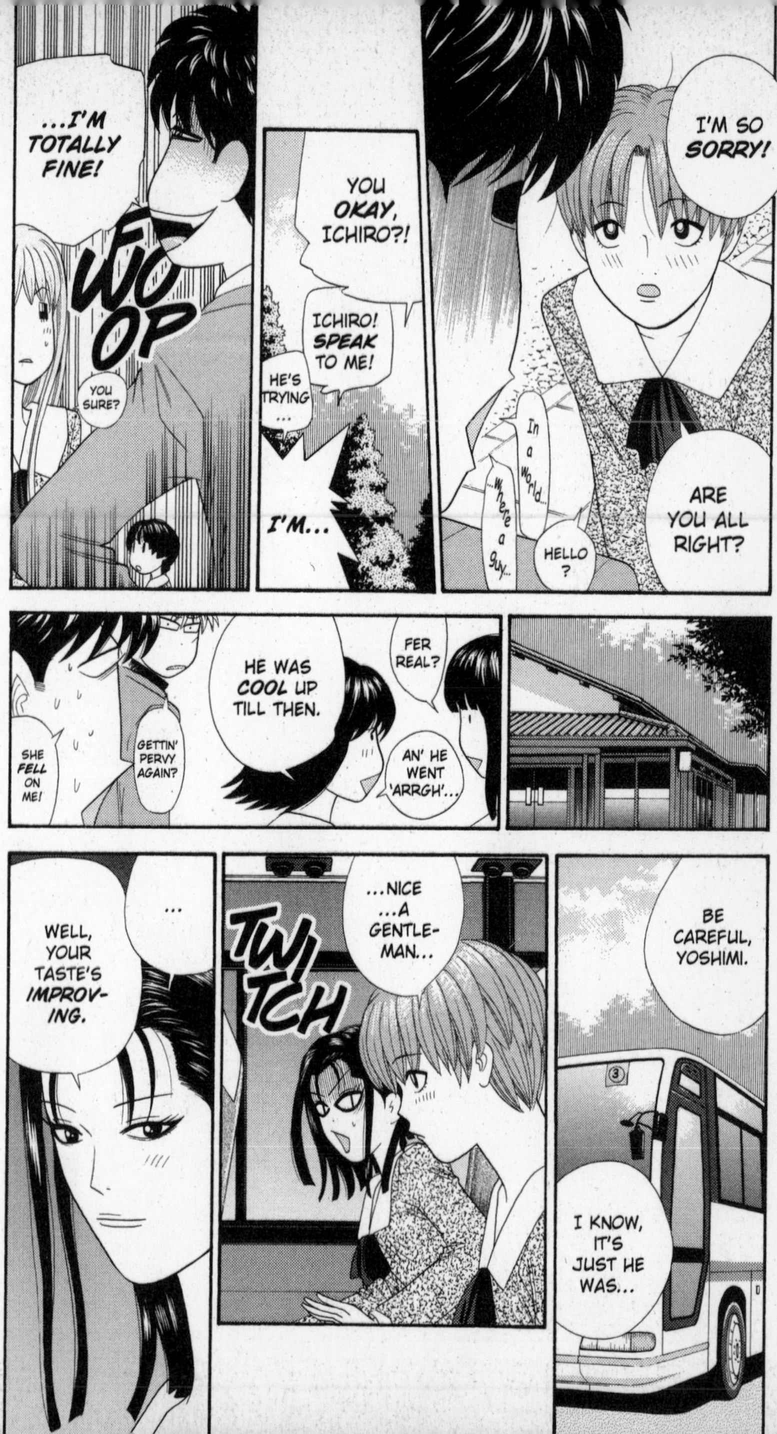
I'M SO SORRY!
ARE YOU ALL RIGHT?
In a world...
...where a guy...
HELLO?
YOU OKAY, ICHIRO?!
ICHIRO! SPEAK TO ME!
HE'S TRYING...
I'M...
...I'M TOTALLY FINE!
WOOP
YOU SURE?
FER REAL?
HE WAS COOL UP TILL THEN.
AN' HE WENT 'ARRGH'...
GETTIN' PERVY AGAIN?
SHE FELL ON ME!
BE CAREFUL, YOSHIMI.
I KNOW, IT'S JUST HE WAS...
...NICE ...A GENTLEMAN...
TWITCH
...
WELL, YOUR TASTE'S IMPROVING.

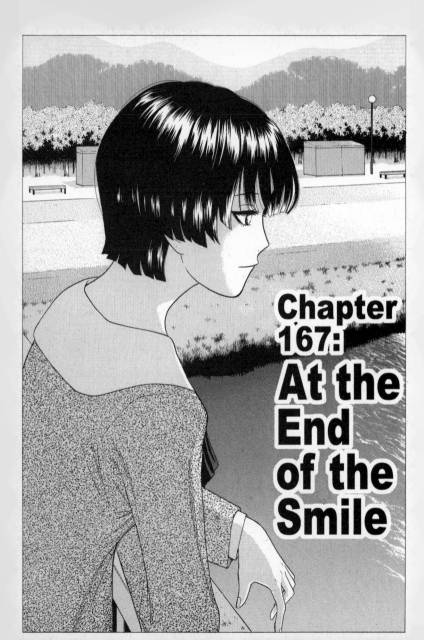

Chapter 167:
At the
End
of the
Smile

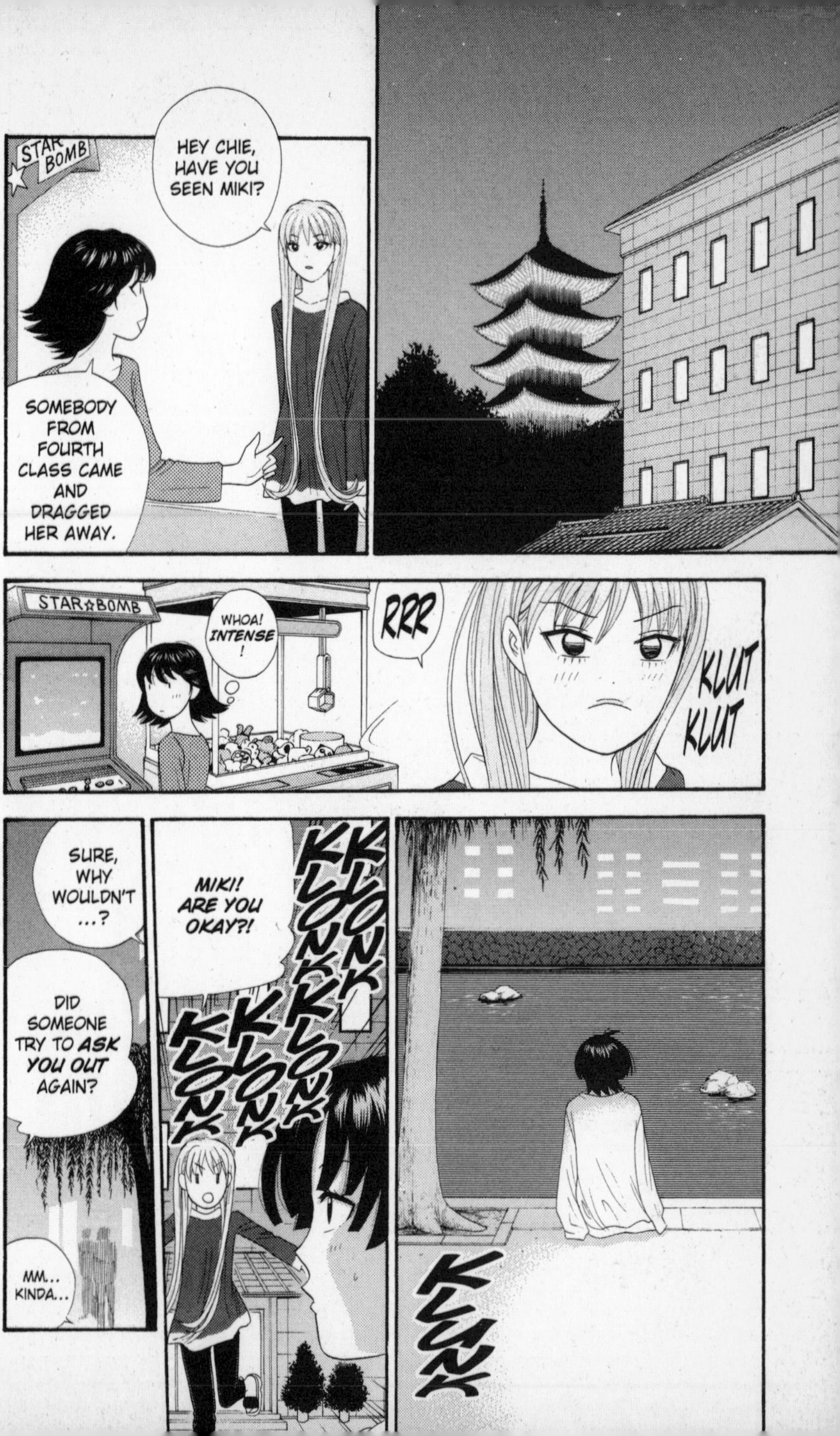

STAR BOMB
HEY CHIE, HAVE YOU SEEN MIKI?
SOMEBODY FROM FOURTH CLASS CAME AND DRAGGED HER AWAY.
KLUT KLUT
RRR
STAR☆BOMB
WHOA! INTENSE!
KLUNK
KKLONK KLONK
KKLONK KLONK
KKLONK
KLONK
MIKI! ARE YOU OKAY?!
SURE, WHY WOULDN'T...?
DID SOMEONE TRY TO ASK YOU OUT AGAIN?
MM... KINDA...

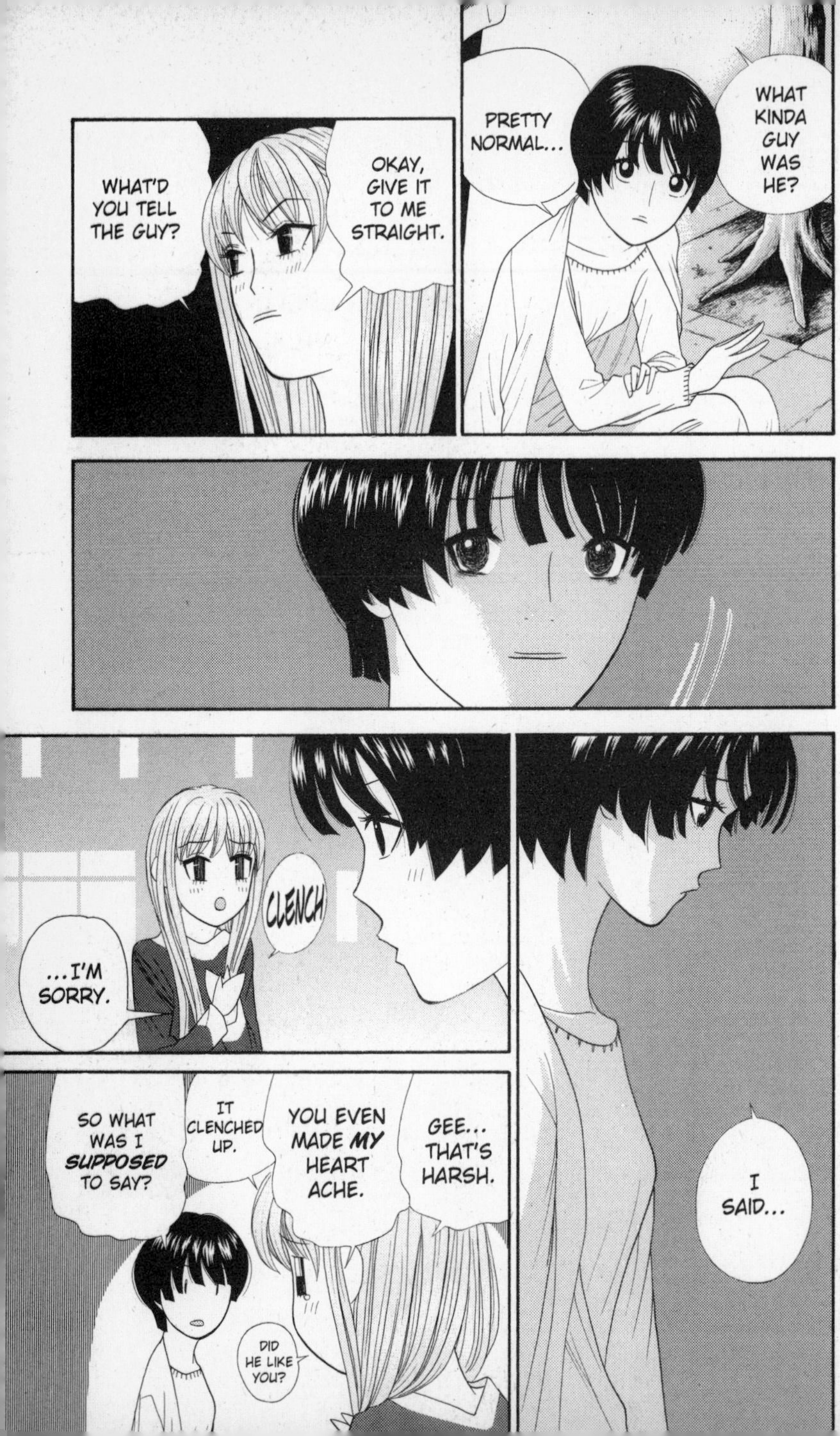
WHAT KINDA GUY WAS HE?
PRETTY NORMAL...
OKAY, GIVE IT TO ME STRAIGHT.
WHAT'D YOU TELL THE GUY?
I SAID...
CLENCH
...I'M SORRY.
GEE... THAT'S HARSH.
YOU EVEN MADE MY HEART ACHE.
IT CLENCHED UP.
SO WHAT WAS I SUPPOSED TO SAY?
DID HE LIKE YOU?

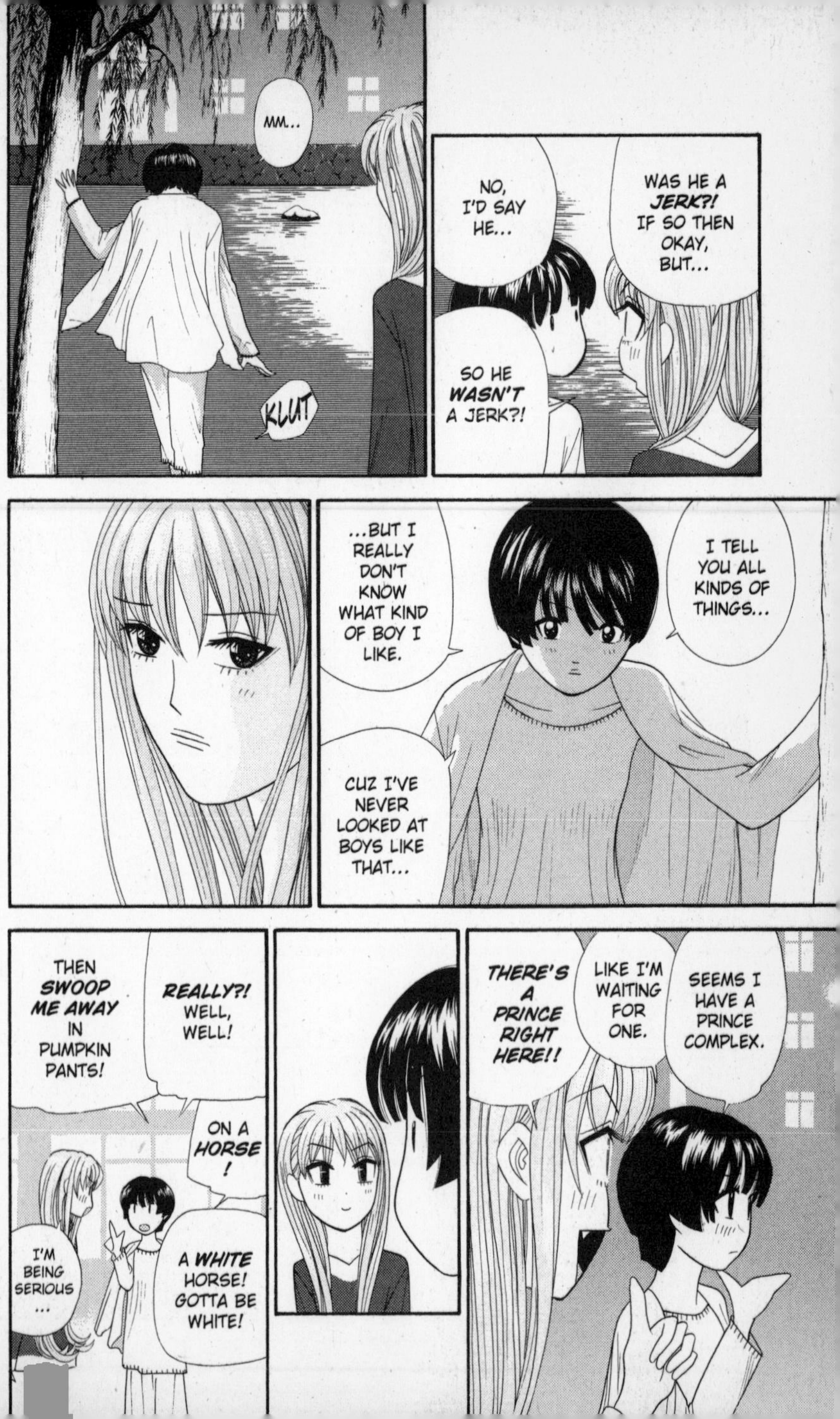
WAS HE A JERK?! IF SO THEN OKAY, BUT...
NO, I'D SAY HE...
SO HE WASN'T A JERK?!
MM...
KLUT
I TELL YOU ALL KINDS OF THINGS...
...BUT I REALLY DON'T KNOW WHAT KIND OF BOY I LIKE.
CUZ I'VE NEVER LOOKED AT BOYS LIKE THAT...
SEEMS I HAVE A PRINCE COMPLEX.
LIKE I'M WAITING FOR ONE.
THERE'S A PRINCE RIGHT HERE!!
REALLY?! WELL, WELL!
THEN SWOOP ME AWAY IN PUMPKIN PANTS!
ON A HORSE!
A WHITE HORSE! GOTTA BE WHITE!
I'M BEING SERIOUS...

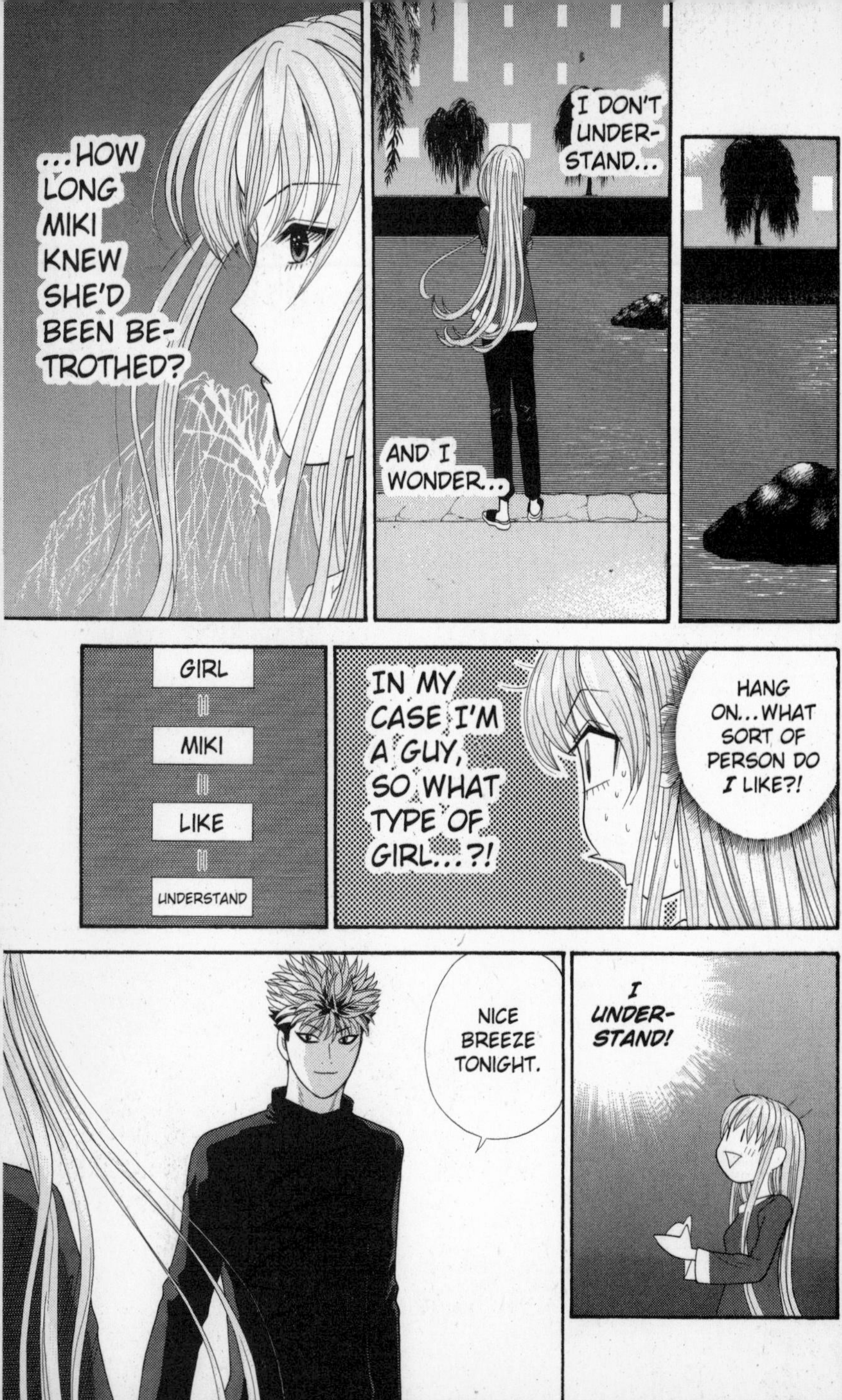
I DON'T UNDER-STAND...
AND I WONDER...
...HOW LONG MIKI KNEW SHE'D BEEN BE-TROTHED?
HANG ON...WHAT SORT OF PERSON DO I LIKE?!
IN MY CASE I'M A GUY, SO WHAT TYPE OF GIRL...?!
GIRL
=
MIKI
=
LIKE
=
UNDERSTAND
I UNDER-STAND!
NICE BREEZE TONIGHT.

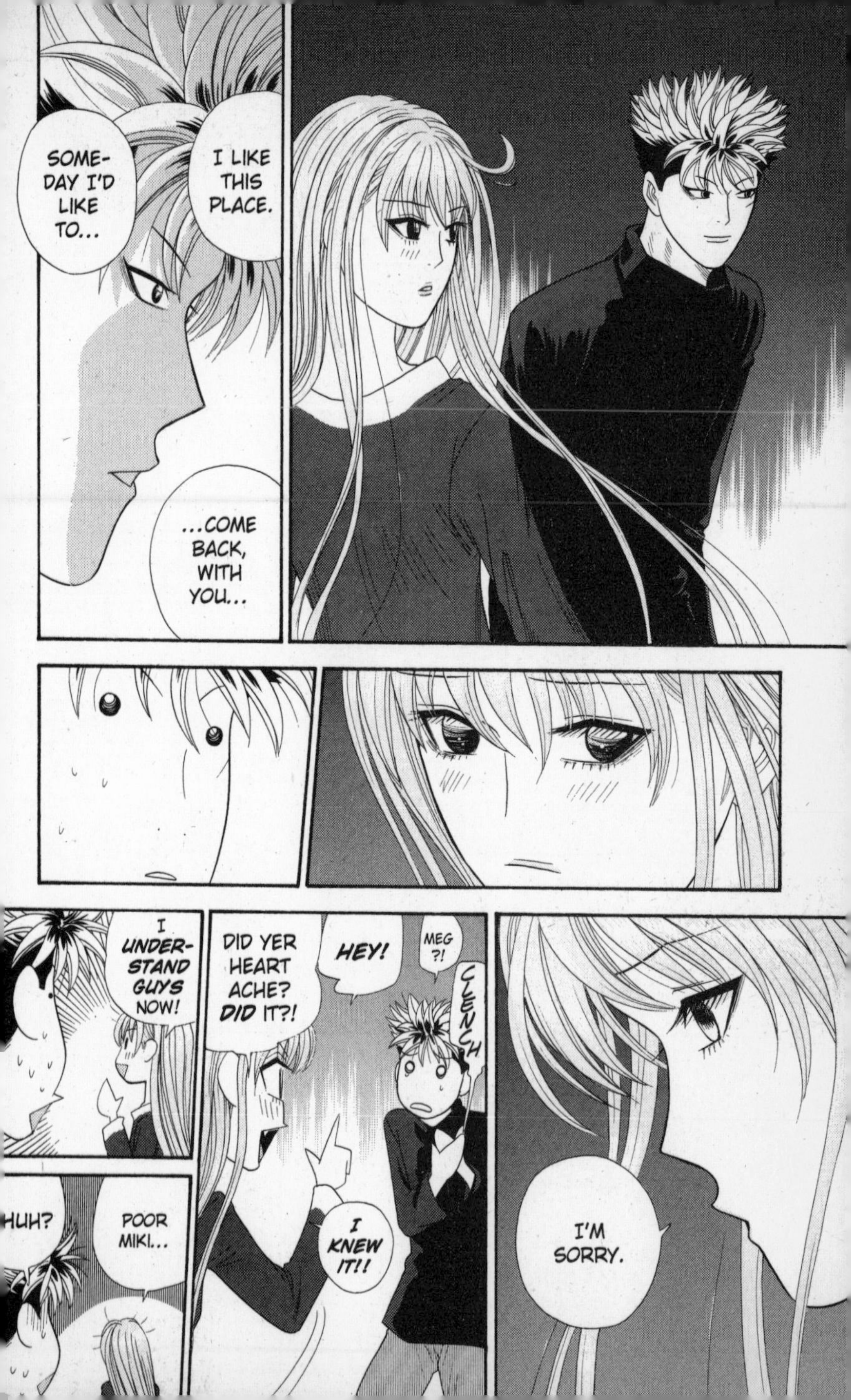
I LIKE THIS PLACE.
SOME-DAY I'D LIKE TO...
...COME BACK, WITH YOU...
I'M SORRY.
MEG ?!
CLENCH
HEY!
DID YER HEART ACHE? ***DID*** IT?!
I KNEW IT!!
I ***UNDER-STAND GUYS*** NOW!
POOR MIKI...
HUH?

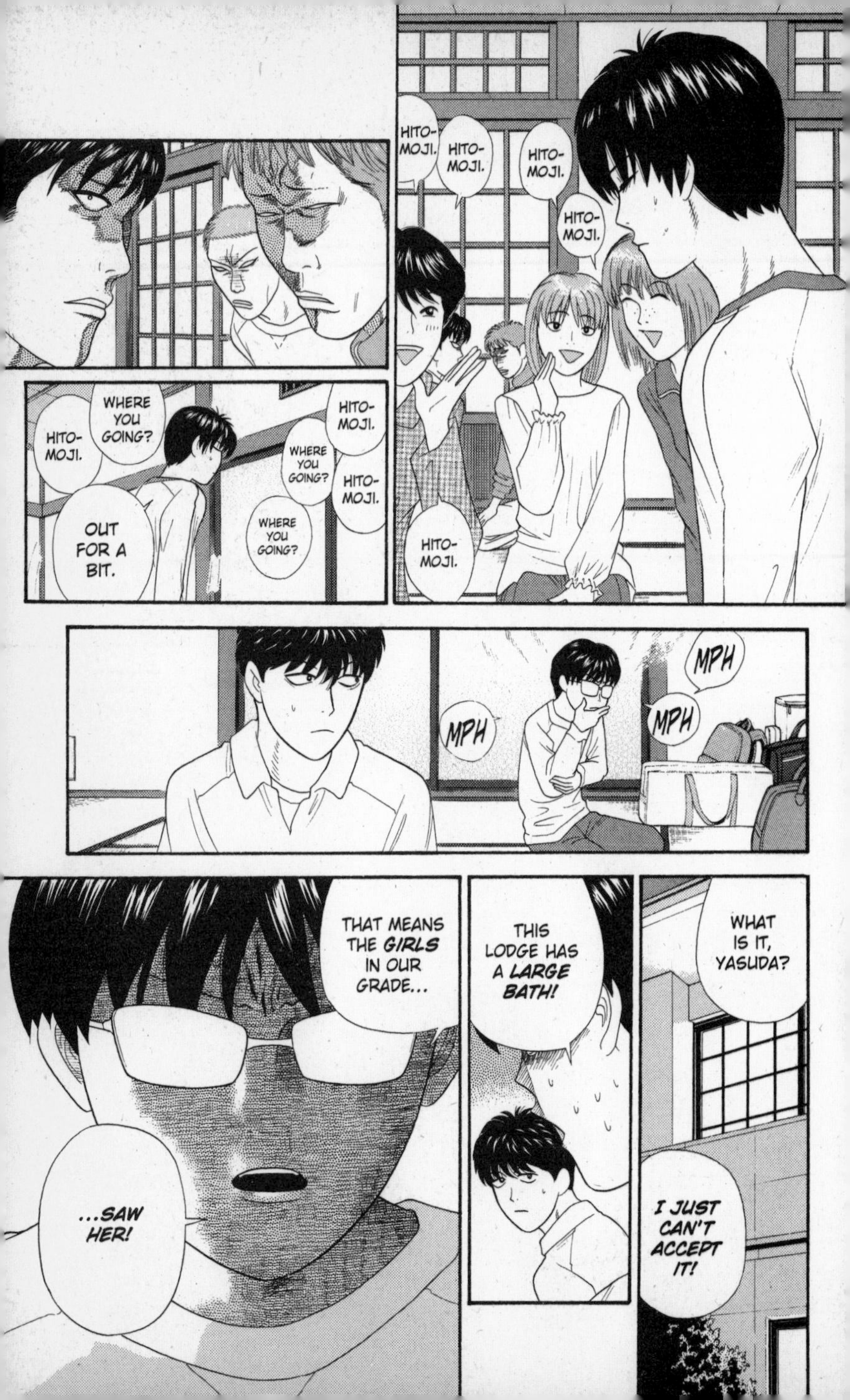
HITO-MOJI.
HITO-MOJI.
HITO-MOJI.
HITO-MOJI.
HITO-MOJI.
HITO-MOJI.
WHERE YOU GOING?
HITO-MOJI.
WHERE YOU GOING?
WHERE YOU GOING?
HITO-MOJI.
WHERE YOU GOING?
HITO-MOJI.
OUT FOR A BIT.
MPH
MPH
MPH
WHAT IS IT, YASUDA?
I JUST CAN'T ACCEPT IT!
THIS LODGE HAS A LARGE BATH!
THAT MEANS THE GIRLS IN OUR GRADE...
...SAW HER!

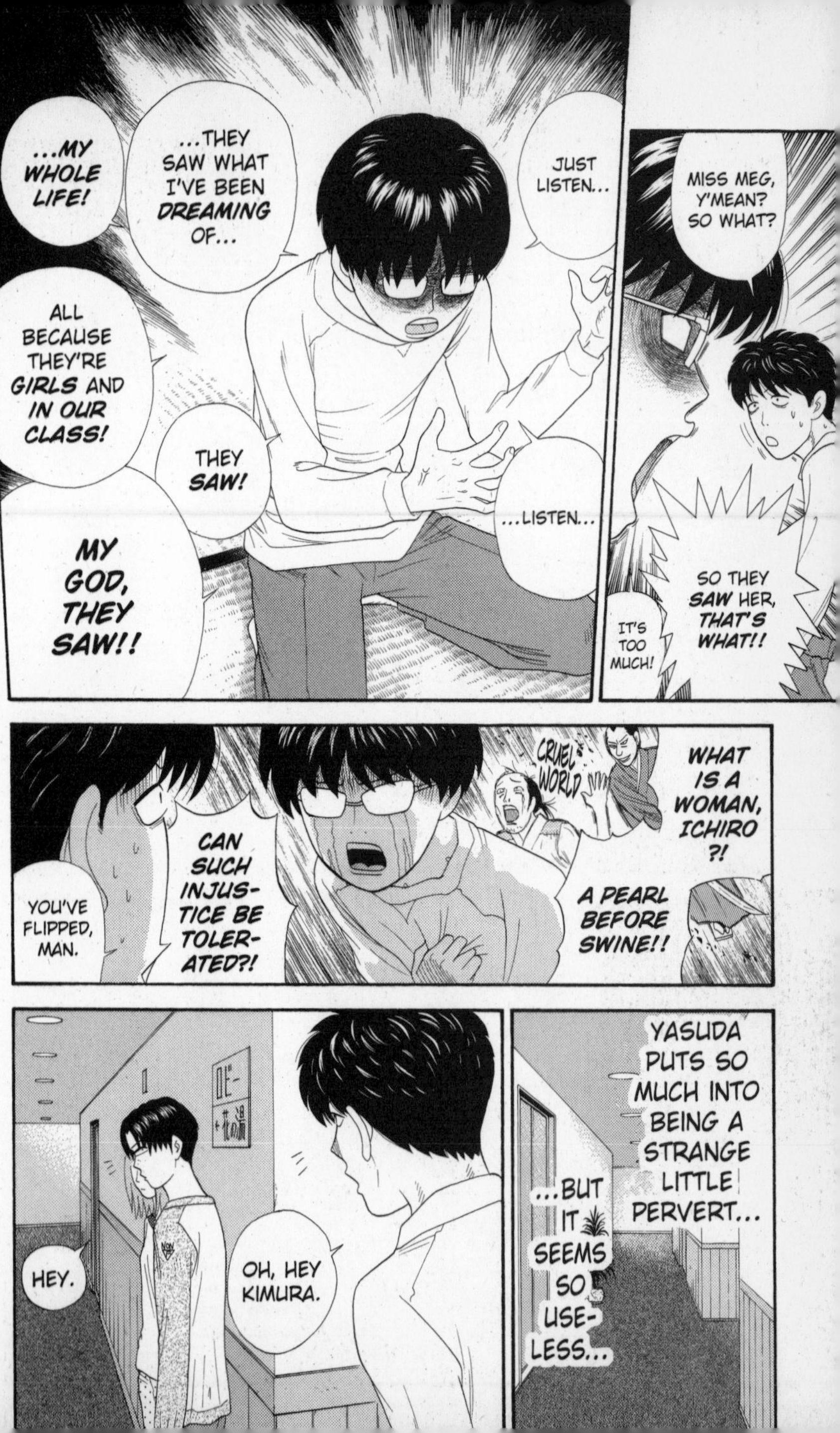
MISS MEG, Y'MEAN? SO WHAT?
SO THEY SAW HER, THAT'S WHAT!!
IT'S TOO MUCH!
JUST LISTEN...
...THEY SAW WHAT I'VE BEEN DREAMING OF...
...MY WHOLE LIFE!
ALL BECAUSE THEY'RE GIRLS AND IN OUR CLASS!
...LISTEN...
THEY SAW!
MY GOD, THEY SAW!!
WHAT IS A WOMAN, ICHIRO?!
CRUEL WORLD
A PEARL BEFORE SWINE!!
CAN SUCH INJUSTICE BE TOLERATED?!
YOU'VE FLIPPED, MAN.
YASUDA PUTS SO MUCH INTO BEING A STRANGE LITTLE PERVERT...
...BUT IT SEEMS SO USELESS...
OH, HEY KIMURA.
HEY.

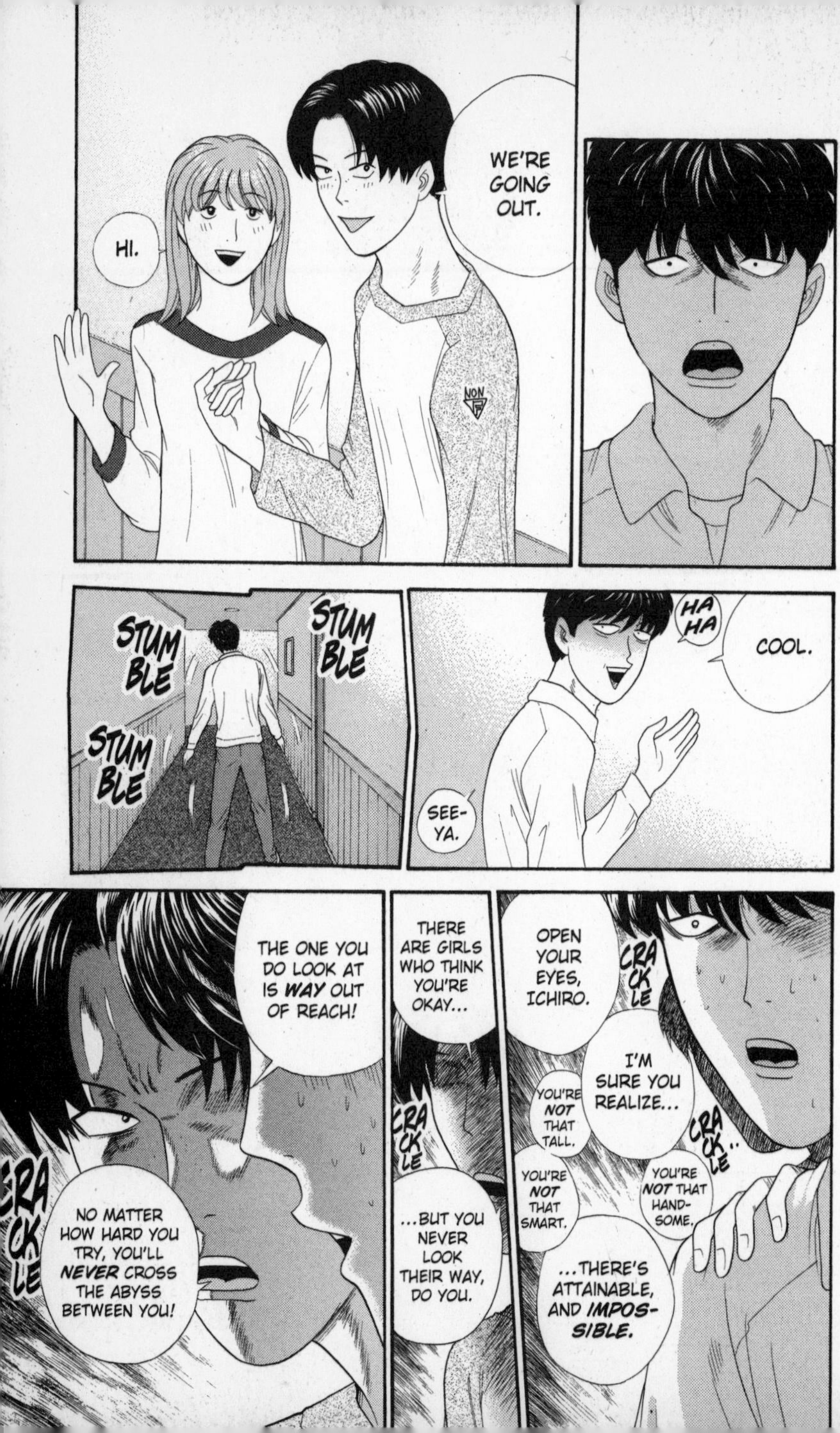
WE'RE GOING OUT.
HI.
HA HA
COOL.
SEE-YA.
STUMBLE
STUMBLE
STUMBLE
OPEN YOUR EYES, ICHIRO.
CRACKLE
I'M SURE YOU REALIZE...
YOU'RE *NOT* THAT TALL.
CRACKLE..
YOU'RE *NOT* THAT HANDSOME.
YOU'RE *NOT* THAT SMART.
...THERE'S ATTAINABLE, AND ***IMPOSSIBLE.***
THERE ARE GIRLS WHO THINK YOU'RE OKAY...
CRACKLE
...BUT YOU NEVER LOOK THEIR WAY, DO YOU.
THE ONE YOU DO LOOK AT IS ***WAY*** OUT OF REACH!
CRACKLE
NO MATTER HOW HARD YOU TRY, YOU'LL ***NEVER*** CROSS THE ABYSS BETWEEN YOU!

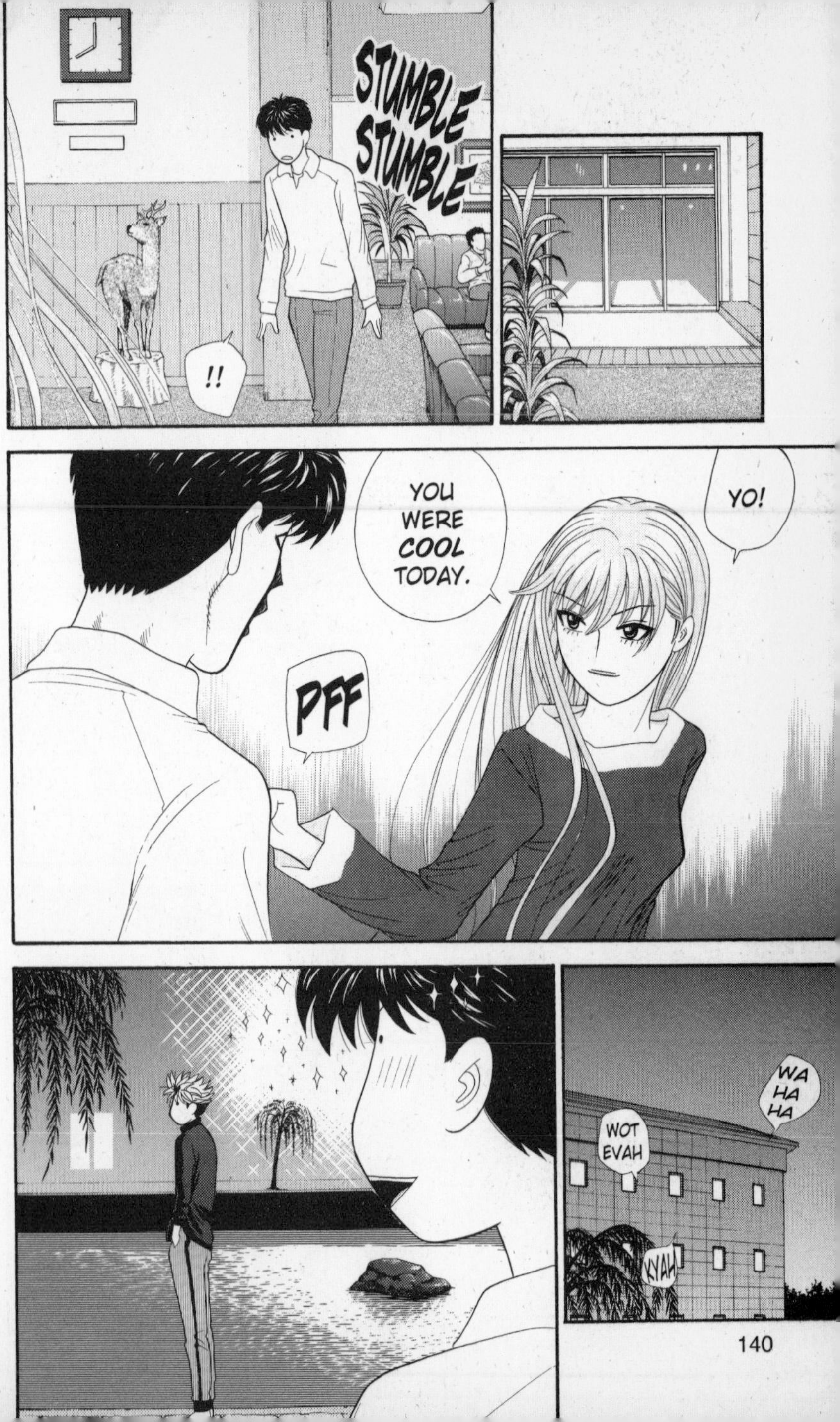
STUMBLE STUMBLE
!!
YO!
YOU WERE COOL TODAY.
PFF
WA HA HA
WOT EVAH
KYAH

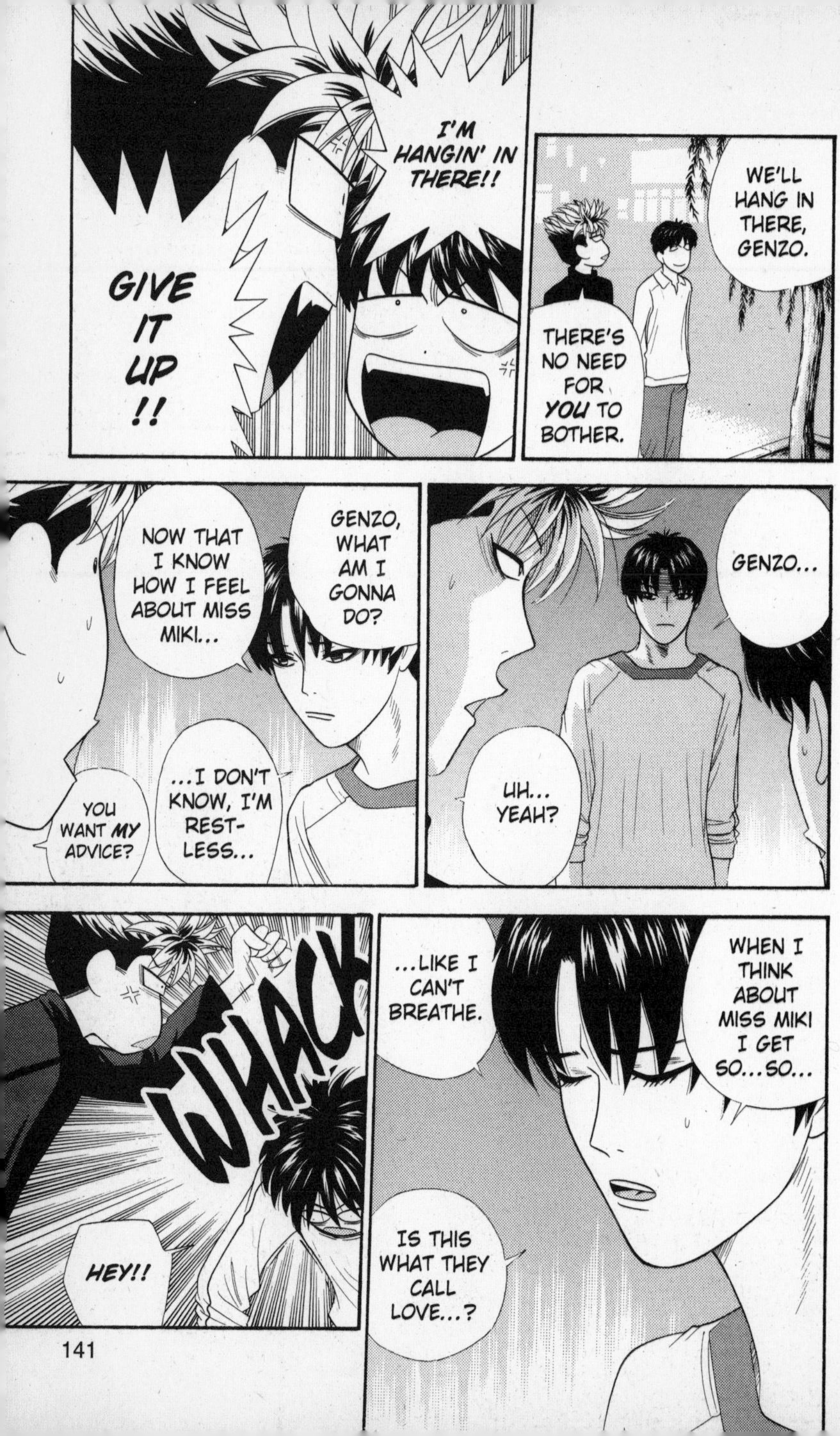
WE'LL HANG IN THERE, GENZO.
THERE'S NO NEED FOR YOU TO BOTHER.
I'M HANGIN' IN THERE!!
GIVE IT UP!!
GENZO...
UH... YEAH?
GENZO, WHAT AM I GONNA DO?
NOW THAT I KNOW HOW I FEEL ABOUT MISS MIKI...
...I DON'T KNOW, I'M RESTLESS...
YOU WANT MY ADVICE?
WHEN I THINK ABOUT MISS MIKI I GET SO...SO...
...LIKE I CAN'T BREATHE.
IS THIS WHAT THEY CALL LOVE...?
WHACK
HEY!!

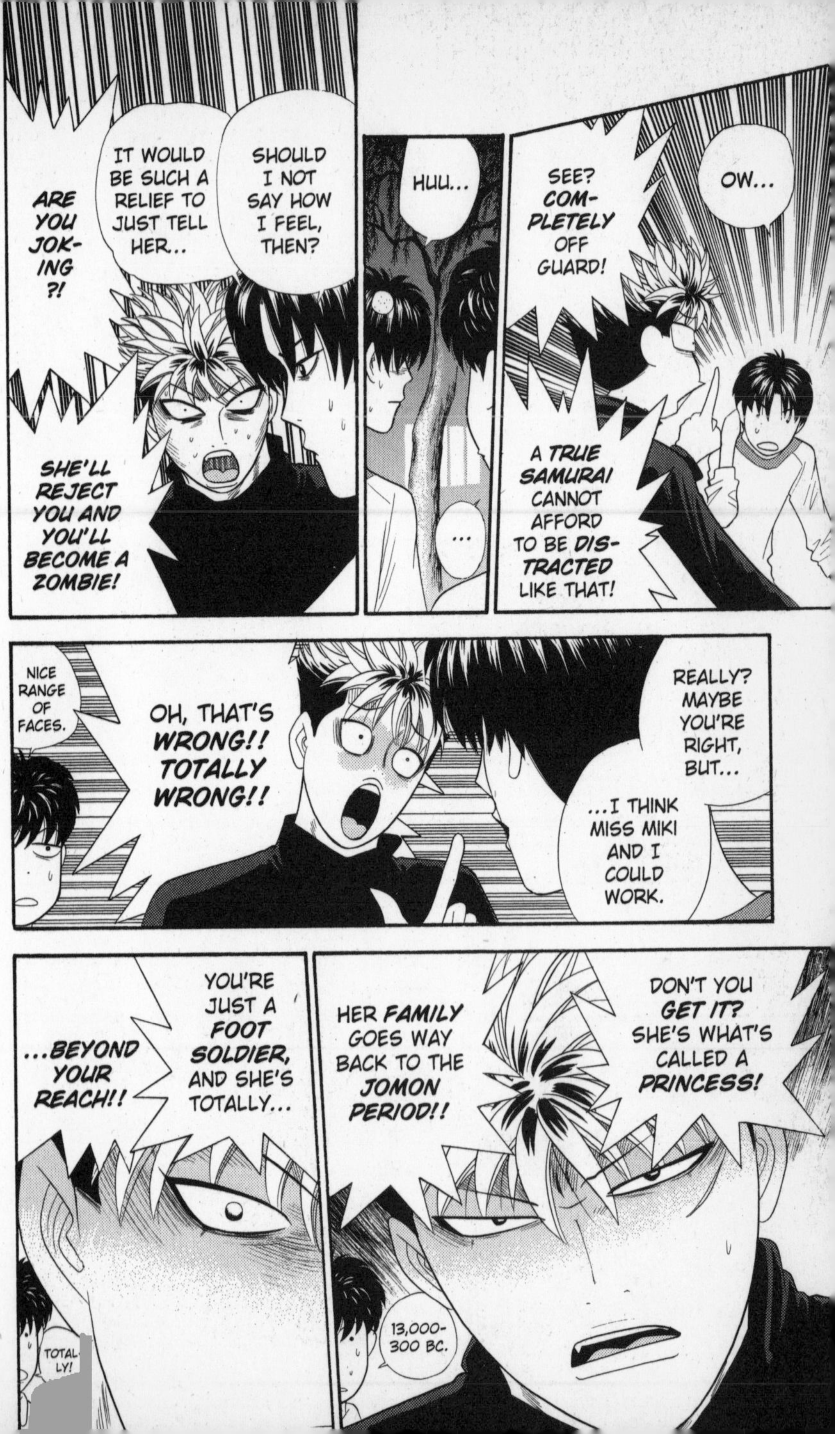
OW...
SEE? COMPLETELY OFF GUARD!
A TRUE SAMURAI CANNOT AFFORD TO BE DISTRACTED LIKE THAT!
HUU...
...
SHOULD I NOT SAY HOW I FEEL, THEN?
IT WOULD BE SUCH A RELIEF TO JUST TELL HER...
ARE YOU JOKING?!
SHE'LL REJECT YOU AND YOU'LL BECOME A ZOMBIE!
REALLY? MAYBE YOU'RE RIGHT, BUT...
...I THINK MISS MIKI AND I COULD WORK.
OH, THAT'S WRONG!! TOTALLY WRONG!!
NICE RANGE OF FACES.
DON'T YOU GET IT? SHE'S WHAT'S CALLED A PRINCESS!
HER FAMILY GOES WAY BACK TO THE JOMON PERIOD!!
13,000-300 BC.
YOU'RE JUST A FOOT SOLDIER, AND SHE'S TOTALLY...
...BEYOND YOUR REACH!!
TOTALLY!

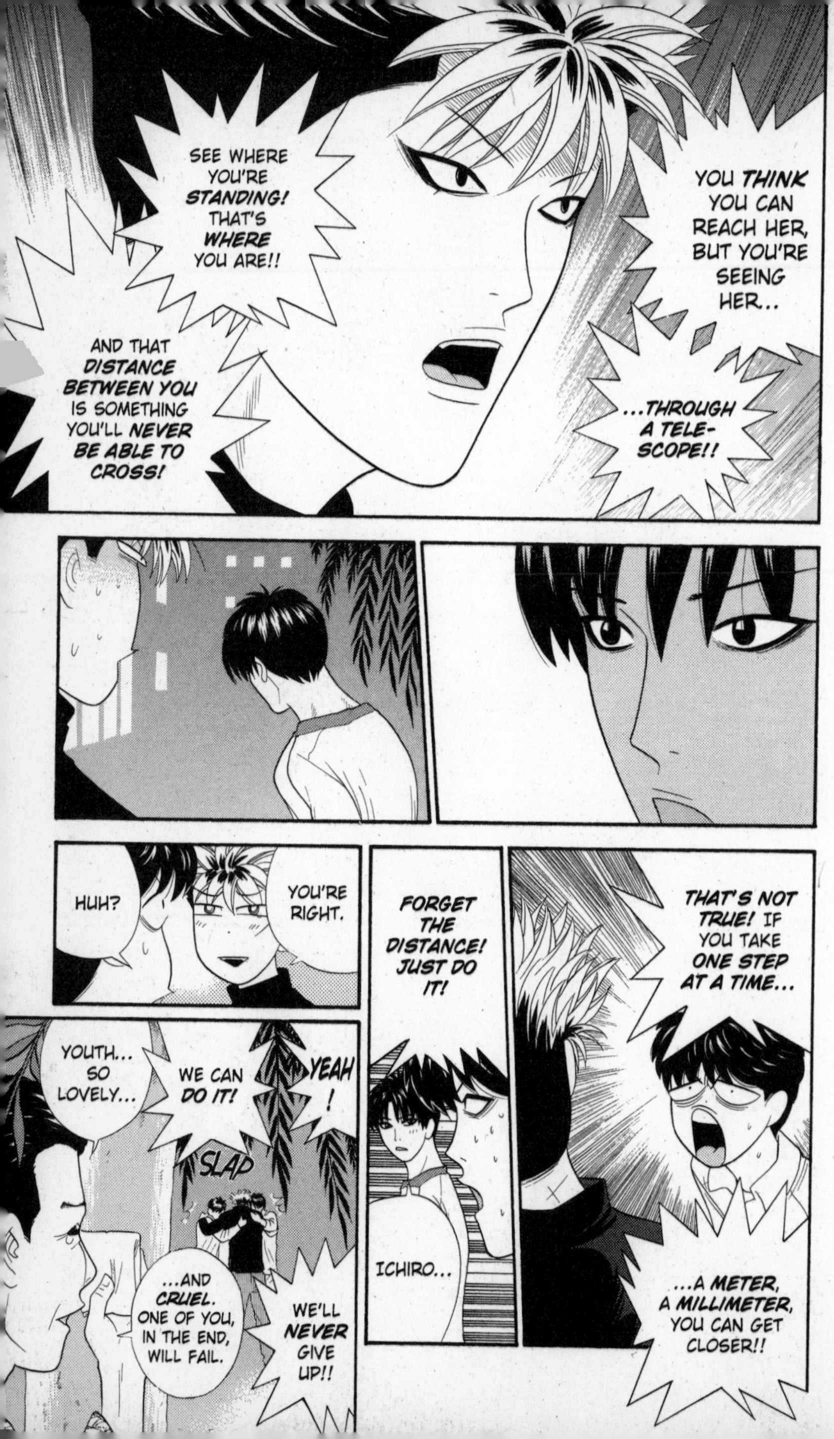
YOU THINK YOU CAN REACH HER, BUT YOU'RE SEEING HER...
...THROUGH A TELE-SCOPE!!
SEE WHERE YOU'RE STANDING! THAT'S WHERE YOU ARE!!
AND THAT DISTANCE BETWEEN YOU IS SOMETHING YOU'LL NEVER BE ABLE TO CROSS!
THAT'S NOT TRUE! IF YOU TAKE ONE STEP AT A TIME...
...A METER, A MILLIMETER, YOU CAN GET CLOSER!!
FORGET THE DISTANCE! JUST DO IT!
ICHIRO...
YOU'RE RIGHT.
HUH?
YEAH!
WE CAN DO IT!
YOUTH... SO LOVELY...
SLAP
WE'LL NEVER GIVE UP!!
...AND CRUEL. ONE OF YOU, IN THE END, WILL FAIL.

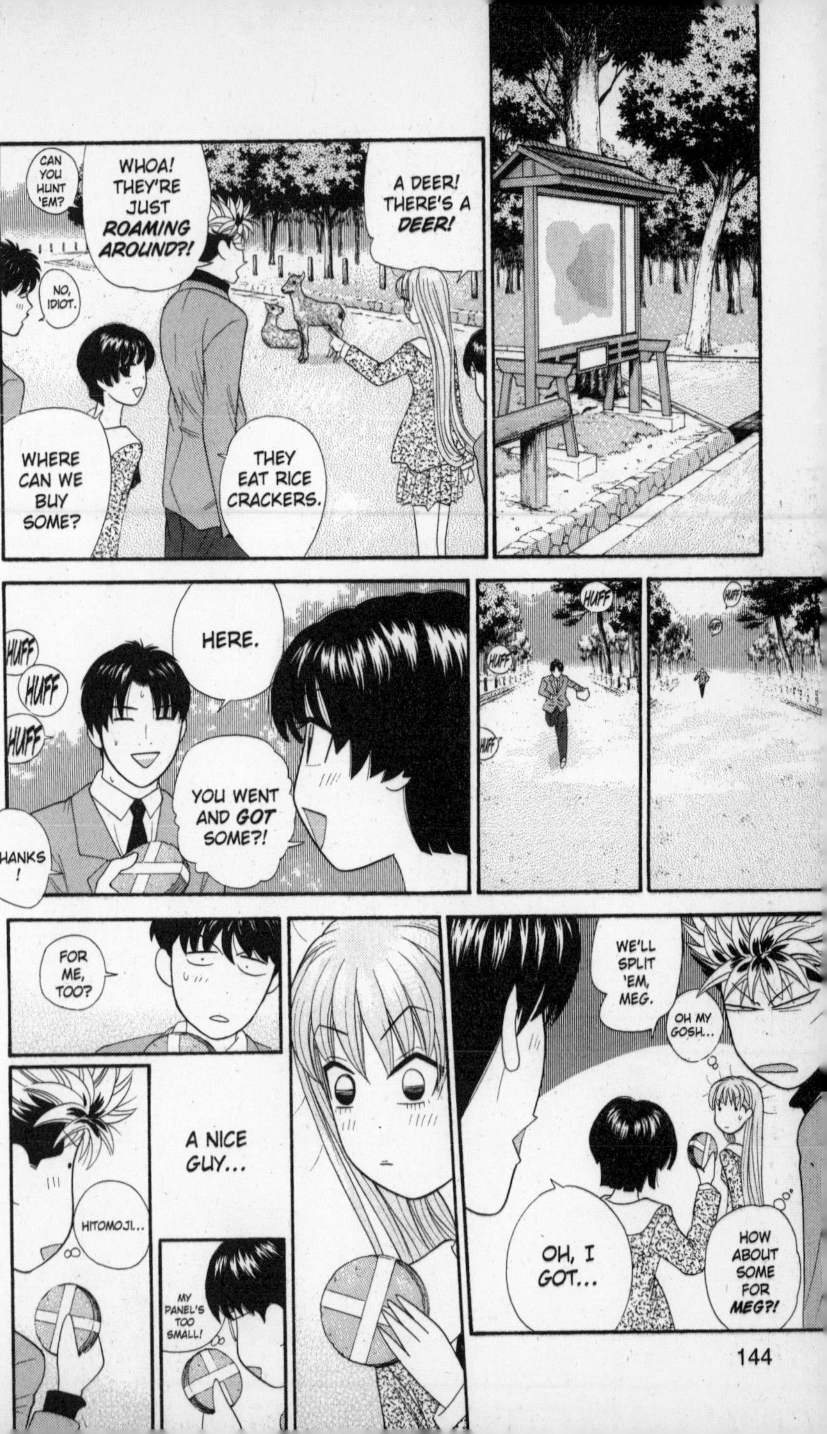
A DEER! THERE'S A DEER!
WHOA! THEY'RE JUST ROAMING AROUND?!
CAN YOU HUNT 'EM?
NO, IDIOT.
THEY EAT RICE CRACKERS.
WHERE CAN WE BUY SOME?
HUFF
HUFF
HUFF
HUFF
HERE.
HUFF
HUFF
HUFF
YOU WENT AND GOT SOME?!
THANKS!
WE'LL SPLIT 'EM, MEG.
OH MY GOSH...
HOW ABOUT SOME FOR MEG?!
OH, I GOT...
FOR ME, TOO?
A NICE GUY...
HITOMOJI...
MY PANEL'S TOO SMALL!

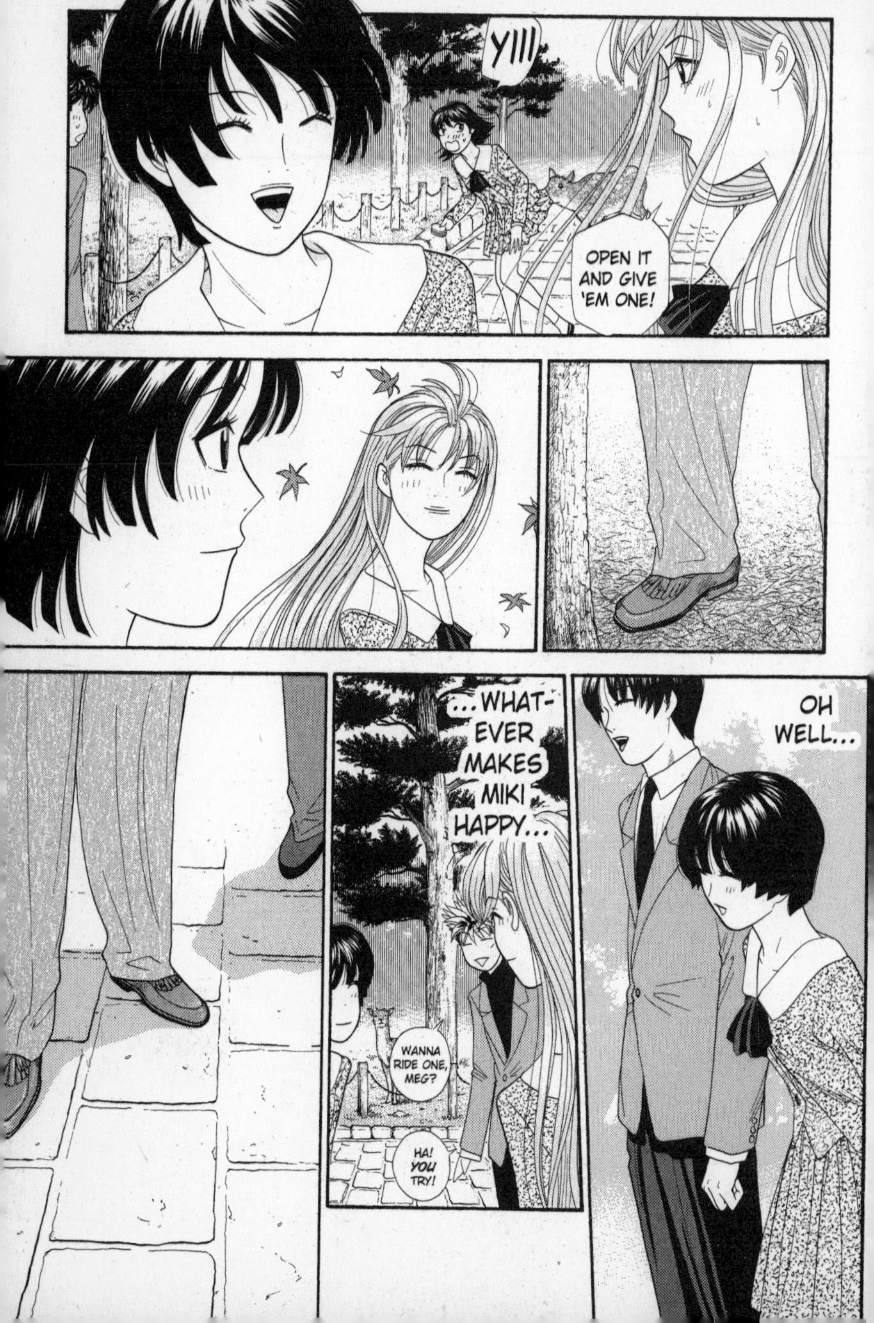
YIII
OPEN IT AND GIVE 'EM ONE!
OH WELL...
...WHAT-EVER MAKES MIKI HAPPY...
WANNA RIDE ONE, MEG?
HA! YOU TRY!

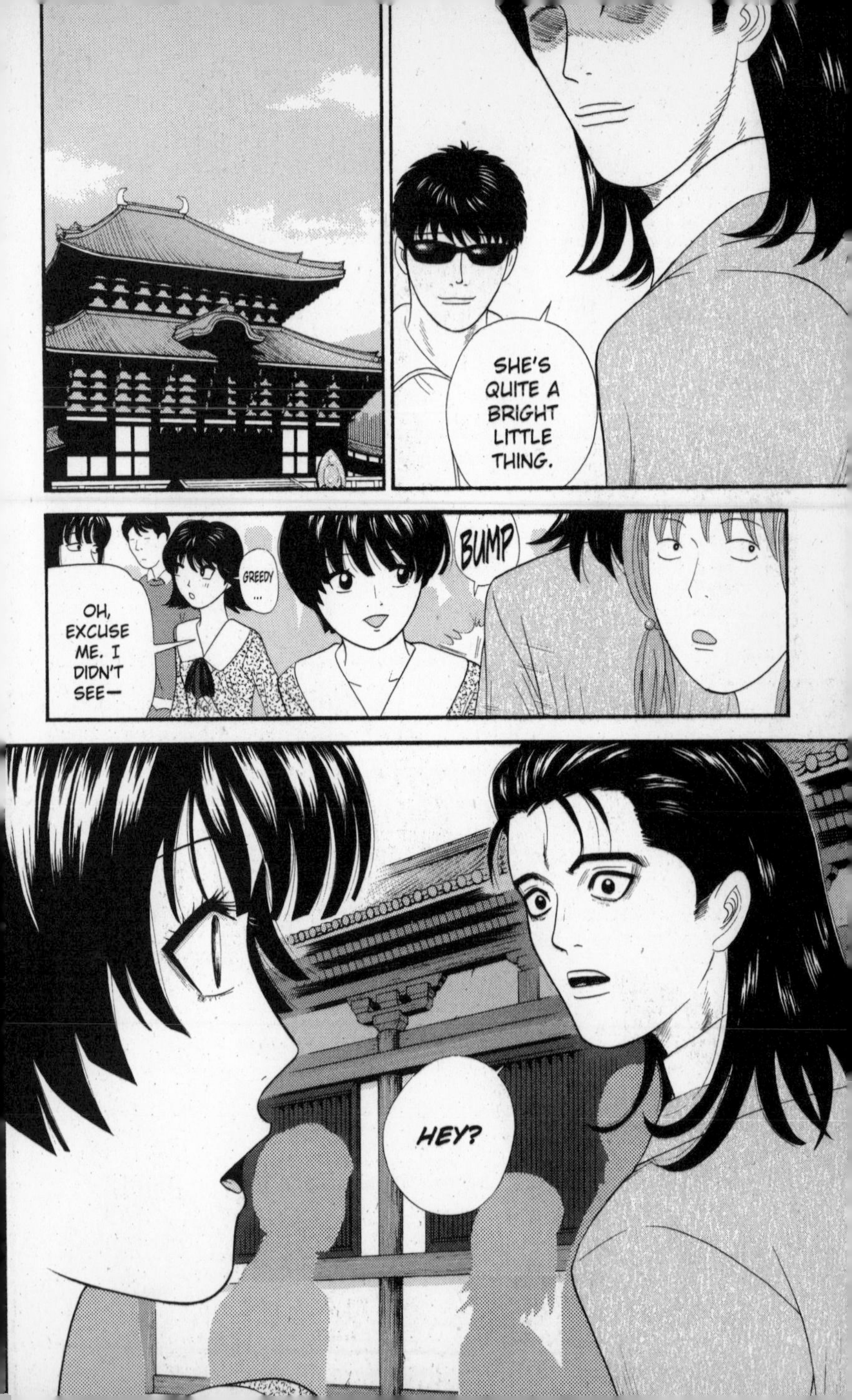
SHE'S QUITE A BRIGHT LITTLE THING.
BUMP
GREEDY ...
OH, EXCUSE ME. I DIDN'T SEE—
HEY?

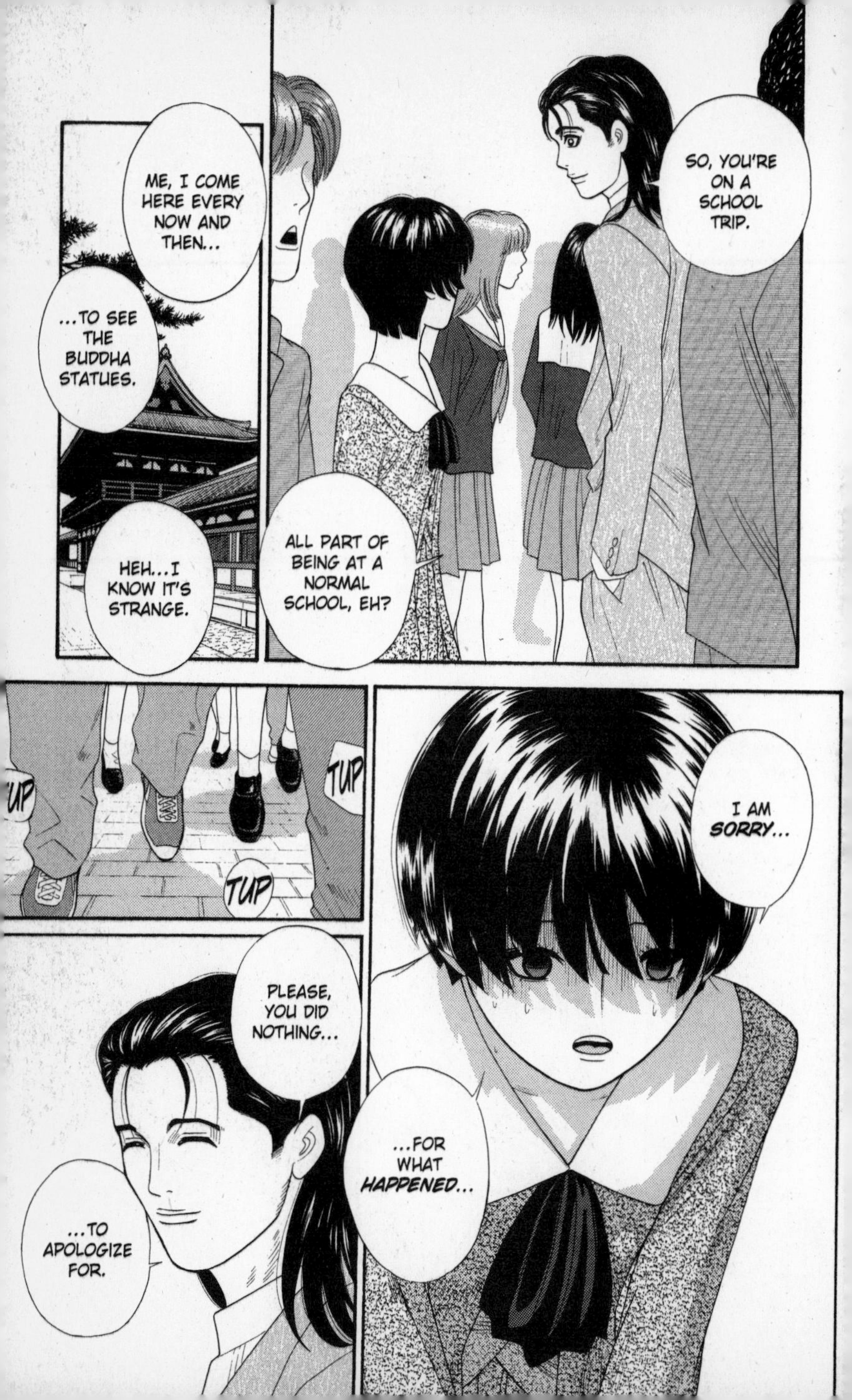
SO, YOU'RE ON A SCHOOL TRIP.
ALL PART OF BEING AT A NORMAL SCHOOL, EH?
ME, I COME HERE EVERY NOW AND THEN...
...TO SEE THE BUDDHA STATUES.
HEH...I KNOW IT'S STRANGE.
I AM *SORRY*...
...FOR WHAT *HAPPENED*...
TUP
TUP
PLEASE, YOU DID NOTHING...
...TO APOLOGIZE FOR.

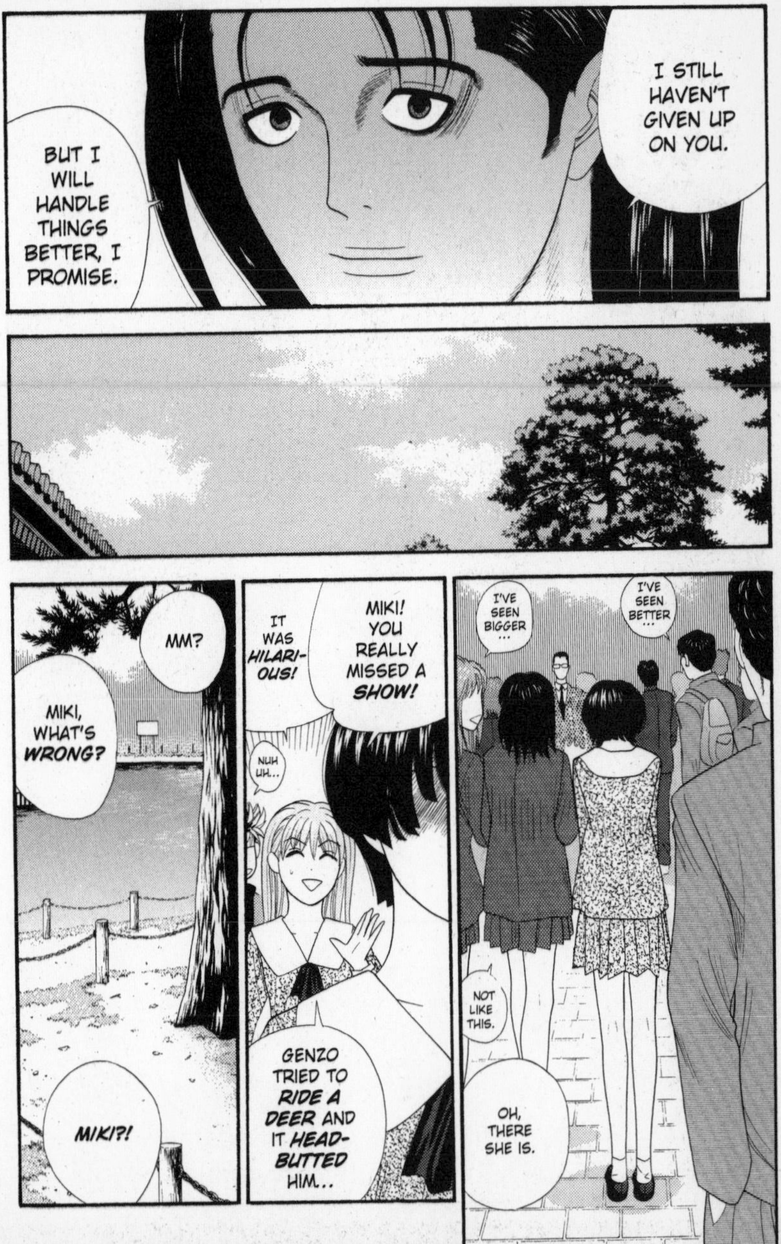
I STILL HAVEN'T GIVEN UP ON YOU.
BUT I WILL HANDLE THINGS BETTER, I PROMISE.
I'VE SEEN BETTER...
I'VE SEEN BIGGER...
NOT LIKE THIS.
OH, THERE SHE IS.
MIKI! YOU REALLY MISSED A SHOW!
IT WAS HILARI-OUS!
NUH UH...
GENZO TRIED TO RIDE A DEER AND IT HEAD-BUTTED HIM..
MM?
MIKI, WHAT'S WRONG?
MIKI?!

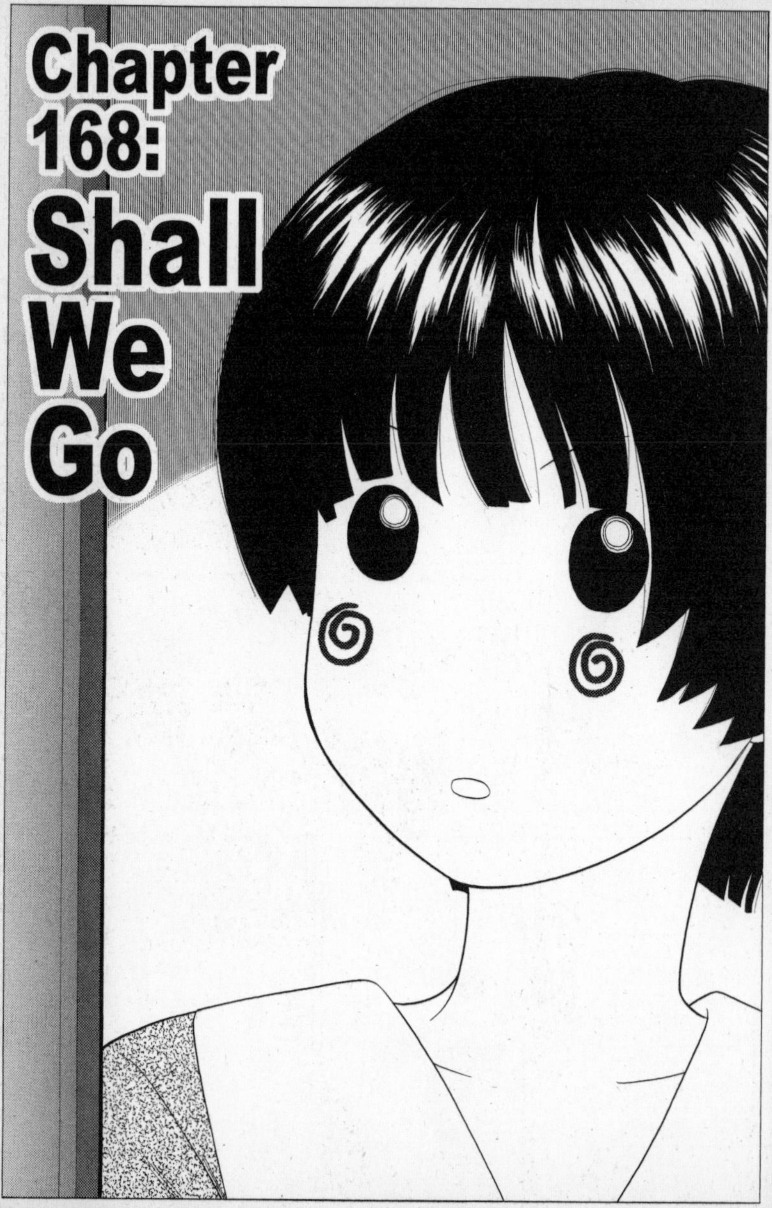
Chapter 168: Shall We Go

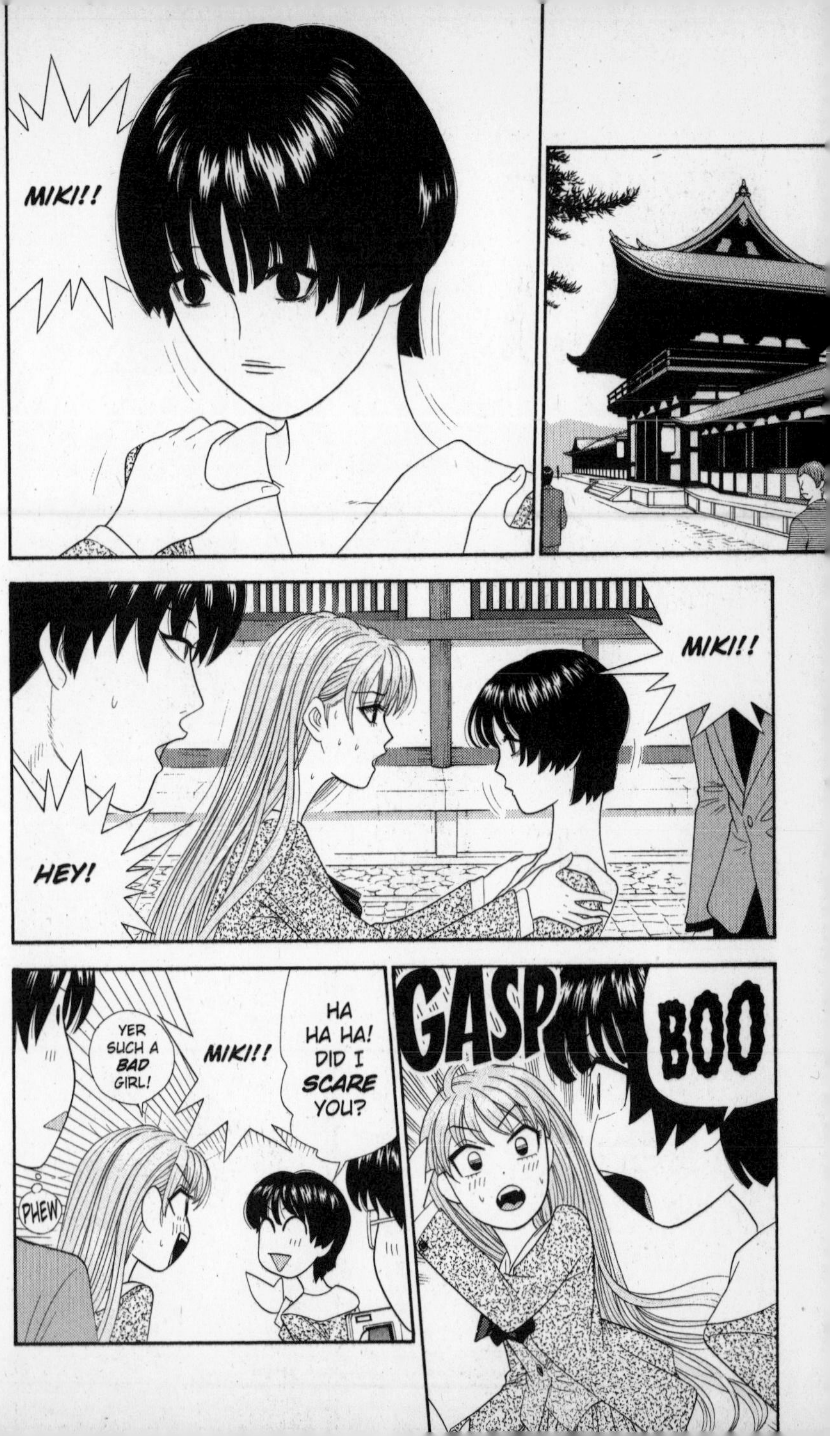
MIKI!!
MIKI!!
HEY!
BOO
GASP
HA HA HA! DID I SCARE YOU?
MIKI!!
YER SUCH A BAD GIRL!
PHEW

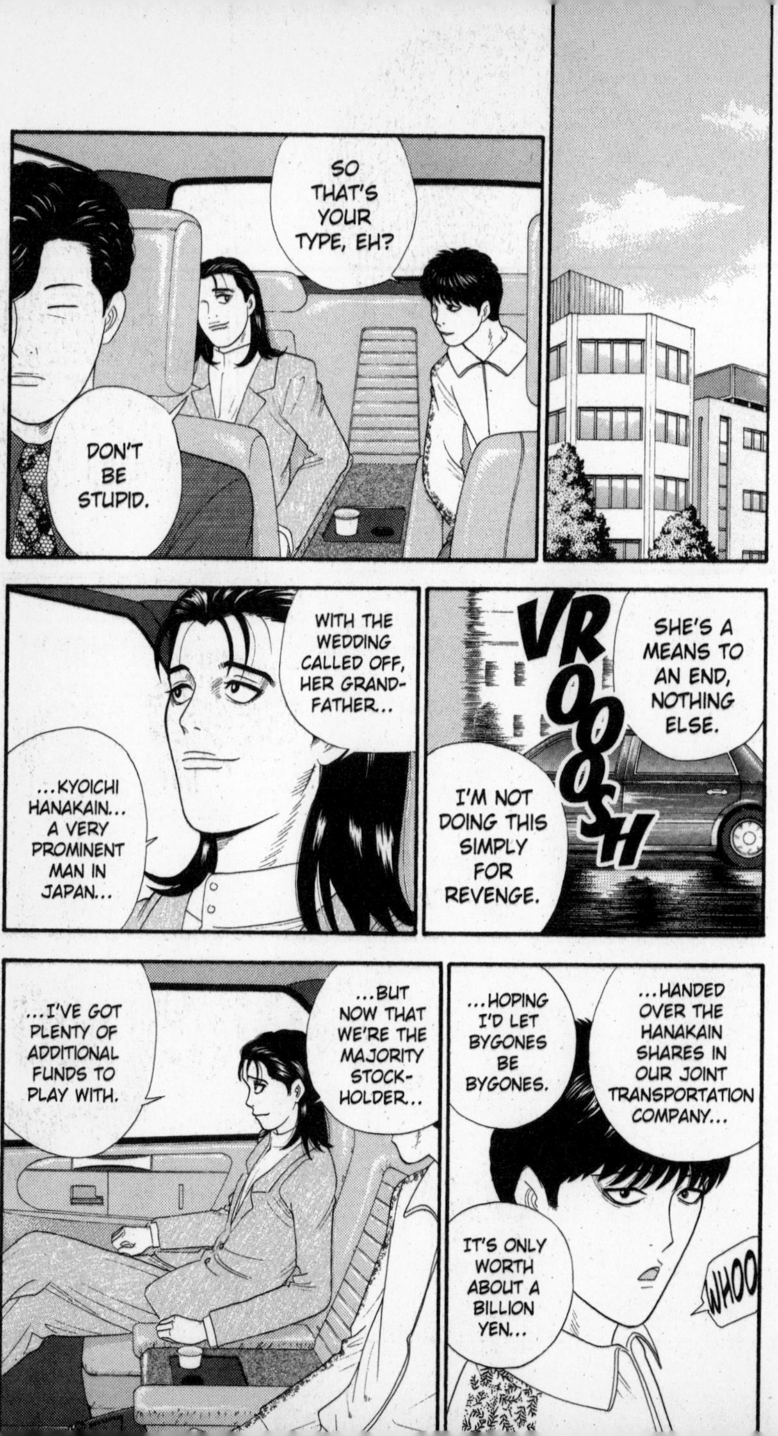
SO THAT'S YOUR TYPE, EH?
DON'T BE STUPID.
VROOOSH
SHE'S A MEANS TO AN END, NOTHING ELSE.
I'M NOT DOING THIS SIMPLY FOR REVENGE.
WITH THE WEDDING CALLED OFF, HER GRAND-FATHER...
...KYOICHI HANAKAIN... A VERY PROMINENT MAN IN JAPAN...
...HANDED OVER THE HANAKAIN SHARES IN OUR JOINT TRANSPORTATION COMPANY...
...HOPING I'D LET BYGONES BE BYGONES.
IT'S ONLY WORTH ABOUT A BILLION YEN...
WHOO
...BUT NOW THAT WE'RE THE MAJORITY STOCK-HOLDER...
...I'VE GOT PLENTY OF ADDITIONAL FUNDS TO PLAY WITH.

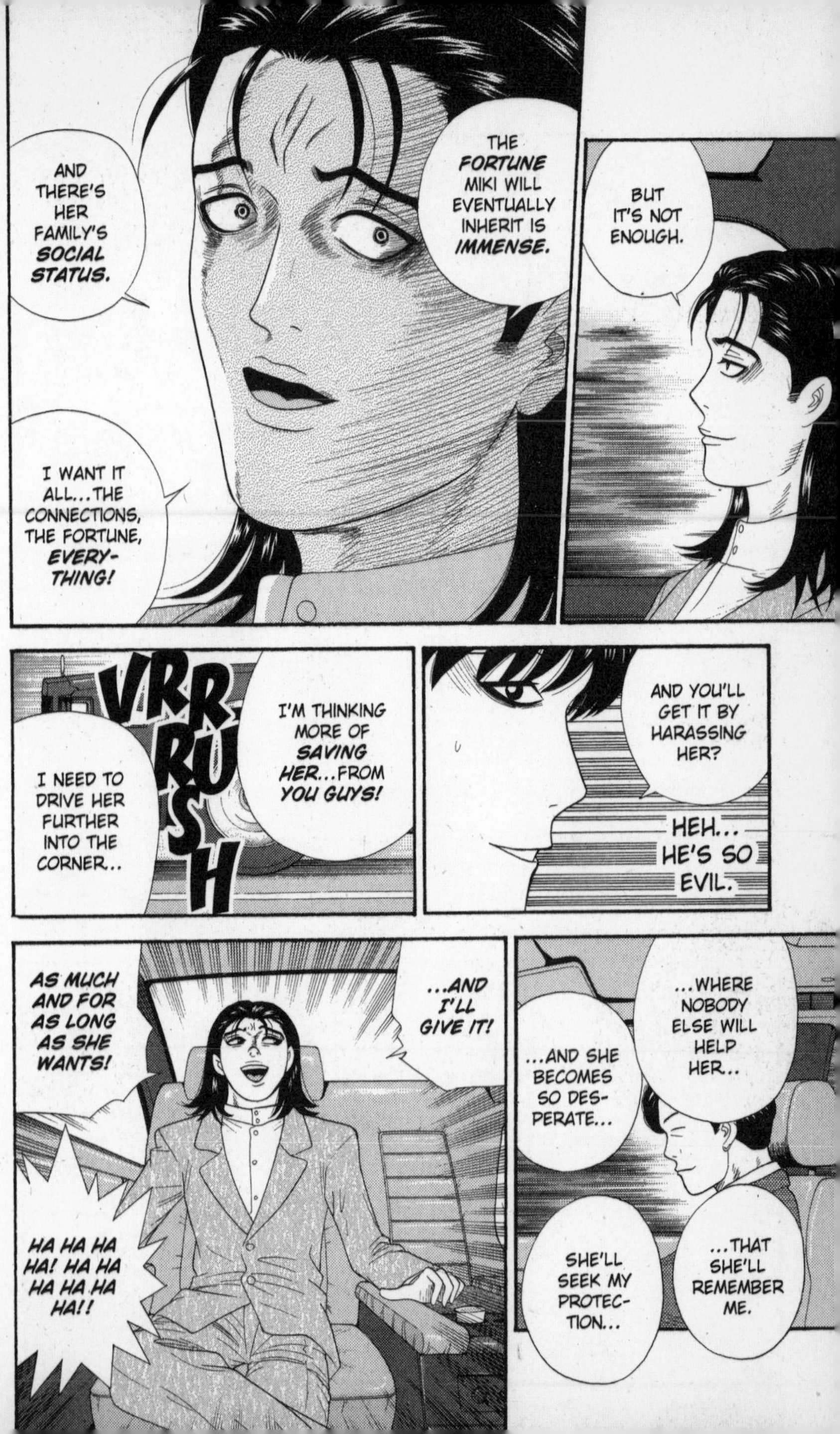
BUT IT'S NOT ENOUGH.
THE FORTUNE MIKI WILL EVENTUALLY INHERIT IS IMMENSE.
AND THERE'S HER FAMILY'S SOCIAL STATUS.
I WANT IT ALL...THE CONNECTIONS, THE FORTUNE, EVERY-THING!
AND YOU'LL GET IT BY HARASSING HER?
HEH... HE'S SO EVIL.
VRRRUSH
I'M THINKING MORE OF SAVING HER...FROM YOU GUYS!
I NEED TO DRIVE HER FURTHER INTO THE CORNER..
...WHERE NOBODY ELSE WILL HELP HER..
...AND SHE BECOMES SO DES-PERATE...
...THAT SHE'LL REMEMBER ME.
SHE'LL SEEK MY PROTEC-TION...
...AND I'LL GIVE IT!
AS MUCH AND FOR AS LONG AS SHE WANTS!
HA HA HA HA! HA HA HA HA HA HA!!

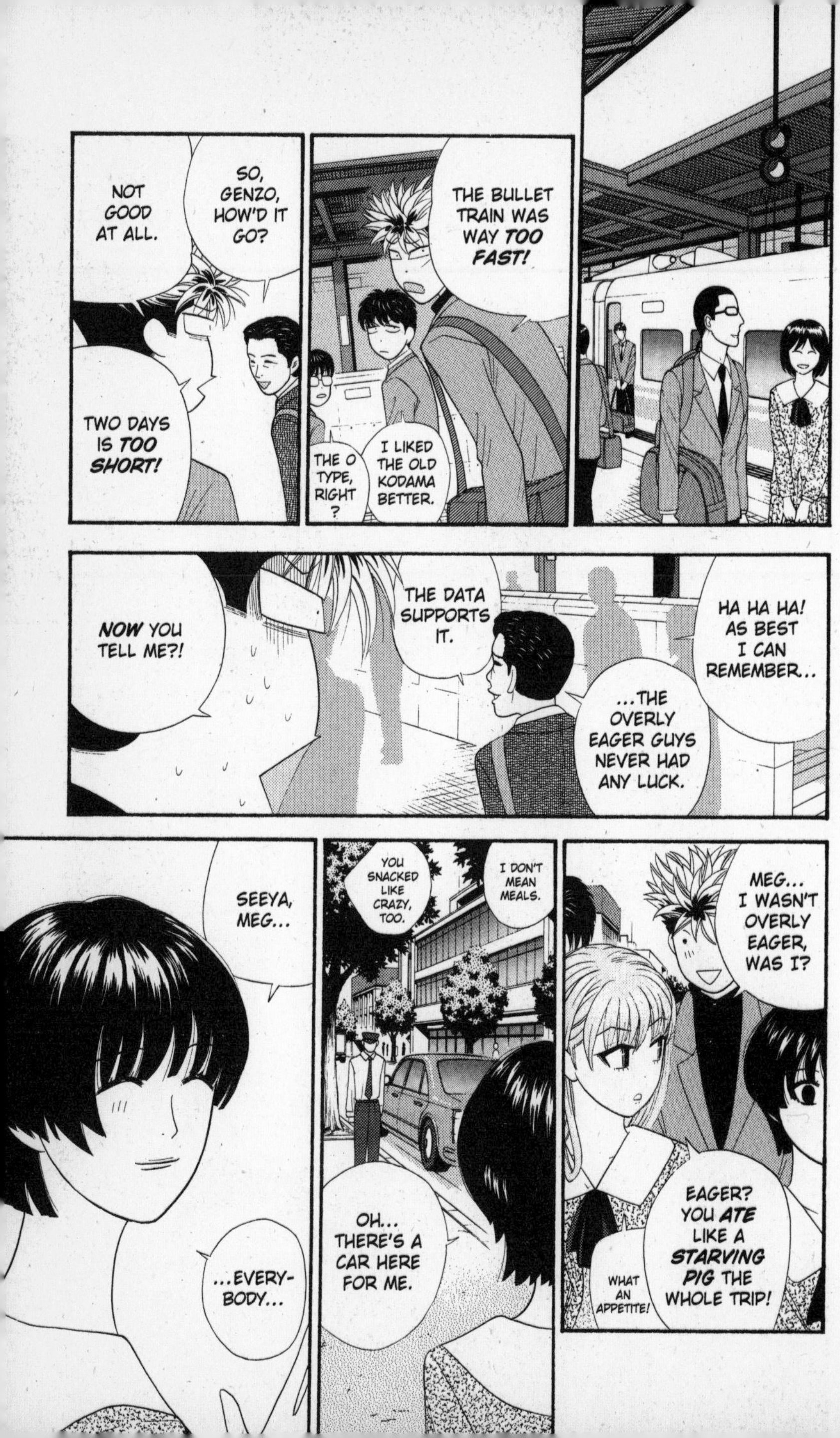
THE BULLET TRAIN WAS WAY TOO FAST!
I LIKED THE OLD KODAMA BETTER.
THE O TYPE, RIGHT?
SO, GENZO, HOW'D IT GO?
NOT GOOD AT ALL.
TWO DAYS IS TOO SHORT!
HA HA HA! AS BEST I CAN REMEMBER...
...THE OVERLY EAGER GUYS NEVER HAD ANY LUCK.
THE DATA SUPPORTS IT.
NOW YOU TELL ME?!
MEG... I WASN'T OVERLY EAGER, WAS I?
EAGER? YOU ATE LIKE A STARVING PIG THE WHOLE TRIP!
WHAT AN APPETITE!
I DON'T MEAN MEALS.
YOU SNACKED LIKE CRAZY, TOO.
OH... THERE'S A CAR HERE FOR ME.
SEEYA, MEG...
...EVERYBODY...

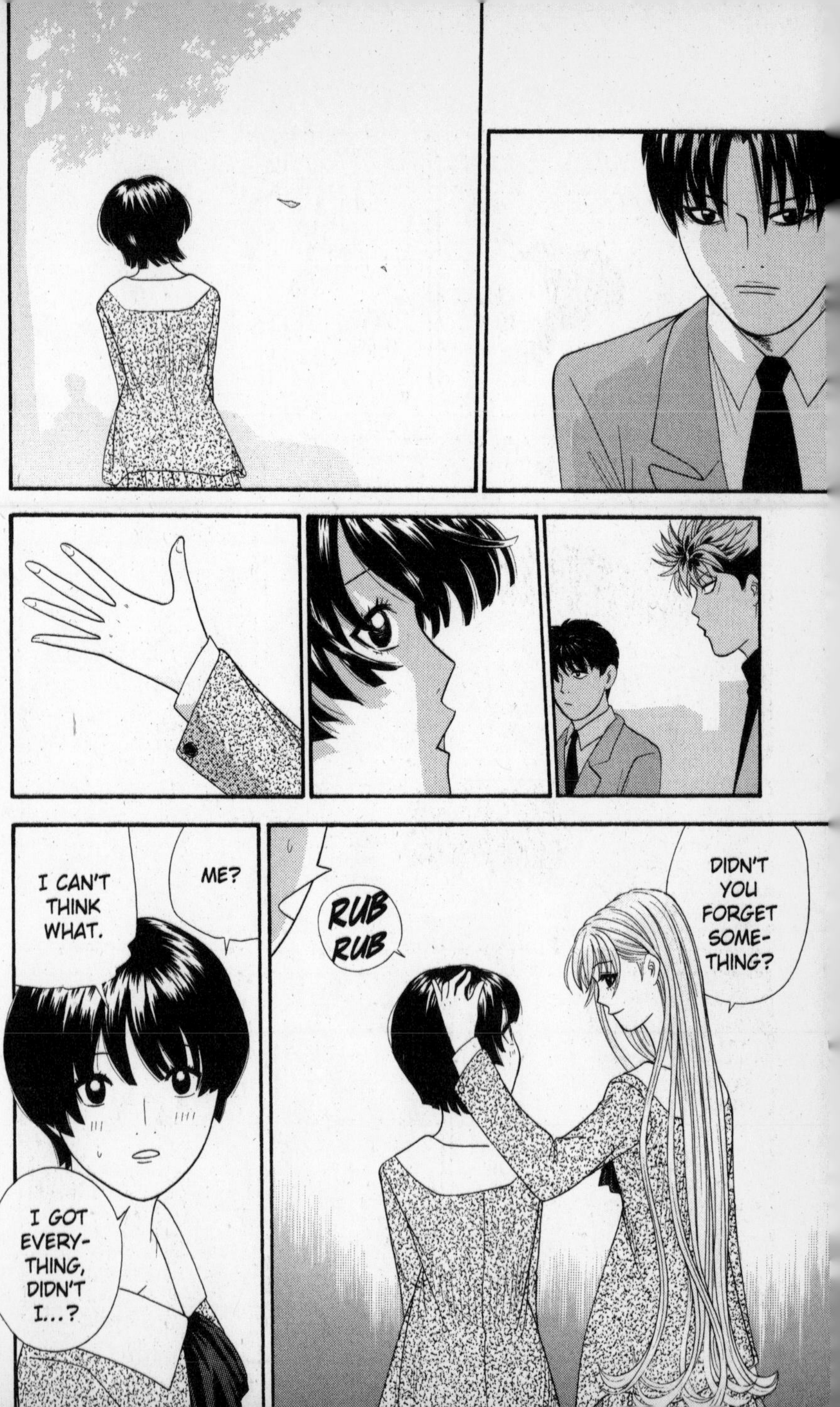
DIDN'T YOU FORGET SOME-THING?
RUB RUB
ME?
I CAN'T THINK WHAT.
I GOT EVERY-THING, DIDN'T I...?

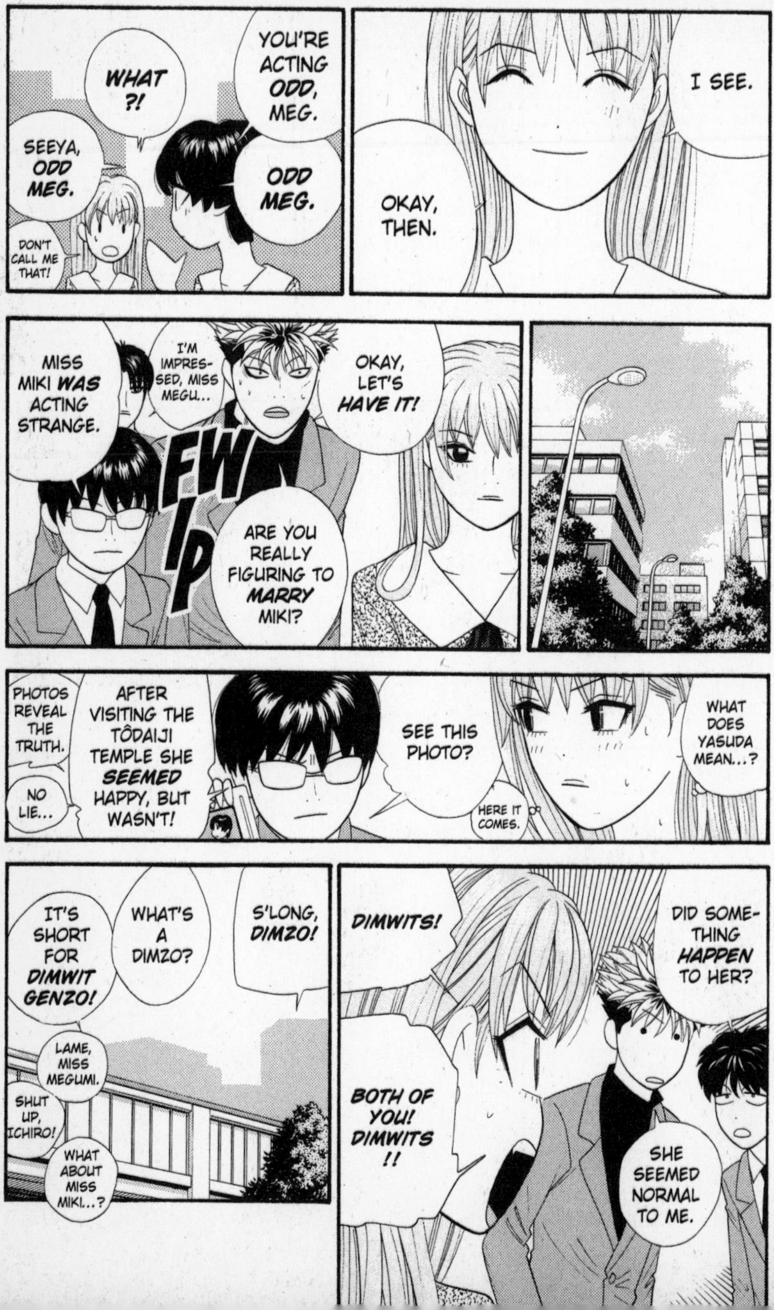
I SEE.
OKAY, THEN.
YOU'RE ACTING ODD, MEG.
WHAT ?!
ODD MEG.
SEEYA, ODD MEG.
DON'T CALL ME THAT!
OKAY, LET'S HAVE IT!
I'M IMPRES-SED, MISS MEGU...
MISS MIKI WAS ACTING STRANGE.
FWIP
ARE YOU REALLY FIGURING TO MARRY MIKI?
WHAT DOES YASUDA MEAN...?
SEE THIS PHOTO?
HERE IT COMES.
AFTER VISITING THE TÔDAIJI TEMPLE SHE SEEMED HAPPY, BUT WASN'T!
PHOTOS REVEAL THE TRUTH.
NO LIE...
DID SOME-THING HAPPEN TO HER?
SHE SEEMED NORMAL TO ME.
DIMWITS!
BOTH OF YOU! DIMWITS !!
S'LONG, DIMZO!
WHAT'S A DIMZO?
IT'S SHORT FOR DIMWIT GENZO!
LAME, MISS MEGUMI.
SHUT UP, ICHIRO!
WHAT ABOUT MISS MIKI...?

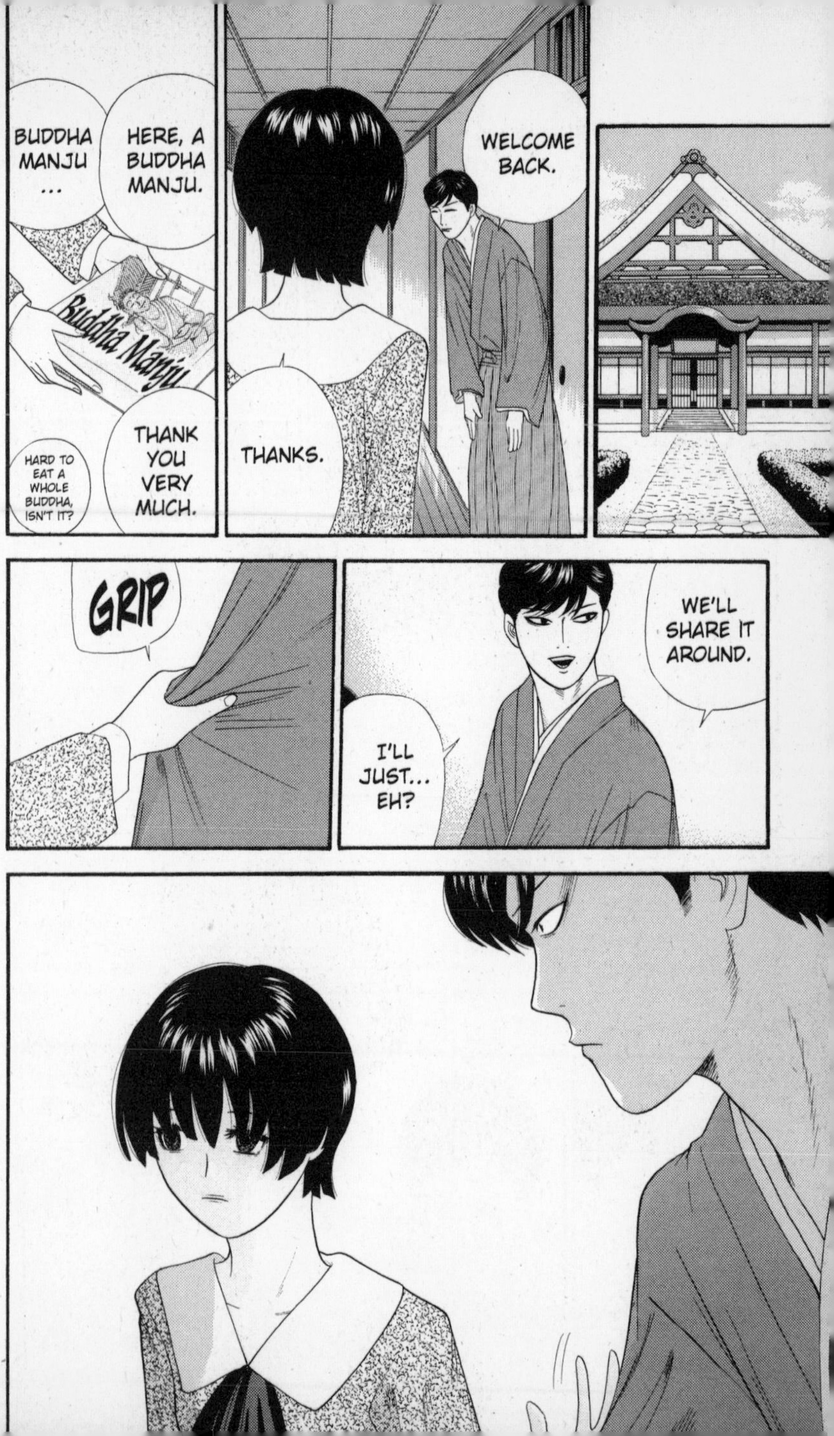
WELCOME BACK.
THANKS.
HERE, A BUDDHA MANJU.
BUDDHA MANJU ...
Buddha Manju
THANK YOU VERY MUCH.
HARD TO EAT A WHOLE BUDDHA, ISN'T IT?
WE'LL SHARE IT AROUND.
I'LL JUST... EH?
GRIP

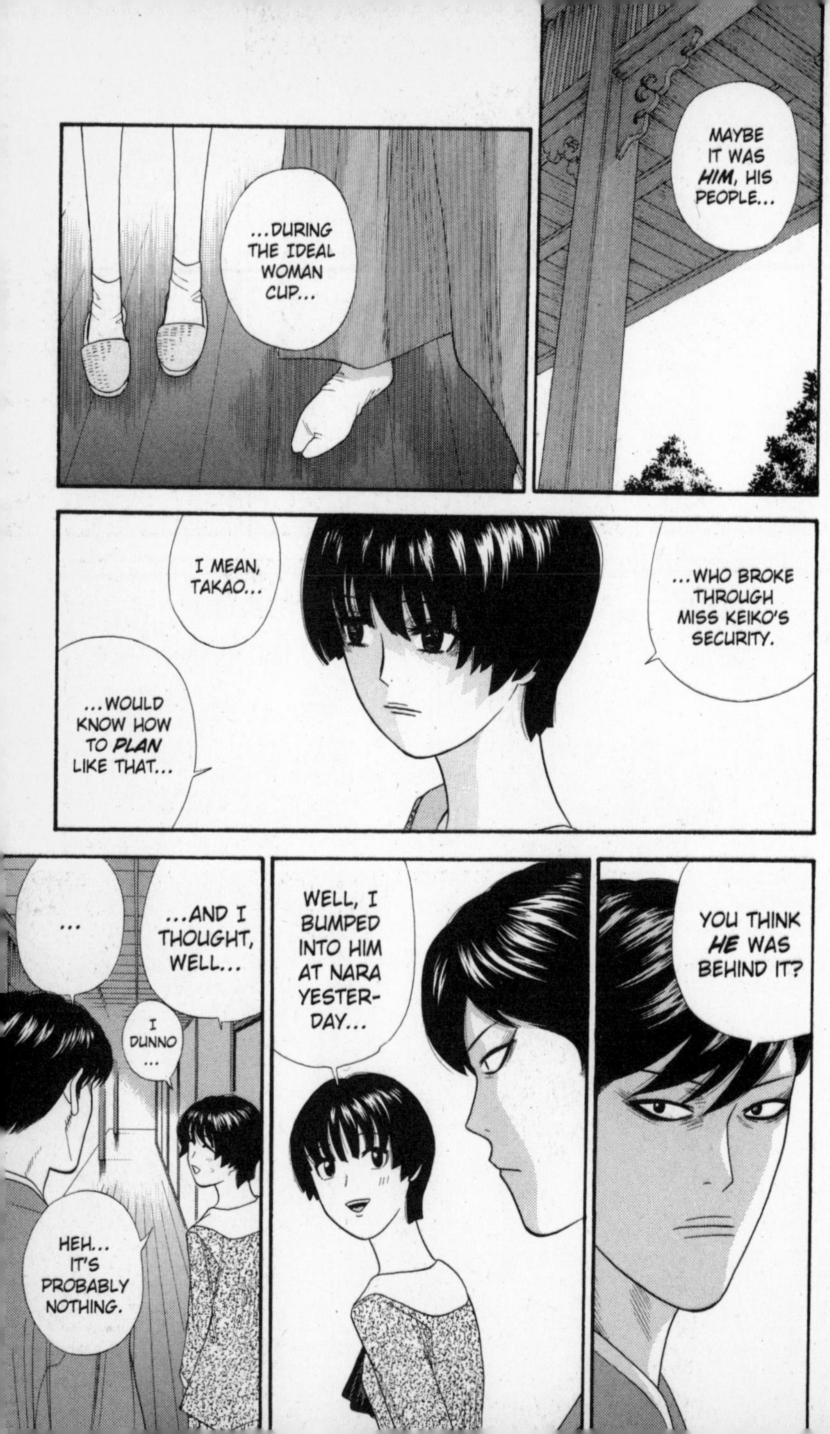
MAYBE IT WAS *HIM*, HIS PEOPLE...
...DURING THE IDEAL WOMAN CUP...
...WHO BROKE THROUGH MISS KEIKO'S SECURITY.
I MEAN, TAKAO...
...WOULD KNOW HOW TO *PLAN* LIKE THAT...
YOU THINK *HE* WAS BEHIND IT?
WELL, I BUMPED INTO HIM AT NARA YESTER-DAY...
...AND I THOUGHT, WELL...
...
I DUNNO ...
HEH... IT'S PROBABLY NOTHING.

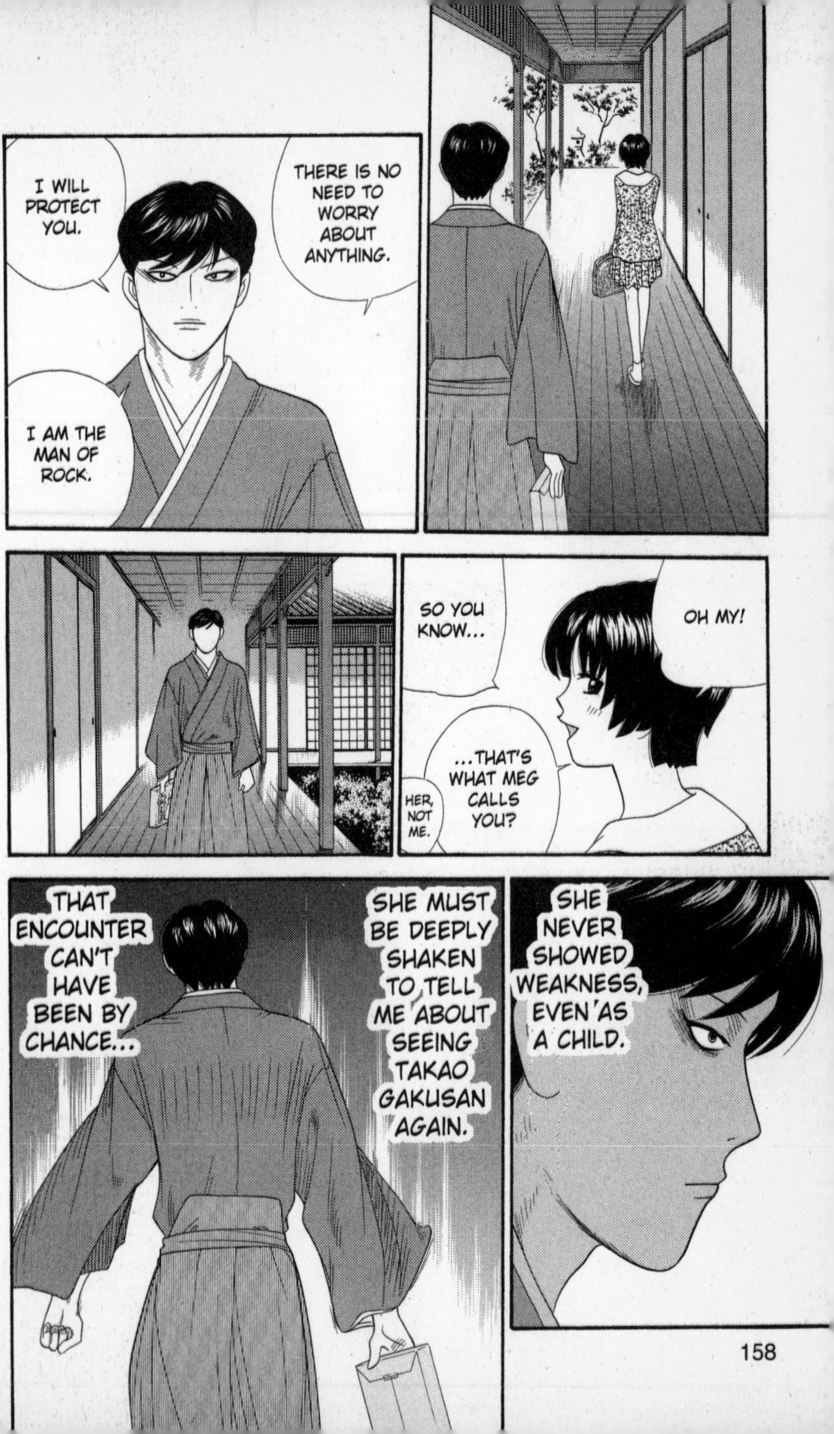
THERE IS NO NEED TO WORRY ABOUT ANYTHING.
I WILL PROTECT YOU.
I AM THE MAN OF ROCK.
OH MY!
SO YOU KNOW...
...THAT'S WHAT MEG CALLS YOU?
HER, NOT ME.
SHE NEVER SHOWED WEAKNESS, EVEN AS A CHILD.
SHE MUST BE DEEPLY SHAKEN TO TELL ME ABOUT SEEING TAKAO GAKUSAN AGAIN.
THAT ENCOUNTER CAN'T HAVE BEEN BY CHANCE...

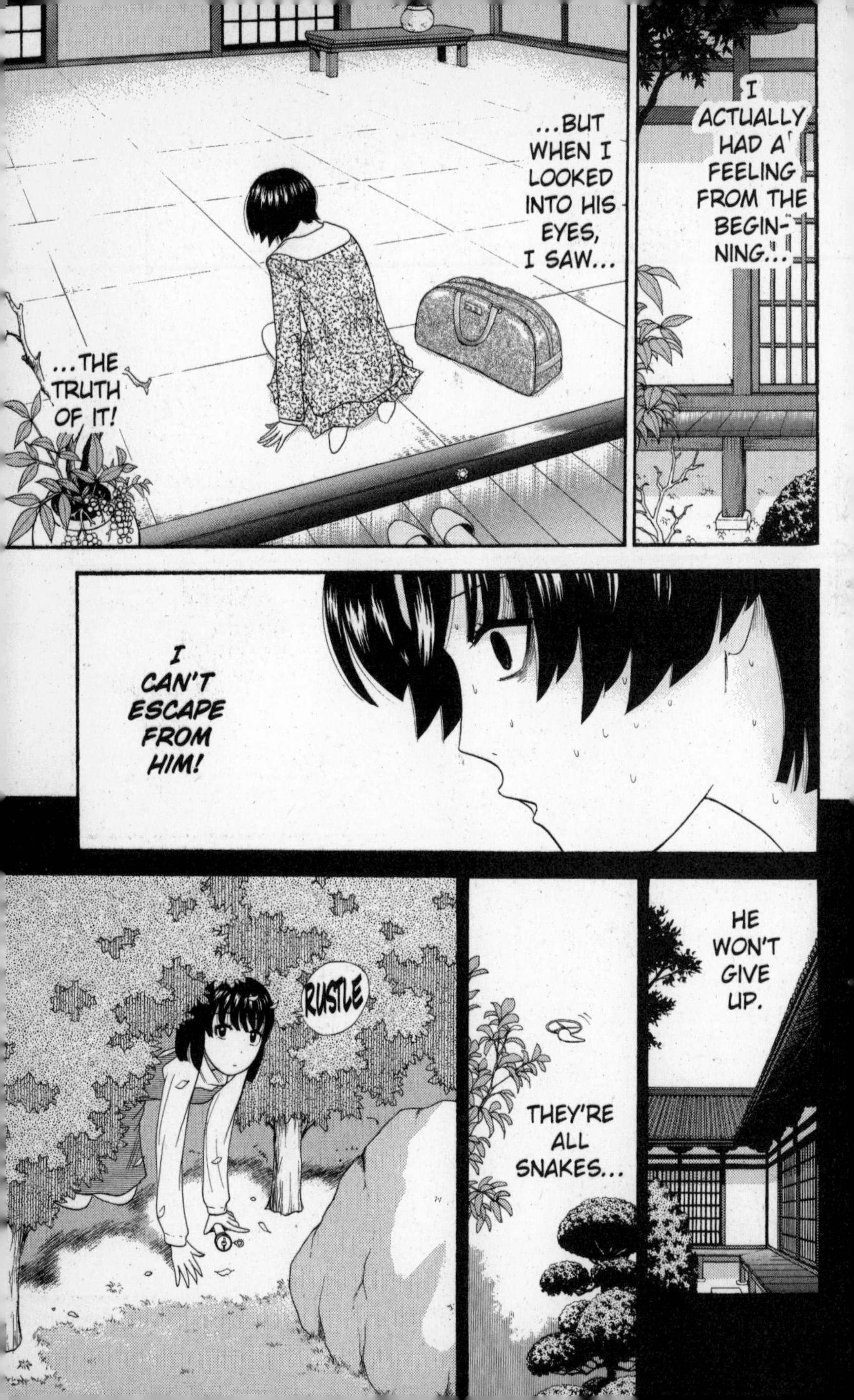
I ACTUALLY HAD A FEELING FROM THE BEGINNING...
...BUT WHEN I LOOKED INTO HIS EYES, I SAW...
...THE TRUTH OF IT!
I CAN'T ESCAPE FROM HIM!
HE WON'T GIVE UP.
THEY'RE ALL SNAKES...
RUSTLE

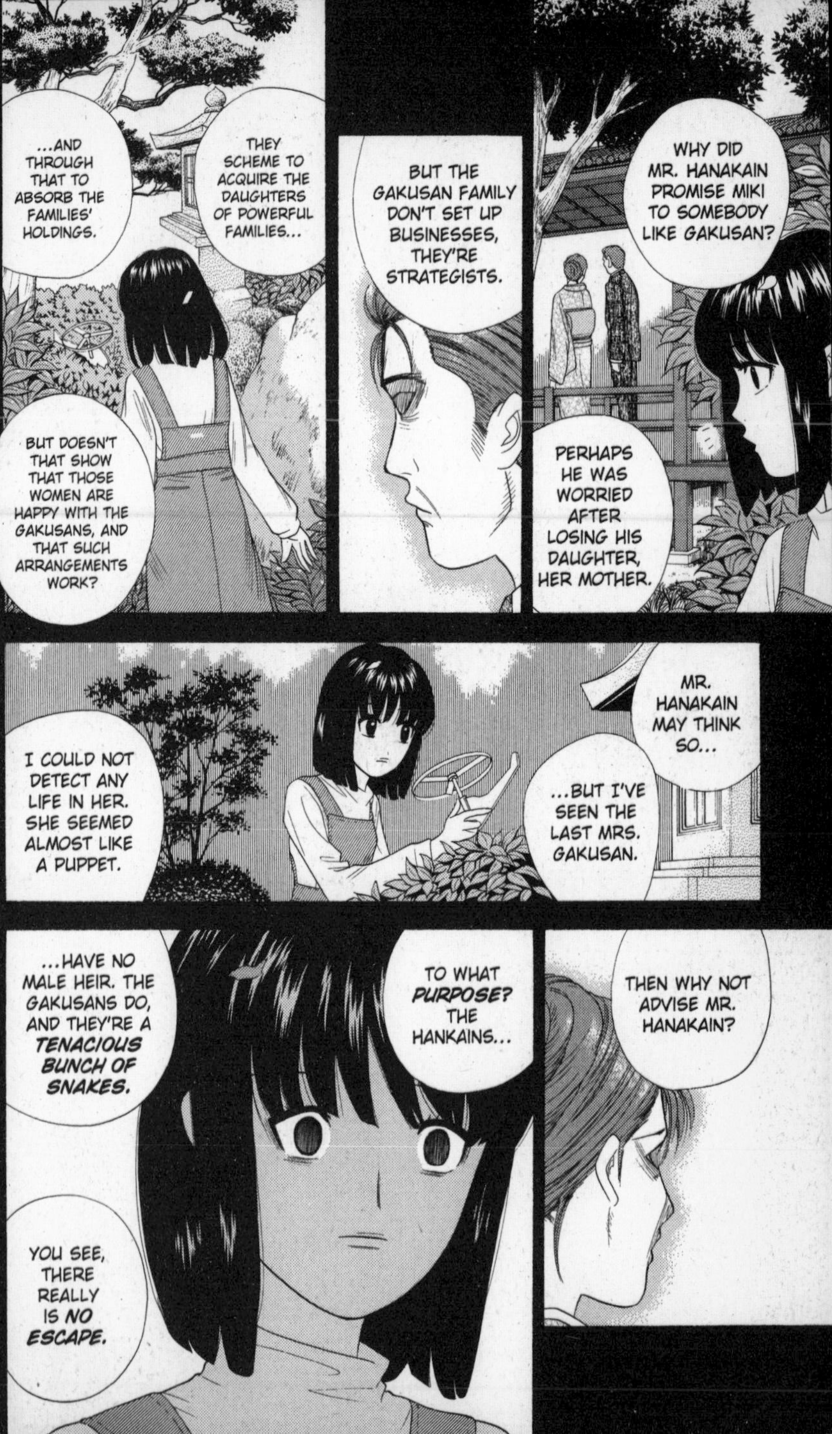
WHY DID MR. HANAKAIN PROMISE MIKI TO SOMEBODY LIKE GAKUSAN?
PERHAPS HE WAS WORRIED AFTER LOSING HIS DAUGHTER, HER MOTHER.
BUT THE GAKUSAN FAMILY DON'T SET UP BUSINESSES, THEY'RE STRATEGISTS.
THEY SCHEME TO ACQUIRE THE DAUGHTERS OF POWERFUL FAMILIES...
...AND THROUGH THAT TO ABSORB THE FAMILIES' HOLDINGS.
BUT DOESN'T THAT SHOW THAT THOSE WOMEN ARE HAPPY WITH THE GAKUSANS, AND THAT SUCH ARRANGEMENTS WORK?
MR. HANAKAIN MAY THINK SO...
...BUT I'VE SEEN THE LAST MRS. GAKUSAN.
I COULD NOT DETECT ANY LIFE IN HER. SHE SEEMED ALMOST LIKE A PUPPET.
THEN WHY NOT ADVISE MR. HANAKAIN?
TO WHAT *PURPOSE?* THE HANKAINS...
...HAVE NO MALE HEIR. THE GAKUSANS DO, AND THEY'RE A ***TENACIOUS BUNCH OF SNAKES.***
YOU SEE, THERE REALLY IS ***NO ESCAPE.***

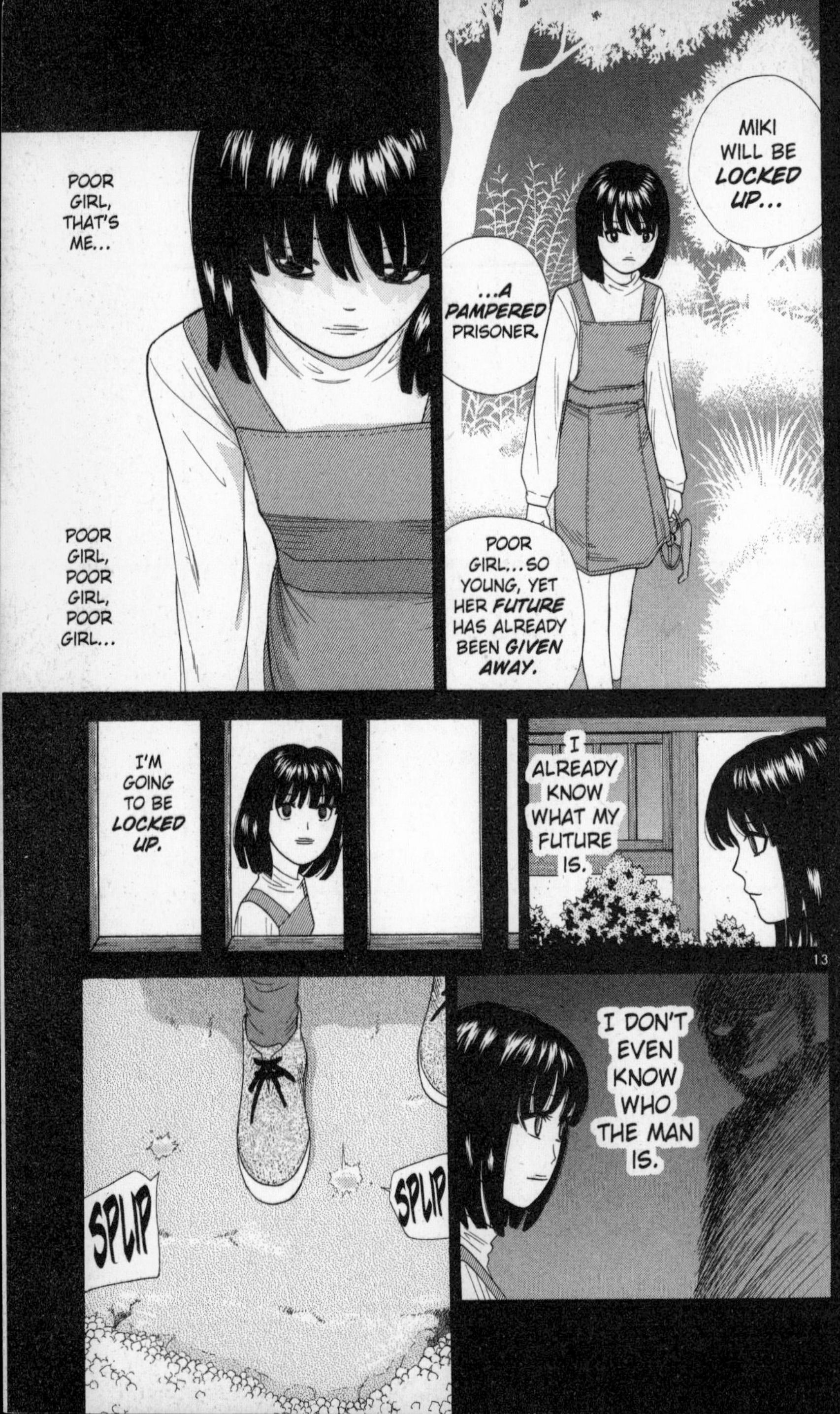
MIKI WILL BE LOCKED UP...
...A PAMPERED PRISONER.
POOR GIRL...SO YOUNG, YET HER FUTURE HAS ALREADY BEEN GIVEN AWAY.
POOR GIRL, THAT'S ME...
POOR GIRL, POOR GIRL, POOR GIRL...
I ALREADY KNOW WHAT MY FUTURE IS.
I'M GOING TO BE LOCKED UP.
I DON'T EVEN KNOW WHO THE MAN IS.
SPLIP
SPLIP

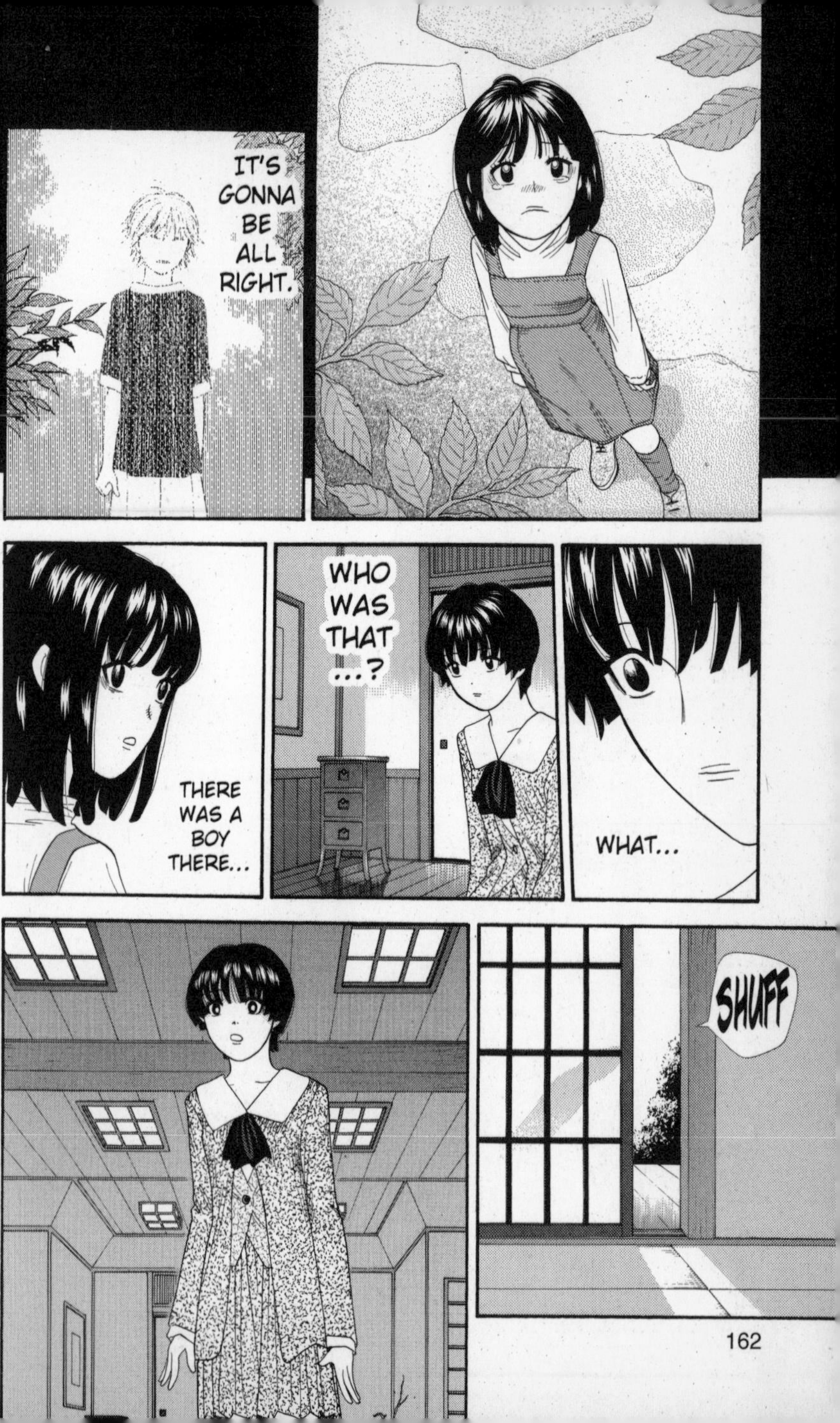
IT'S GONNA BE ALL RIGHT.
WHAT...
WHO WAS THAT ...?
THERE WAS A BOY THERE...
SHUFF

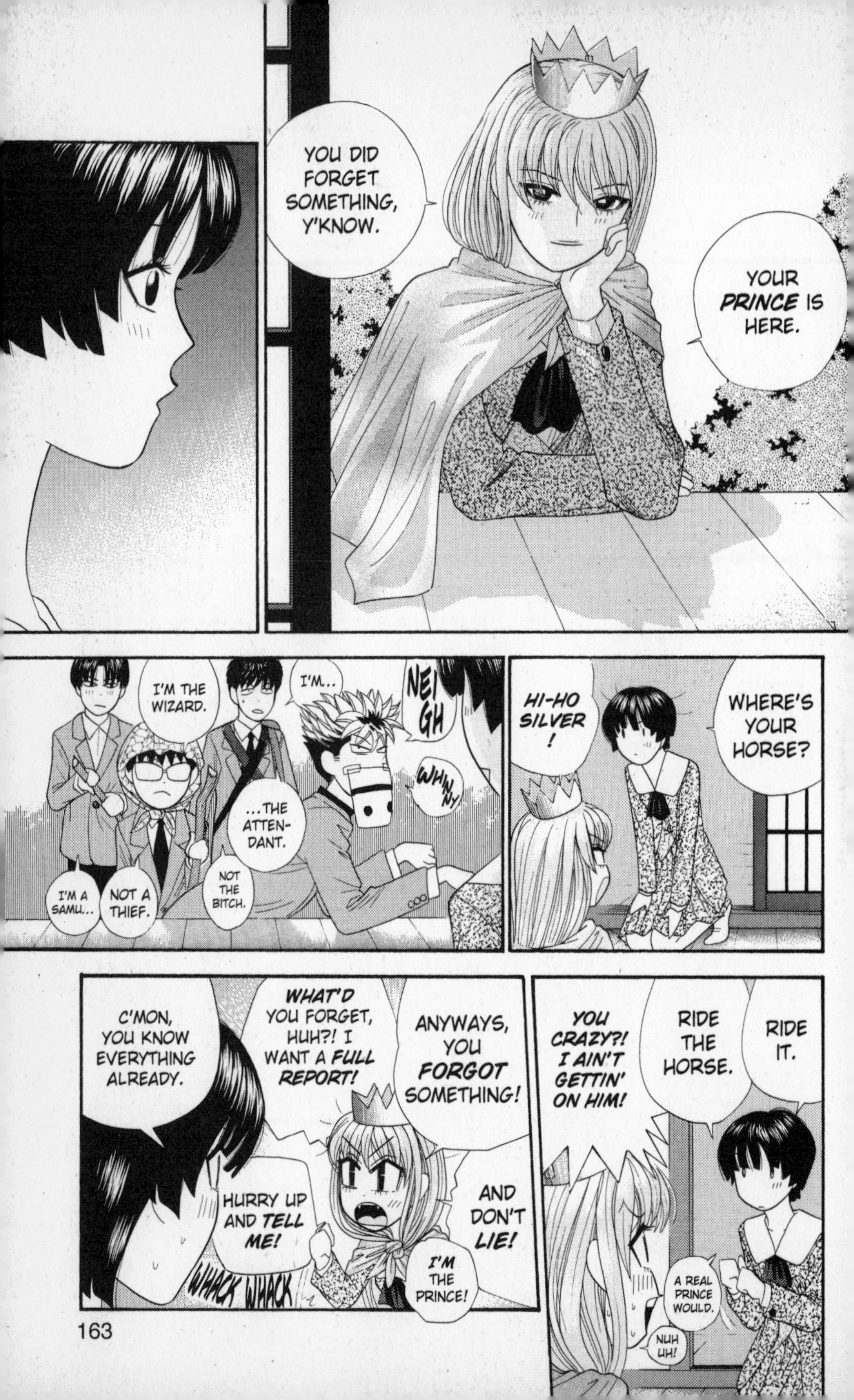
YOU DID FORGET SOMETHING, Y'KNOW.
YOUR *PRINCE* IS HERE.
WHERE'S YOUR HORSE?
HI-HO SILVER!
NEIGH
WHINNY
I'M...
I'M THE WIZARD.
...THE ATTENDANT.
NOT THE BITCH.
NOT A THIEF.
I'M A SAMU...
RIDE IT.
RIDE THE HORSE.
YOU CRAZY?! I AIN'T GETTIN' ON HIM!
A REAL PRINCE WOULD.
NUH UH!
ANYWAYS, YOU *FORGOT* SOMETHING!
WHAT'D YOU FORGET, HUH?! I WANT A FULL REPORT!
C'MON, YOU KNOW EVERYTHING ALREADY.
AND DON'T *LIE!*
HURRY UP AND *TELL ME!*
I'M THE PRINCE!
WHACK WHACK

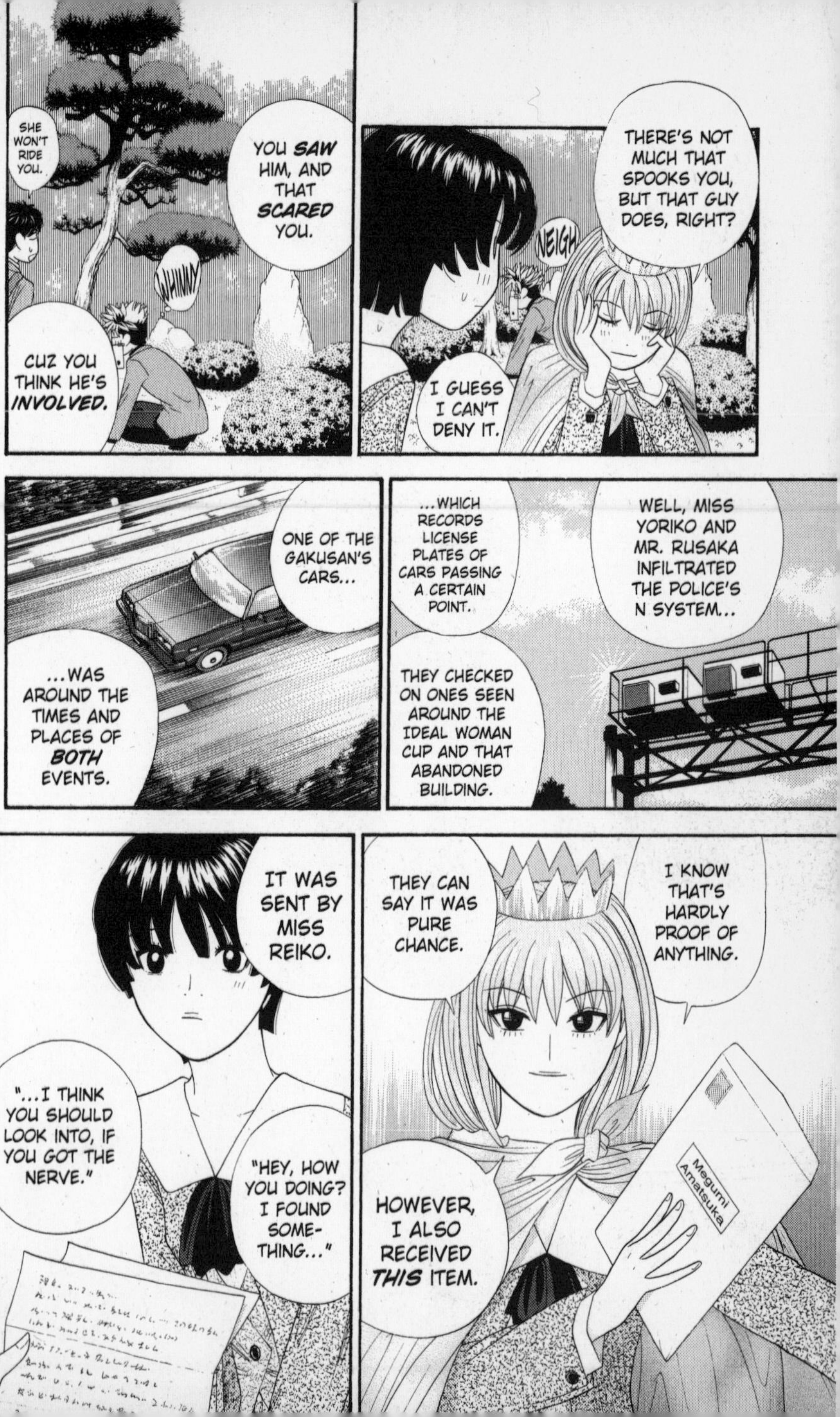
THERE'S NOT MUCH THAT SPOOKS YOU, BUT THAT GUY DOES, RIGHT?
NEIGH
I GUESS I CAN'T DENY IT.
YOU SAW HIM, AND THAT SCARED YOU.
SHE WON'T RIDE YOU.
WHINNY
CUZ YOU THINK HE'S INVOLVED.
WELL, MISS YORIKO AND MR. RUSAKA INFILTRATED THE POLICE'S N SYSTEM...
...WHICH RECORDS LICENSE PLATES OF CARS PASSING A CERTAIN POINT.
THEY CHECKED ON ONES SEEN AROUND THE IDEAL WOMAN CUP AND THAT ABANDONED BUILDING.
ONE OF THE GAKUSAN'S CARS...
...WAS AROUND THE TIMES AND PLACES OF BOTH EVENTS.
I KNOW THAT'S HARDLY PROOF OF ANYTHING.
THEY CAN SAY IT WAS PURE CHANCE.
HOWEVER, I ALSO RECEIVED THIS ITEM.
Megumi Amatsuka
IT WAS SENT BY MISS REIKO.
"HEY, HOW YOU DOING? I FOUND SOMETHING..."
"...I THINK YOU SHOULD LOOK INTO, IF YOU GOT THE NERVE."

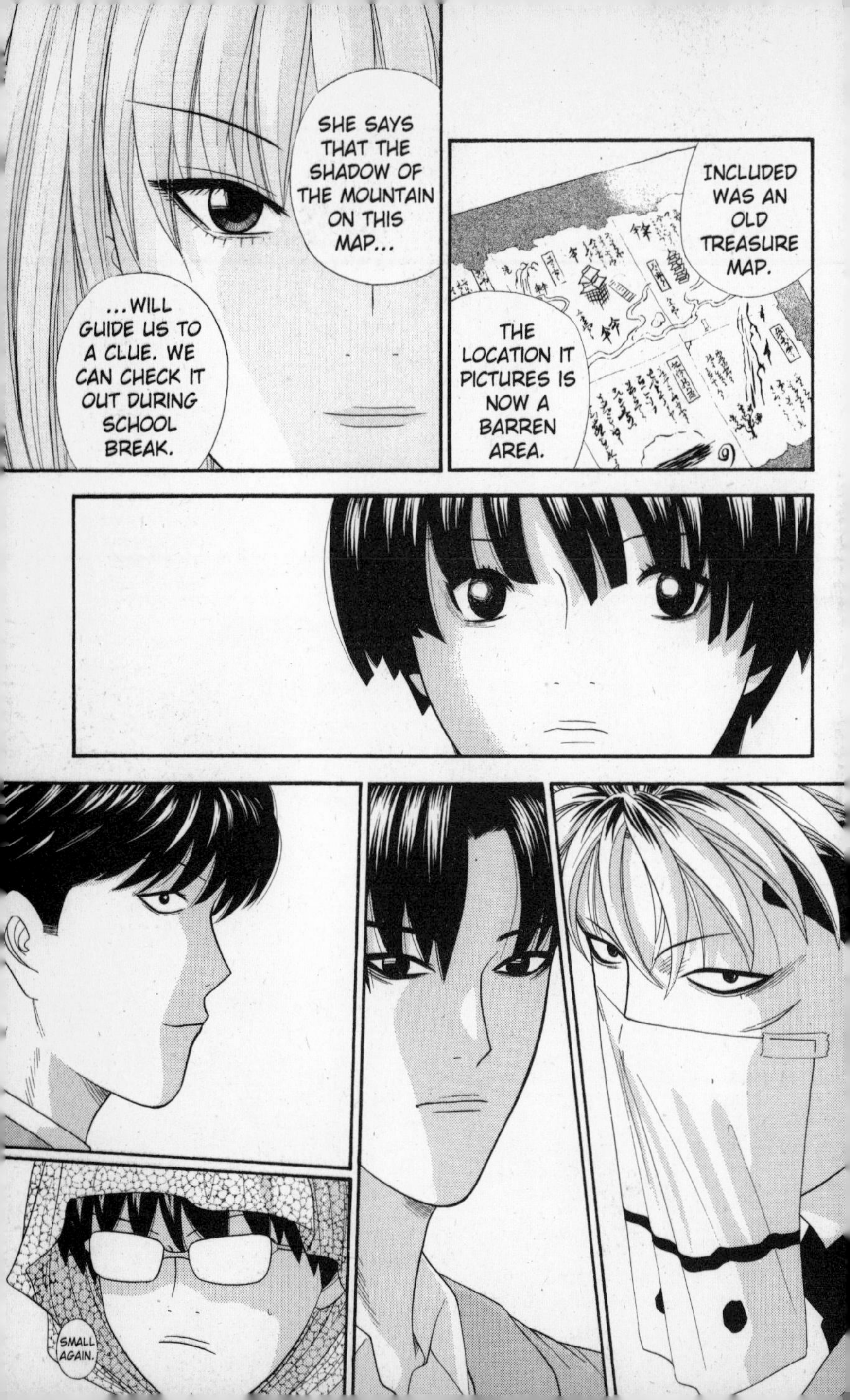
INCLUDED WAS AN OLD TREASURE MAP.
THE LOCATION IT PICTURES IS NOW A BARREN AREA.
SHE SAYS THAT THE SHADOW OF THE MOUNTAIN ON THIS MAP...
...WILL GUIDE US TO A CLUE. WE CAN CHECK IT OUT DURING SCHOOL BREAK.
SMALL AGAIN.

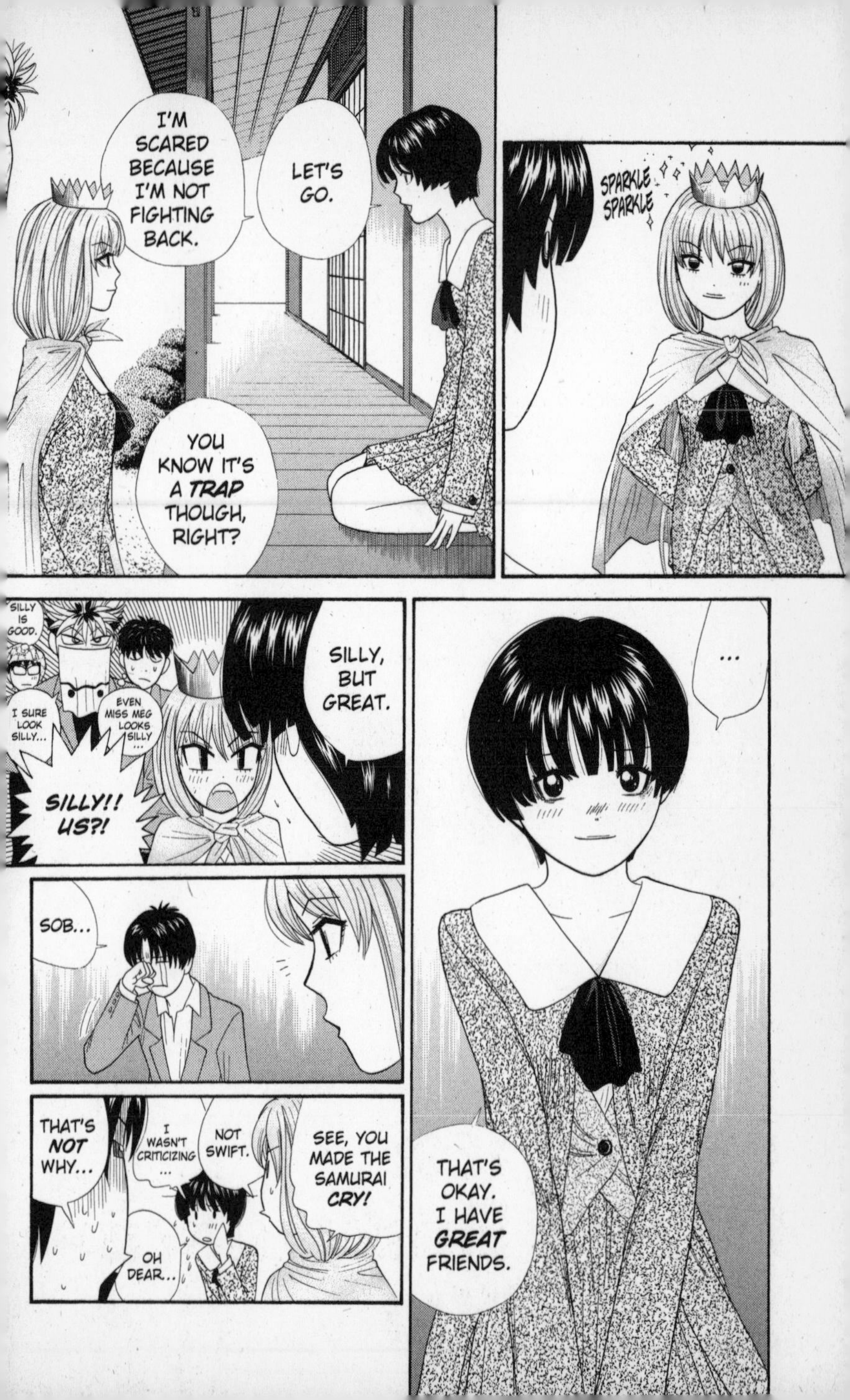
SPARKLE SPARKLE
LET'S GO.
I'M SCARED BECAUSE I'M NOT FIGHTING BACK.
YOU KNOW IT'S A *TRAP* THOUGH, RIGHT?
...
THAT'S OKAY. I HAVE **GREAT** FRIENDS.
SILLY, BUT GREAT.
SILLY!! US?!
EVEN MISS MEG LOOKS SILLY...
SILLY IS GOOD.
I SURE LOOK SILLY...
SOB...
SEE, YOU MADE THE SAMURAI *CRY!*
NOT SWIFT.
I WASN'T CRITICIZING...
THAT'S *NOT* WHY...
OH DEAR...

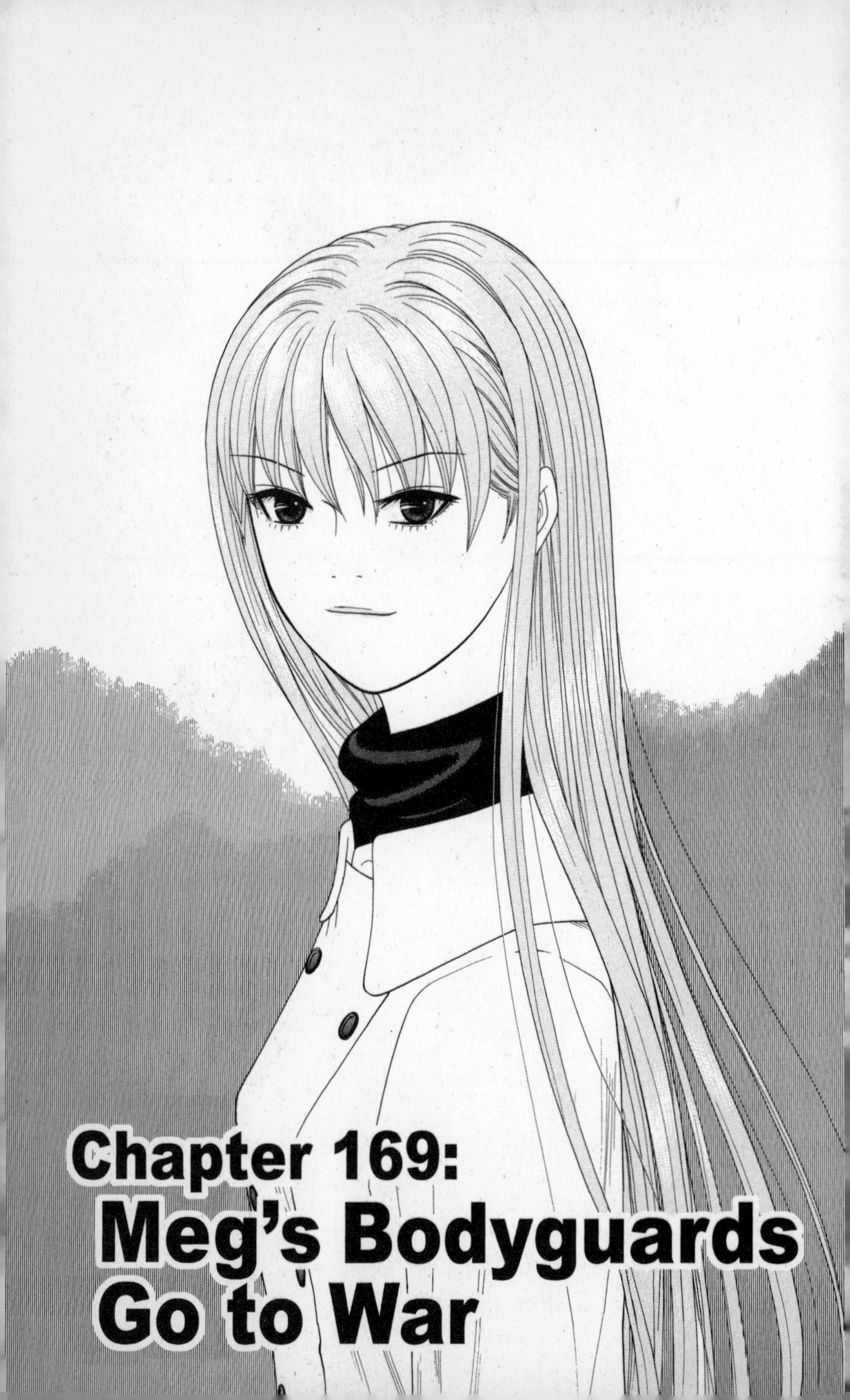
Chapter 169:
Meg's Bodyguards Go to War

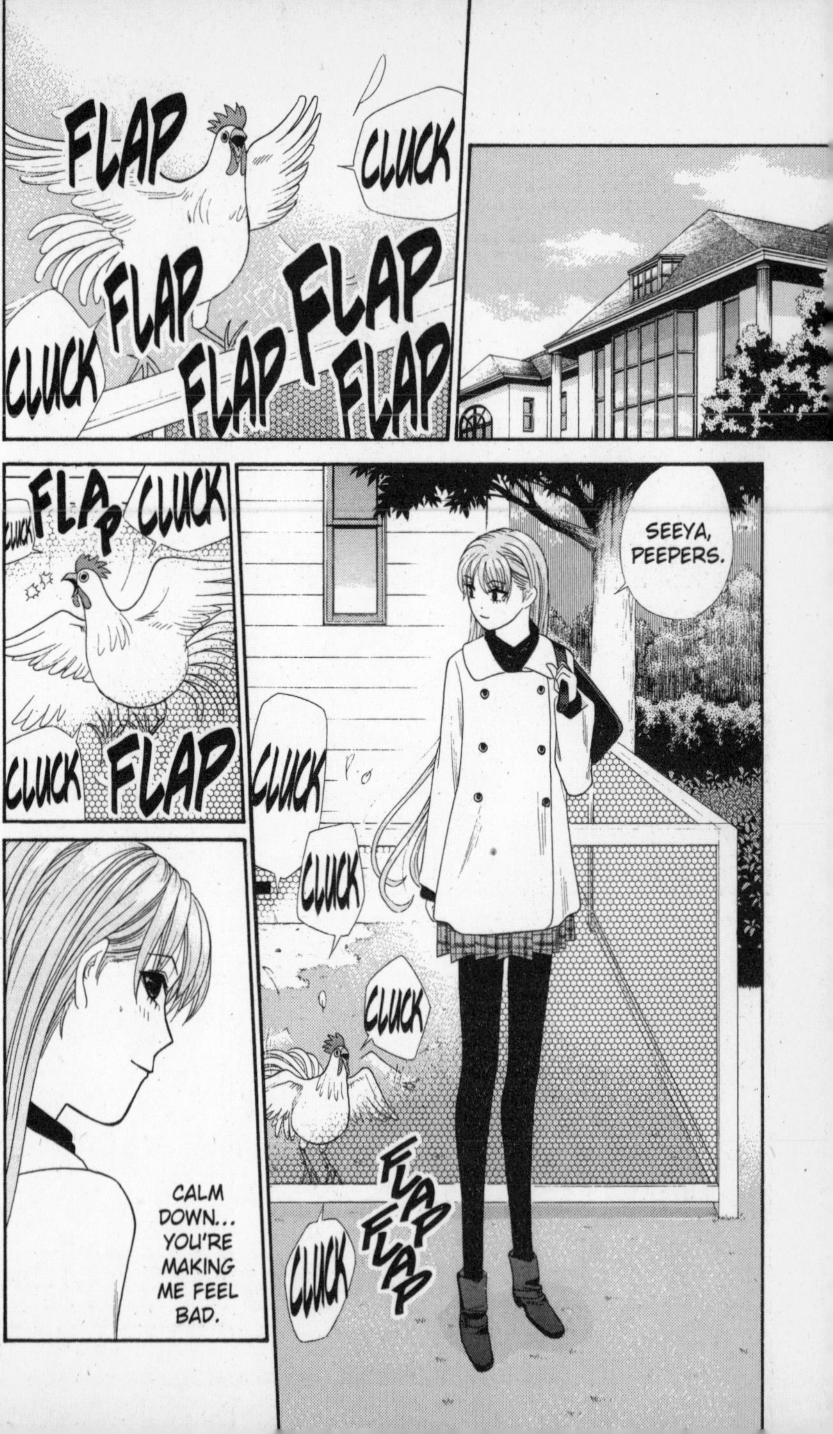

CLUCK
FLAP
FLAP
FLAP
FLAP
FLAP
CLUCK
SEEYA, PEEPERS.
CLUCK
CLUCK
CLUCK
CLUCK
FLAP FLAP
CLUCK
CLUCK
FLAP
CLUCK
CLUCK
FLAP
CALM DOWN... YOU'RE MAKING ME FEEL BAD.

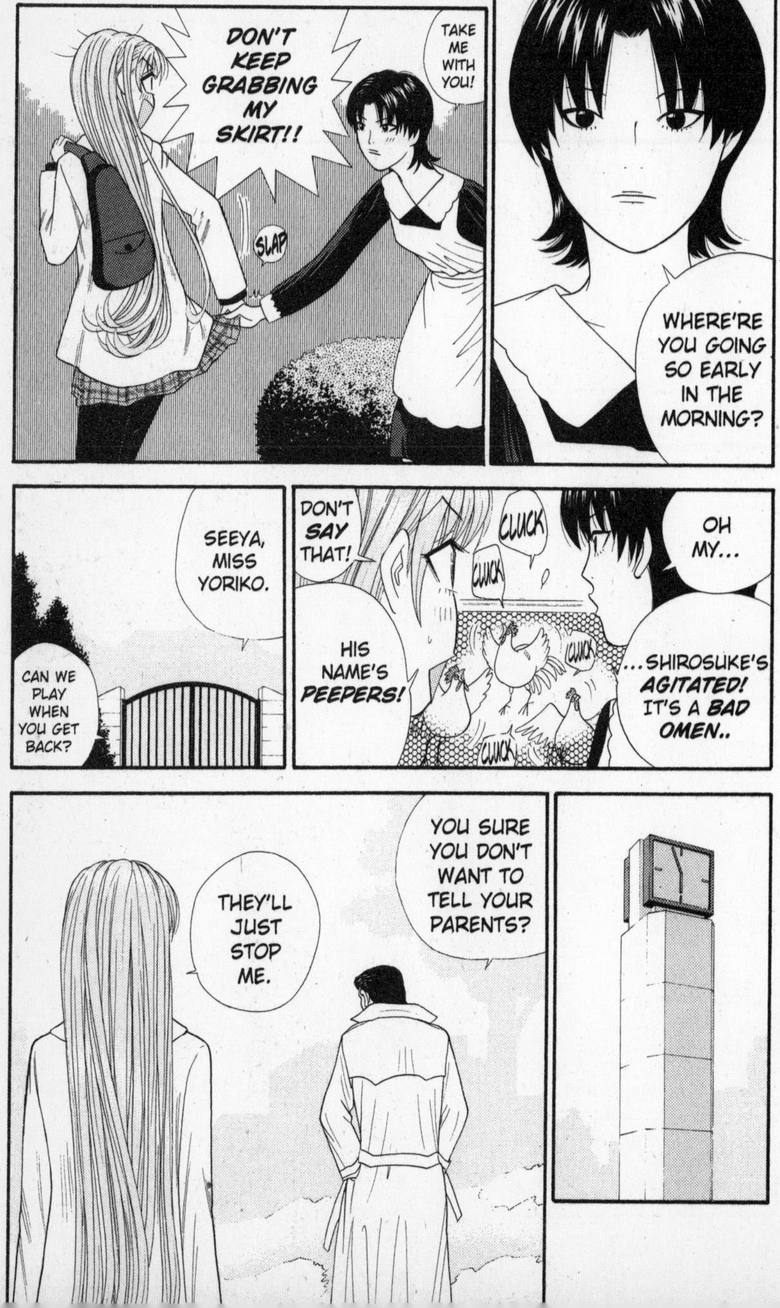
WHERE'RE YOU GOING SO EARLY IN THE MORNING?
TAKE ME WITH YOU!
DON'T KEEP GRABBING MY SKIRT!!
SLAP
OH MY...
...SHIROSUKE'S AGITATED! IT'S A BAD OMEN..
CLUCK
CLUCK
CLUCK
CLUCK
DON'T SAY THAT!
HIS NAME'S PEEPERS!
SEEYA, MISS YORIKO.
CAN WE PLAY WHEN YOU GET BACK?
YOU SURE YOU DON'T WANT TO TELL YOUR PARENTS?
THEY'LL JUST STOP ME.

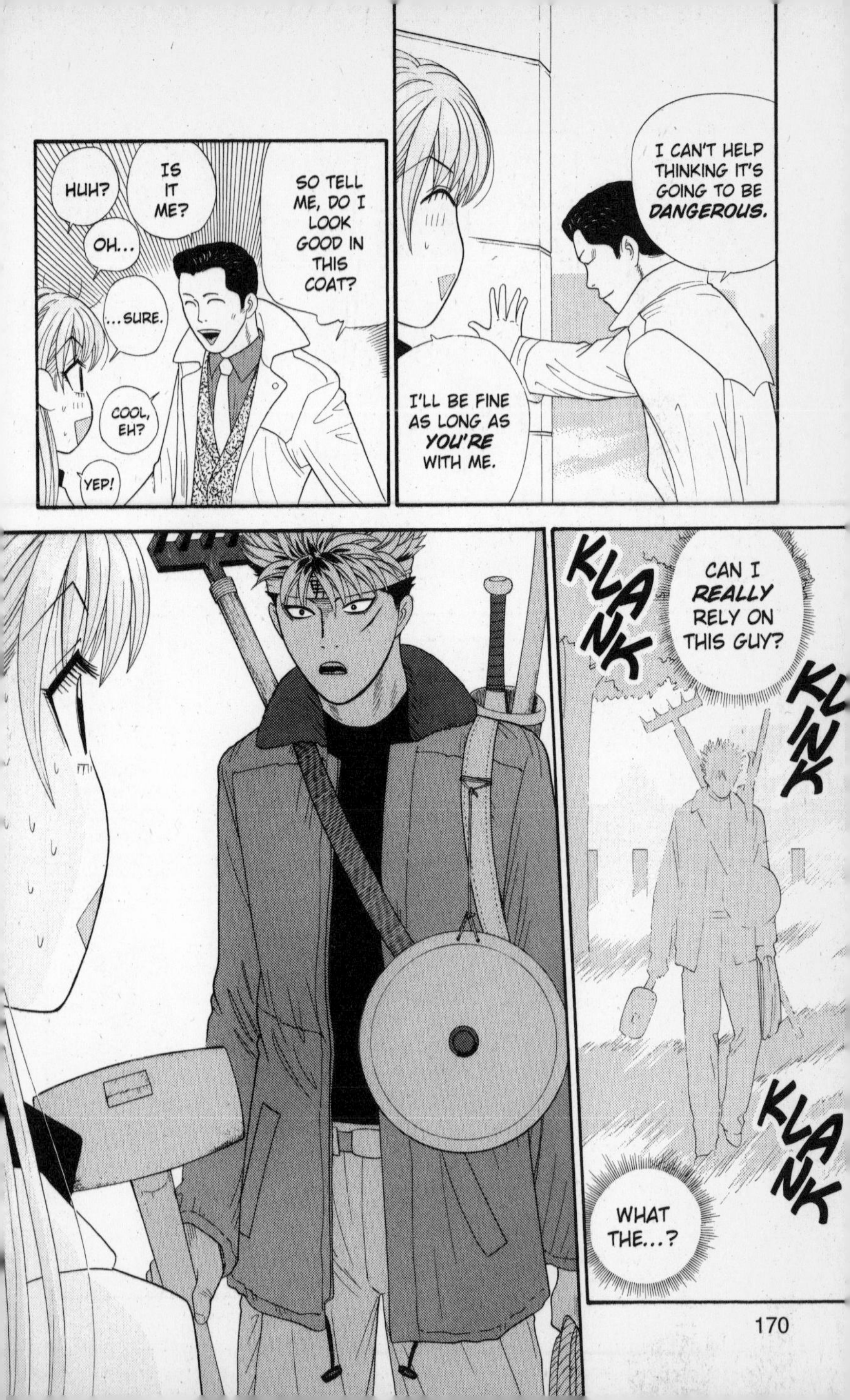
I CAN'T HELP THINKING IT'S GOING TO BE *DANGEROUS.*
I'LL BE FINE AS LONG AS *YOU'RE* WITH ME.
SO TELL ME, DO I LOOK GOOD IN THIS COAT?
IS IT ME?
HUH?
OH...
...SURE.
COOL, EH?
YEP!
KLANK
CAN I *REALLY* RELY ON THIS GUY?
KLINK
KLANK
WHAT THE...?

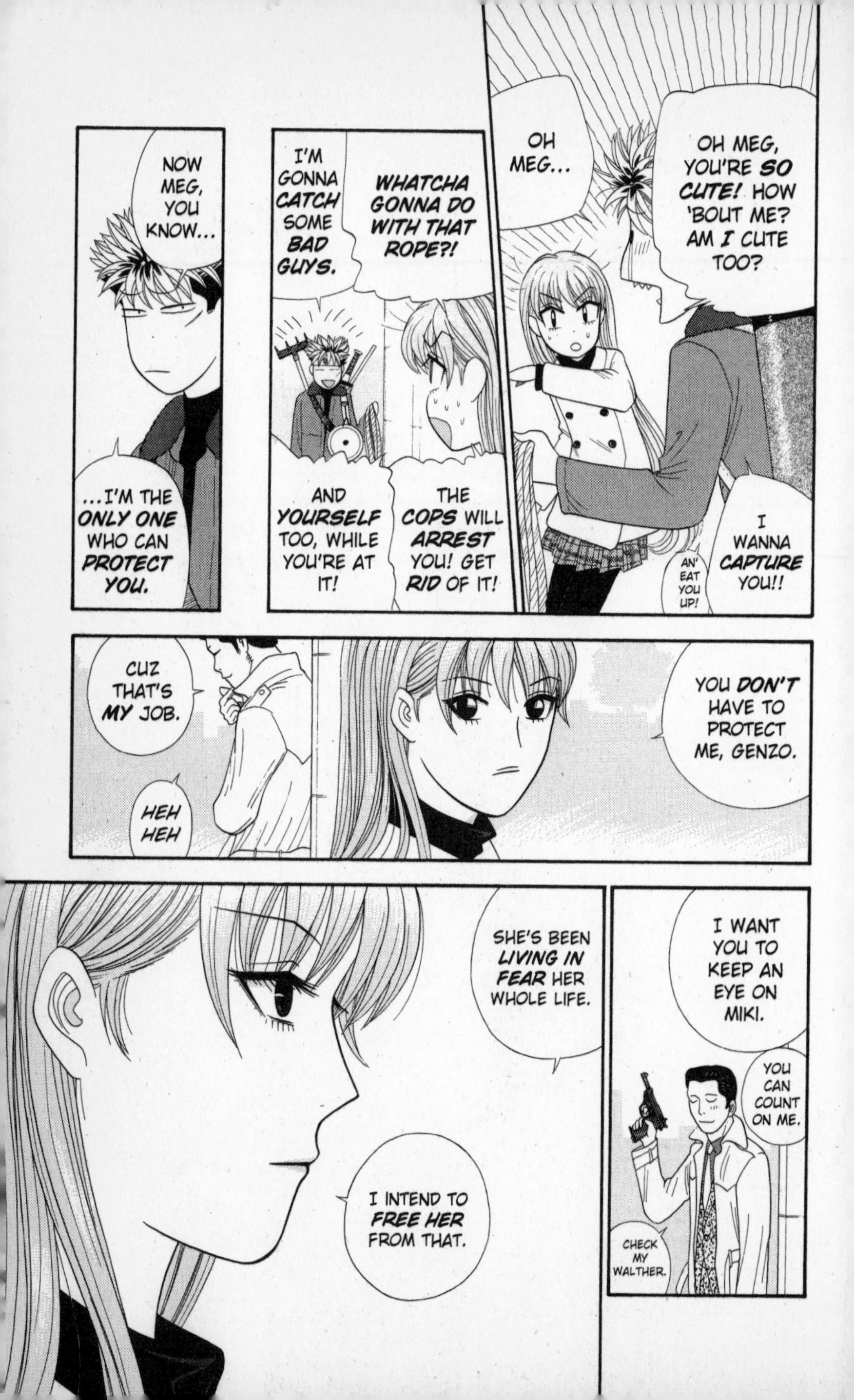
OH MEG, YOU'RE SO CUTE! HOW 'BOUT ME? AM I CUTE TOO?
OH MEG...
I WANNA CAPTURE YOU!!
AN' EAT YOU UP!
WHATCHA GONNA DO WITH THAT ROPE?!
I'M GONNA CATCH SOME BAD GUYS.
THE COPS WILL ARREST YOU! GET RID OF IT!
AND YOURSELF TOO, WHILE YOU'RE AT IT!
NOW MEG, YOU KNOW...
...I'M THE ONLY ONE WHO CAN PROTECT YOU.
YOU DON'T HAVE TO PROTECT ME, GENZO.
CUZ THAT'S MY JOB.
HEH HEH
I WANT YOU TO KEEP AN EYE ON MIKI.
YOU CAN COUNT ON ME.
CHECK MY WALTHER.
SHE'S BEEN LIVING IN FEAR HER WHOLE LIFE.
I INTEND TO FREE HER FROM THAT.

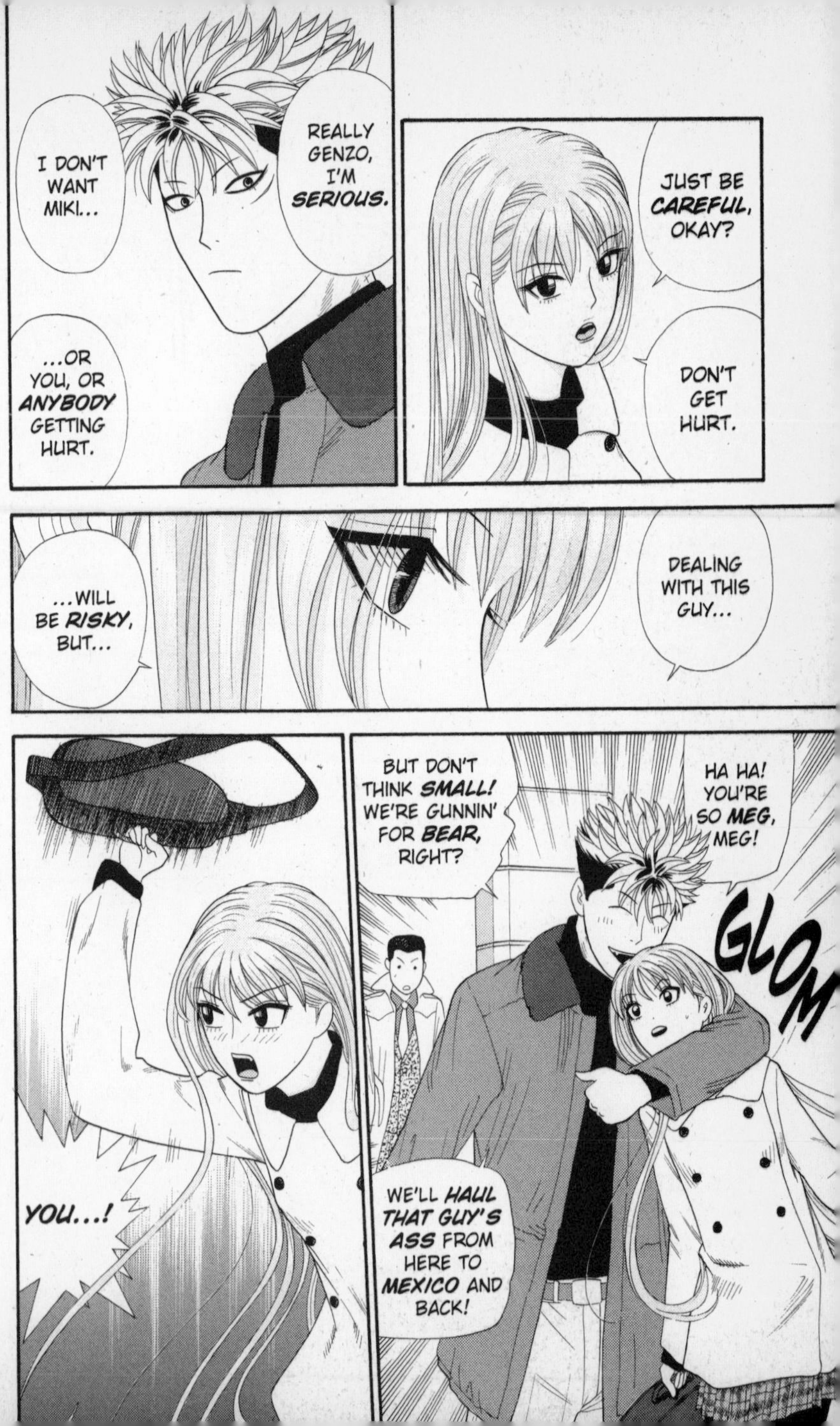
JUST BE CAREFUL, OKAY?
DON'T GET HURT.
REALLY GENZO, I'M SERIOUS.
I DON'T WANT MIKI...
...OR YOU, OR ANYBODY GETTING HURT.
DEALING WITH THIS GUY...
...WILL BE RISKY, BUT...
HA HA! YOU'RE SO MEG, MEG!
GLOM
BUT DON'T THINK SMALL! WE'RE GUNNIN' FOR BEAR, RIGHT?
WE'LL HAUL THAT GUY'S ASS FROM HERE TO MEXICO AND BACK!
YOU...!

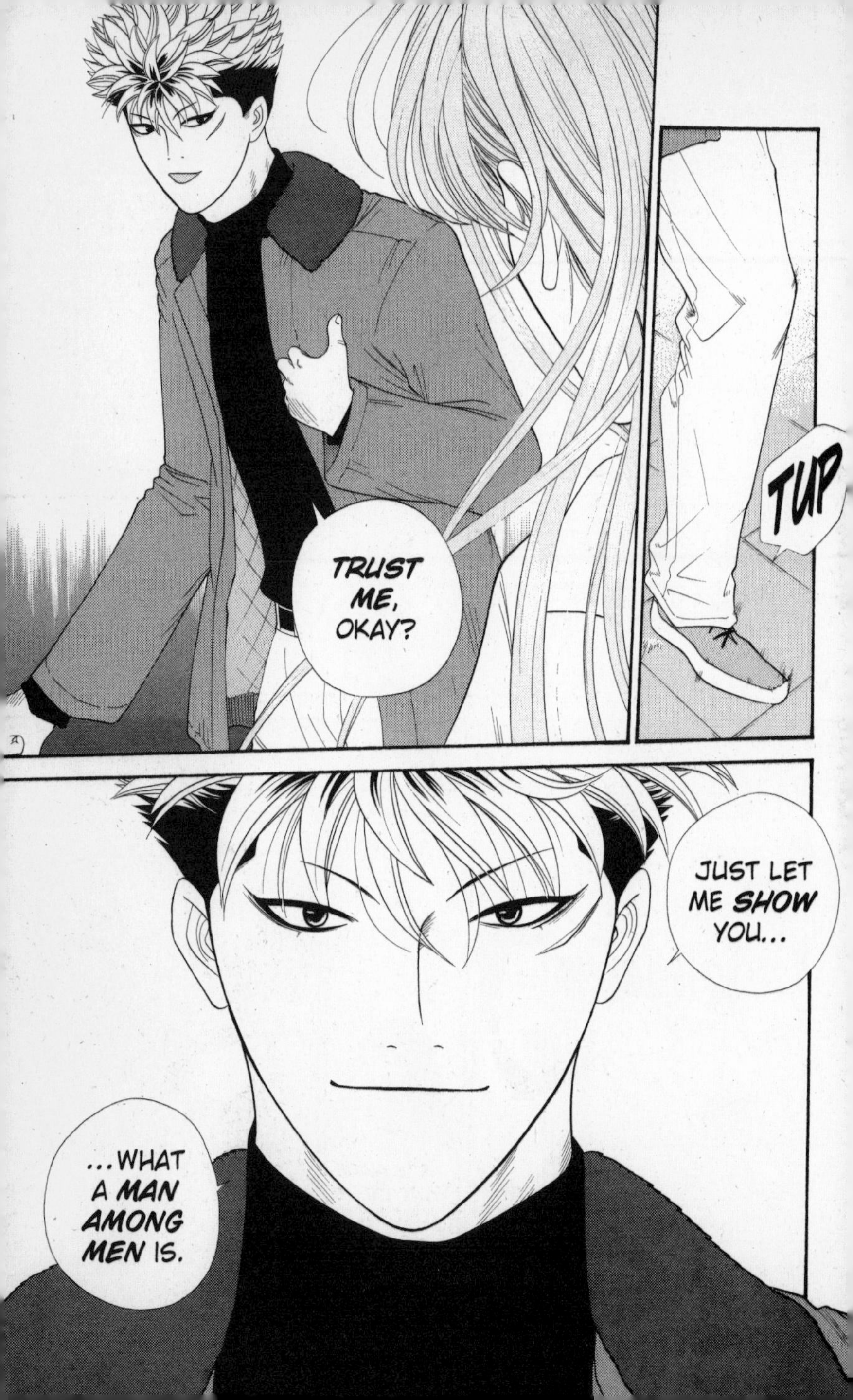
TUP
TRUST ME, OKAY?
JUST LET ME SHOW YOU...
...WHAT A MAN AMONG MEN IS.

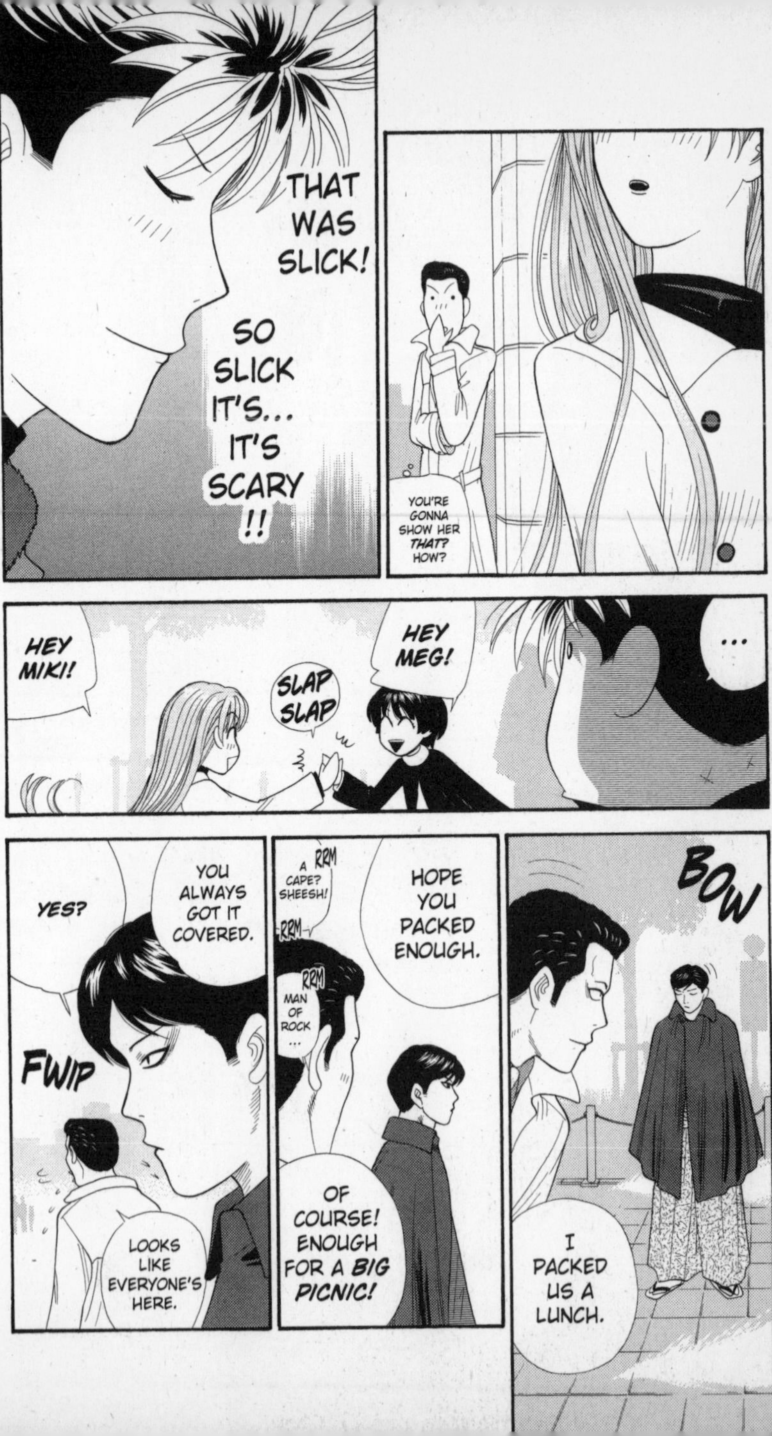
YOU'RE GONNA SHOW HER *THAT?* HOW?
THAT WAS SLICK!
SO SLICK IT'S... IT'S SCARY!!
...
HEY MEG!
SLAP SLAP
HEY MIKI!
BOW
I PACKED US A LUNCH.
HOPE YOU PACKED ENOUGH.
A CAPE? SHEESH!
RRM
RRM
RRM
MAN OF ROCK...
OF COURSE! ENOUGH FOR A *BIG PICNIC!*
YOU ALWAYS GOT IT COVERED.
YES?
FWIP
LOOKS LIKE EVERYONE'S HERE.

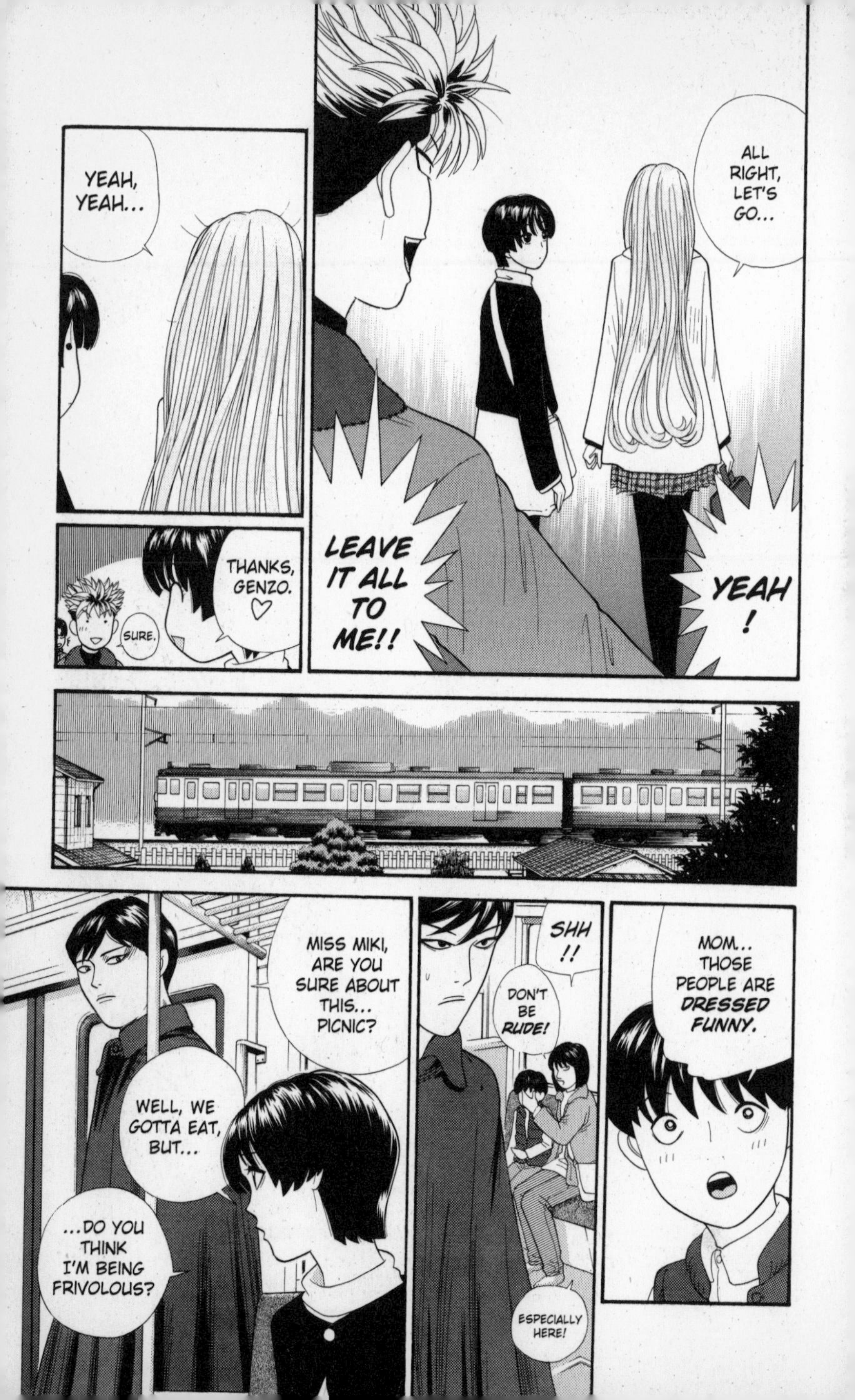
ALL RIGHT, LET'S GO...
LEAVE IT ALL TO ME!!
YEAH!
YEAH, YEAH...
THANKS, GENZO. ♡
SURE.
MOM.. THOSE PEOPLE ARE DRESSED FUNNY.
SHH!!
DON'T BE RUDE!
ESPECIALLY HERE!
MISS MIKI, ARE YOU SURE ABOUT THIS... PICNIC?
WELL, WE GOTTA EAT, BUT...
...DO YOU THINK I'M BEING FRIVOLOUS?

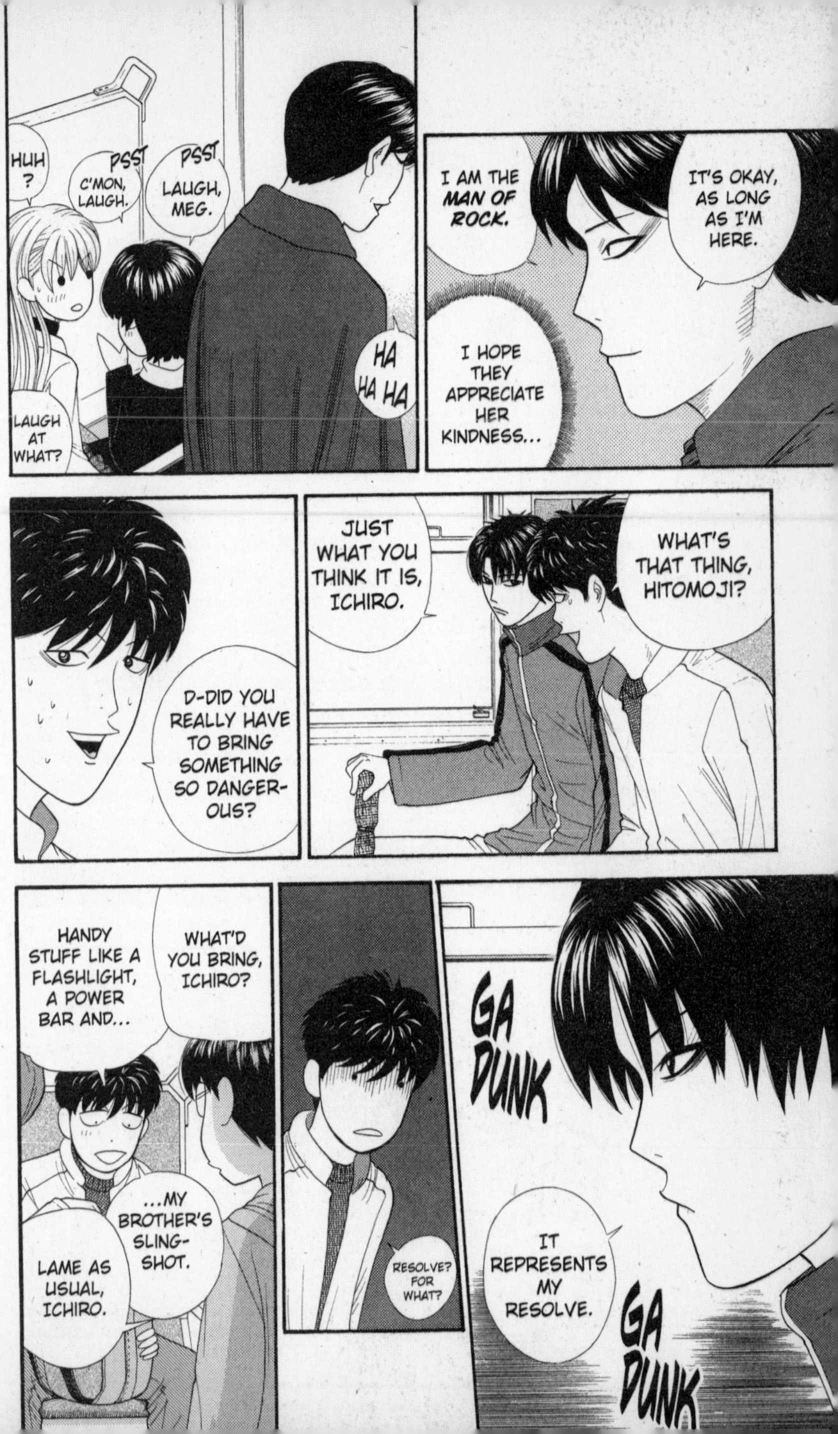
IT'S OKAY, AS LONG AS I'M HERE.
I AM THE MAN OF ROCK.
I HOPE THEY APPRECIATE HER KINDNESS...
PSST
LAUGH, MEG.
PSST
C'MON, LAUGH.
HUH?
HA HA HA
LAUGH AT WHAT?
WHAT'S THAT THING, HITOMOJI?
JUST WHAT YOU THINK IT IS, ICHIRO.
D-DID YOU REALLY HAVE TO BRING SOMETHING SO DANGER-OUS?
GA DUNK
IT REPRESENTS MY RESOLVE.
GA DUNK
RESOLVE? FOR WHAT?
WHAT'D YOU BRING, ICHIRO?
HANDY STUFF LIKE A FLASHLIGHT, A POWER BAR AND...
...MY BROTHER'S SLING-SHOT.
LAME AS USUAL, ICHIRO.

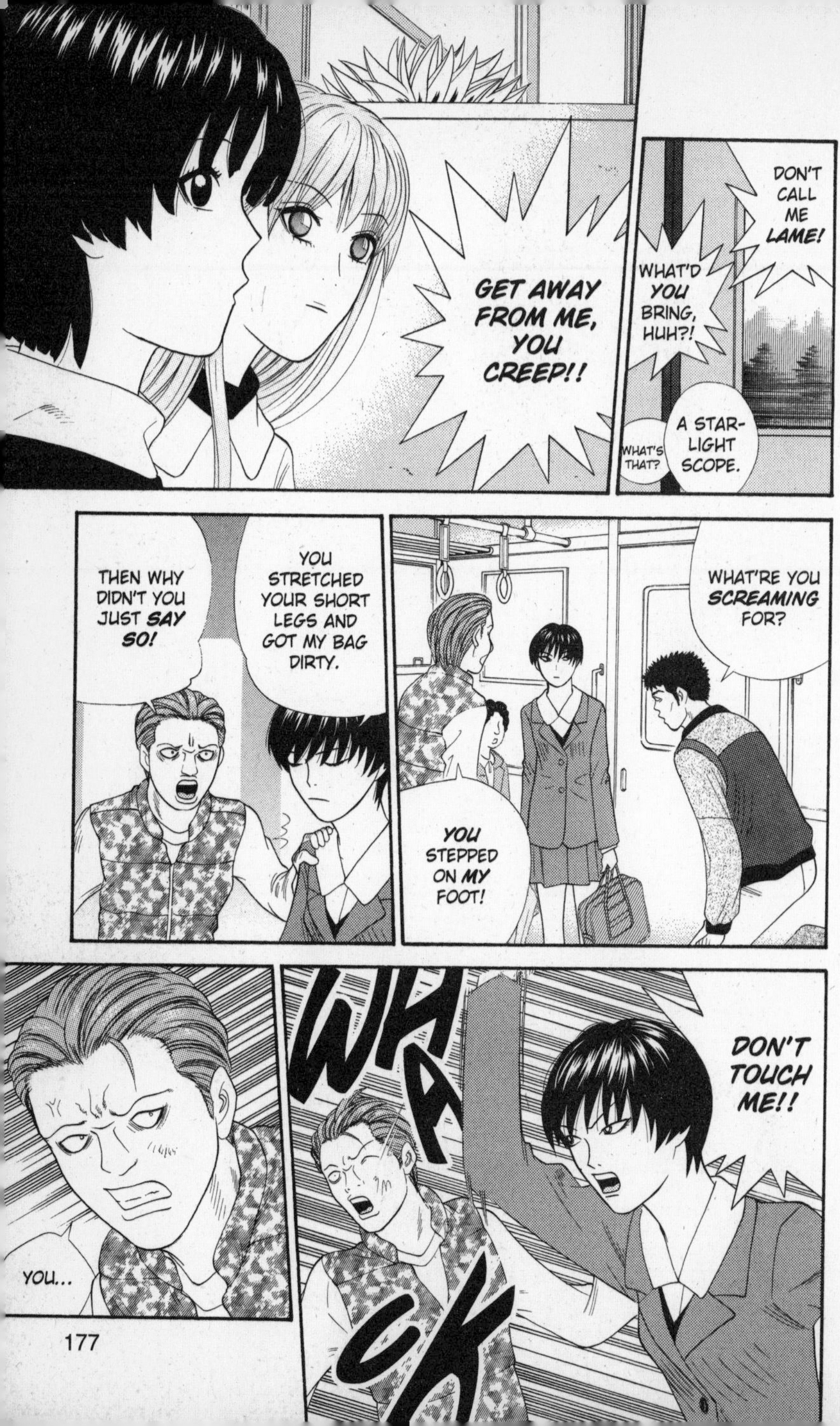
DON'T CALL ME LAME!
WHAT'D YOU BRING, HUH?!
A STAR-LIGHT SCOPE.
WHAT'S THAT?
GET AWAY FROM ME, YOU CREEP!!
WHAT'RE YOU SCREAMING FOR?
YOU STEPPED ON MY FOOT!
YOU STRETCHED YOUR SHORT LEGS AND GOT MY BAG DIRTY.
THEN WHY DIDN'T YOU JUST SAY SO!
DON'T TOUCH ME!!
WHACK
YOU...

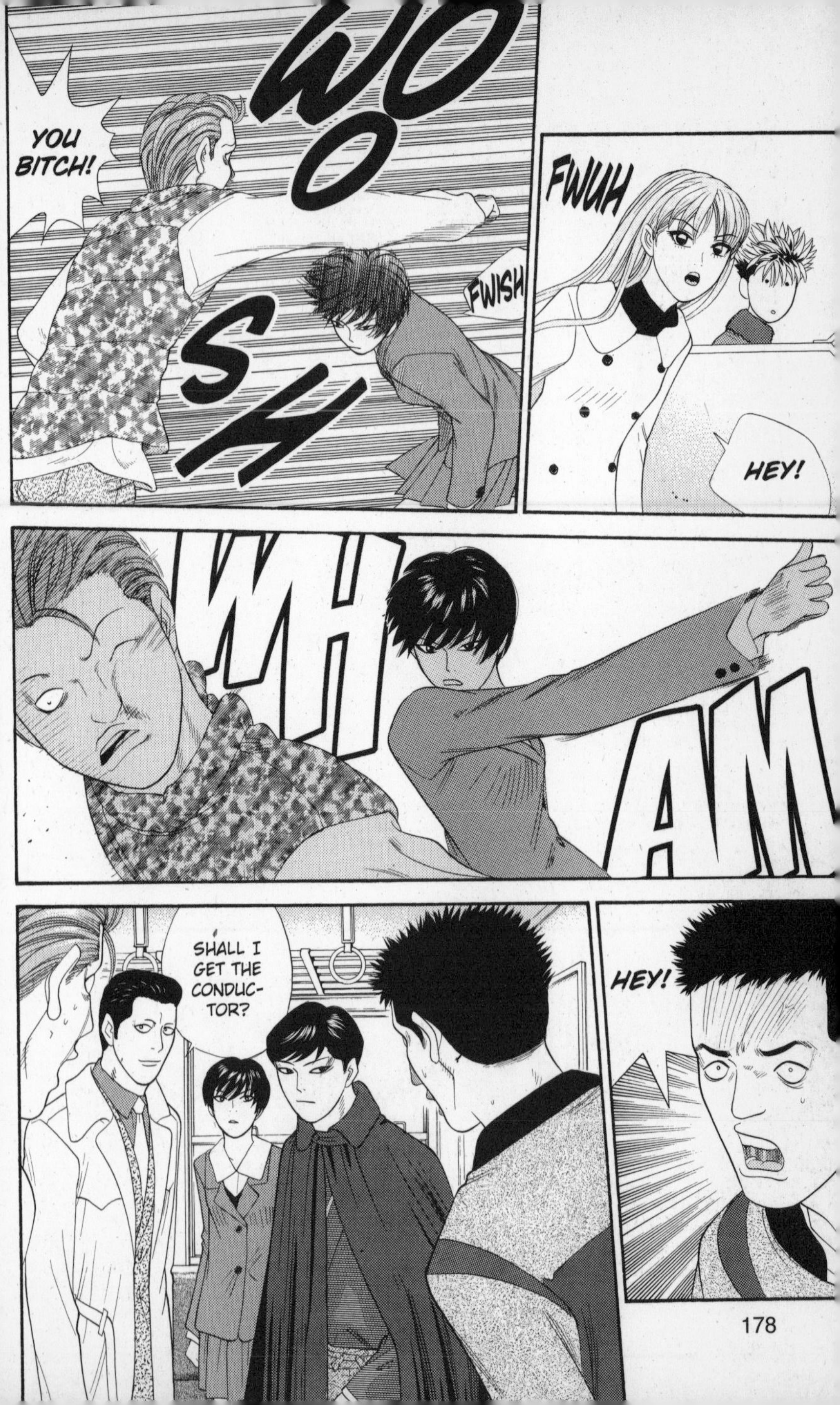
FWUH
HEY!
YOU BITCH!
WOOSH
FWISH
WHAM
HEY!
SHALL I GET THE CONDUCTOR?

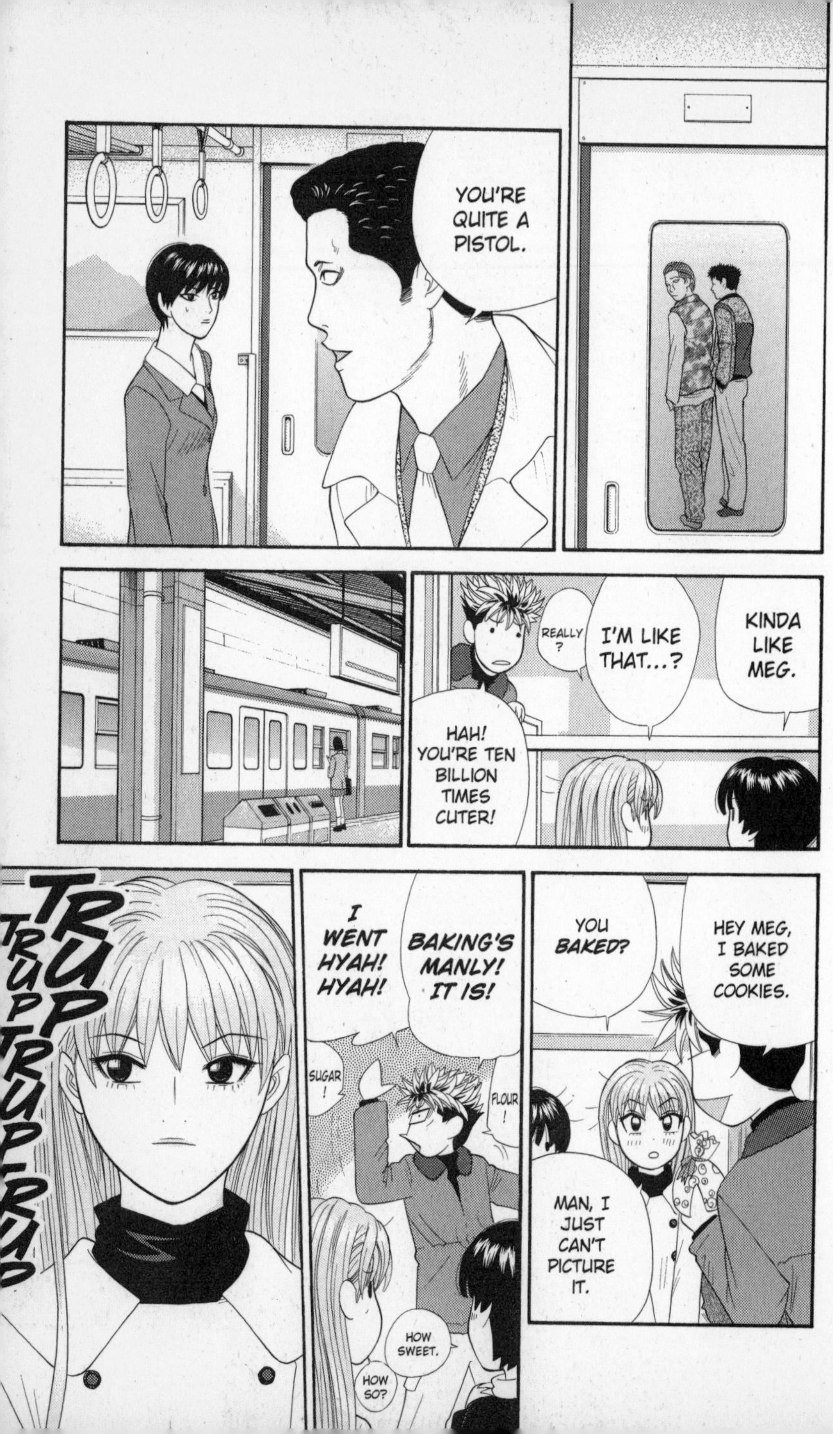
YOU'RE QUITE A PISTOL.
KINDA LIKE MEG.
I'M LIKE THAT...?
REALLY?
HAH! YOU'RE TEN BILLION TIMES CUTER!
HEY MEG, I BAKED SOME COOKIES.
YOU BAKED?
MAN, I JUST CAN'T PICTURE IT.
BAKING'S MANLY! IT IS!
I WENT HYAH! HYAH!
FLOUR!
SUGAR!
HOW SWEET.
HOW SO?
TRUP
TRUPTRUPTRUP

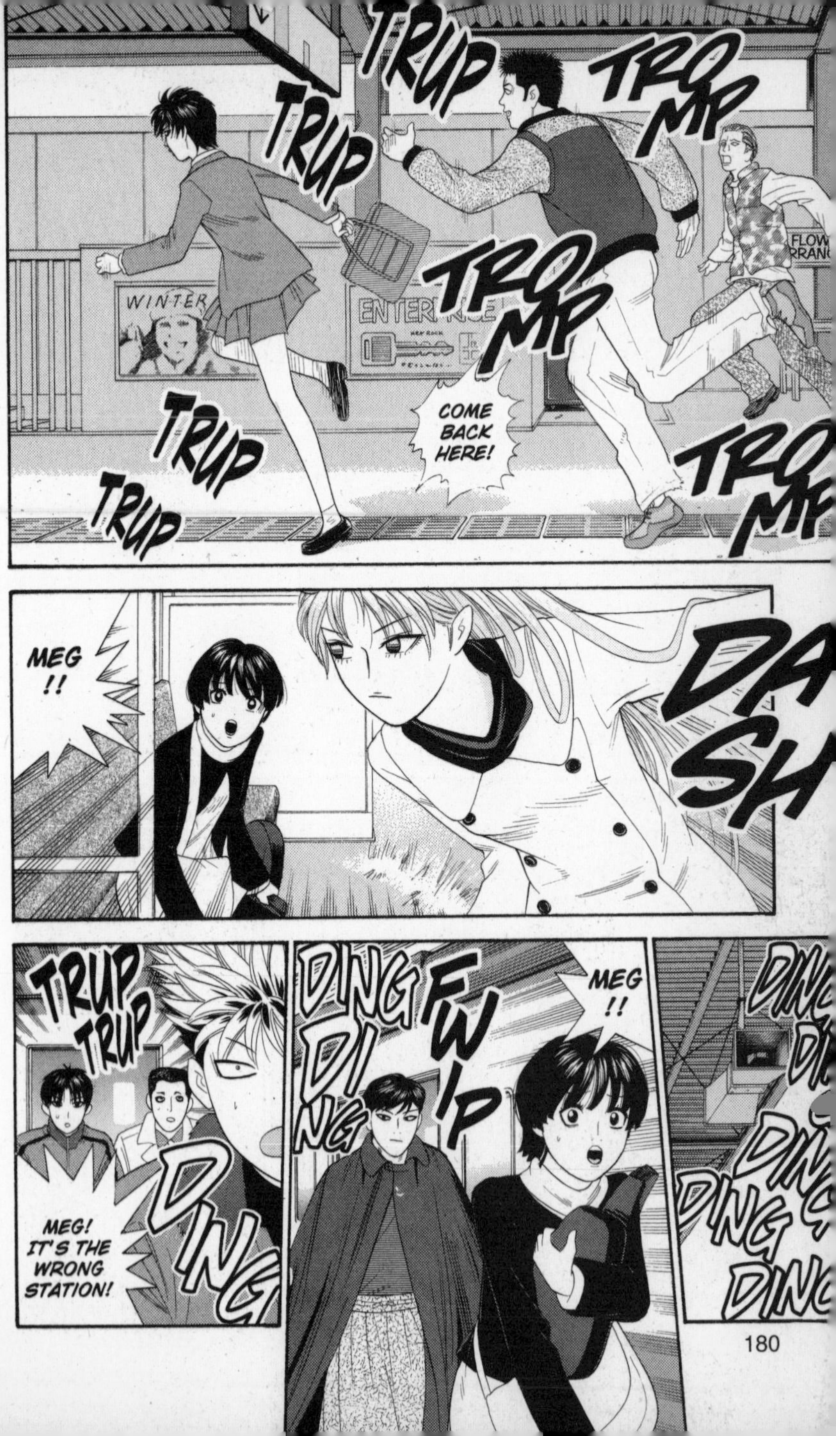
TROMP
TRUP
TRUP
TROMP
COME BACK HERE!
TROMP
TRUP
TRUP
DASH
MEG !!
DING DING
MEG !!
FWIP
DING DING DING
TRUP TRUP
DING
MEG! IT'S THE WRONG STATION!

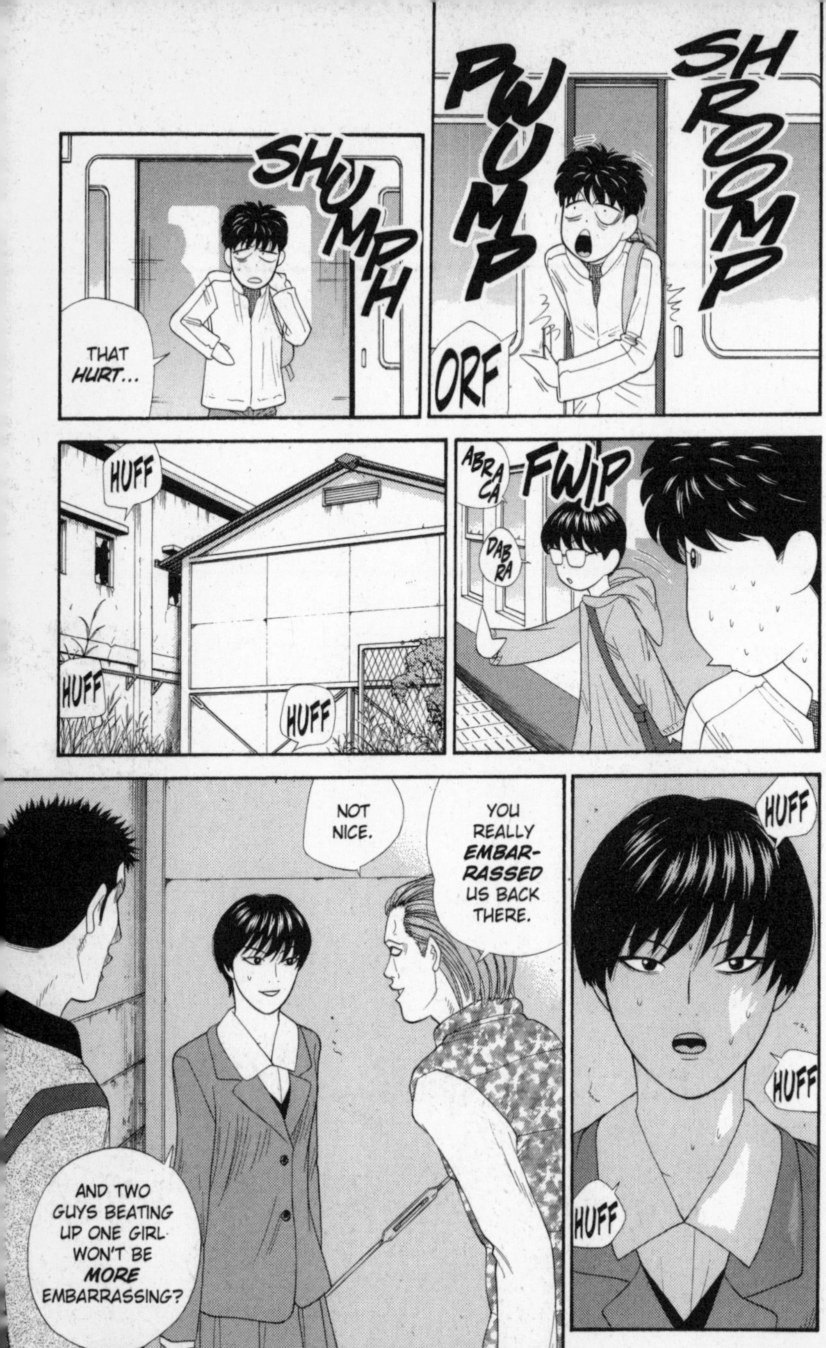
SHROOMP
PWUMP
ORF
SHUMPH
THAT HURT...
FWIP
ABRACA
DABRA
HUFF
HUFF
HUFF
HUFF
HUFF
HUFF
YOU REALLY EMBARRASSED US BACK THERE.
NOT NICE.
AND TWO GUYS BEATING UP ONE GIRL WON'T BE MORE EMBARRASSING?

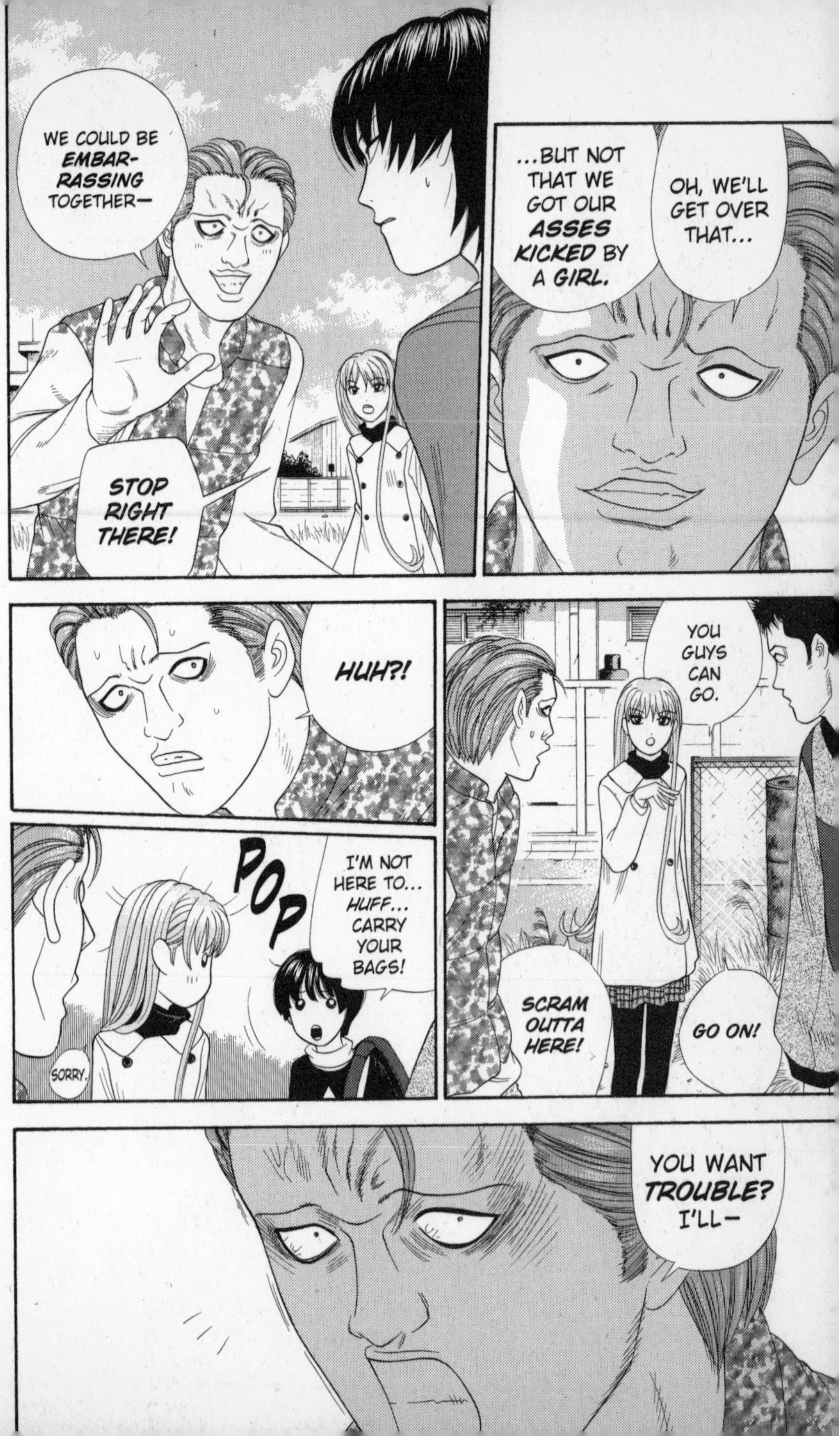
OH, WE'LL GET OVER THAT...
...BUT NOT THAT WE GOT OUR ASSES KICKED BY A GIRL.
WE COULD BE EMBARRASSING TOGETHER—
STOP RIGHT THERE!
YOU GUYS CAN GO.
GO ON!
SCRAM OUTTA HERE!
HUH?!
I'M NOT HERE TO... HUFF... CARRY YOUR BAGS!
POP
SORRY.
YOU WANT TROUBLE? I'LL—

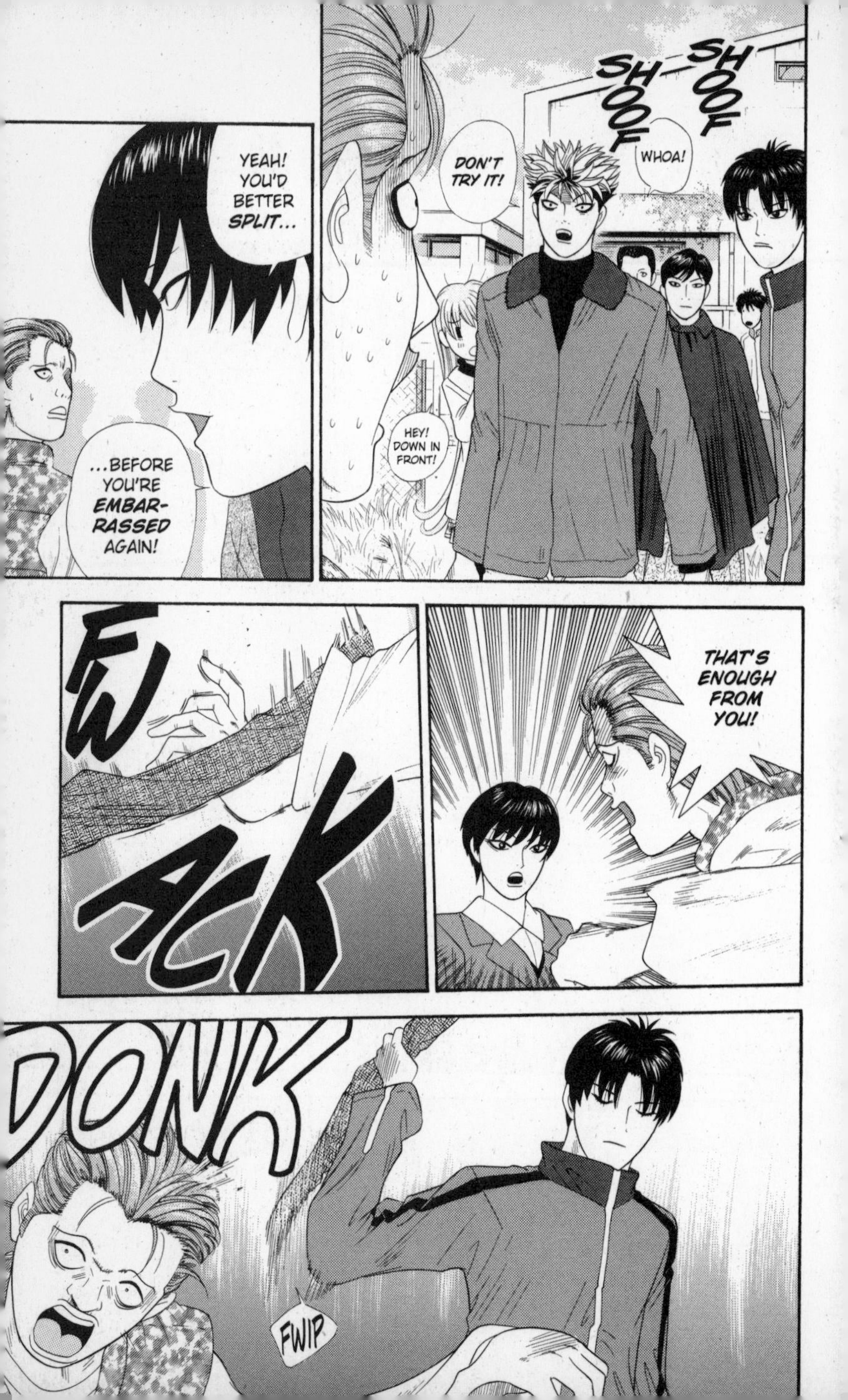
SHOOF SHOOF
WHOA!
DON'T TRY IT!
HEY! DOWN IN FRONT!
YEAH! YOU'D BETTER SPLIT...
...BEFORE YOU'RE EMBARRASSED AGAIN!
THAT'S ENOUGH FROM YOU!
FWACK
DONK
FWIP

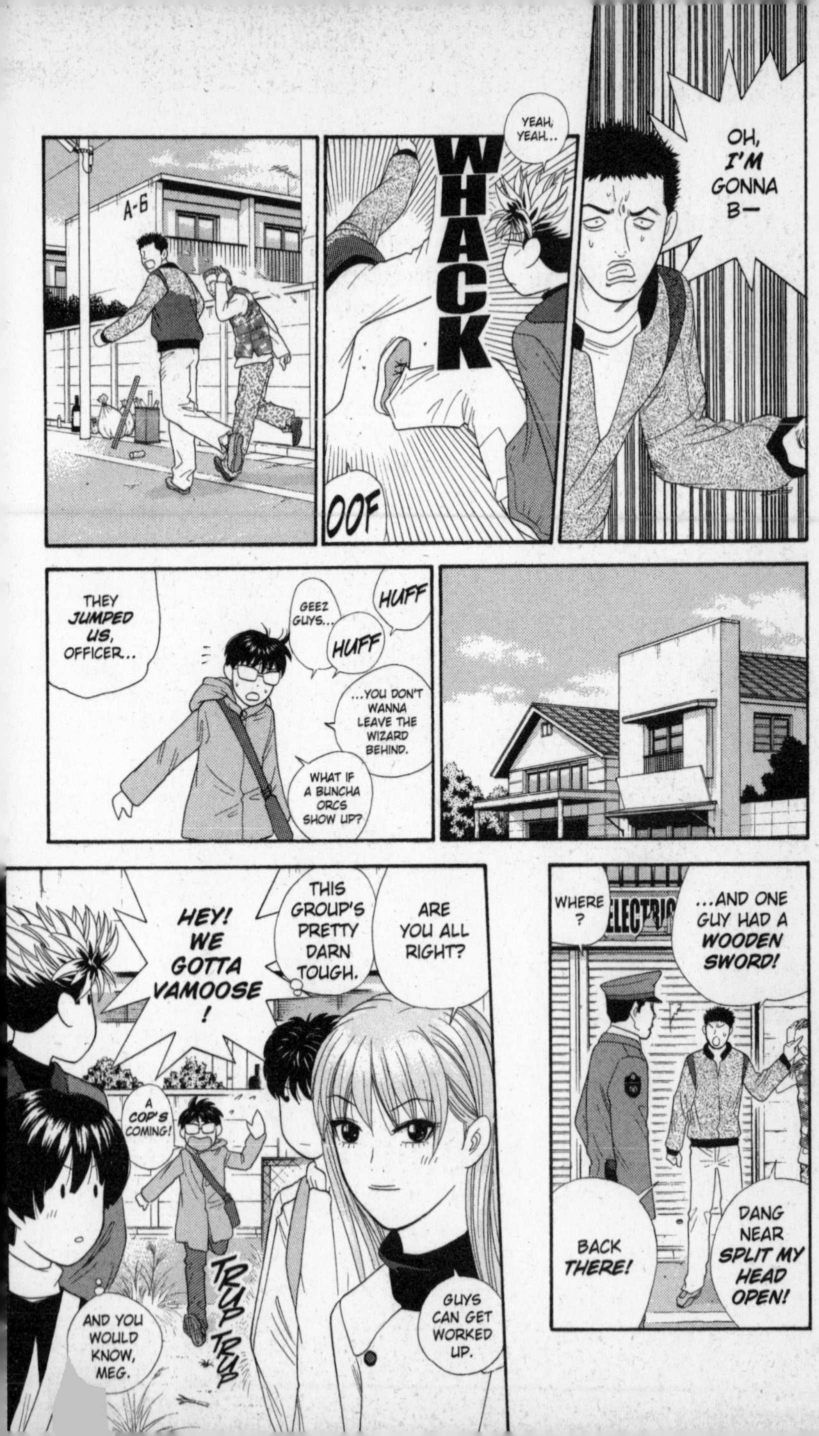
OH, I'M GONNA B—
YEAH, YEAH...
WHACK
OOF
A-6
HUFF
GEEZ GUYS...
HUFF
...YOU DON'T WANNA LEAVE THE WIZARD BEHIND.
WHAT IF A BUNCHA ORCS SHOW UP?
THEY JUMPED US, OFFICER...
...AND ONE GUY HAD A WOODEN SWORD!
WHERE?
DANG NEAR SPLIT MY HEAD OPEN!
BACK THERE!
ARE YOU ALL RIGHT?
THIS GROUP'S PRETTY DARN TOUGH.
HEY! WE GOTTA VAMOOSE!
A COP'S COMING!
GUYS CAN GET WORKED UP.
TRUP TRUP
AND YOU WOULD KNOW, MEG.

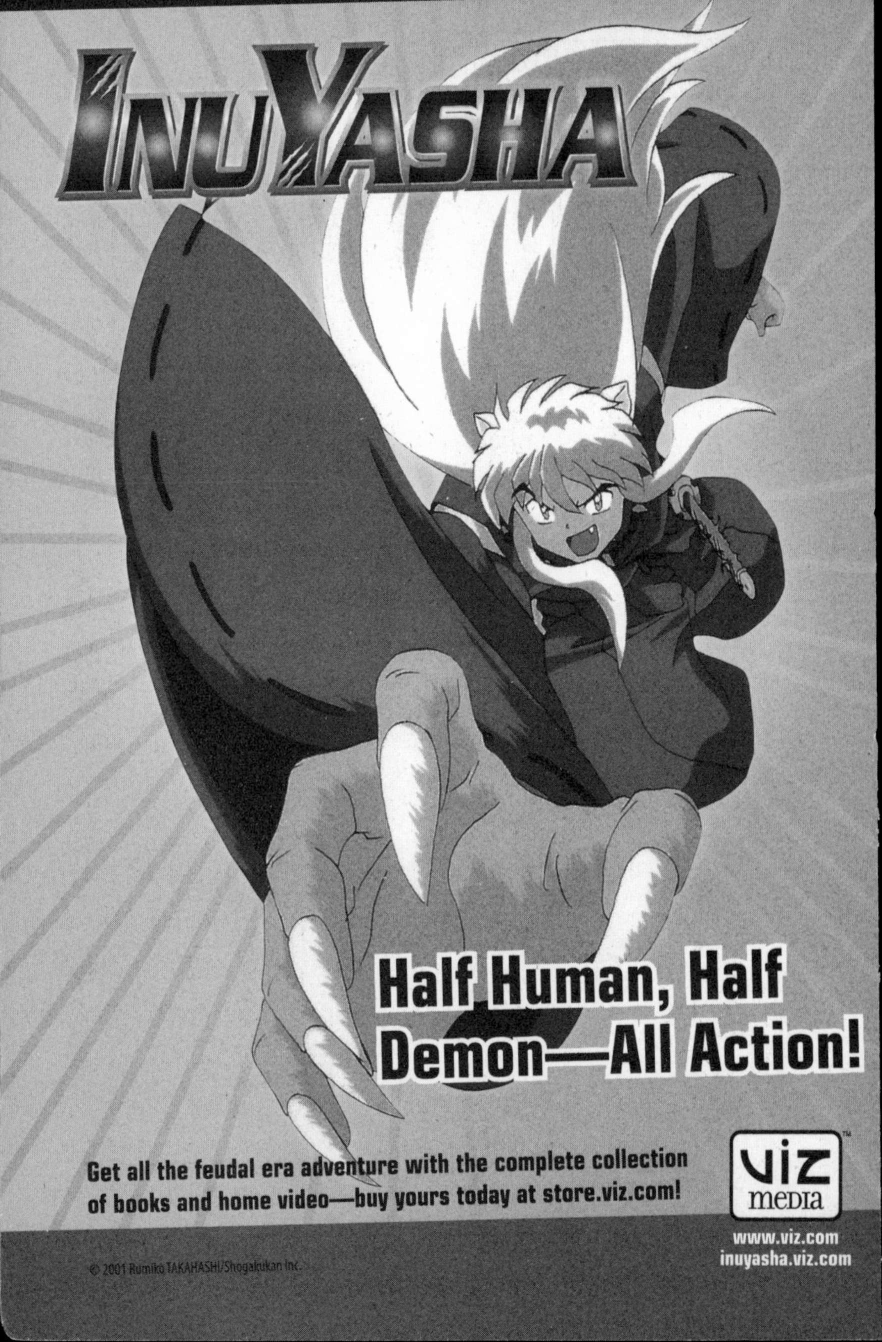
INUYASHA
Half Human, Half Demon—All Action!
Get all the feudal era adventure with the complete collection of books and home video—buy yours today at store.viz.com!
viz media
www.viz.com
inuyasha.viz.com
© 2001 Rumiko TAKAHASHI/Shogakukan Inc.

INUYASHA

Read the action from the start with the original manga series

Full color adaptation of the popular TV series

Art book with cel art, paintings, character profiles and more

TV SERIES & MOVIES ON DVD!

See more of the action in Inuyasha full-length movies

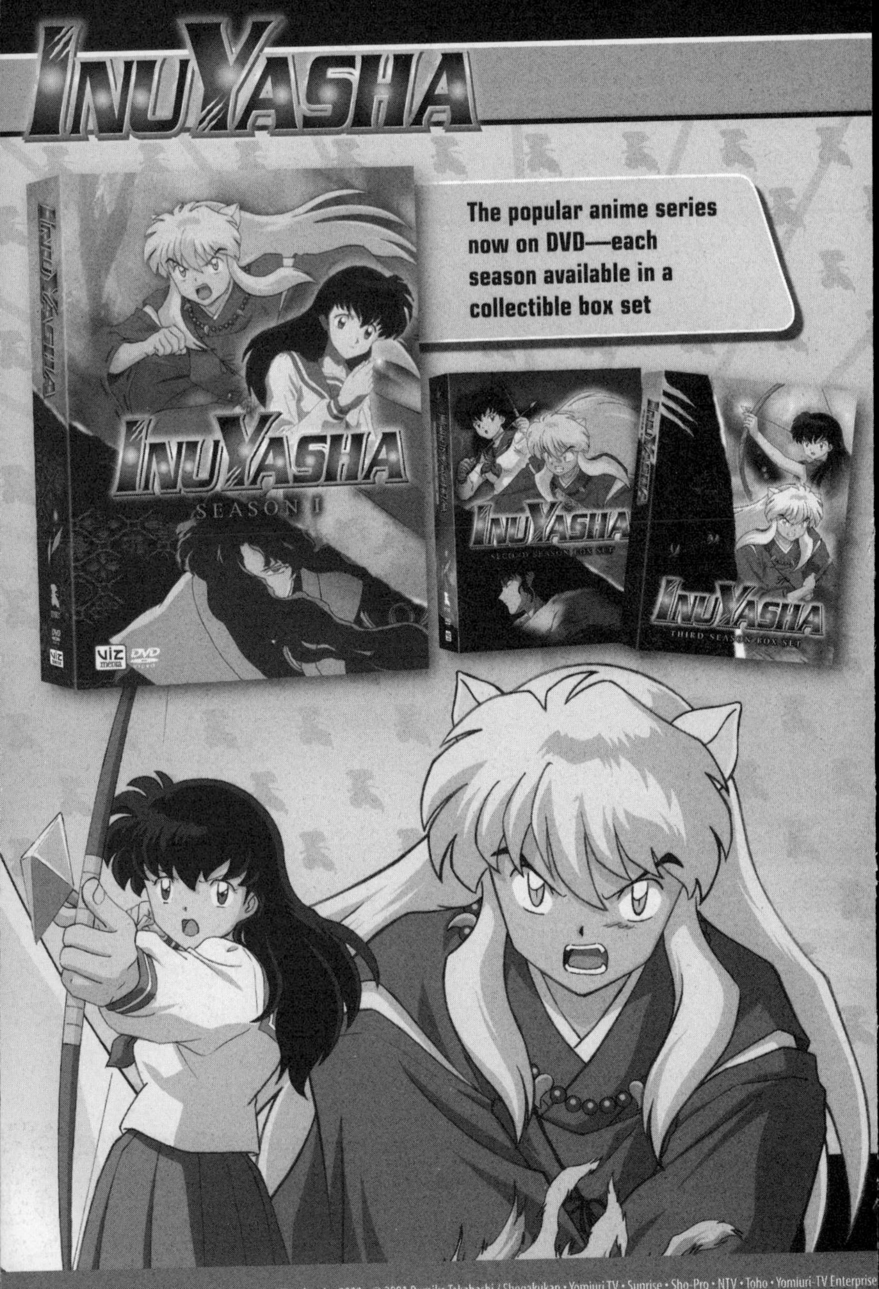

INUYASHA
The popular anime series now on DVD—each season available in a collectible box set
INUYASHA SEASON I
INUYASHA SECOND SEASON BOX SET
INUYASHA THIRD SEASON BOX SET

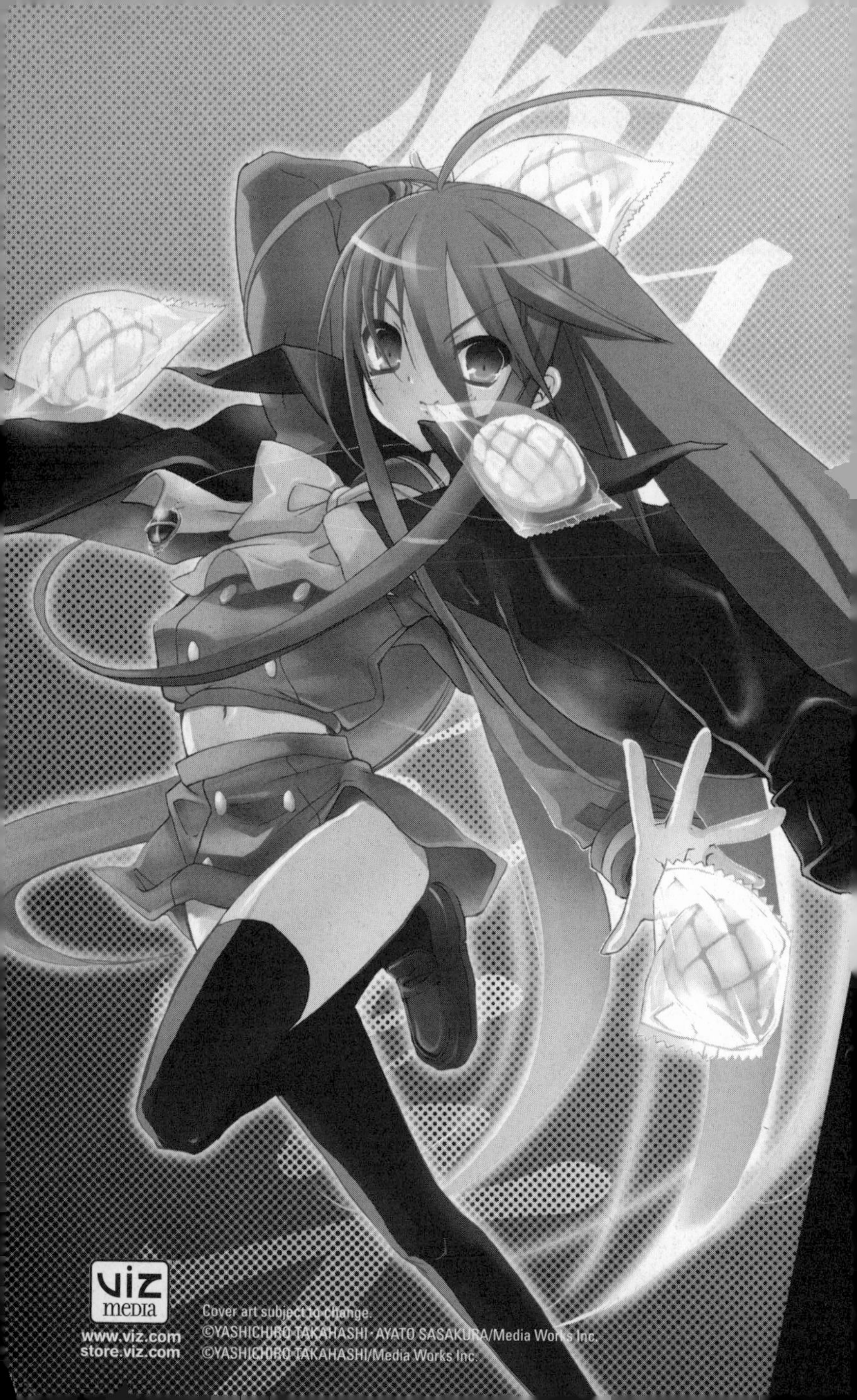

www.viz.com
store.viz.com

Cover art subject to change.

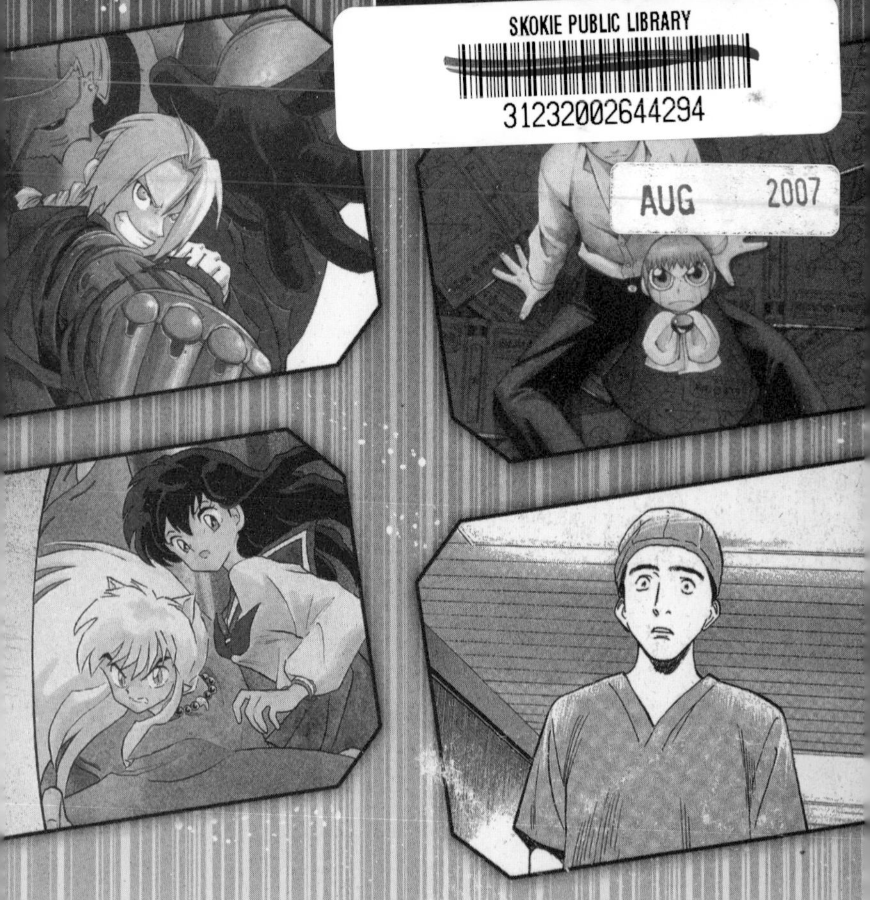